The Roman Cavalry

The Roman Cavalry

From the First to the Third Century AD

Karen R. Dixon
and
Pat Southern

London and New York

Dedicated to the Memory
of
Caesar and Napoleon

and also

from K.R.D. for:
my grandfather Edward Ramsey,
my parents and
Richard Underwood

from P.S. for:
my parents and both Bobbies

First published 1992 by B. T. Batsford

First published in paperback 1997
by Routledge
11 New Fetter Lane, London EC4P 4EE

Simultaneously published in the USA and Canada
by Routledge
29 West 35th Street, New York, NY 10001

Typeset by Servis Filmsetting Ltd, Manchester
Printed in Great Britain by Biddles Ltd, Guildford, Surrey

British Library Cataloguing in Publication Data
A catalogue record for this book is available from the British Library

Library of Congress Cataloguing in Publication Data
A catalogue record for this book is available from the Library of Congress

ISBN 0–7134–6396–1 (hbk)
ISBN 0–415–17039–7 (pbk)

Contents

Illustrations

Plates

(*between pages 112 and 113*)

Preface and acknowledgements

The literature on the Roman army is already vast, but the authors make no apology for adding yet another title to the list. The Roman cavalry has not been dealt with as a separate entity; this book aims to bring together the evidence in a form suitable for the interested general reader and for students of ancient history and archaeology. The information presented is necessarily selective, both for reasons of space and some kind of balance. The evidence for the various aspects of the Roman cavalry is uneven. The origins and early organization of Roman mounted units is briefly discussed from the first use of tribal contingents, but the majority of the information concerns the regular formations of *alae* and *cohortes equitatae* from the first to the third century AD.

The authors have considered it necessary to utilize literary evidence from earlier and later periods. Obviously, such evidence must be used with caution, but it is nevertheless a valuable exercise in that it offers informative comparisons and suggestions where contemporary information is lacking.

Whilst it is easy to imbue everything to do with warfare, and especially cavalry, with a kind of radiant glory, the authors are aware that the subject is also one of suffering and distress. It sometimes seems that dry artefactual studies and archaeological investigations have lost sight of the fact that the finds of equipment, armour and personal belongings, and the ground-plans of barracks and fortifications, all represent the daily lives of countless people and animals, not dissimilar to their modern counterparts.

Since no book can ever be the product of a single mind, we must render our thanks to the numerous people who have helped us. First and foremost we would like to express our gratitude to Peter Kemmis Betty of B.T. Batsford Ltd. for his prompt attention to all our queries, however minor. Among our colleagues at the University of Newcastle upon Tyne, Dr Kevin Greene has been of inestimable help in continually answering our questions on points of detail and presentation; Dr Jeremy Johns kindly translated passages from Greek; Mr Charles Daniels discussed aspects of Wallsend fort.

Peter Connolly, Dr Brian Dobson and Professor John Mann are gratefully acknowledged for reading drafts of the text, discussing detail and saving us from errors. Without the continual support, unflagging derision and cruel honesty of Richard Underwood, Philip 'semi-colon' Clark, and Ian Peter Stephenson this book would have been much easier to write, but not half so much fun.

It is difficult for anyone without first-hand experience of horses to attempt to write about them, particularly at a remove of two thousand years. Consequently we have sought advice from those whose knowledge is greater than ours. In this respect we must thank Mrs Ann Hyland, who very kindly went over most of the text and saved us from mistakes. She also made available to us her interpretation of Arrian's *Ars Tactica*.

Graeme Stobbs produced many of the plans and drawings almost within hours of being asked for them. Further plans were produced at the same speed and level of competence by Richard Underwood. Wendy Young typed the first drafts of the second half of the book, despite the hieroglyphics in which it was written.

Special thanks go to the staff at the Library of the University of Newcastle upon Tyne, especially those on the Inter-Library Loan desk. We would also like to acknowledge the following museums for providing photographs: Museum für Vor-und Frühgeschichte, Frankfurt; Corinium Museum, Cirencester; British Museum, London; Grosvenor Museum, Chester; Württembergisches Landesmuseum, Stuttgart; Saalburgmuseum, Bad Homburg; Rijksmuseum van Oudheden, Leiden; Kunsthistorisches Museum Antikensammlung, Vienna; Prähistorische Staatssammlung, Munich; Museum of Antiquities, Newcastle upon Tyne; Mittelrheinisches Landesmuseum Mainz; National Museum, Damascus; Castle Museum, Norwich; Romisch-Germanisches Museum, Cologne; Gäuboden-Museum, Straubing; Staatliches Amt für Vor-und Frühgeschichte, Koblenz.

Any mistakes and errors of judgement remaining belong to us, but for a small fee they can be yours too. Anyone who feels incensed enough to argue might like to write to us so that we too can share in pushing back the frontiers of knowledge.

1 The sources

The sources of information for the Roman cavalry are the same as those commonly used for any history of the Roman army as a whole. The evidence is sometimes fragmentary and therefore incomplete for any period of the Empire, and all the available information should anyway be used with caution.

Documentary evidence includes the writings of the ancient authors, military records and letters on papyrus or writing tablets, and inscriptions on stone, such as tombstones, altars and permanent records of special events, for example Hadrian's speech to the Numidian army, set out as a huge inscription at Lambaesis. A tombstone often conveys details of the deceased's career and also a 'portrait', and is therefore just as much a document as a papyrus or the text of an ancient writer. The reliability of sculptural evidence is questionable (Fig.1), but artistic representations of cavalrymen and their horses are so abundant all over the Roman Empire that they cannot be ignored. In addition to the documentary evidence, archaeological discoveries have revealed much about Roman forts and about the military equipment of the soldiers who manned them.

All these sources taken together can be used to reconstruct, tentatively, a history of the Roman cavalry. It is probably true to say that there are more questions than answers, and so the gaps in our knowledge can be filled only by speculation. If future discoveries reveal that any or all of this is wrong, the reader will no doubt make his or her own subtractions and additions.

Perhaps one of the greatest problems connected with the use of any of the aforementioned evidence is that the history of the Roman Empire stretched over both an enormous time-span and a large geographical area. The evidence from one or two provinces at a specific date is not necessarily relevant to the rest of the Empire, either at the same or at different times. Whilst it is important to try to evaluate what the ancient authors wrote about the Roman army, this can be misleading if it is not explained how far they are separated from each other by time and place. For example, if the information from the works of, say, Polybius, Josephus and Vegetius

1 Tombstone of Silicius Catus, Oran Museum. Basing arguments about armament styles and breeds of horses on such sculptures clearly has its limitations. Comparison with more elaborate and (possibly) more accurate gravestones reveals the primitive style of Catus' portrait, but it should be remembered that all the tombstones depicting Roman soldiers shared the same purpose, namely that of honouring the dead. (Drawn by K.R. Dixon.)

(*Epitoma Rei Militaris*) is lumped together without a cautionary word about when and why each of them wrote, the resultant composite picture of the army will be distorted if not false. Polybius was a Greek of the second century BC who observed the Roman army of the Republic. Josephus was a Jew who recorded in meticulous detail the army of Vespasian and Titus in Judaea in the AD 60s. Vegetius, writing in the fourth century AD, described how he thought the army *should* operate, and not necessarily how it did, in his day. Such a procedure would be much like trying to reconstruct a history of the English army using firstly the work of Ordericus Vitalis who wrote in the twelfth century about the exploits of William the Conqueror; secondly a few documents concerning the campaign leading up to the battle of Agincourt; and thirdly the musings of Marshal de Saxe, who wrote down his thoughts on how an army should be run in the 1730s (though the work was not published until 1756). It does not need to be said that such a project would be patently ridiculous, but the time-span was roughly the same as that covered by the Greek and Latin authors previously mentioned. Even if the invention of firearms is discounted, the changes which occurred in military operations between the twelfth and the eighteenth centuries could not be properly documented from such sparse and widely divergent sources. The Roman army also changed over the centuries and we are allowed merely a glimpse of it from time to time; the rest is obscure.

None the less, though the details of organization and equipment may have changed, there are certain broad principles that would have remained the same over several centuries. For instance, troops must be taught to work together and trained in the various manoeuvres and duties they are to perform. Horses have to be obtained, looked after and fed, and eventually disposed of. For this reason comparative evidence from other periods of history has been used in this book. Until roughly the Second World War, horses were indispensable all over the world in many walks of life, in transport and agriculture as well as warfare, therefore first-hand knowledge of horses was much more widespread than it is today. In this mechanized age the majority of people have no contact with horses, and are still further removed from cavalry and its use. The military manuals published by the British War Office up to the 1930s, and the works of eighteenth- and nineteenth-century soldiers who had direct knowledge of cavalry, can usefully supplement the sometimes scanty information that exists on the Roman mounted units. The problems faced by all armies until the age of mechanization were often quite similar. Communications, transport and supply, together with disease and accidents among men and animals, probably limited the activities of the Roman army just as much as any other, and it is of interest to compare how other armies dealt with such problems. It is unlikely, for instance, that in the provinces of the Rhine and Danube the grass grew any earlier or later for the Romans than it did for Marlborough in the first decade of the eighteenth century. Dependent as it is on supplies of fodder and forage, cavalry is sometimes restricted in its actions by seasons and locations. This is yet another reason why several provinces should not be studied together without sufficient differentiation between their geography and climate, which affect agriculture, transport and food supply.

Literary sources

Concerning ancient literature, all manuscripts are subject to the same dangers of miscopying over the centuries, and even worse, of complete loss of certain sections. The wonder is that so much has survived, and it is perhaps not surprising that there are so many uncertainties surrounding that which does. Even the authorship of some works is disputed. There are those who say, for instance, that Xenophon did not write *The Art of*

Horsemanship and *The Cavalry Commander*. It is an opinion that should be noted but the finer details of the dispute are best left to classicists and philologists. The main points are that someone did write these two works; that they are very useful; and that Xenophon is as good a code word as any with which to identify them. The books concern the cavalry of ancient Greece, not the later Roman cavalry; and although the information is useful it should be remembered that Xenophon was concerned with how the cavalry should be organized. There were evidently many faults he would have liked to correct, and there is not infrequently a note of exasperation in his writings. But documentation of common failings is useful in itself.

For yet other works not only the authorship but also the date is disputed. Hyginus' book, formerly known as *De Munitionibus Castrorum* and more recently corrected to *De Metatione Castrorum*, is often referred to as pseudo-Hyginus, because it is not certain who was responsible for it. This in turn means that it is impossible to date it accurately: it has been placed variously in the reigns of Domitian, Trajan, Marcus Aurelius, and in the third and fourth centuries. The only certain fact about it is that it concerns a campaign on the Danube, when the Emperor was present, accompanied by his entourage.

The documentary sources can be divided into two broad categories, consisting of those in which the author recorded his own observations or first-hand knowledge, and those which were compilations, usually narrative histories, that owe their origin to a variety of sources, not all of which can be identified.

In the first category Polybius and Josephus have already been mentioned. They were not Romans and they recorded their observations of the army at a particular point in time. If there were facts which they misunderstood, or even deliberately misrepresented, these are difficult to identify at this distance in time. Such a possibility, combined with modern misreadings, precludes unrestricted use of such sources. Perhaps more reliable are Caesar's commentaries on the Gallic and Civil Wars. However much it may be possible to level at him the accusation that the works were undertaken primarily for self-aggrandizement and political advancement, the places, personalities and events of his books are probably not overly distorted. The fact that he was able to record the names of officers and soldiers who had distinguished themselves suggest that he used military records compiled at the time, or that he kept notes himself, or both. In any case these books provide first-hand experience of late Republican army practice and the problems faced on campaign.

Arrian was another author who wrote from his own experience. He was a friend of Hadrian and his work includes both the description of the battle order employed by him against the Alans, a tribe from south-east Russia who threatened the eastern Roman provinces while he was governor of Cappadocia, and the *Tactica*. The latter specifically concerns cavalry and is therefore extremely valuable as a source, but it is once again restricted to one specific time and place, and it is not certain how widely applicable it might have been. On the whole Arrian has a good reputation as a plain and straightforward writer, who tried to use the most reliable sources of information.

Narrative histories such as Tacitus' *Annals* and *Histories*, and the books of Appian and Cassius Dio, can provide information on how cavalry was used, and illuminate administrative details of army life which are not accessible from epigraphic or papyrological sources. The Romans kept a central records office in Rome (the *Tabularium*), where official archives were deposited, and there may have been similar record offices in each provincial headquarters. It is not certain how far writers would be allowed access to such information. Perhaps it depended largely upon circumstances and personal connections. In general, it could be said that the authors quoted above are more reliable than, for instance, Suetonius, who wrote *The Twelve Caesars*, and those who were responsible for the *Scriptores Historiae Augustae* dealing with the later Emperors.

Military writers of the late Roman Empire include Vegetius, who wrote in the fourth century; Procopius whose work belongs to the mid-sixth century; and Maurice whose *Strategikon* may have been written about the end of the sixth century. These writers lived and worked at times very remote from the age of the late Republic and early Empire and it is to be expected that the armies they described would be quite different from what had gone before. Flavius Vegetius Renatus was not a soldier but a civilian official who had read widely. He is sometimes confused with Publius Vegetius Renatus who wrote *Ars Mulomedicinae*. Flavius Vegetius' military manual, *Epitoma Rei Militaris* consists of four books classified by subject: recruits; organization; strategy; and fortifications. They are so packed with information that it seems wasteful to reject any of it, but Vegetius' books were compiled from widely differing sources of all periods, without discrimination and sometimes without acknowledgement, making it difficult to assess the precise value of what he says.

Procopius' *History of the Wars* seems to be based on somewhat better foundations. In this he tried to record events of which he himself had knowledge or he used information from eye-witnesses to try to arrive at the truth. He was clearly a supporter of Belisarius and in opposition to Justinian, with the result that another of his works, the *Secret History*, is less reliable because it was devoted to an attack on the latter.

The *Strategikon* is a military manual, the authorship of which is not definitely established but is usually attributed to the Emperor Maurice. It belongs to the end of the sixth or the beginning of the seventh century, and documents not only Byzantine methods of waging war but also contains information on the peoples against whom the Byzantines were fighting, such as the Lombards, Avars and Franks. Much of the work consists of sound common sense and covers general principles which to some extent may be applied retrospectively to the previous two or three centuries.

Sources for Roman law which have some relevance to the army are the *Codex Theodosianus*, dating to the end of the fifth century, and the *Digest* of Justinian, which came into force at the beginning of the sixth. The *Codex Theodosianus* of AD 438 is a compilation of earlier laws and enactments and contains material from the time of Constantine onwards. The *Digest* is composed of a much wider range of material, not laws but legal opinions, for the most part drawn from the works of writers of the second and third centuries. One of the most useful aspects of the *Digest* is that the original author is noted, so that it is possible to arrive at a better evaluation of the information. The *leges militares* of Ruffus are a compilation of laws found in a Byzantine collection called *Iuris Graeco-Romani* by Johannes Leunclavius, published in 1596 (Brand 1968, xxxii). The author Ruffus is unknown; he may possibly be identified with Sextus Ruffus (or Rufius) Festus, who was a provincial governor under Valentinian II. If this is so, his wide experience of military matters would have given him the basis for his compilation of laws (Brand 1968, 138). It has also been suggested that whoever wrote the laws may be the same person as the author of the *Strategikon*, mentioned above as attributed to the Emperor Maurice. In this case, Ruffus may have been a military officer serving under Maurice. The laws themselves do not appear to have been merely extracted from the *Digest*, the wording is different and there is reason to think that they derive from an independent source (Brand 1968, 136–41). In the present work, however, the name cited in connection with these laws is Ruffus (despite its doubtful authenticity) because it is a convenient and distinctive label.

Specialist literature not primarily concerned with the cavalry but which has some bearing on it, includes the agricultural works of Cato (Marcus Porcius), Varro and Columella, and the veterinary authors such as Vegetius (Publius) and Pelagonius. Cato wrote his *De Agricultura* in about 160 BC and although it is not much concerned with horses he did list fodder crops available at his time. Varro and Columella whose works date to roughly AD 37 and AD 60–5 respectively, dealt with farm animals in more detail, giving information on feeding, housing and breeding horses. Though they both acknowledged the importance of horses for warfare, they kept to their civilian farming themes. The veterinary authors' work can be properly evaluated only by a trained specialist with veterinary knowledge and also deep experience of horses. In the absence of these two qualities, it is merely possible to repeat what the books contain. Vegetius derived most of his information from other sources, notably Pelagonius, who in turn had used Columella's work. The result is a compilation not based on direct veterinary experience.

Inscriptions

The many inscriptions that have survived from the Roman Empire can provide details about army units and individual soldiers. Inscriptions from forts naming the units that built them and/or occupied them can help to distinguish 'cavalry' forts, but this useful information is quite rare and the identification of forts intended for *cohortes peditatae*, *cohortes equitatae* and *alae* is not as straightforward as it may seem.

Altars and tombstones provide information about individual soldiers, sometimes merely their names but they often include further details. On some altars, the soldiers related their reasons for dedicating them to particular gods or goddesses, and occasionally they added the names of the consuls of the year, from which it is possible to establish an exact date. On tombstones it is usual to find the soldier's name, rank and the unit he was serving in at the time, sometimes with an account of other units in which he had served, his age at death and his length of service. Some men are described as veterans, others presumably died while still in service. Only very rarely is the cause of death included on the funerary monument.

One inscription which is often quoted in connection with the Roman cavalry is Hadrian's *Adlocutio*, or address to the army of Numidia, which he gave at Lambaesis in AD 128. The legionaries and auxiliaries put on a display for the emperor which he described and praised in his speech. Much of it survives, inscribed on a column (*CIL* VIII 18042 = *ILS* 2487; 9133–5). The valuable information it provides about the *equites legionis* and the exercises of the *cohortes equitatae* and *alae* will be discussed in the relevant contexts.

Pictorial sources

The sculptures on numerous Roman monuments vary enormously in style and competence of execution, and should not be used as evidence to support any theory without a note of caution. Some monuments, such as Trajan's Column, have been quoted as authentic depictions of the soldiers, their equipment and horses. This is somewhat dubious: the very perfection of the human figures and the horses ought to warn against the acceptance of the sculptures as realistic portrayals. Some of the funerary monuments to be found in museums include a wealth of detail on horse trappings and soldiers' equipment. A number of these may be entirely accurate, executed by craftsmen who knew the finer details of the military equipment that they intended to show. Others may have been made by sculptors who were instructed in general terms what the customer required and then improvised within these terms of reference. It is impossible to be sure. Perhaps it depended upon the price charged, with skill and accuracy being at the top of the scale.

Papyrus

The survival rate of papyrus is naturally greater in hot dry climates than in wet northern European ones, and so most of the surviving military records of this kind concern the eastern provinces. Notable collections are those from Oxyrhynchus, which lay 200km (120 miles) south of Cairo, and from Dura-Europos on the Euphrates. The Oxyrhynchus papyri comprise many public, official and private documents. The Dura collection is much smaller, and likewise contains much private material, but its importance for military matters is enormous because of the two detailed duty rosters of *Cohors XX Palmyrenorum*, stationed at Dura in the early third century AD (Pl.1); (*P. Dur*. 100; 101). Fink (1971) has collected together, discussed and translated Roman military papyrus records. The information contained in them about daily life in the army and its administrative and financial machinery is invaluable, but there are problems of interpretation, not least because of all the abbreviations used. The soldiers who were responsible for keeping the records merely needed to know who was where at a given time or who had been paid an amount of money for something. They did not imagine that 2000 years later someone would try to interpret what they had written, without their background knowledge of what the abbreviated terms meant. There is still discussion and disagreement about some of the records.

Archaeological evidence

Archaeology is sometimes a very imprecise tool and the interpretation of fort sites and artefacts is hazardous, even when reasonably accurate dates are obtainable from inscriptions, or pottery and coin evidence. It is not possible to reconstruct the history of a fort except on broad general lines. Excavation can reveal that buildings were pulled down and re-erected and that a fort's defences underwent several changes but it is not always clear how these changes fitted into the known history of the province. In many instances it is not known which unit occupied the fort. The number of rooms in a barrack block has been advanced as a theoretical guide to the type of unit in occupation, but this is not wholly reliable. The number of *contubernia* per barrack varies and it cannot be asserted that there is consistency between numbers of rooms and type of unit. The presence or absence of stables has not been proved at most forts simply because very few have been completely excavated. At a small number of forts where excavation has been more extensive, some buildings have been identified as stables usually because of the presence of internal drains or troughs, or the lack of internal partitions, which could be taken to indicate that these buildings were not barracks.

Archaeological evidence is silent on the matters of recruitment, organization and employment of cavalry. In the latter case, the weapons and armour that have been found assist in reconstructing probable fighting methods, but are not relevant to the more mundane tasks such as convoy duty, police work and scouting, which it is likely that the cavalry also habitually performed.

It is therefore necessary to utilize and try to evaluate selections from all the aforementioned types of information. This has both strengths and weaknesses, and different opinions are permissible provided they are based on ascertainable facts.

2 Origins, organization and titulature

Origins

Evidence regarding the precise details of the development of the Roman cavalry is scant. Various ancient authors offer fragmentary glimpses of the changes that occurred through time, but the information that would enable us to view this progression as a continual process is lacking. The source dealing with the earliest period is Livy (1.13), who records that under Romulus (traditionally 753 BC), the legendary founder of Rome, three centuries of knights (*equites*) were created, each being named after one of the three 'tribes' that existed at this time: the Ramnenses, Titienses and Luceres. Later, under Tarquinius Priscus, the strength of these centuries was increased to 1800 men in total.

It was not until Servius (traditionally 578–535 BC), however, that a substantial reorganization of the cavalry took place. The *equites* were now organized into 18 centuries (incorporating the three created under Romulus). According to Livy (1.43), service in the cavalry was restricted to those men who possessed 100,000 *asses* or more, and could furnish themselves with a 'helmet, round shield, greaves and cuirass, all of bronze, for the protection of their bodies . . .' The state treasury granted each *eques* ten thousand *asses* towards the purchase of a mount, and further financial help for the feeding and maintenance of the horse was provided by rich spinsters who were each obliged to pay 2000 *asses* annually (Livy 1.43).

One of the results of the expansion of Rome was her being able to recruit from a larger geographical area. Initially the army was largely supplemented by the Italian allies. These troops were organized and equipped in a similar manner to the Romans, and served in accordance with the treaty obligations drawn up either when they submitted to Rome, or when they were accepted into her alliance (Keppie 1984, 22). Gradually, however, an increasing number of foreign troops, particularly cavalry, were raised from the Celtic regions as will be seen below.

By Polybius' time in the second century BC, the structure of the cavalry had apparently undergone further change. The *equites* were now recruited before the *pedites*, and 300 were assigned to each legion (Polybius *Histories* 6.20). Their equipment was also greatly improved by being modelled on Greek examples: the lances were now provided with stronger shafts and spikes on the butt-ends, the shields were more solidly constructed, and Polybius implies that some sort of body armour was introduced (*Histories* 6.25). Furthermore, the rations for cavalrymen and their horses were reorganized. A Roman *eques* received seven *medimni* of barley and two of wheat, whilst an allied *eques* was allocated one and one-third *medimni* of wheat and five of barley. These rations were given free of charge to the allies, but the Roman troops had the cost deducted from their pay (Polybius *Histories* 6.39).

Although the above changes helped to place the cavalry on a more organized footing, a major weakness still remained. Roman citizens undoubtedly made excellent infantrymen, but as cavalrymen, an arm in which there was seemingly no native tradition, they were apparently less effective. Furthermore, the legionary cavalry were chosen purely on a qualification of wealth, rather than horsemanship. As noted by Hyland (1990, 188), however, wealth and horsemanship were likely to have gone hand-in-hand, since youths from such a background were generally given riding instruction. This deficiency, although somewhat lessened by the addition of allied cavalry, meant that the mounted force fielded by Rome was no match for enemy cavalrymen who had been 'born in the saddle'.

The seriousness of this weakness became disastrously apparent during the third century BC, when Rome was forced to take the field against Carthage in the Second Punic War. Although the main strength of the Carthaginian army lay in the brilliant leadership of its general, Hannibal, the deciding factor in several of its victorious engagements was the Numidian, Spanish and Celtic cavalry. At the Battle of Cannae in 216 BC, for example, the Roman army employed its usual formation, in which the infantry was placed in the centre and the cavalry on the wings. The Roman mounted contingent, however, was soon driven from the field by the Spanish and Celtic horse, who then proceeded to block the rear of the Roman infantry, having also attacked the allied cavalry, who had been fighting the Numidian horse on the other flank. The Romans were hemmed in, and in the massacre that followed an estimated 50,000 Roman and allied troops fell.

The necessity for an efficient cavalry force, together with other changes in Rome's strategy, was realized by the general Publius Scipio. After moving the war to African soil, and gaining the much needed support of the Numidians with their highly skilled horsemen, he finally defeated Hannibal at the Battle of Zama which took place in 202 BC.

Despite the recognized need for an adequate cavalry force to be attached to the Roman army following the Punic Wars, it was not until almost a century later that there appears to have been a decisive move towards the employment of foreign troops. These men, who used their native weapons, were either mercenaries or were levied from friendly states near to the area of campaign. This resulted in the legionary cavalry being used less and less, and they are last mentioned in unaltered form, together with the allied cavalry, by Sallust in his history of the Jugurthine War (95), which lasted from 111 BC until 105 BC. The legionary cavalry was, however, to re-emerge during the first century AD in a slightly different form (see pp.27ff).

The literary sources show that during the first century BC the practice of recruiting large bodies of native troops whilst on campaign became more and more common. The commentaries of Caesar are particularly noteworthy in this regard and contain numerous specific references about cavalry being raised in this way. For example, during his Gallic War (1.15), Caesar raised 4000 cavalry from the whole of the province, the tribe of the Aedui and their allies. Most of these Gallic cavalrymen were young aristocrats who would also have provided Caesar with hostages, which he could use to ensure the good behaviour of the tribes to which they belonged (*pers. comm.* J.C. Mann). A similar situation is recorded by Appian (*Civil Wars* 4.88), who writes that Brutus had been provided with 4000 horse which had been variously obtained from Gaul, Lusitania, Thrace, Illyricum, Parthia and Thessaly, whilst Cassius had gathered a further 2000 cavalry from Spain and Gaul, together with 4000 mounted archers from Arabia, Medea and Parthia.

These foreign troops were given the collective title of *auxilia*, a term which literally means 'help'. Once Rome realized that this was an effective method of remedying the apparent armament and skill deficiencies of the army, it was adopted on an ever increasing scale. Auxiliary troops were usually levied from areas in the vicinity of a campaign, although of necessity they were sometimes called upon to serve outside their homelands if the action had moved to a different theatre of war. They were originally commanded by native leaders, but by the late first century AD, the majority of commanders were young men of equestrian status.

Under the Republic many units levied on a campaign were disbanded on its completion. With the creation of a standing army and the regularization of the *auxilia*, however, which most believe to have been officially sanctioned (although not instigated) by Augustus (Webster 1985, 142; Cheesman 1914, 17), this policy changed, resulting in an increasing number becoming permanent auxiliary units.

Unit strength and organization

The *alae*

The *alae* were auxiliary units composed entirely of cavalry; the name *ala* means 'wing' in Latin, and comes from their deployment in battle on the flanks of an army. Initially the *alae* were formed into quingenary units, nominally 500 strong. Hyginus states that they were divided into 16 *turmae* (*De Metatione Castrorum* 16), a figure further attested by an inscription of AD 199 from Alexandria in Egypt (*CIL* III.6581), which records 16 decurions (*turmae* commanders) in both of the *ala* units mentioned. Uncertainty exists regarding the number of men in a *turma*. A fragment of a *pridianum* (strength report) of *Ala Commagenorum* from the Claudian period (*Ch LA* XI n501) records 434 men and 12 decurions, giving a figure of 36 men per *turma*. It is possible, however, that not all the decurions were present, and thus the *turma* strength may in actuality have been lower (Holder 1980, 9). A hay receipt on papyrus for a *turma* of the *Ala Veterana Gallica*, dating to AD 130 (Fink 1971, no.80), lists 30 men excluding the decurion. Furthermore, Arrian, a governor of Cappadocia under Hadrian, stated that there were 512 men in an *ala quingenaria* (*Tactica* 18). When divided by 16, this gives a total of 32 (including the officers) per *turma*. Unfortunately archaeology can shed no more light on the problem, owing to the lack of completely excavated *quingenaria* forts. The evidence would therefore seem to suggest that a figure of approximately 32 men (inclusive of officers) was the *turma* strength of a quingenary unit (Keppie 1984, 183; Breeze and Dobson 1987, 154–5; Webster 1985, 146; Holder 1982, 34; Dobson 1981, 224; Cheesman 1914, 26–7).

The creation of milliary units, nominally 1000 strong, occurred during the Flavian period (Breeze and Dobson 1987, 155; Holder 1982, 34; 1987, 13; Dobson 1981, 224; Birley 1966, 349–56). It has been suggested that the *ala milliaria* was the last of the six unit types to be established within the *auxilia* (Breeze and Dobson 1987, 156). The *alae milliariae* were the elite cavalry units of the Roman army. There were only a few throughout the Empire (Holder 1987, 13), no province holding more than one at any given time. In Britain, the *Ala Augusta Gallorum Petriana milliaria civium Romanorum bis torquata* was stationed at Stanwix on Hadrian's Wall. Milliary units were raised either from new recruits plus a small core of experienced men, or by increasing an established *quingenaria* unit (Holder 1982, 33). The latter method was the most economical, as a large proportion of the men were already trained.

Owing to the lack of full-scale archaeological excavation of forts known to have housed *milliariae*, information on their organization comes solely from Hyginus, who states that these units were divided into 24 *turmae* (*De Metatione Castrorum*. 16). Yet again problems arise concerning the number of men in a *turma*. If the term *milliaria* is taken literally, a *turma* strength of 42 is required to produce an appropriate total, implying that there were two different sizes of *turma* (Birley 1966, 349; Cheesman 1914, 26). Evidence suggests, however, that *milliaria* and *quingenaria* were not precise but approximate terms (Breeze and Dobson 1987, 156; Holder 1982, 37). For example, by the mid-80s AD, the first cohort of a legion contained five double centuries and was given the title *milliaria* (Hyginus *De Metatione Castrorum* 3. 4; Vegetius *Epitoma Rei Militaris* 2.8); if, however, each single century contained 80 men, as was normal in the other legionary cohorts, the total paper strength would be 800 and not 1000 (Breeze and Dobson 1987, 155). Similarly, the infantry *quingenaria* units had six centuries of 80 men, giving a total of 480, not 500, whilst the mixed infantry and cavalry *quingenaria* units (see below) contained approximately 608. Furthermore, the fact that there were only 24 *turmae* in a *milliaria* unit and not 32, implies that the Romans did not intend the unit to be double the strength of an *ala quingenaria*, being in actuality one-and-a-half times the size (Breeze and Dobson 1987, 156). It therefore seems likely that *turma* strengths were similar in all types of unit, numbering approximately 32, and that the term *milliaria* was merely a way of denoting a larger unit (Breeze and Dobson 1987, 16; Holder 1982, 38).

The commander of an *ala* was called a *praefectus equitum*. Originally he would have been a native leader of the tribe from which the unit had been raised, but by the late first century AD the majority of *praefecti* were young men of equestrian status, a status which they gained through a property qualification, and one which by this time had nothing to do with horses (see p.20). To attain the position of *praefectus equitum* of an *ala*, a number of civil and military posts had usually to be undertaken sequentially, with cavalry commands ranking higher than infantry ones. The commander of an *ala milliaria* unit was the highest of all (Keppie 1984, 184). There does not appear to have been a fixed term of service for any of the posts, although the average was three or four years (Webster 1985, 146). After holding such commands it was then possible to rise to a post in the imperial service, or even a seat in the senate (Dobson 1981, 224; Webster 1985, 146).

Although *praefecti* were primarily drawn from the equestrian class, it was possible during the early years of the first century AD for the chief centurions of legions (*primipili*), who automatically gained equestrian status on attaining this rank, to become auxiliary commanders (Webster 1985, 146). From the reign of Claudius onwards, all *praefecti* were of equestrian status, but it was possible for auxiliarymen, by gaining Roman citizenship on their discharge, to enable their families gradually to rise towards a higher position in civil or military life.

Each *turma* within the unit was commanded by a *decurio*. This post was usually held by a man promoted from the ranks, or one from a legion, for whom it was a step towards the centurionate. Aemilius Macer, in *The Digest*, outlines the tasks of this officer (49. 16. 12. 2): 'To keep the troops in camp, to bring them out for training, to keep the keys of the gates, to go round the guards from time to time, to attend the soldiers' mealtimes and sample the food to prevent the quartermasters from cheating, to punish offences, to hear complaints and inspect sick quarters.'

The officers below the decurions can be divided into two groups: the *principales* and the *immunes*. The former are distinguished by their ability both to stand in for the decurions and to command small detachments of men. The highest ranking officer of this group was the senior standard bearer, the *vexillarius*, who took his name from the small square flag he carried, called a *vexillum*. Other officers included in this group are the *imaginifer*, whose duty it was to carry an image of the Emperor; the *signifer* (standard bearer), one being attached to each *turma*; the *cornicularius* (secretary to a senior officer); the *duplicarius* (the second-in-command of a *turma*) and *sesquiplicarius* (the third-in-command of a *turma*), one of each being attached to every *turma*. The titles of the latter two posts denote their respective pay scales, that is double and one-and-a-half times a trooper's pay. There is evidence to suggest, however, that the *signifer* and *cornicularius* would also receive double pay (Breeze 1971). The *immunes*, as their name implies, were immune from doing certain duties in return for the execution of various tasks. They did not, however, rank higher than their fellow soldiers, or receive any extra pay (Breeze 1971, 133). The following posts belong to this group: the *curator* (accountant), one of which was attached to every *turma*; the *custos armorum* (keeper of the armoury); and the commander's clerical and administrative staff which comprised the *actarius* (the second-in-command of the staff), *strator* (see p.157–8), *stator* (messenger), *librarius* (clerk) and *beneficiarius* (assistant to the *praefectus*).

The *cohortes equitatae*

The *cohors equitata* was a unit composed of both infantry and cavalry, introduced into the Roman army during the Julio-Claudian period. It has been suggested that the idea may have been derived from the German mixed units, in which the infantry fought alongside the cavalry, reportedly holding on to the horse's mane in combat (Caesar, *Gallic War* 1.48; Dobson 1981, 224). Although it is true that Caesar employed a contingent of this type during the Gallic War (7.65), and an inscription from Augustus' reign records such a unit as having existed within the Roman army (*CIL* x.4862), it is believed that the *equites* and *pedites* of the later mixed units fought independently of each other in battle (see Chapter 8).

Information on the number of men in the two contingents of the *cohortes equitatae* comes from various sources. The *De Metatione Castrorum* of Hyginus states that a *cohors milliaria equitata* had 240 cavalry and 760 infantry, the numbers being halved in a *cohors quingenaria equitata* to 120 and 380 respectively. Josephus, in his account of the Jewish War, gives a total of 120 cavalry and 600 infantry for a *quingenaria* unit in AD 67 (3.2.67). The *pridiana* of three *quingenaria* units, ranging in date from the early second to the early third century AD, give cavalry totals of 119, 114 and 100 (the latter after the loss of 11); for the infantry the totals, with new admissions, are 427, 363 and 334 (the latter, after the loss of 16) (Fink 1971, nos. 63 and 64; Thomas and Davies 1977, 50–61). The discrepancies in the numbers of men in both branches of the units are possibly due, as Holder suggests (1982, 30–1), to the figures representing respectively, a unit at full strength ready to engage in war; one during peacetime conditions; and one recorded directly after combat.

What does become apparent from the evidence cited above is that although the total number of cavalry in a *quingenaria* unit deviates little from the writers' stated 120, the infantry figure differs considerably. A reason for this anomaly may lie in the fact that both Hyginus and Josephus appear to have believed that *milliaria* did indeed mean 1000 men and 'century' 100, when in reality this does not seem to have been the case (see p.23; Holder 1980, 7; Cheesman 1914, 30). On the other hand, it may be that under certain circumstances, such as during a campaign, the numbers of *pedites* and *equites* were increased. This may account for the considerably larger infantry complement of 600 men mentioned by Josephus (*Jewish War* 3.2.67).

A fragmentary pre-Flavian inscription from Ankara, Turkey (*CIL* III.6760), provides information on the organization of the cavalry within a quingenary unit. It records four decurions as belonging to *Cohors II Hispanorum*, implying that there was a corresponding number of *turmae*. This would equate well with both the literary and papyrological evidence, with each *turma* comprising approximately 30 troopers. From this, it may be postulated that a milliary unit would have had double this number of decurions and *turmae*.

The organization of the infantry has caused some debate among scholars (Holder 1980, 7–8; 1982, 30; Webster 1985, 149; Cheesman 1914, 29–30). The majority believe that the foot-soldiers were organized into centuries of 80 men in a similar manner to the legions, being arranged, as Hyginus states, into ten centuries in a *cohors milliaria equitata*, and six in a quingenary unit (*De Metatione Castrorum* 27).

Archaeology may be able to provide further evidence on the organization of the cavalry and infantry. A *cohors quingenaria equitata* is thought to have been in garrison on Hadrian's Wall at Wallsend during the Hadrianic period. Most of the fort's ground-plan is now known from excavation which has revealed nine rectangular barrack blocks, approximately 49m (150ft) long by 9m (28ft) wide. One of these could possibly be identified as a stable on the basis that it has a good drainage system but no partitions (*pers. comm.* C.M. Daniels). At Birrens, Dumfriesshire, the fort of a *milliaria* unit was excavated and 22 buildings were found, of which it is suggested 18 would have been required for the men, leaving four to serve as stables (Webster 1985, 149). Until, however, more excavation is undertaken on the forts of mixed units, it is inadvisable to attempt to calculate the amount of space each branch would have required, since the actual size of both complements appears to fluctuate.

The *equites legionis*

Although the legionary cavalry are attested by both literary and epigraphic evidence, many problems still exist, particularly with regard to their organization. The only reference for the number of cavalry per legion in the early Empire comes from Josephus writing in the first century AD (*Jewish War* 3.6.2.120): 'Then came the cavalry units of the legion; for to each legion are attached a hundred and twenty horse'. This sentence has led to the belief that during the early Empire, all legions had a cavalry contingent of 120 men (Pitts and St Joseph 1985, 169; Parker 1958, 210; Webster 1985, 111; Dobson 1981, 217; Holder 1982, 24). There are a number of factors relating to this reference, however, that have to be taken into consideration before it can be so generally applied. Firstly, Josephus was writing specifically about the legions in Judaea in AD 67, and his statement may be only a direct reflection of what he saw, and not a general comment on the cavalry strength of legions throughout the whole Empire, and at all periods. Secondly, these legions were engaged in a serious, prolonged war, and thus the number of both infantry and cavalry present may have differed from the peacetime complement. All that can be said with any certainty regarding this reference, therefore, is that according to Josephus, 120 cavalry were attached to the legions present in Judaea in AD 67; whether such a situation existed elsewhere is by no means certain.

One further reference exists regarding the numbers of *equites legionis*. Vegetius (*Epitoma Rei Militaris* 2.6; Pitts and St Joseph 1985, 169; Breeze 1969, 53) states that there were 132 *equites* in the first cohort and 66 in each of the other nine cohorts, giving a total paper strength of 726 cavalry per legion. Such an increase in the mounted contingent may reflect the growing need for the legion to become a more mobile force.

Exactly how the *equites legionis* were organized is still far from clear. Vegetius states (2.6; 14) that the 66 *equites* in each cohort (the first cohort had 132) formed two *turmae* of 32 men, under the command of a *decurio*. A ring from Baden in Germany, bearing the inscription *eq.leg.XXI Sexti t.*, has been cited in support of Vegetius' statement, with the suggestion that the *t.* may be an abbreviation for *turma (CIL* VIII, 10024, 31). Owing, however, to both its position in the text (the word *turma* usually coming before the officer's name), and the very abbreviated form of the engraving, doubt has been cast on the validity of this interpretation (Breeze 1969, 53; Pitts and St Joseph 1985, 169). Furthermore, epigraphic evidence would seem to imply that from the first to the middle of the third century, *equites* were carried on the books of centuries, at least for purposes of administration (Pitts and St Joseph 1985, 169; Breeze 1969, 54; Parker 1958, 210; 1932, 140; Holder 1982, 24; Webster 1985, 111). A number of tombstones mention *equites* as belonging to centuries, such as that of Quintus Cornelius of *Legio IX Hispana* from Lincoln, dating from AD 47–71 (Pitts and St Joseph 1985, 169), who served in the century of Cassius Martialis (*RIB* 254); and a *laterculus* of AD 220 (*CIL* VIII 2568, 18) which states that an *optio equitum* of *Legio III Augusta*, was in the fifth century of the seventh cohort. That some *equites* at least were placed on the books of centuries, and were not organized into *turmae* is, from the cited evidence, undeniable. We must therefore assume that Vegetius was either describing a situation which came into being after a third century reform (Breeze 1969, 54; Pitts and St Joseph 1985, 169), or that he was confusing the organization of the legionary cavalry with that of an *ala* (Pitts and St Joseph 1985, 169).

Why the *equites* were kept on the books of centuries is not altogether clear, particularly when it appears that for much of the time they worked together as a unit, completely independent of the legionary infantry (see p.29–30). It has been suggested that on recruitment into the legions, all soldiers had to undergo basic training as infantrymen, before they could become *equites* (Breeze 1969, 54, n.19). Thus, on attaining places in the cavalry, they simply stayed on the books of the century into which they had initially enrolled (Pitts and St Joseph 1985, 170). If such a situation did exist, then there is no need to try to allocate a specific number of cavalrymen to each century, the number possibly being dictated by nothing more than the personal choice of the men themselves, and the availability of places in the cavalry of the legion in which they were serving.

The problem of whether or not there was an overall commander in charge of the *equites legionis* is as yet unresolved (Breeze 1969, 55; Speidel 1970, 144; Pitts and St Joseph 1985, 170). If such a post did exist it has been postulated that the officer in question would have held the rank of centurion (Pitts and St Joseph 1985, 170; Speidel 1970, 144). Domaszewski, however, argued that the *optio*, which is attested for the legionary cavalry (*CIL* VIII 2568), would have been the highest ranking officer (1967, 47). In opposition to this theory, according to Speidel (1970, 145), is an inscription recording the career of a praetorian guard (*CIL* VI 32709a = *ILS* 9190), who held the posts of *optio equitum* and *vexillarius equitum*, amongst others; which has led him to suggest that owing to the order in which the offices were recorded, the *vexillarius equitum* must rank higher than, or at least equal to an *optio equitum*. Whether it is correct, however, to assume that the order in which the titles are listed on inscriptions, is the order in which they were held, is questionable. Caution must therefore be exercised regarding theories based on such evidence.

Precisely how independent the *equites legionis* were within the legion is uncertain. A tombstone recording the career of T. Claudius Maximus is thought to include the first known reference to a *quaestor* in the legionary *equites* (Speidel 1970, 144). A separate treasurer for the cavalry would obviously imply a greater degree of organizational independence from the infantry than was hitherto thought. It is known, however, from both literary and epigraphic sources, that the *equites* trained, marched and fought as a unit (Speidel 1970, 144). Two inscriptions, one of a *magister kampi* (*CIL* VIII.2562, 6) and another of a *magister equitum* (*CIL* V.8278), may imply specific training for the cavalry in the legions concerned.

Further support for the *equites* receiving individual training, comes from Hadrian's *Adlocutio* (*CIL* VIII.2532; 18042 = *ILS* 2487; 9133–35), which records how he congratulated the legionary cavalry on their display: 'Military exercises have, I may say, their own rules, and if anything is added to or taken away from these rules, the exercise becomes either of little value or too difficult. The more elaborateness is added, the poorer a show it makes. But you performed the most difficult of all exercises, namely, javelin throwing, clad in cuirass . . . In addition, I congratulate you on your spirit . . .' It is reasonable to deduce from this that only by tuition from cavalry instructors, and the *equites* training as a body, could the degree of skill required to undertake such a performance be made possible. Evidence for the *equites legionis* marching together comes from Arrian's *Acies Contra Alanos*, and the first-century writer Josephus (*Jewish War* 5.2.1.47–50):

> As Titus advanced into enemy territory, his vanguard consisted of the contingents of the kings with the whole body of auxiliaries. Next to these were the pioneers and camp-measurers, then the officers' baggage-train; behind the troops protecting these came the

> commander-in-chief, escorted by the lancers and other picked troops, and followed by the legionary cavalry. These were succeeded by the engines, and these by the tribunes and prefects of cohorts with picked escort; after them and surrounding the eagle came the ensigns preceded by their trumpeters, and behind them the solid column, six abreast. The servants attached to each legion followed in a body, preceded by the baggage-train. Last of all came the mercenaries with a rearguard to keep watch on them.

The *equites legionis*, therefore, do appear to have marched separately from the legionary infantry, a similar order of march still occurring in Arrian's time (Dent 1974, 571).

Despite a certain degree of unit identity, the legionary cavalry were not always employed as a group, serving mainly as mounted messengers and scouts (Pitts and St Joseph 1985, 170; Breeze 1969, 55; Webster 1985, 111; Dobson 1981, 217; Bishop 1988, 112). In such a situation, it was not necessary for them to be housed together, each *eques* continuing to live in the barracks of the century into which he had initially enrolled. It is possible that they were accommodated as a unit (Breeze 1969, 55), but owing to the fact that only two legionary fortresses have been fully excavated (Neuss in Germany and Inchtuthil in Scotland), evidence is extremely limited. Furthermore, both excavators and scholars seem still to be searching for enough barrack space to house 120 men, despite the fact that at Inchtuthil barrack blocks A and B had 20 *contubernia*, when it was thought that only 16 were necessary: in this instance it was suggested that the extra four may have belonged to the commander, assuming one existed (Pitts and St Joseph 1985, 170). Yet again, it would appear that too much reliance is being placed on Josephus' statement, thus not allowing for the possibility that more than 120 cavalrymen were present in the fortress.

As mentioned above, Vegetius states that the legionary cavalry numbered 726 per legion (*Epitoma Rei Militaris*, 2.6). It is believed that this substantial increase occurred during the reign of Gallienus (AD 253–68) (Parker 1932, 145; Holder 1982, 97). It is a matter of debate as to whether or not it was under this Emperor that the legionary cavalry became separate units. It may be that a gradual process of independence was begun under Gallienus, but that the final severance of all ties with the legionary infantry did not occur until the time of Constantine I (AD 324–37) (Parker 1932, 145).

The *equites singulares*

The Emperor and the provincial governors had a contingent of cavalry and infantry attached to them for their personal service and protection. The cavalry who served the Emperor were seconded from the *alae*, and were called *equites singulares Augusti*. The infantry equivalent was the Praetorian Guard. During the first and second centuries AD, men serving within the Guard usually came from Italy and were recruited directly. From the time of Severus (AD 193–211) onwards, however, some Praetorians were drawn from the legions, and of those still recruited directly most now came from Thrace (*pers. comm.* J.C. Mann). The provincial governors' cavalry contingents, the *equites singulares*, were also drawn from the *alae*, but the infantry, the *pedites singulares*, were seconded from the *auxilia*.

The strength of *singulares* units is not known for certain, but it has been argued that a governor in charge of a strong military province would have had a milliary guard unit comprising an equal number of infantry and cavalry (Speidel 1976).

There are further problems regarding the internal organization of these units. Officers within the *singulares* gained the additional title of *consularis*, to distinguish them as serving in these elite units. The cavalry contingent appears to have been commanded by a *praepositus*. Decurions are attested for the *singulares*, implying that the men were divided into *turmae*. A *signifer* is recorded, however, and this may indicate the presence of tactical squadrons, a situation which would presumably be necessary since the *singulares* did engage in combat (Speidel 1981, 406; Davies 1976, 142). Furthermore, it is known that the men still belonged to the *turma* or century of their regular unit, to which they would probably return on completion of their service in the guard. *Singulares* could therefore have simultaneously belonged to two *turmae* or centuries.

It is not known if there was a specified term of service in the guard, although it appears that the officers could remain in the *singulares* until, and sometimes beyond, their 25 years of service, unless they wished to make themselves available for further promotion within the army (Holder 1982, 75). The men serving in these units received no extra pay (Davies 1976, 135).

The *numeri, exploratores* and *cunei*

The *numeri* and *exploratores* of the Roman army may have contained a mounted element. The title *numerus* covers a wide variety of different troops, some of whom were drawn from the *auxilia* to perform special tasks, while others, the so-called ethnic units, were recruited from peoples on the fringes of the Empire and stationed in areas of low population probably to guard routes. Not much is known about their organization and they may have differed vastly in size and strength. Two decurions are attested on inscriptions, one serving in a *numerus Maurorum* in Dacia (*CIL* III 7695) and another from Africa in a *numerus Palmyrenorum*. This may indicate that some *numeri* were divided into *turmae* commanded by the appropriate officer.

Exploratores, literally 'scouts', would probably be mounted units, but this may not have always been the case. At Dura-Europos, Syria, 15 men were listed as scouts from the *Cohors XX Palmyrenorum*, and of these five men were *pedites* (Speidel 1970, 74). The *exploratores* at Walldürn in Germany in AD 232 may have been mounted; no less than four reliefs of the horse goddess Epona were found there. If the buildings at Niederbieber are correctly identified as stables, the troops attested there, a *numerus Brittonum* and the *numerus exploratorum Germanicianorum Divitiensium* may have been wholly or partly mounted.

Units with the title *cuneus*, which means wedge, are usually described as the mounted counterparts of the *numeri*, but this is not strictly accurate. The use of the title *cuneus* seems to have developed in the third century AD, some time later than the formation of the *numeri* which may already have contained mounted men, at least in part. Nothing is known of the numbers of men in a *cuneus*. There may have been no standard figures for each unit, and their organization may have been likewise unstandardized. The *cunei equitum* of the *Notitia Dignitatum* were quite different from the smaller ethnic units. These were all stationed on the Danube and probably developed from the older cavalry vexillations.

Camel units (*dromedarii*)

Dromedarii were only used in the east, and could serve either as a whole camel unit, such as the *Ala I Ulpia dromedariorum milliaria*, which was raised by Trajan to serve in Syria (Holder 1987, 14), or with a *cohors equitata*.

Information regarding the strength and organization of camel, and part-camel units, is slight. Two duty rosters of *Cohors XX Palmyrenorum milliaria equitata* from Dura-Europos record the presence of approximately 20 *dromedarii* on *P. Dur*. 100, and approximately 35 on *P. Dur*. 101 (Gilliam 1965, 76). Although they are listed separately, they are assigned to infantry centuries, and it seems that the new *dromedarii* who are recorded on *P. Dur*. 101, enlisted as *pedites*, and only attained the post of camel troops after having served a number of years as infantry (Gilliam 1965, 76).

Unit titulature

Auxiliary units were most often distinguished by the use of epithets relating to the province or tribe from which they were originally raised. Where more than one unit was raised from the same tribe or province a number was added. From the reign of Tiberius, units sometimes added the name of either their most distinguished, or their original commander, as, for example, the *Ala Augusta Gallorum Petriana milliaria civium Romanorum bis torquata*, which was named after T. Pomponius Petra. This '-iana' form (eg. *Petriana*), usually only appears in the titles of *alae* units (*pers. comm.* J.C. Mann). Alternatively, they could take the name of the province in which they had served, such as the *Cohors I Thracum Syriaca*, which is attested in Moesia Superior (*CIL* III 14575; 14579). A unit could also be given the name of the Emperor under whom it was raised, or have it bestowed on them for outstanding bravery and loyalty in battle.

If all the men involved in combat from a particular unit had fought with great courage, then a block grant of Roman citizenship could be awarded, together with the title *civium Romanorum*. Although it is often thought that this award was begun under Vespasian (AD 69–79), an inscription from Bath (*RIB* 159), probably records such a grant being made during the censorship of Claudius and Vitellius (AD 47–8) (*pers. comm.* J.C. Mann). Although the unit kept this title, only the men serving at the time of the award received the citizenship.

Torques, which were previously given to individuals, were now awarded to entire units, usually at the same time as the reward of citizenship (Holder 1982, 22). Both the rewards of torques and citizenship were granted to the *Ala Augusta Gallorum Petriana milliaria civium Romanorum bis torquata*, and such honorific titles may have instilled the men serving in this, and other similarly awarded units, with a great sense of pride.

During the third century it was common practice for the *cognomen* of the Emperor to be added to all unit titles (Maxfield 1981, 17; Holder 1982, 24). On the death of an Emperor units would exchange the old name for that of the new Emperor.

3 Equipment and unit armament styles

The equipment of the Roman army was not as uniform as is often believed, a considerable amount of variation in both style and decoration being found in most items. It would have been necessary for the army to enforce some regulations on the basic equipment required to fight within a particular unit, but it seems unlikely that any restrictions would have been placed on surface ornamentation or the style of accoutrements, such as scabbard suspension loops or reinforcements, provided they did not impair the functional ability of the equipment. Furthermore, although certain items, such as helmets, underwent changes in style, it would be wrong to assume that any new design would be simultaneously adopted throughout the Empire. Regional variations were always present in such a cosmopolitan army, and at any one time there was probably a wide range of designs in existence.

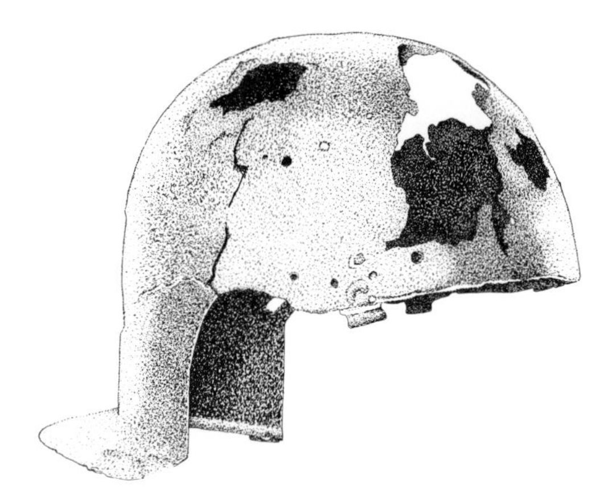

2 Iron auxiliary cavalry helmet from Newstead, believed by Robinson to date from the Flavian period (1975, 94–5). A fragment of silver sheathing remains on the neck-flange, suggesting that originally the helmet may have been covered in silver or bronze. Although the cheek-pieces have not survived, the hinges which held them are still attached. (National Musueum of Scotland, Edinburgh. Drawn by K.R. Dixon.)

Protective equipment: the men

The helmet

A typology exists for Roman cavalry helmets (Robinson 1975, 89–106), which can be seen gradually to offer greater protection to the wearer. The earliest examples, dating to the Flavian period (AD 69–92), consist of a simple iron skull-piece, cheek-pieces, no reinforcing peak, and a narrow neck-flange. A helmet of this type was found at Newstead in Scotland (Fig.2) (Curle 1911, 164, Pl.XXVI; Robinson 1975, 89). The rivet holes encircling the skull-piece suggest that originally it might have been sheathed in silver or bronze (Robinson 1975, 89).

In the late first or early second century AD, cavalry helmets began to be fitted with reinforcing strips across the forehead. These over time gradually rose more and more at the front, eventually forming a peak (Dobson 1981, 235; Robinson 1975, 89). A very unusual example of this type was found at Witcham Gravel, England (Fig.3) (Robinson 1975, 89). The sides and neck-flange of this bronze-plated iron helmet are decorated with large bosses. The left cheek-piece is still extant.

Later in the second century the cheek-pieces became larger, fitting round the face, and leaving only the eyes, nose and mouth visible, such as in the helmet from Heddernheim, Germany (Pl.2) (Robinson 1975, 90, Pl.259). Helmets were now also fitted with crossed reinforcing bars over the skull-

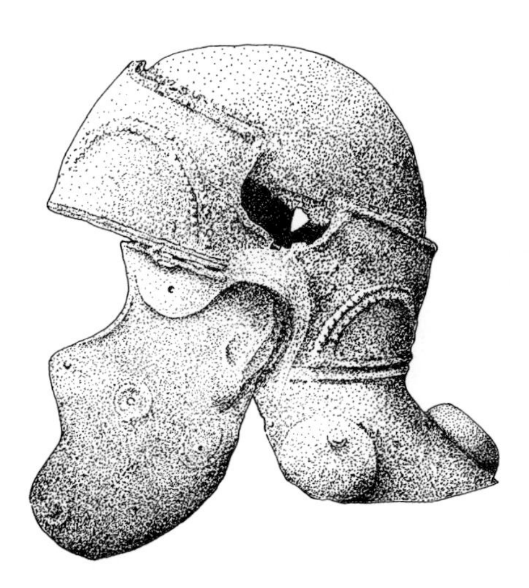

3 Cavalry helmet dating to the late first or early second century AD from Witcham Gravel, Cambridgeshire. Made of iron with four covering sections of bronze it is adorned with large bronze bosses. (British Museum, London. Drawn by K.R. Dixon.)

4 Cavalryman from the Arch of Galerius, Thessaloniki, Greece. Erected between AD 297 and 311. He wears a tall, conical helmet, not unlike the later *Spangenhelmen*, and a long scale shirt (*lorica squamata*). (Redrawn by K.R. Dixon from Robinson 1975.)

piece and deep neck-flanges, as again can be seen on the Heddernheim example.

Further variations exist, and an interesting style can be seen on the Arch of Galerius, Thessaloniki, which was erected between AD 297 and 311. Here the helmets (Fig.4), believed by Robinson (1975, 93) to be worn by *cataphractarii*, are segmentally panelled, tall and conical with check-pieces and neck-guards, and are the forerunners of the later *Spangenhelmen* (James 1986, 113–134).

Mail armour

Mail armour, *lorica hamata*, is made from rings of iron or bronze, each one passing through the two rings directly above and the two directly below. A common method of construction uses alternate downward rows of wire rings, with the flattened ends riveted together, and solid rings. It is uncertain whether the solid rings were punched out of sheet metal, or were made of wire with the butt ends welded together. Examples of this type of mail have been found at The Lunt, England (Fig.5) (Hobley 1969, 116, 13, fig.21, no.13), Carlingwark Loch (Piggott 1955, 38, 50, Pl.II) and Newstead, Scotland (Curle 1911, 161, Pl.XXXVIII). External ring diameters range from 3mm to 9mm ($\frac{1}{8}$ to $\frac{1}{3}$in.).

Several sites have produced another type of mail, consisting of bronze rings faced with very small scales, such as the shirt from Augsburg, Germany, which had alternate scales of bronze and iron (Robinson 1975, 173). Fragments have also been found at Newstead, Scotland (Curle 1911, 161, Pl.XXXVIII, Fig.8) and Ouddorp, Holland (Robinson 1975, 173).

Pictorial evidence is abundant for cavalrymen wearing *loricae hamatae*. A late Augustan relief in the Palazzo Ducale at Mantua shows Romans fighting Gauls, and depicts the horsemen wearing mail shirts with extensive shoulder reinforcements which fall half way down the upper arm (Strong 1961, Fig.41; Robinson 1975, 157, 164). These reinforcements were fitted with hooks, by which they were attached to a disc positioned in the centre of the shirt (Pl.3). Examples of this type of fastening have been found at Chassenard, France (Robinson 1975, pl.480), and Neuss, Germany (Fig.6) (Bishop and Coulston 1989, 32). Shoulder reinforcements appear to be particularly associated with the cavalry.

Late first-century tombstones, such as that of the cavalryman Bassus from Cologne, Germany, depict short-sleeved, hip-length shirts, with side slits (Fig.7) (Schleiermacher 1984, no.17). As can be seen from both the columns of Trajan and Marcus Aurelius, this simple style continued into the second century, changing only slightly by having jagged rather than straight

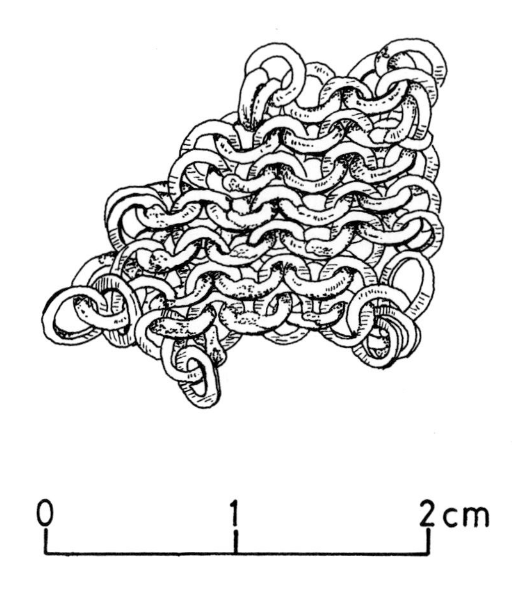

5 A fragment of Roman mail from The Lunt, Baginton, Warwickshire. Made of bronze with rows of riveted wire rings alternating with ones punched out of sheet metal. (Redrawn by K.R. Dixon from Hobley 1969).)

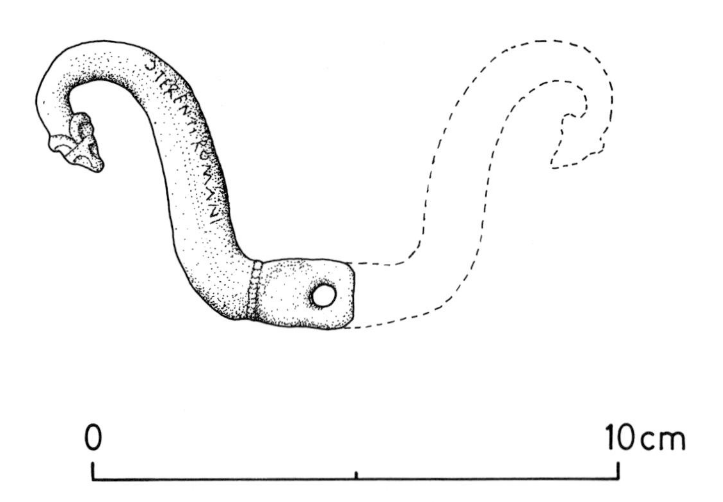

6 Hook fastening from Neuss, Germany. A hook was attached to the lower inner edge of each shoulder reinforcement, by which they were fastened to a disc in the centre of the shirt. This prevented the reinforcements from flapping around and troubling the wearer. (Redrawn by K.R. Dixon from Bishop and Coulston 1989.)

edges round the sleeves and the bottom of the shirt. By the 200s AD, however, the cavalry had begun to wear longer *loricae hamatae*, such as that depicted on a tombstone from Chester (Pl.4) (Schleiermacher 1984, no.73).

Scale armour

The making of scale armour, *lorica squamata*, required only a minimum of skill as the cutting of each individual scale from iron or bronze sheets, and the mounting of them on linen or leather, demanded patience rather than craftsmanship.

The size and shape of the scales vary greatly, although the most common type is rectangular and flat with a rounded end. To strengthen the scales a central ridge could be embossed on them, creating the appearance of feathers. It is believed that this type of scale would only have been worn by officers (Robinson 1975, 156). Scales could also be made more decorative by tinning every alternate one, producing a silver and gold chequerboard effect, like those found at Ham Hill, England, and Augsburg, Germany.

The scales were pierced with a number of holes, usually grouped in pairs; those on the sides were used to link the scales to each other in overlapping horizontal rows, and those at the top were to attach the rows to the backing, which could be either of leather or linen (Fig.8). In some cases, however, the holes in the top were wired to the corresponding holes in the lower end of the scale below, producing an extremely rigid body armour: a fragment of this

7 *T[itus] FLAVIVS BASSVS MVCALAE / F[ilius] DANSALA EQ[ues] ALAE NORI/ CORV[m] TVR[ma] FABI PVDENTIS / AN[norum] XXXXVI STIP[endiorum] XXVI H[eres] F[aciendum] C[vrauit]*
'Titus Flavius Bassus, son of Mucala, of the tribe of Dansala, trooper of the *Ala Noricorum*, and the *turma* of Fabius Pudentis, 46 years old, of 26 years' service. His heir had this erected.'
This tombstone, which dates to the last decade of the first century AD, is the most detailed Roman cavalry tombstone to survive. The rider is shown wearing a short-sleeved hip-length shirt, with side slits. He carries an oval shield and a spear, and has a long sword (*spatha*) hanging from a belt around his waist. The horse is depicted wearing a hackamore, a type of muzzle, bifurcated harness, on which hang lunate and lozenge-shaped pendants, and a decorative fringed chest band (peytral). (Römisch-Germanisches Museum, Cologne, Germany. Drawn by K.R. Dixon.)

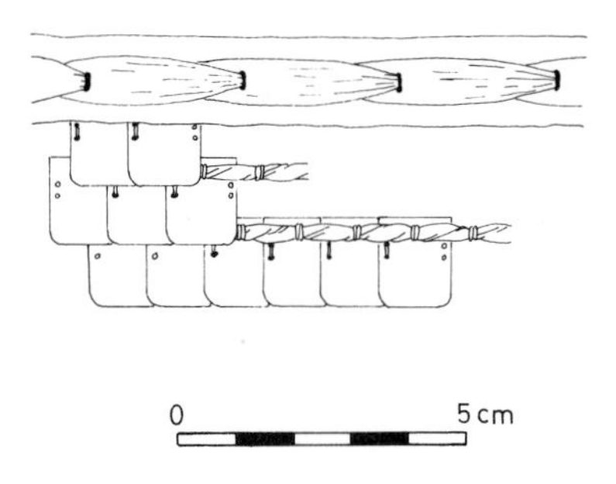

8 An extremely well-preserved example of scale armour, from Carpow, Perthshire, Scotland. The scales are still attached to the linen and some of the leather edging round the neck has also survived. The cord, visible on the drawing, was sewn onto each scale which was in turn pierced with holes in horizontal lines, the thread catching in the lining at the same time. Owing to the unusual weave of the shirt and the amount of care taken with the binding of the edge it is believed that the owner must have held a high rank (Wild 1981, 305–6.) Redrawn by K.R. Dixon from Wild 1981.)

type was found at Krefeld-Gellep, Germany (Ruger 1971, 290–2, Fig.13, Taf.14).

Some uncertainty remains regarding the position of the opening in scale shirts to enable soldiers to put them on. The suggestion of a back opening was rejected by Robinson on the basis that the soldier would have required assistance to do up the fastenings (1975, 156). Recent investigations, however, using a reconstructed *lorica squamata* with a back opening, have demonstrated that the wearer *can* fasten the garment completely unaided (*pers. comm.* J.R.A. Underwood). The left-side opening is favoured by both Robinson and Connolly, the latter basing his preference on the fact that Greek cuirasses, from the Bronze Age to the Hellenistic period, were fastened in this manner, and he suggests that the Romans may have continued this tradition (*pers. comm.* P. Connolly).

The style of *lorica squamata* prevalent during the first and second centuries AD, appears to have been a thigh-length shirt with two breast plates joined together on the chest, with short side slits in order to facilitate it being worn on horseback (Fig.9) (Schleiermacher 1984, no.9). The shirt is sleeveless, although there is a fringe of short *pteruges*.

During the third and fourth centuries the style of *loricae squamatae* appears to have changed. The Arch of Galerius at Thessaloniki (AD 297 to 311), shows dismounted cavalrymen (see Fig.4), possibly Sarmatians, wearing almost knee-length shirts with sleeves, and a tight waist-belt which would reduce the strain on the shoulders. No side slits are shown on these

9 *VONATORIX DV/CONIS F[ilius] EQVES ALA/LONGINIANA AN/NORVM XLV STIPEN/DIORVM XVII H[ic] S[itus] E[st]*
'Vonatorix, son of Duco, trooper of the *Ala Longiniana*, 45 years old, of 17 years' service. Here lies buried.'

This tombstone, dating to the middle of the first century AD, depicts the style of scale shirt which continued in use from the first to the second century. Vonatorix wears a sleeveless shirt with the arm holes fringed with short *pteruges* (strips of leather) and he carries an 'hexagonal' shield. The horse's bridle and harness are adorned with metal discs (*phalerae*). (Rheinisches Landesmuseum, Bonn, Germany. Drawn by K.R. Dixon.)

10 Grafitto from Dura-Europos, Syria, believed to depict a *clibanarius*. The rider appears to be encased in armour, including some form of thigh protection, possibly similar to the lamellar *cuisses* found at the same site. On his head he wears a conical helmet, apparently constructed in small panels. The horse is covered in a scale barding (coat), not unlike those actually discovered at this site. (Drawn by K.R. Dixon.)

loricae, and in the absence of front and back slits it is difficult to envisage how a cavalryman would have managed to sit astride his horse. This style of scale armour is also depicted on the Arch of Constantine, again apparently without slits.

Lamellar armour

Lamellar armour is constructed from elongated rectangular scales of iron, bronze, bone, rawhide or wood, laced together through holes pierced in the scales. The size of the scales depended on what part of the body they were intended to protect; those for the upper arms and shoulders were generally quite small, whilst those for the body were much longer (Robinson 1975, 162). The best surviving examples of lamellae come from Dura-Europos, Syria, where two thigh guards (*cuisses*) of rawhide were found (Pl.5) (see below; Rostovtzeff *et al.* 1936, 450–2, Pl.XXIII; Robinson 1975, 162, Pl.457–8).

Thigh guards

The Dura-Europos graffito of a heavy-armoured cavalryman (*clibanarius* or *cataphract*) (Fig.10), is thought to be wearing some form of thigh protection. Such a belief is supported by the find of two lamellar *cuisses* of rawhide from the same site (see Pl.5). Both thigh guards are lacquered, one red and one black, and are of 'leg-of-mutton' shape. They are laced with hide in horizontal rows, and attached vertically by red leather laces on the exterior. The *cuisses* were only intended to cover and protect the outsides of the rider's legs.

Shields

Roman cavalry shields could be oval (see Fig.7), hexagonal (see Fig.9), rectangular or round (see Fig.1). Sculptural evidence appears to imply that the three former shapes were mainly employed from the first to the third centuries AD, with the round shield becoming the more dominant style from then onwards.

Oval shields were not restricted to the cavalry, as from the second century onwards legionaries began to use this flat type in preference to the semicylindrical rectangular shield (Tomlin 1981, 259). The oval shield covers from Valkenburg in the Netherlands (Groenman-van Waateringe 1967, 52–73), therefore, need not have belonged to cavalry; the same can be said of the five oval shields which were found at Dura-Europos (Rostovtzeff *et al.* 1939, 326–69, Figs.83–4, Pls.XLI–VI). The oval shape was, however, ideally suited to the cavalry, protecting the rider from shoulder to ankle in a fairly narrow strip, with the widest part of the shield covering the trunk and thigh.

Flat shields were constructed either from laminated strips of wood, or from planks of wood, held together with glue, with the possible addition of strengthening struts across the back (*pers. comm.* P. Connolly). A further preventative measure against the shield splitting was provided by binding, either of hide (Fig.11) or bronze (Fig.12), which could be attached round the circumference. This also served to present a neat finish (*pers. comm.* J.R.A. Underwood). Extant finds would seem to suggest that bronze binding was

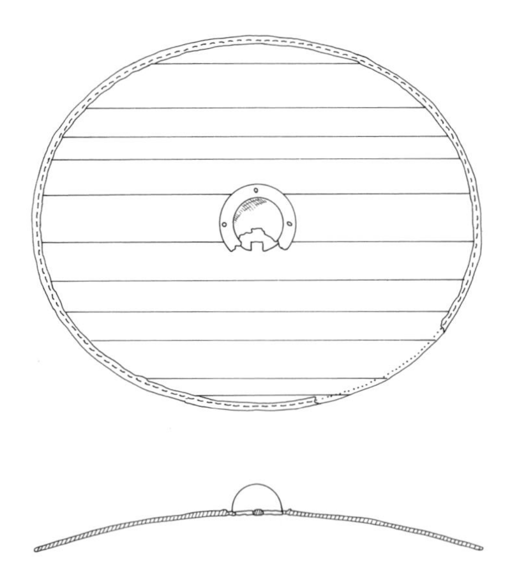

11 Oval shield from Dura Europos, Syria. It is constructed of wooden planks glued together longitudinally. In the middle of the shield is a circular hole, over which the boss (*umbo*) would have been placed. The circumference of the shield is bound with a leather edging (Rostovtzeff *et al.* 1939, 326–69, Figs.83–4, Pls.XLI–VI. Redrawn by K.R. Dixon.)

the most common material employed. This may, however, be the result of a bias in the archaeological record, since organic edgings are less likely to survive.

Before the binding was attached, the shield was sometimes covered on both sides with hide and linen, as was the case with the semicylindrical

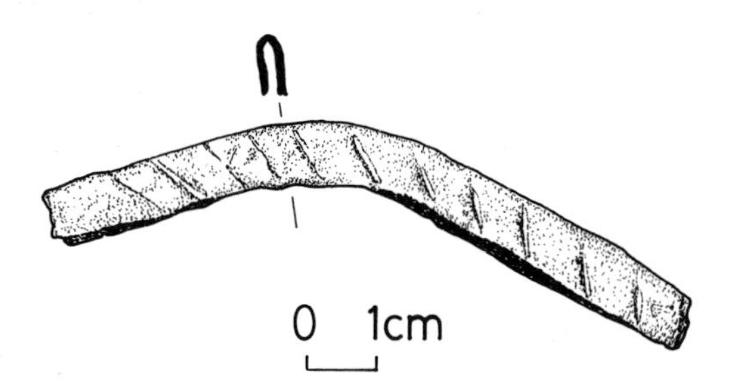

12 Fragment of bronze shield binding from Colchester. It has been suggested that it may have come from a hexagonal shield, although the bend may have been caused by pre- or post-deposition damage. (Redrawn by K.R. Dixon from Crummy 1981.)

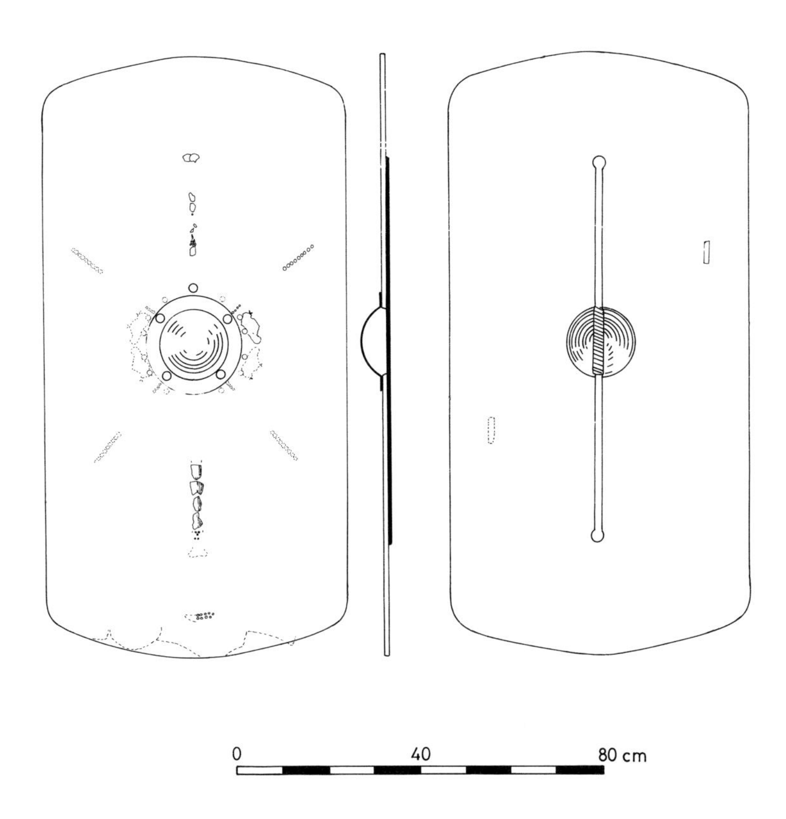

13–14 Reconstruction of the external and internal faces of the Doncaster shield: note the extended shield grip. (Redrawn by J.R.A. Underwood from Buckland 1978).

rectangular one from Dura (Rostovtzeff *et al.* 1936, 456–66, Pl.xxv). This could then be painted, possibly to show either the *turma* or larger unit to which the trooper belonged. Three of the shields from Dura were elaborately and colourfully decorated with patterns and figures, including one depicting scenes of Amazons fighting Greeks (Rostovtzeff *et al.* 1939, 326–69, Figs.83–4, Pls.xli–vi).

The shield was held by a grip, usually of wood, although occasionally strengthened with metal, which ran across a central hole. The grip was sometimes extended beyond the hole on either side, as is demonstrated by the example from Doncaster (Figs 13–14) (Buckland 1978, 248–51, Fig.7). The carrying hand was protected by a hemispherical metal boss (*umbo*) which was fixed to the outside of the shield by four or six rivets.

Some uncertainty exists concerning the size of shields. The leather shield covers from Valkenburg ranged in length from 1m ($3\frac{1}{4}$ft) to 1.5m (5ft) and from 52cm (21in) to 64cm (26in) wide (Groenman-van Waateringe 1967,

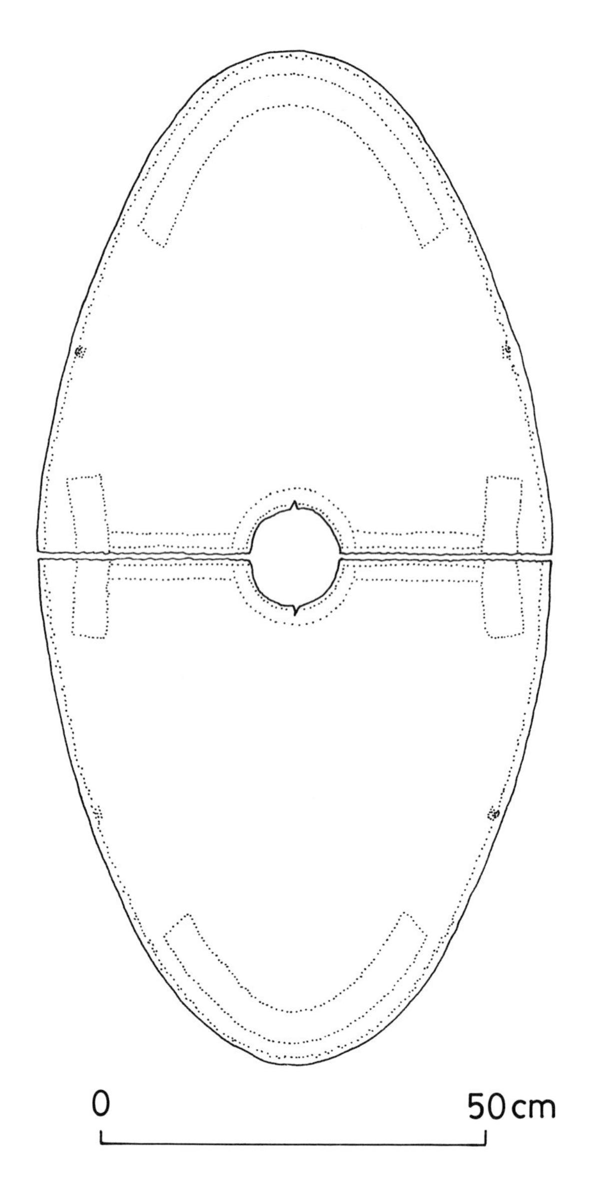

15 Reconstruction of an oval leather shield cover from Valkenburg, the Netherlands. (Redrawn by K.R. Dixon from Groenman-van Waateringe 1967.)

209). It must be remembered, however, that these measurements would include the edge that folded over the shield for the drawstring to pass through, which would therefore result in the shield being 7.5–10cm (3–4in) less than the size of the cover.

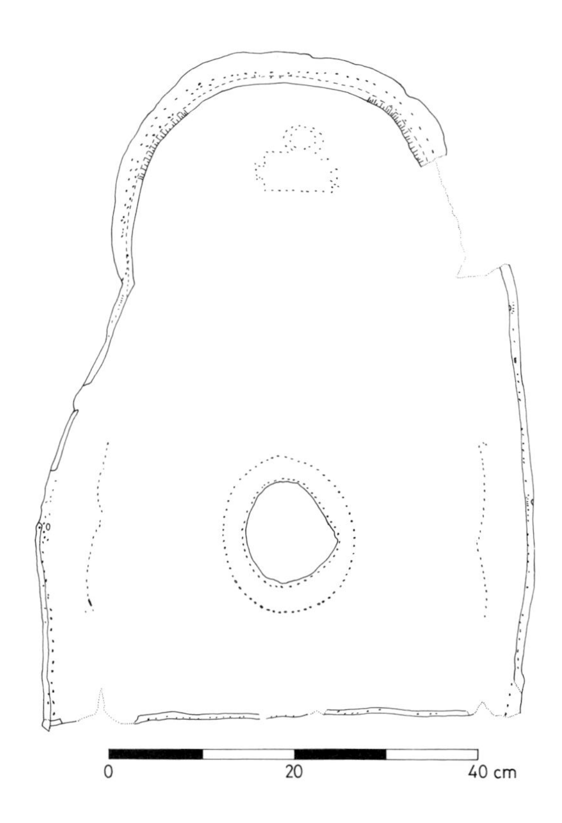

16 Large section of an oval leather shield cover from Valkenburg, the Netherlands. Note the flap of leather through which the drawstring would have passed to secure the cover to the shield, and the stitch-holes which indicate that originally a leather *tabula ansata* (unit/name tag) was attached. (Redrawn by K.R. Dixon from Groenman-van Waateringe 1967).

Shield covers

When a shield was not in use it was protected by a leather shield cover which was tightened round the edge of the shield back by a drawstring. A number of these covers were found at Valkenburg in the Netherlands (see above) (Fig.15) (Groenman-van Waateringe 1967, 52–73). One example from this site bore stitch-holes in the distinctive shape of a *tabula ansata* (name/unit tag) (Fig.16) (Groenman-van Waateringe 1967, 56–7, no.6).

A carrying strap was probably attached to these covers, enabling the cavalryman to sling the shield over his back when not in use. A number of scenes on Trajan's Column depict shields hung from the two side horns of the saddle, sometimes placed beneath the saddle cloth (Lepper and Frere 1988, Pl.VIII, scene V; Pl.IX, scene IX; Pl.XXXIII, scene XLII; Pl.XXXVI, scene XLIX; Pl.LXV, scene LXXXIX; Pl.LXXVII, scene CIV; Pl.LXXVIII, scene CIV).

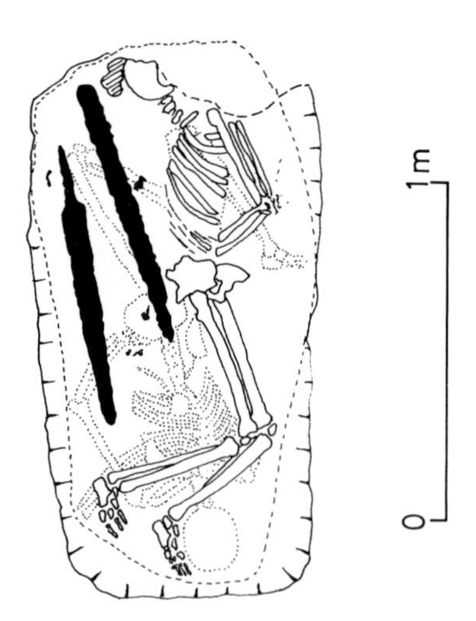

17 Plan of the double inhumation burial from Canterbury, Kent. The burial consists of two males, aged between 20 and 30, who appear to have been hurriedly thrown into a roughly-cut grave. Two swords, still in their scabbards, together with iron and bronze fittings, presumably from belts, were then thrown on top of the bodies. The cause of death is not known in either case, but the hurried nature of their deposition, and the inclusion of weapons (a rare feature in Roman burials), led the excavators to suggest murder, execution or possibly a ritual killing (Tatton-Brown 1979, 361. Redrawn by K.R. Dixon.)

Armament

Swords

The cavalry used a long slashing sword called the *spatha*, which ranged in overall length from 65cm (26in) to 90cm (36in), and in width from 4cm ($1\frac{1}{2}$in) to 8cm (3in). Two examples of these swords were recovered from a second-century burial of two cavalrymen in Canterbury (Fig.17); (Bennett *et al.* 1982, 43–6, 185–90; *Britannia* 1978, 9, 468–71; Tatton-Brown 1979, 361–4).

By the late second or early third century, the *spatha* was also being employed by the Roman infantry, which had previously used the *gladius*, a short stabbing sword. From this period onwards, therefore, it is difficult to ascertain whether a long sword belongs to an infantryman or a cavalryman, unless it is found with distinguishing associated artefacts. Probably the best preserved example of a *spatha* comes from Cologne, Germany, and dates to the fourth century (Pl.6) (Coussin 1926, 490; Tomlin 1981, 260; Petrikovits 1967, 23; *pers comm.* V. Heimburg). It has a total length of 90.5cm (36in), and still possesses a circular silver reinforcement for the tip of the scabbard and a ridged ivory grip.

The *spatha* was suspended from a waist belt or a baldric. During the first century AD the sword was worn on the right side of the body, as numerous cavalry tombstones of the period show. From the second century onwards, however, the *spatha* started to be worn on the left side, although not exclusively so.

The *contus*

The *contus* was a heavy lance, approximately 3.5m (12ft) long, which was held two-handed without a shield. It has been suggested that owing to the lack of stirrups during the Roman period the later method of holding the lance one-handed under the armpit (couching) could not be employed. This position required the rider to maintain a rigid posture, bracing himself with

18 Tombstone of Aduitor, *eques* of *Ala I Caninafatium*. Aduitor carries the *contus*, an extremely long lance of approximately 3.5m (12ft) long. Note the two-handed method by which the rider carries the *contus*. (Tipasa Museum, Algeria, North Africa. Drawn by K.R. Dixon.)

the stirrups to prevent him from being knocked backwards out of the saddle by the force of impact on hitting the target (Coulston 1986, 63). Alternatively, it may be that without any historical precedent this style had simply not developed (*pers. comm.* J.R.A. Underwood).

Contarii in the Roman army were therefore restricted to using the two-handed method, holding the *contus* either underarm and horizontally along the horse's right side (Fig.18), or overarm and diagonally across the horse's neck (Coulston 1986, 65, Pl.6, 1–2).

The lance

The Roman lance was approximately 1.8m (6ft) long (Fig.19). It could be used either as a shock weapon (i.e. in a charge where impact is required), or it could be hurled. The grip used to hold the lance was determined by the way it was to be employed. When throwing the lance or stabbing

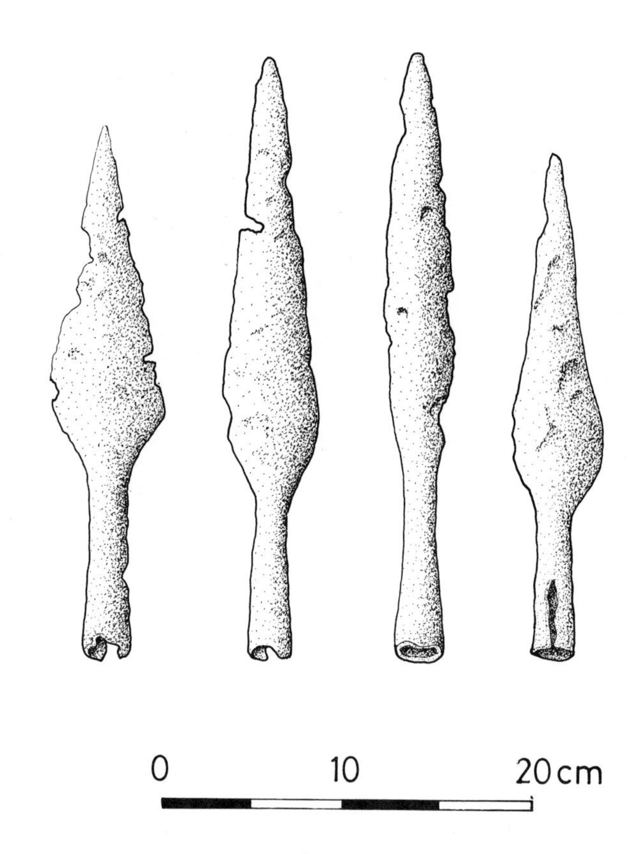

19 A selection of socketed lance heads from Saalburg, Germany. (Saalburgmuseum, Bad Homburg, Germany. Redrawn by K.R. Dixon from Jacobi 1897.)

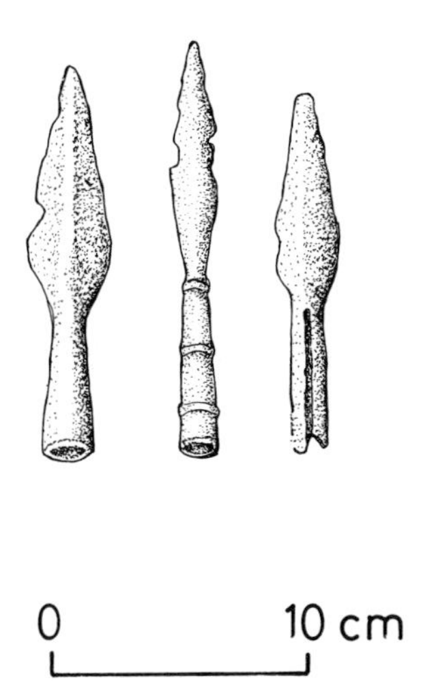

20 A selection of socketed javelin heads from Saalburg, Germany. (Saalburgmuseum, Bad Homburg, Germany. Redrawn by K.R. Dixon from Jacobi 1897.)

downwards, it was held overarm with the thumb pointing backwards, and when using it as a shock weapon it was held underarm with the thumb pointing forwards (Holder 1987, 14).

The lance has always been a weapon credited with great 'moral effect' (Strachan 1985, 57), and of all the arms used by cavalry, the lance was the one guaranteed to strike terror into both infantry and cavalry alike, particularly when used as either a shock weapon or when pursuing fleeing opponents. A cavalry officer during the Crimean War wrote in his diary after the battle of Balaclava: 'I don't care about their [the Russians'] swords, they use them so slowly and only cut, but I don't like their lances' (Warner 1977, 102).

There are numerous references to the use of lances in ancient works. Tacitus in his account of the Boudiccan rebellion records an incident which occurred during the final battle (*Annals* 14.37): 'and the cavalry, with lances extended, broke a way through any parties of resolute men whom they encountered.'

The javelin

According to Josephus (*Jewish War* 3.92.5) the cavalry carried 'in a quiver slung beside them three or more darts with broad points and as long as lances' (Fig.20). It is believed that these javelins had an effective throwing range of approximately 25m (82ft) (Holder 1987, 14).

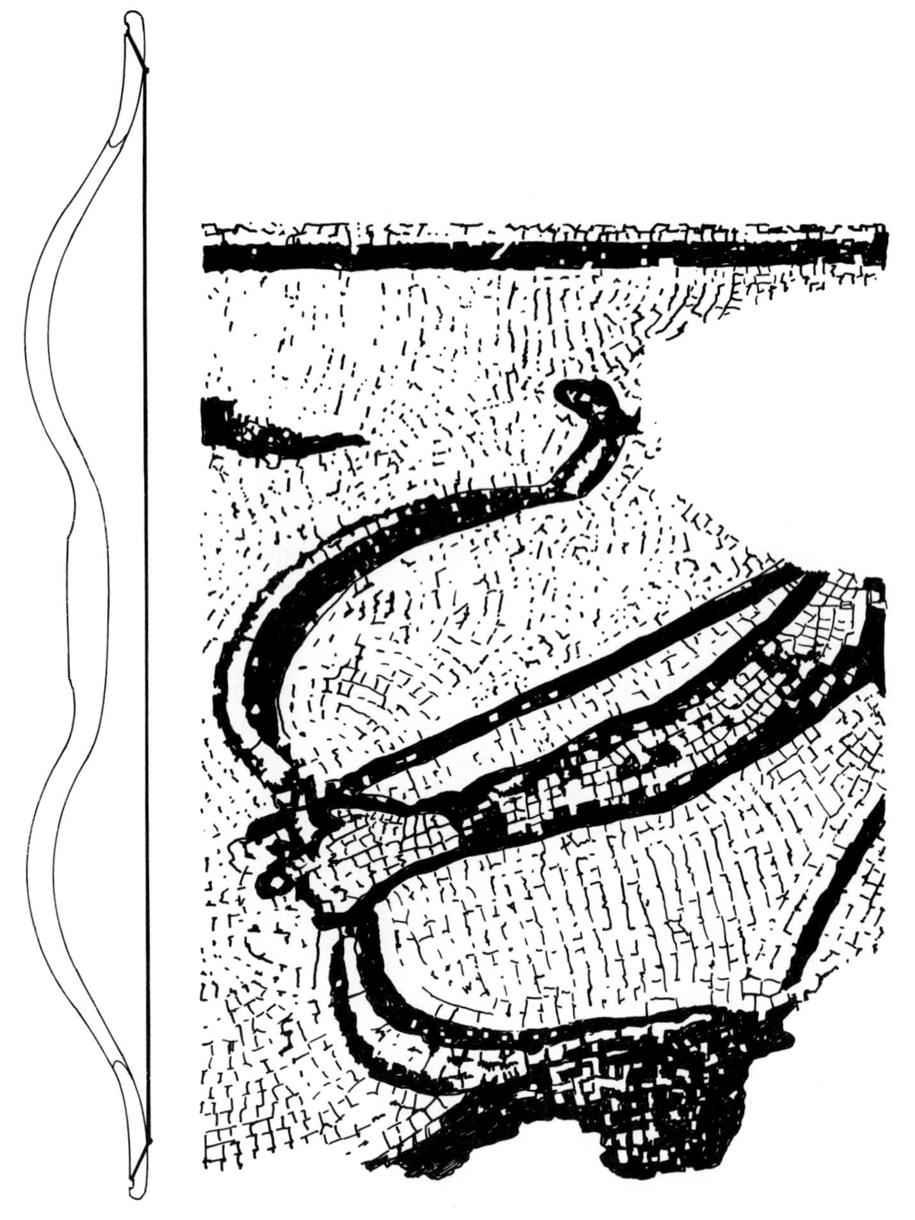

21 (*Left*) An illustration showing the basic shape of a composite bow when strung with the bowstring. Note the laths on the tips of the bow. (Redrawn by J.R.A. Underwood from Coulston 1985.)

22 (*Right*) Details of the 'Triclinos' hunt mosaic from Apamea Syriae, now housed in the Musées Royaux, Brussels. This depiction shows how the bow shape changes from that shown in Fig. 21 once the bowstring is pulled into a firing position by the archer (Drawn by K.R. Dixon.)

Archery equipment

The bow

Roman horse-archers used the composite bow, so called because of the many parts required in its construction. The basic shape (Fig.21) was supplied by a wooden core, which then had horn, bone and sinew adhered to it. Great skill is necessary to produce a composite bow of high quality and specialist archer units would probably have been supplied by particular *fabricae* dealing specifically with the construction of bows (Coulston 1985, 258).

The bows used on horseback were probably both shorter and lighter than those used on foot, as mounted archers lost the stability of the ground which enabled foot-archers to use larger and more powerful bows. Thus horse-archers shot lighter arrows, which had a shorter effective range than those shot by the infantry (Coulston 1985, 245–6).

There is little archaeological evidence for Roman composite bows, usually only the antler or bone laths that were attached to the tips of the bow survive (see Fig.21). The greatest sources of information, other than comparative, are sculptural representations and mosaics (Fig.22). Several tombstones depict horse-archers, but apart from showing the basic shape of the composite bow they are of little help in defining any greater detail. What does become apparent from two of these gravestones, however, is that the sculptors were not necessarily very familiar with archery, since one from Mainz, Germany, depicts the archer as nocking three arrows together (Schleiermacher 1984, no.25; Coulston 1985, 237), and another, also from Mainz, shows the horse's head through the bow whilst the archer draws the bowstring around its neck (Fig.23) (Schleiermacher 1984, no.23; Coulston 1985, 237).

Bow-cases

Bow-cases are an essential piece of equipment for the archer, as both the glue which binds the parts of the stave together and the bowstring can be badly damaged by moisture. There are recorded instances of archers being caught off-guard by sudden downpours, rendering their bows useless (Frontinus *Strategems* 4.7.30; Dio 56.21.3).

Although there is no direct Roman evidence for the bow-case, there are some Parthian and Sassanid reliefs that may depict a style employed by some archers within the army (Coulston 1985, 271). These reliefs show the Scythian-developed *gorytus*. This piece of equipment consisted of a combined quiver and bow-case, and was primarily employed by cavalrymen (Coulston 1985, 271).

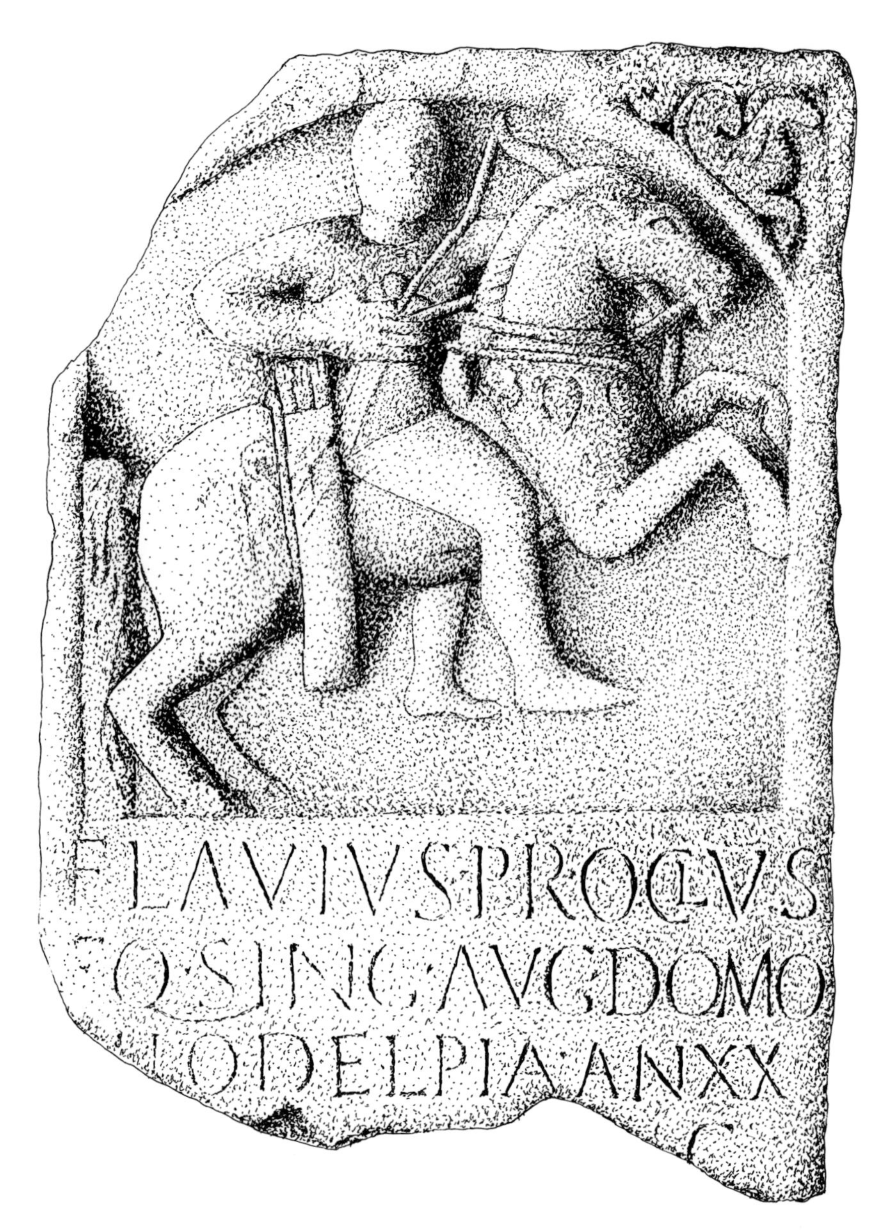

23 *FLAVIVS PROCLVS/EQ[ues] SING[ularis] AVG[usti] DOMO / [pi]LODELPIA AN[norum] XX / STIP[endiorum] . . . H[eres] F[aciendum] C[uravit]*
'Flavius Proclus, Mounted Guard to the Emperor, from Philadelphia [Amman], 20 years of age, of . . . years' service. His heir had this erected.'

The sculptor of this tombstone appears to have been rather unfamiliar with the rudiments of archery, having carved the horse's head through the bow, with the rider drawing his bowstring around its neck. First half of the first century AD (Landesmuseum Mainz, Germany. Drawn by K.R. Dixon.)

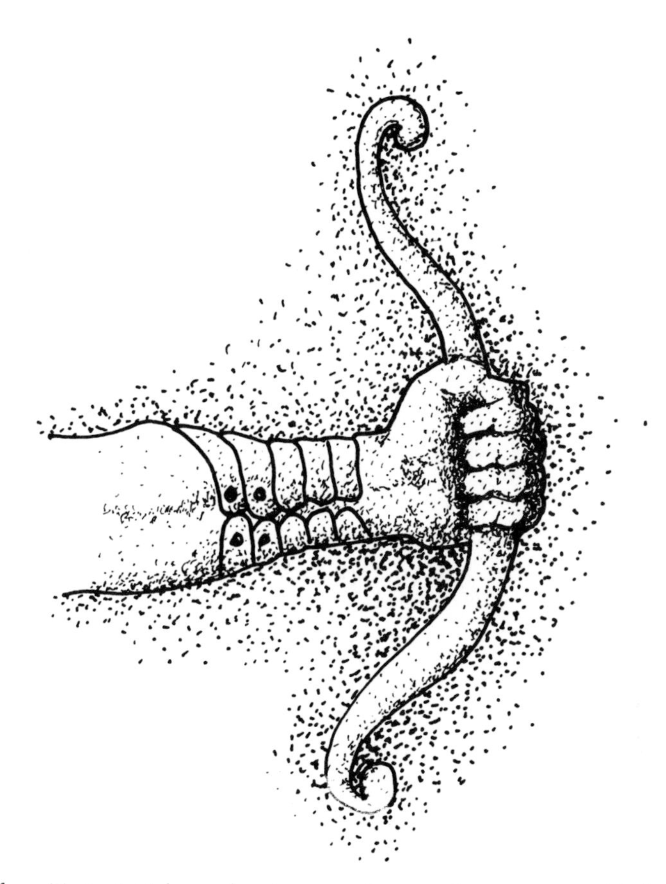

24 Detail from Trajan's Column showing an archer wearing a bracer on his forearm. A bracer afforded protection to archers using the Mediterranean release, which brought the bowstring back close to the arm, sometimes causing bruising or burns to the forearm. (Drawn by K.R. Dixon.)

Bracers

Bracers were only necessary if the archer used the Mediterranean method of release. This entailed drawing and releasing the string employing two or more fingers whilst keeping the back of the hand vertical (Coulston 1985, 275). With this method the string is brought back close to the left forearm, sometimes catching it and causing a bruise or burn. The leather bracer therefore afforded protection against such an occurrence.

It appears that bracers were made of organic material, as there is no archaeological evidence for their use. A scene on Trajan's Column, however, does clearly depict archers wearing them (Fig.24) Lepper and Frere 1988, Pl.L, Scene LXX; Coulston 1985, 277).

Thumb-rings

Thumb-rings were only required by archers if they were employing the Mongolian release, and although the most popular release in the Roman army was the Mediterranean one, it is possible that the Mongolian system was adopted by some archers by the late fourth century (Coulston 1985, 278).

The Mongolian release takes the arrow on a rightward path, and in order to protect the thumb, and make the holding of the string between the thumb and the index finger more comfortable, a ring was worn (Coulston 1985, 275–6). These rings could be made from bone or leather, and are distinguished by a flange to hold the string. It was previously believed that a bone ring from Chesters on Hadrian's Wall was used for such a purpose (Robinson 1976, 29, 39), but Coulston has dismissed this suggestion as it lacks a flange (1985, 276).

Arrows

There is abundant archaeological evidence for Roman arrows since the very nature of their use dictated that large quantities would be lost during training and in battle. The metal arrowheads constitute the bulk of the material found, particularly from the West, but some examples where both the shafts and fletchings survive have been discovered in the Eastern Roman territories, in areas where the arid conditions are excellent for the preservation of organic material.

The weight, size, style of head and type of fletchings used for the arrows depended on the archer's size, how the bow was being employed, and the amount of protection the target had (Coulston 1985, 264). In battle, the archer would initially have shot his personalized arrows, probably a quiver-full, before having to use the mass-produced ones kept in reserve (Coulston 1985, 270).

Arrowheads were usually made of iron, but bone ones were apparently used by the Germans, Huns, Sarmatians and Scythians (Ammianus 31.2.9; Pausanias 1.221.2–6). The best type of heads according to later treatises were those of square or triangular section, barbed heads being more suited for use against unarmoured men and beasts (Fig.25) (Faris and Elmer 1945, 107–9). The question may then be asked why the Romans employed barbed heads and not the more favoured styles. The reason is possibly that there was little incentive to use or develop a more penetrative head in the West, where the enemy was seldom armoured (Coulston 1985, 269). When barbed heads were employed, however, the wounds could be horrific, as to extract such a head would usually necessitate pulling the arrow back through the point of entry. Procopius (*History of the Wars* 6.2.28) notes the technique

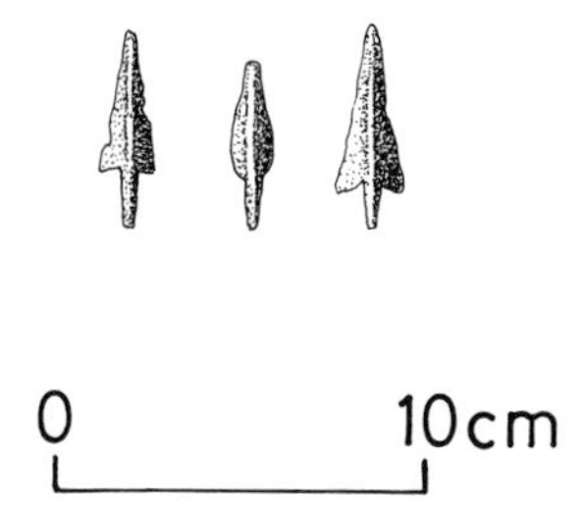

25 A selection of tanged arrowheads from Saalburg, Germany. (Saalburgmuseum, Bad Homburg, Germany. Redrawn by K.R. Dixon from Jacobi 1897.)

used by a surgeon to extract a barbed arrow from a particularly deep face wound: 'Accordingly he cut off that part of the shaft which showed outside and threw it away, cutting open the skin at the back of the head, at the place where the man felt the most pain, he easily drew toward him the barb, which with its three sharp points now stuck out behind and brought with it the remaining portion of the weapon.'

The arrowheads were attached to the shafts by means of either a socket or a tang. Materials used for the shafts included reeds (Pliny *Natural History* 16.65.160), cornel-wood (by the Sarmatians), with pine and hazel being used by the Germans (Pausanias 1.21.5–6). Although the shafts rarely survive in Britain, some examples of arrowheads from Housesteads, Corbridge and Caerleon still have the remains of wood attached to their tangs (Coulston 1985, 268). The best examples, however, come from the East, such as those from Dura-Europos, Syria (Pl.7), where the lower portions of three cane or reed shafts were found, all of which bore painted markings, probably to identify the owner, or denote a matching set (Rostovtzeff *et al.* 1936, 453–5, Pl.xxiv; Coulston 1985, 266–7).

Quivers

Quivers were a necessary part of the archer's equipment, as they protected the fletchings from damage and prevented the glue which attached them from getting damp. Roman sculptural depictions of quivers all show a cylindrical form. It was generally hung from the right-hand side of the saddle behind the trooper, such as is portrayed on a tombstone from Mainz (see Fig.23; Schleiermacher 1984, no.23). A gravestone from Walbersdorf, however, shows the rider wearing the quiver on a *balteus* (shoulder strap), which was the method of suspension usually employed by the infantry (Coulston 1985, 271).

Miscellaneous equipment

Musical instruments

Musical instruments were used by the Roman army in conjunction with standards for relaying commands in the field, and for ceremonial occasions. Four types of horn appear to have been employed: the *tuba*; *cornu*; *bucina*; and the *lituus* (Webster 1985, 140). It has been suggested that the *lituus* (Pl.8), which was a J-shaped horn may have been specifically used by the cavalry (Dobson 1981, 237), although others believe that it was reserved for ceremonies (Webster 1985, 140).

Spurs

To whom the invention of the spur should be attributed remains uncertain: the Celts apparently used them (Azzaroli 1985, 115), and Xenophon refers to them as an aid to jumping (*Art of Horsemanship* 8.5). Roman spurs have been classified into a number of groups based on the means by which they were attached to the horseman's footwear (i.e. rivets, hooks or loops) (Fig.26), and the shape of the arm or prick which protrudes centrally from the back of the spur (Jahn 1921; Shortt 1959; Manning 1985, 69–70, pl.29, H24–9).

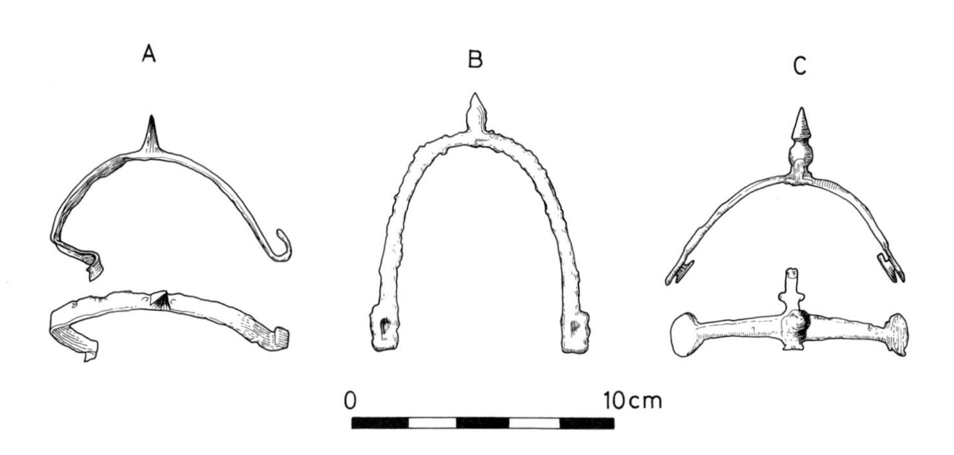

26 The three main types of Roman spur. A: iron hook spur from Corbridge, Northumberland; B: iron loop spur from Hod Hill, Dorset; C: iron rivet spur from Corbridge, Northumberland. (Redrawn by K.R. Dixon from Shortt 1959.)

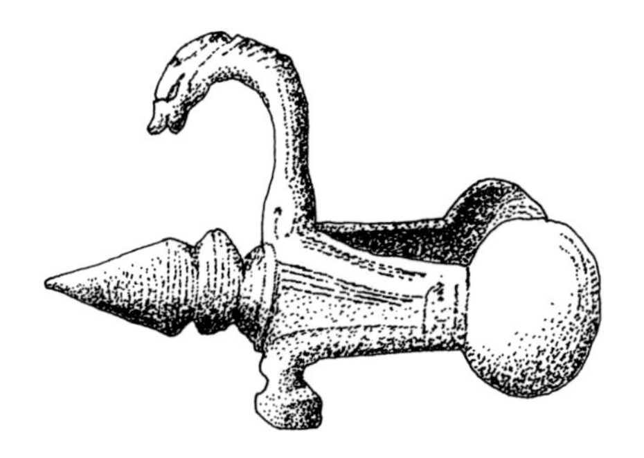

27 An elaborate spur from Saverne in France. It consists of an additional arm positioned above the prick, which terminates in a horse's head. (Redrawn by K.R. Dixon from Vigneron 1968.)

Spurs, which were made of bronze or iron, were sometimes decorated, often with an incised design, such as the one of bronze from Longstock, England (Shortt 1959, 61–2, pl.XIV). An extremely elaborate example was found at Saverne, France, comprising an additional arm situated above the prick, which terminated in a tiny horse's head (Fig.27) (Vigneron 1968, 85, pl.31, c).

Precisely how common the employment of spurs was in the Roman cavalry, or in the Roman Empire in general, is as yet unclear: Vigneron believes that they formed a regular part of the cavalryman's equipment (1968, 61), whilst Shortt argues that they were not in general use (1959, 61). There is certainly an absence of sculptural depictions of spurs, although this may be due to the difficulty of carving such a small item of equipment, and they may, therefore, have been painted on, leaving no subsequent traces. A more probable reason, however, may lie in the fact that not all horses require or respond well to the use of spurs. In such a situation, the choice of employment presumably rested with the rider's assessment of his horse's needs and temperament.

Standards

The standards played a very important role in the Roman army, for not only were they a rallying point for troops and a method of relaying signals in battle, but they also had a religious significance. The known standard types employed by the cavalry were ones also used by the infantry. The *vexillum* was a square piece of red or purple material (Fig.28) with fringing on the bottom edge, which hung from a crossbar attached to a lance (Rostovtzeff 1942, 94–5). *Vexillarii*, the men who carried this standard, are recorded for both the *alae* and the legionary cavalry (*CIL* VI 32709a = *ILS* 9190). The only

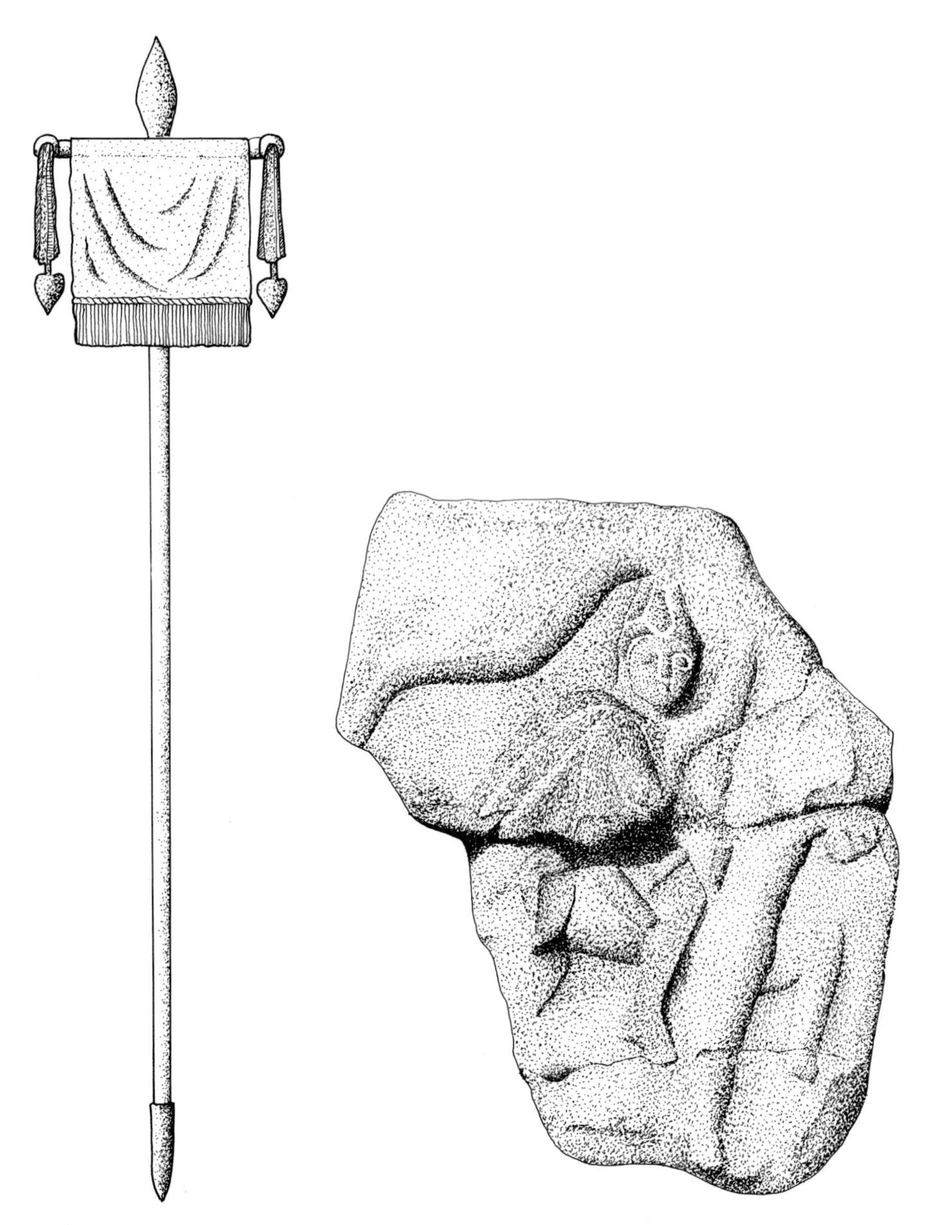

28 (*Left*) The *vexillum*. This flag, carried by the *vexillarius*, consisted of a square piece of purple or red material with a fringed lower edge. It was suspended from a crossbar which was attached to the upper portion of a lance. (Drawn by K.R. Dixon.)

29 (*Right*) Tombstone of a Sarmatian *draconarius* (the bearer of the dragon standard) from Chester. Note the tail of the standard, which was made of material, streaming out behind the rider's head. (Grosvenor Museum, Chester. Drawn by K.R. Dixon.)

known example of a *vexillum* comes from Egypt, and is painted with a figure of Victory (Rostovtzeff 1942, 92–106).

The *imago*, the standard which bore the image of the Emperor, is attested for the *alae*, as the office of *imaginifer*, the carrier of this standard, is recorded on an inscription (*AE* 1906.119). In the legion, a *signa* was carried by each century, but whether this applied to the *turmae* in a cavalry unit is uncertain. The *signa* was carried by the *signifer*, as is recorded on the tombstone of Flavinus, now housed in Hexham Abbey, Northumberland (Pl.9) (*RIB* 1172).

One of the most striking forms of standard used by the cavalry was the dragon standard, the bearer of which was called the *draconarius*. They were introduced into the Roman army by the Sarmatians during the second century AD, and consisted of a hollow, open-mouthed dragon's head, to which was attached a long tube of material, the whole then being mounted on a pole. Their effect when held on horseback in the procession heralding the arrival of Constantius in Rome in AD 357 is described by Ammianus (16.10.4): 'And behind the manifold others that preceded him [Constantius] he was surrounded by dragons, woven out of purple thread and bound to mouths open to the breeze and hence hissing as if raised by anger, and leaving their tails winding in the wind.' An example of one of these dragon heads was found near the Roman fort of Niederbieber, Germany (Pl.10) (Garbsch 1978, 88, Taf.48, 3), and a tombstone from Chester depicts a Sarmatian *draconarius* (Fig.29). The dragon standard was primarily associated with the cavalry of the Roman army, but according to Vegetius (2.13), by the fourth century one was carried by each legionary cohort.

Equipment: the horses

Bardings

Bardings are the 'coats' worn by horses to protect them against injury in battle. Three bardings, two complete and one incomplete, were found at Dura-Europos (Pl.11) (Rostovtzeff *et al.* 1936, 440–9, pl.XXI–II). Of the two complete examples the one constructed of bronze scales is exceptionally well preserved. It comprises two panels of scales, sewn on to a doubled backing of coarse linen, which would hang on either side of the horse's body. The panels are joined down the middle by a strip of red leather, at one end of which is attached a triangular tail piece. A hole has been cut in the barding to allow it to fit over the saddle. The two loops placed either side of this hole at the back are thought to have been used to attach a quiver and sword (Rostovtzeff *et al* 1936, 499). All the edges of the barding were finished in red leather. The other complete example was of iron scales, and

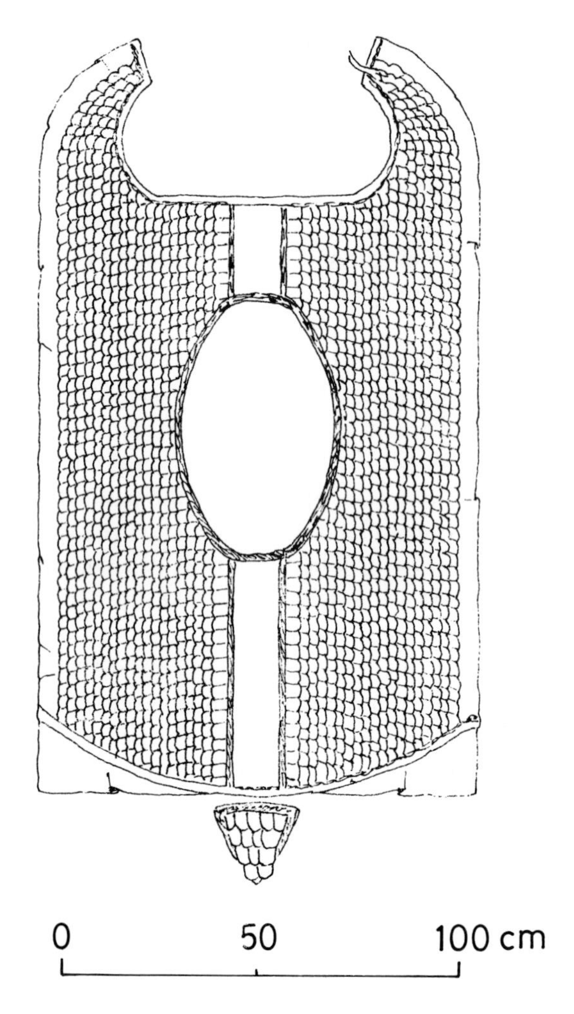

30 Plan of one of the horse bardings from Dura-Europos, Syria (not the one seen in Pl.11). Note the triangular tail piece and the two extensions at the front end, which would have fastened in the centre of the horse's chest. (Redrawn by K.R. Dixon from Rostovtzeff *et al.* 1936.)

differed slightly by having extensions at the front two corners of the barding, which went round the horse's breast (Fig.30).

The only contemporary representation of a *clibanarius*, a heavy-armoured cavalryman, is a graffito from Dura (see Fig.11). It depicts the horse wearing a scale barding which also appears to cover the neck and head. There are several literary references to bardings, such as that from the third-century writer Heliodorus (*Aethiopica* 9.15): 'From its back to its belly on either side hangs a housing of iron mail which both protects it, and by its looseness does not hinder its course.'

No bardings like those from Dura have been found in north-western Europe, although it is possible that fragments of scale may not have been recognized as belonging to horse bardings. The finds of chamfrons in this area, however, would suggest that some form of bardings, perhaps of cloth, might have been employed, since it is thought that it is unlikely that chamfrons were worn in isolation (Driel-Murray 1989, 281).

The bridle

The bridle is an important piece of equipment as it enables the rider to control the reactions and movements of the horse. In battle, however, Roman cavalrymen would have relied on leg control, since their hands would have been occupied holding a shield and spear or sword, rather than the reins (Bishop 1988, 108).

Control is exercised over the horse by the bit, a rod of metal which goes through the mouth and has a ring on either end through which the reins and the straps of the bridle are attached. From the archaeological remains it appears that there were two types of bit in use during the Roman period, the snaffle and the curb (Manning 1985, 66–7; Dobson 1981, 238–9; Liversidge 1968, 399). Snaffle bits (Fig.31), which are of Celtic origin, are simple in form and less severe on the horse's mouth than curb bits. They consist of jointed or solid bars, with free-moving rings on either end, and are designed to be used two-handed (*pers. comm.* A. Hyland; Manning 1985, 66).

Roman curb bits were very severe, and were designed to give riders full control of their mounts using only one hand, which was particularly useful for cavalry (*pers. comm.* A. Hyland). They consist of solid or jointed bars; if

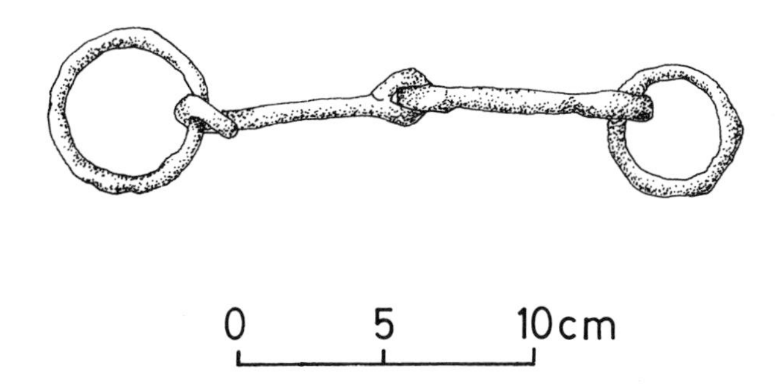

31 Iron snaffle bit from Hod Hill, Dorset. It consists of a jointed bar with a ring on either end. The bar is placed in the horse's mouth and the reins are attached to the rings. (Redrawn by K.R. Dixon from Manning 1985.)

of the former style the bars are occasionally bent into a U-shape in the middle, such as an example from Newstead, Scotland (Fig.32) (Curle 1911, 297, Pl.LXXI no.3; Manning 1985, 68, Fig.17 no.2; Hyland 1990, pl.10). Rings are placed at the top of the bars for the bridle straps, with eyes at the bottom for the reins, and a chain or bar runs under the horse's chin in order to keep the bit in position. Curb bits allowed the rider, with a sharp tug on the reins, to pull the horse's head upwards, giving him greater control.

Hackamores were also employed by the Romans (Taylor 1975, 106–33). These are metal 'muzzles' (Fig.33), which consist of a bar which runs above

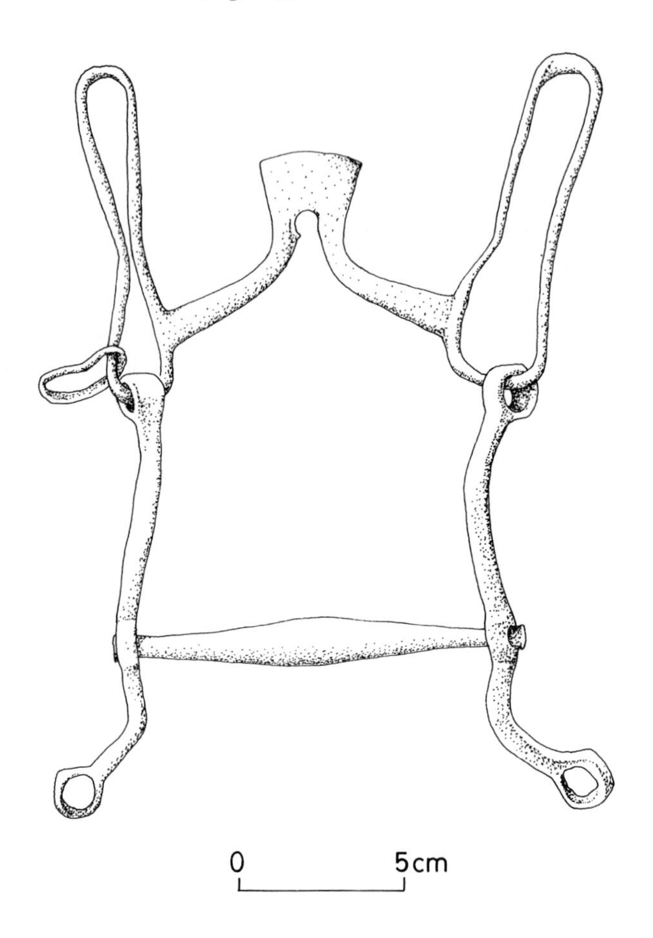

32 Curb bit from Newstead, Scotland. The Roman curb bit was very severe. The bar with the 'U'-shaped bend in the middle was placed in the horse's mouth whilst the other bar was positioned under the horse's chin, enabling the rider to be able to pull the animal's head sharply upwards, facilitating greater control. The rings are for the attachment of the bridle and the reins. (Redrawn by K.R. Dixon from Hyland 1991.)

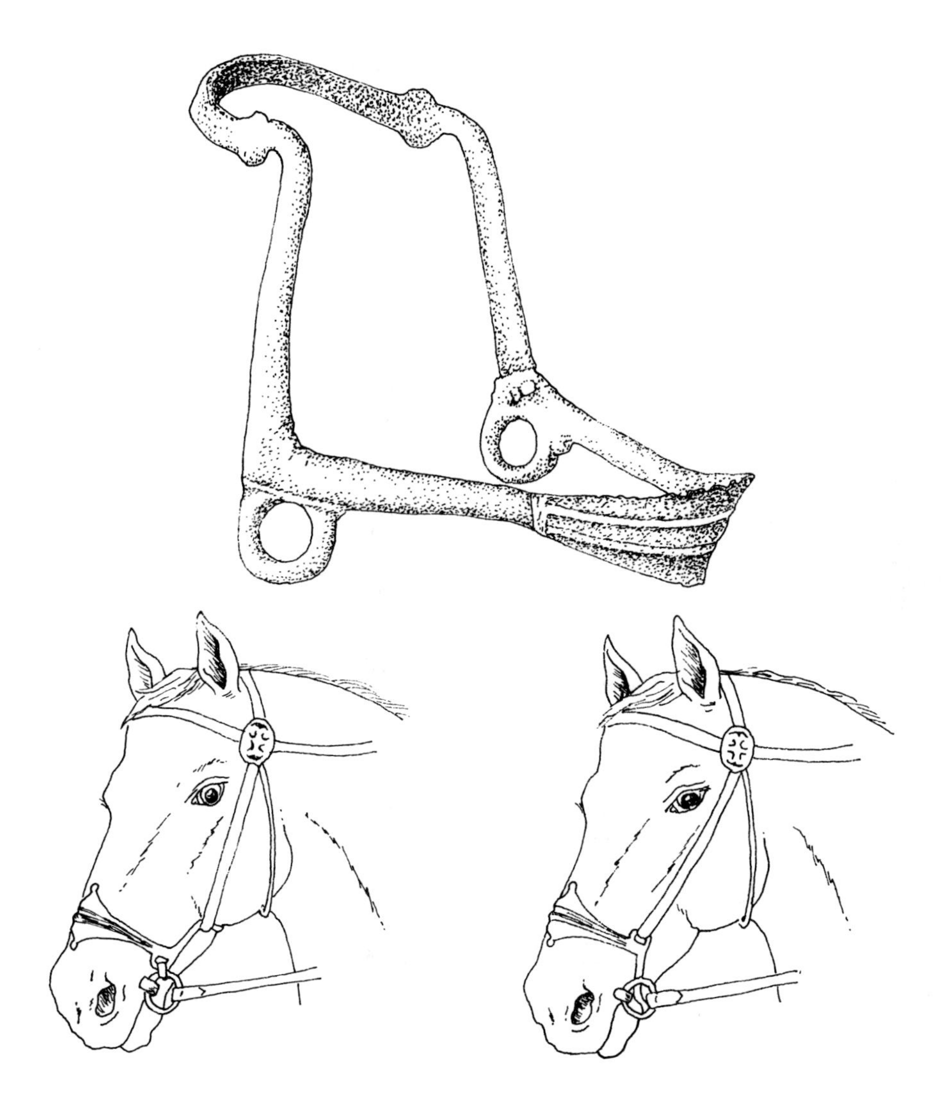

33 Roman hackamore ('muzzle') from Wiesbaden, Germany. There is some uncertainty as to which way this hackamore was worn, as the two drawings illustrate: the first positioning would bring the bar just under the horse's cheek, whilst the second drawing shows the bar resting at the edge of the mouth. Either placement would serve the same purpose. (Redrawn by K.R. Dixon from Taylor 1975.)

the nose and under the chin. They are attached by rings and eyes to the bridle straps and the reins, and prevent the horse from opening his mouth and 'getting away from the bit' (Littauer 1969, 291–2). The Romans employed hackamores in conjunction with bits, as the tombstone of Bassus demonstrates (see Fig.7).

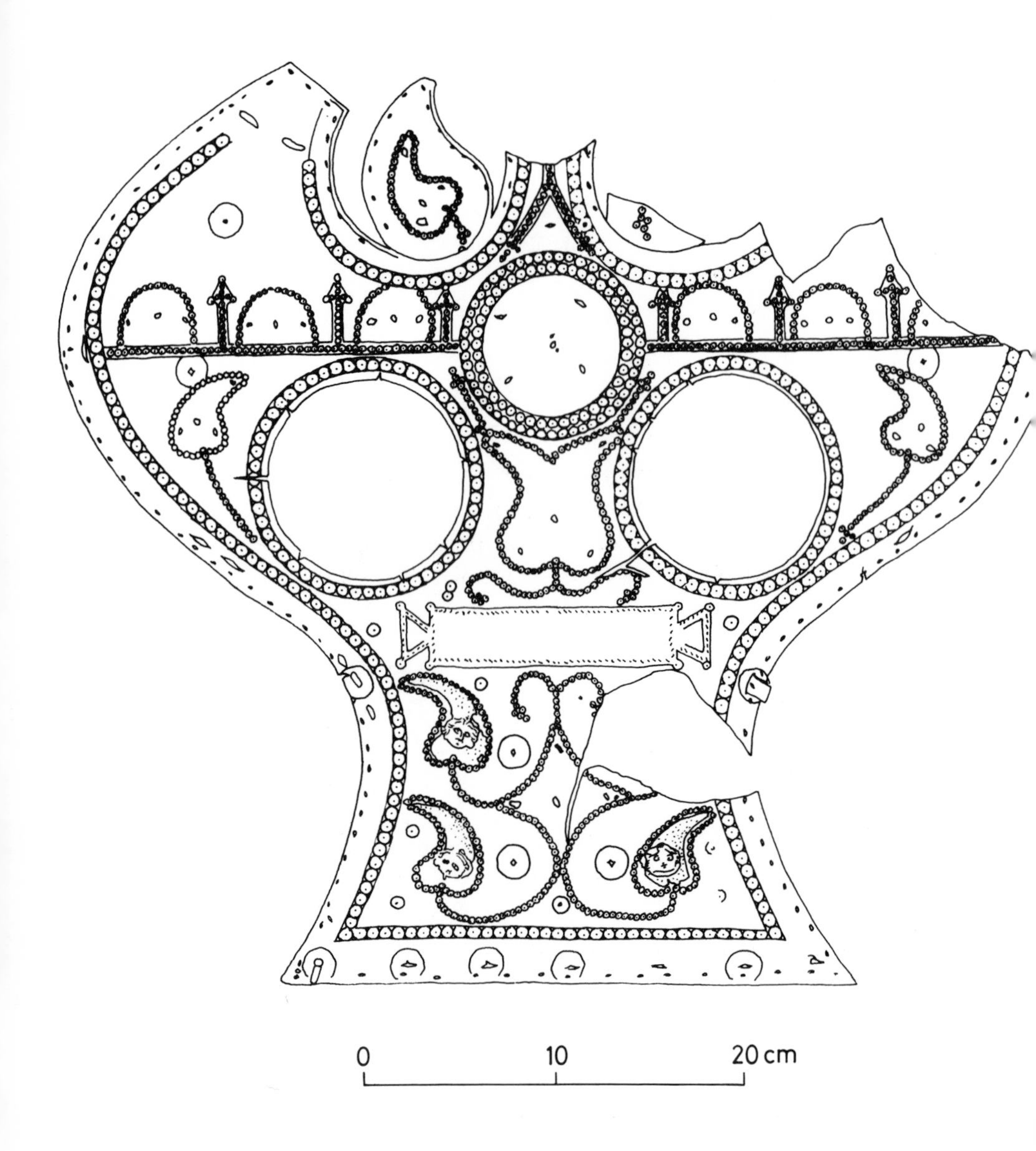

34 The chamfron from Vindolanda (Chesterholm), Northumberland. Made from leather with a covering decoration executed in metal studs. Note the *tabula ansata* (name tag) just below the eye-holes. The chamfron would have been secured to the horse's head by leather straps. (Redrawn by K.R. Dixon from Driel-Murray 1989.)

The leather straps of the bridle have not survived in the archaeological record, but there are numerous sculptural depictions, which often show the bridle with small decorative metal discs (*phalerae*) on them, a number of which have been found (see p.69). The tombstone of Vonatorix from Bonn (see Fig.9) clearly shows a *phalera* on the middle of the brow band and one at the junction of the brow band and the cheek straps, together with another where the straps meet at the horse's mouth (Ulbert 1968, Taf.24; Schleiermacher 1984, no.9).

The chamfron

Chamfrons are the protective head covers worn by horses, of which several leather examples have been found in Britain, notably the one from Newstead, Scotland (Curle 1911, 153–5, Pl.xxi; 1913, 400–5, Fig.11–12), and the most complete one from Vindolanda, England (Fig.34) (Driel-Murray 1989, 283–90, Fig.5–6). Both of these chamfrons are almost identical in design, consisting of a leather face piece, with two circular holes for the eyes, two flaps for the ears and an overall pattern executed in metal studs. Stitch-holes indicate that originally a name-plate (*tabula ansata*), probably of leather, had been sewn on to the frontlet.

It was previously assumed that the loose eye-guards, which have been recovered from a number of sites (Pl.12), would have been attached to the eye-holes of these leather chamfrons. There is, however, no direct evidence to substantiate such a belief (Driel-Murray 1989, 291), although it is possible that the damage detectable around the eye-holes on one of the Vindolanda chamfrons may have been caused by metal eye-guards.

The more elaborate metal chamfrons are believed to have been reserved for the *hippika gymnasia*, when extremely elaborate equipment was worn by both the men and the horses (for a full discussion see Chapter 7).

The harness

Evidence for the Roman harness, which was probably of Celtic origin, comes from both archaeological and pictorial sources. The function of the harness is to secure the saddle to the horse by a system of straps (Fig.35), the major one being the girth strap, which runs around the horse's middle and holds the saddle in a central position. In order to prevent the saddle slipping backwards, a strap extends round the horse's breast, and to prevent the saddle sliding forwards, a further one, the crupper strap, passes under the tail. Sculpture depicts some of the breast and crupper straps as being bifurcated, such as the tombstone of Bassus (see Fig.7) (Schleiermacher 1984, no.17; Bishop 1988, 71–4 no.6, Fig.1).

At the junctions where the straps met, rings or discs (*phalerae*) were

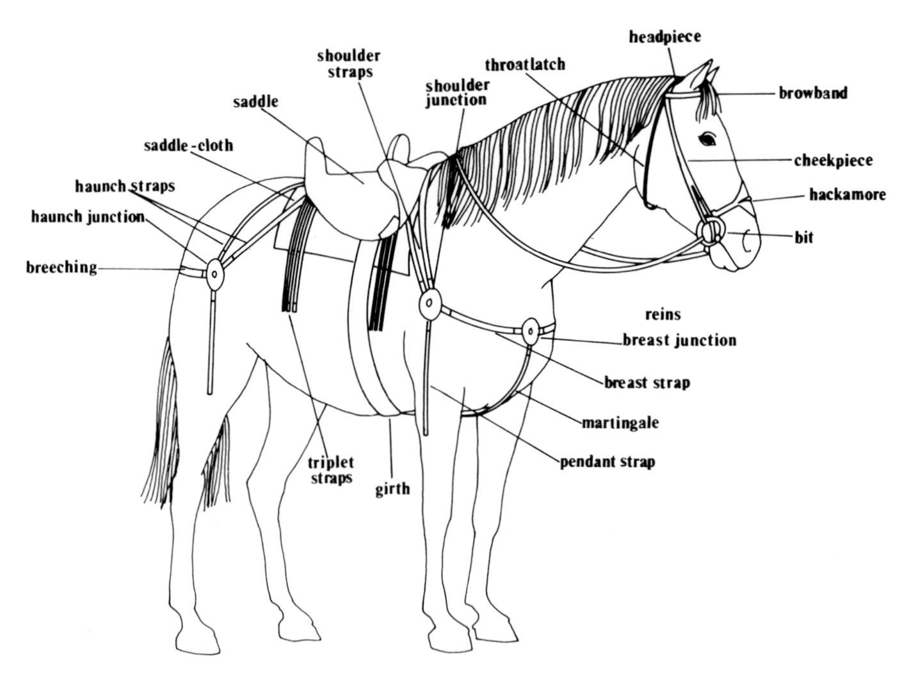

35 Reconstruction of a typical Roman harness system. (Redrawn by K.R. Dixon from Bishop 1988.)

provided to connect them together. A large number of these junction fitments have been found (Fig.36). The find of first-century harness fitments from Doorwerth, the Netherlands included examples of the *phalerae* type (Pl.13), which had rings fixed to the back to hold the straps.

Roman harness fittings also included non-functional items such as pendants. These came in a variety of forms, including lunate (Fig.37) and 'trifid' (Fig.38). Although a number of methods were employed in the suspension of these pendants, the latter style is always found attached to a *phalera*, such as an example from Doorwerth (Pl.14). There is abundant pictorial evidence for these pendants, a particularly good example being the tombstone of Bassus (see Fig.7) (Schleiermacher 1984, no.17) which shows the horse wearing a harness with lunate and lozenge-shaped pendants.

It has been suggested that pendants, as well as enhancing the horse's appearance, were worn for symbolic reasons, since it is known that the *lunula* represented the moon and femininity and that the *phalera* symbolized the sun and masculinity (Bishop 1988, 107). Such a motive would not have been alien in the Roman army, where symbolism appears to have played an important role in the motifs which adorned military equipment (Toynbee 1964, 298).

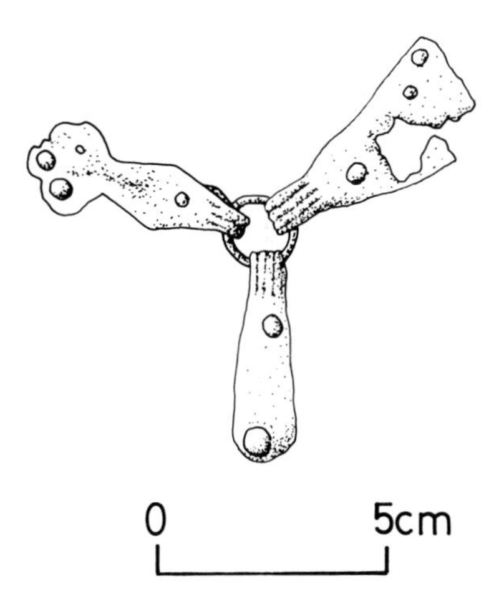

36 Bronze strap junction from Baden, Germany. This example may have served as a breast, shoulder or haunch junction (see Fig. 35). (Redrawn by K.R. Dixon from Unz 1971.)

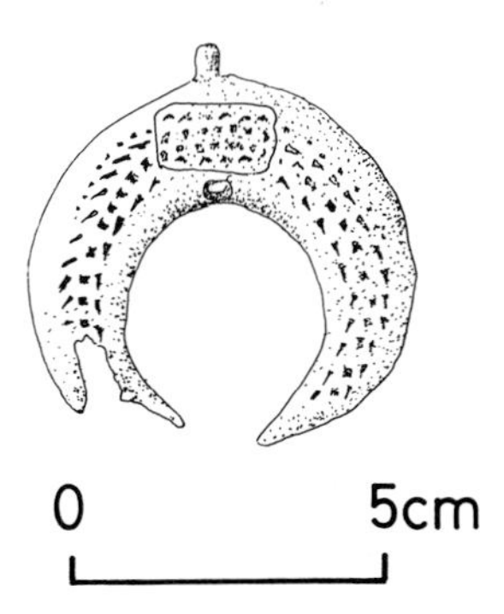

37 Bronze lunate pendant from Windisch, Austria, with niello decoration. (Redrawn by K.R. Dixon from Unz 1973.)

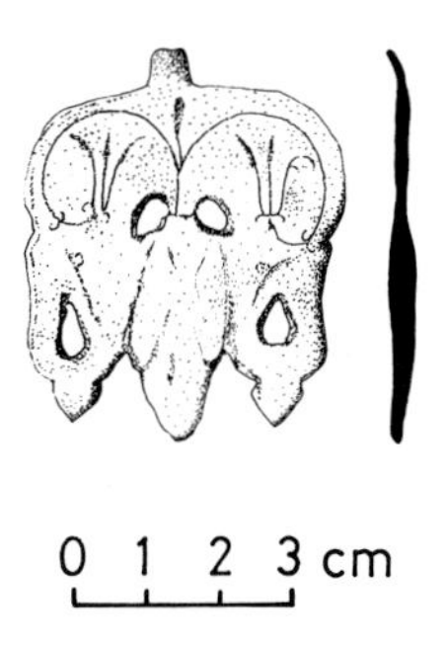

38 Silvered-bronze 'trifid' pendant with niello decoration from Rottweil, Germany. (Redrawn by K.R. Dixon from Planck 1975.)

Peytrals

It is believed that a peytral, which protects the front of the horse's chest, would probably have been worn by Roman cavalry horses, although there is little evidence for such a belief (Driel-Murray 1989, 281–3). The tombstone of Bassus (see Fig.7) clearly depicts the horse wearing a fringed peytral, although this example is considered to be decorative. A fragment of a leather peytral, similar to the one worn by Bassus' horse, was found at Vindolanda (Fig.39) (Driel-Murray 1989, 282, Fig.1). Despite their seemingly decorative nature, these soft leather peytrals may have afforded some protection to the horse from the harness pendants, which would have constantly banged against the horse whenever it was in motion (Bishop 1988, 111).

The saddle

Our knowledge of the Roman saddle has advanced greatly due to the extensive research and reconstructive work undertaken by Peter Connolly (1986; 1987; 1988). The purpose of the saddle is to transfer the weight of the rider from the horse's spine to its flanks, and to provide the rider with a secure and comfortable seat. In order to fulfil these requirements, a rigid saddle is thought necessary, consisting of a wooden frame (tree) with padding (Fig.40) (Connolly 1986; 1987; 1988). Although no tree has been found, the leather saddle covers from Vindolanda, Britain (Driel-Murray 1989, 309), and Valkenburg in the Netherlands (Fig.41) (Groenman-van Waateringe 1967, 106, Fig.35) have stress lines, which would only occur if the leather was stretched over a rigid frame (*pers. comm.* P. Connolly; Driel-Murray 1989, 294, 301, 309–10).

A saddle with a rigid frame must be made to fit a particular build of horse

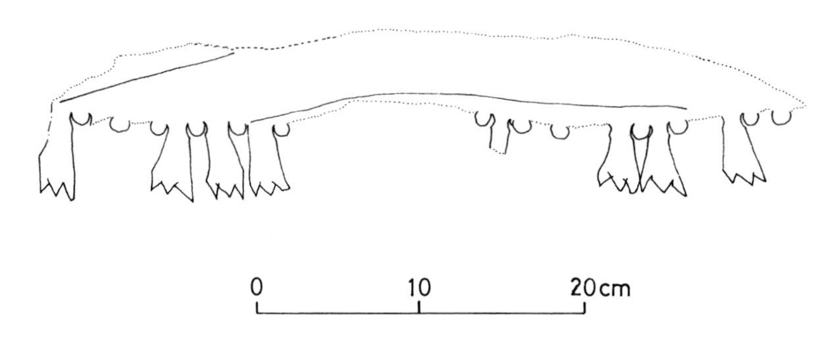

39 Leather fragment, possibly from a horse's peytral (breast band), from Vindolanda (Chesterholm), Northumberland. A depiction of a horse wearing a peytral similar to this example, can be seen on the tombstone of Bassus (Fig.7). (Redrawn by K.R. Dixon from Driel-Murray 1989.)

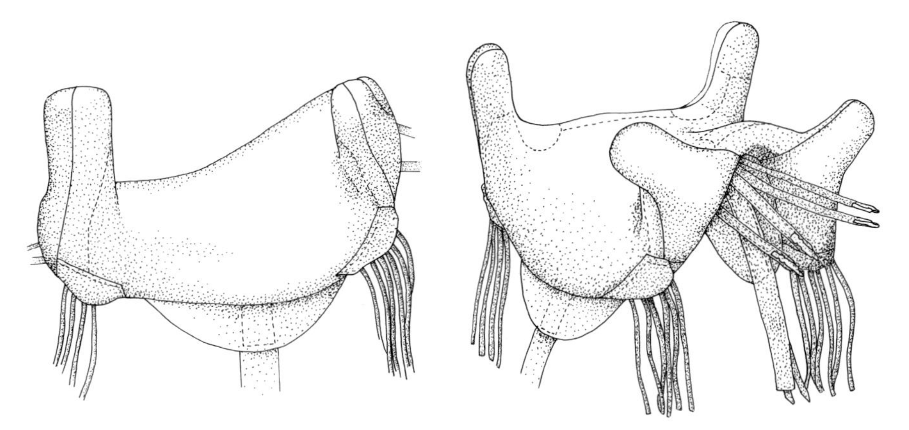

40 Peter Connolly's reconstruction of a Roman saddle. It has a wooden frame (tree) which is then padded to fit the measurements of a particular horse. Although no saddle tree has yet been found, leather saddle covers recovered from a number of sites (Fig.41) show stress lines, implying that they were stretched over a rigid frame. (Redrawn by K.R. Dixon from Connolly 1987.)

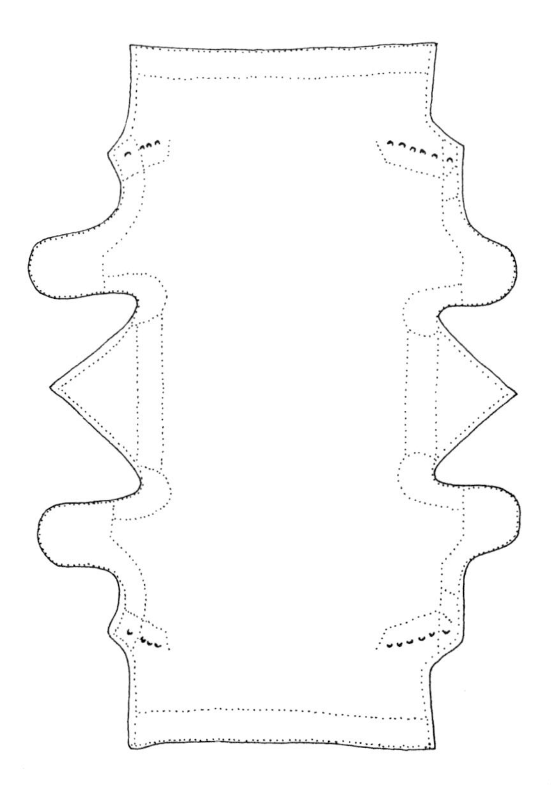

41 Reconstruction of a leather saddle cover from Valkenburg, the Netherlands. (Redrawn by K.R. Dixon from Groenman-van Waateringe 1967.)

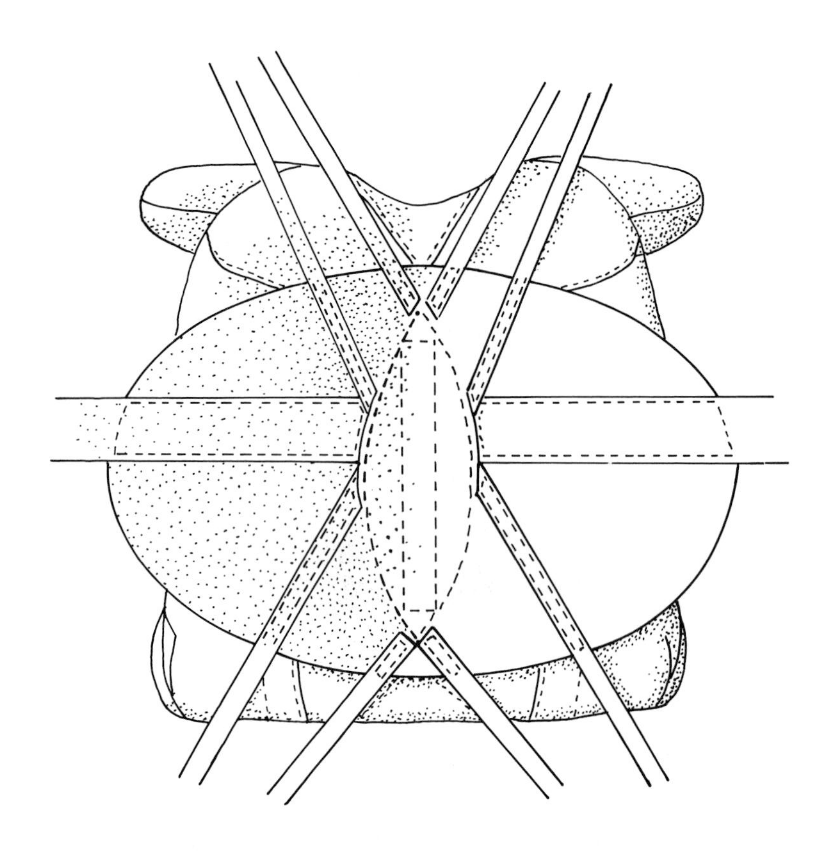

42 The underside of Peter Connolly's reconstructed Roman saddle, showing the attachment of the harness straps to the leather flaps of the saddle cover. (Redrawn by J.R.A. Underwood from Connolly, 1987.)

(Connolly 1987, 7), and it has been suggested that the Roman army may have had several standard sizes which would have been padded to suit individual horses' requirements (*pers. comm.* A. Hyland). The tree of the reconstructed saddle, which it must be remembered is only an interpretation, is made of strips of laminated wood, to which the girth, crupper and breast straps are attached to flaps extending from the leather cover (Fig.42) (Connolly 1987, 11, Fig.9e).

The exact function of the bronze horn plates, such as those from Newstead, Scotland (Fig.43) (Curle 1911, 177–8, Pl.xxxii, Fig.17; Connolly 1987, 11; 1991, forthcoming) is not certain. They may have been used as shapers for the horns of saddles, or alternatively they may have been used to protect the horns against damage (Bishop 1988, 104). Until recently it was

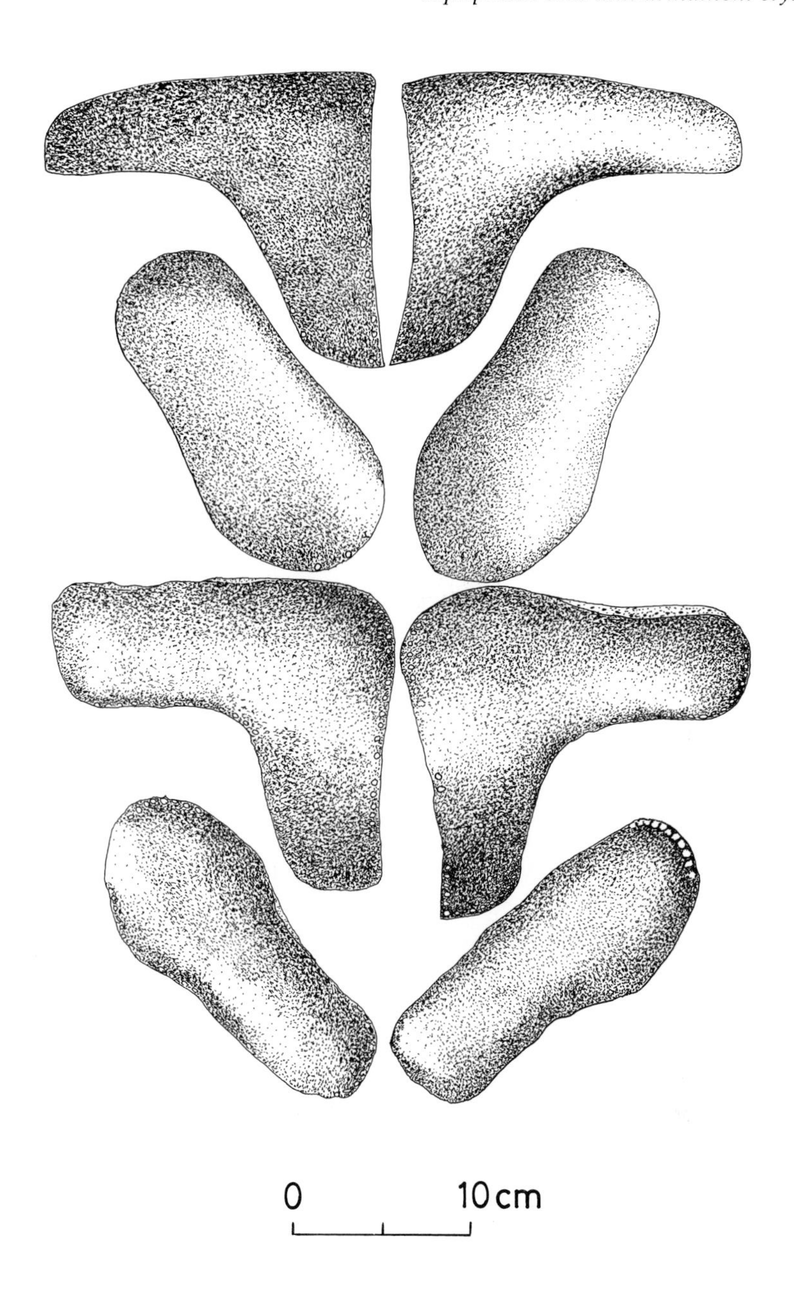

43 Bronze horn plates from a saddle from Newstead, Scotland. Each one is inscribed with a number and a name, probably to identify to the saddler which saddle they belong to. They may have served as shapers or as protection against damage. (Drawn by K.R. Dixon.)

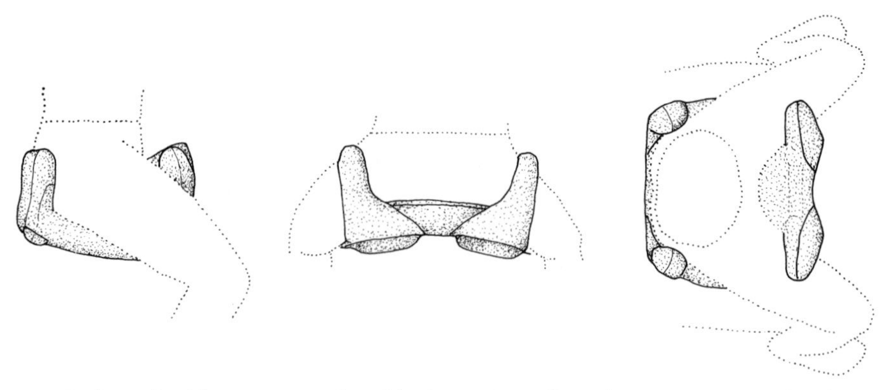

44 Sculptural evidence was employed by Peter Connolly in his reconstruction for the position of the saddle horns. As this illustration shows, when angled in this manner the horns provide excellent security in the saddle for the rider. (Redrawn by K.R. Dixon from Connolly 1987.)

not known whether they were fitted to the outside or the inside of the saddle cover. Further speculation arose from the occurrence of inscribed names on the examples from Newstead (Curle 1911, 177–8, Pl.xxxii, Fig.17). After a recent examination of these plates, however, it is known that the names were punched on the inside face, and were probably meant to identify to the saddler the saddle to which they belonged, implying that they were placed inside the saddle cover (Connolly 1991, forthcoming).

Evidence for the angle of the horns is slight, although tombstones, such as that of Romanius from Mainz, Germany (see Pl.3), show the back pair of horns hugging the seat of the rider, whilst those at the front appear to come over the thighs. A reconstruction saddle with the horns in such a position provides the rider with an extremely secure seat, serving a similar function to stirrups (Fig.44). It would have permitted the rider to employ greater force in weapon thrusts and blows, and parry attacks from the enemy, without the danger of being easily knocked from the saddle. Due to this advancement in our knowledge of the Roman saddle, the effectiveness of the Roman cavalry, particularly regarding the use of shock tactics, is now no longer in doubt.

The saddle-cloth

Sculpture provides much evidence for a Roman saddle-cloth which was worn under the saddle; it is possible that a smaller cloth of fur may have been placed beneath a more elaborate outer one, to give the horse greater protection from chafing (Connolly 1988, 30). Various styles of saddle-cloth can be recognized, with the majority of sculptured examples covering the horse's flanks and terminating in tassels or fringing (Fig.45). In some cases, however, they are extremely long and have a shorter second cloth on top, as can be seen on the tombstone of Primigenius (Pl.15), and on numerous scenes on Trajan's Column, which is notably the only sculpture which depicts cavalrymen riding with long saddle-cloths. It may be, as suggested by Bishop (1988, 108–9), that the sculptors of the Column were basing their cavalry horses on 'the partially-understood equipment of horses in parade gear', rather than representing the equipment used in combat.

In some instances, saddle-cloths are not portrayed as a carved feature, and in such cases they may have been painted on, traces of which rarely survive, one exception being the tombstone of Silius from Mainz, Germany, on which the saddle-cloth was painted green (Curle 1911, 295).

Triplet straps

Sets of straps, usually depicted in groups of three, are frequently shown on the front and rear of saddles on Roman sculpture, such as on the tombstone of Primigenius (see Pl.15). Their function was probably purely decorative and they are believed to be Celtic in origin, owing to their appearance on the Gundestrup Cauldron which dates from the second to the first century BC. (Bishop 1988, 89; Klindt-Jensen 1961), and two monumental Roman reliefs showing Celtic military equipment.

It has been suggested that the presence of holes at the lower edges of the Valkenburg and Vechten saddle covers may have been for the attachment of these straps (Bishop 1988, 109).

The straps on the horse of Primigenius (see Pl.15) appear to have three plates positioned close to the saddle on either side, and it is possible that the rectangular plates from the Doorwerth find of horse equipment may have served such a function (Bishop 1988, 110).

Unit armament styles

Contarii

Units such as the *Ala I Ulpia contariorum milliaria* were equipped with the *contus* or heavy lance (see p.49–50). These units appear to have been created

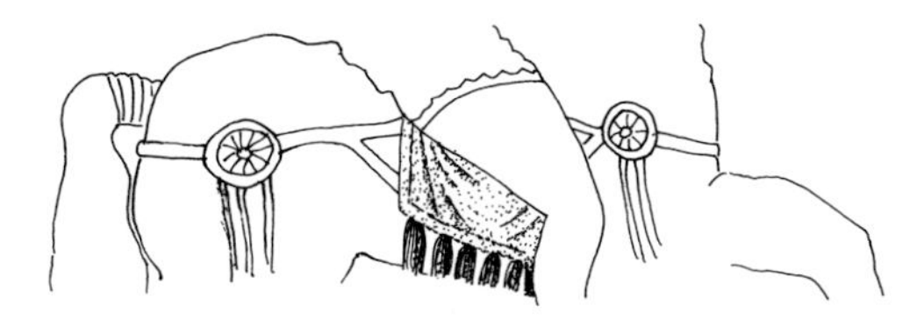

45 Detail from the tombstone of Longinus showing the fringed saddle-cloth. (Colchester Museum, Essex. Drawn by K.R. Dixon.)

under Trajan or Hadrian, probably in response to the conflict with the Sarmatians, from whom the *contus* was adopted (Coulston 1986, 69).

Heavy-armoured cavalry (*cataphractarii* and *clibanarii*)

Heavy-armoured cavalry, as their name suggests, were cavalry where both man and horse were protected by armour. Much debate has centred around the terms *cataphractarii* and *clibanarii*, and whether they denoted two distinct types of heavy-armoured cavalry or were simply two different words for the same thing. Speidel (1984), basing his argument on a tombstone from Claudiopolis, Bithynia, and the *Notitia Dignitatum* which mention both terms, states that the term *cataphractarii* was used for all heavy-armoured cavalry, but that the term *clibanarii* was reserved for heavy-armoured cavalry from Persia, Parthia and Palmyra, who were also *cataphractarii*. Coulston, however, suggested that the distinction may lie in the armament, with the *cataphractarii* being less heavily armoured and using lance and shield in the western style, and the *clibanarii* being more in the eastern tradition, employing bow and lance (1986, 63).

Heavy-armoured cavalry were of eastern origin, where the extensive use of bows encouraged the wearing of armour by both man and horse (Coulston 1986, 62). Rome came disastrously into contact with Parthian *cataphractarii* in 53 BC, when Crassus led his army to annihilation at the Battle of Carrhae. The impact of these heavy-armoured cavalry on the Roman army at Carrhae is recorded by Plutarch (*Lives*, *Crassus* 24): '[the Parthians] were seen to be themselves blazing in helmets and breastplates, their Marginian steel glittering keen and bright, and their horses clad in plates of bronze and steel.'

Although units of heavy-armoured cavalry may have existed in the Roman period prior to the reign of Hadrian (AD 117–38), the first known *ala cataphractariorum* was created during the rule of this Emperor (Dobson 1981, 235).

A grafitto from Dura-Europos (see Fig.10) shows a *clibanarius* or *cataphract*, with the rider in full body armour carrying a lance, and the horse wearing what appears to be a scale barding very similar to the ones found at the same site (see p.61–3). A description of *clibanarii* which accords perfectly with the rider in the Dura grafitto is given by Ammianus (16.10.8):

> scattered among them were the full-armoured cavalry (whom they call *clibanarii*), all masked, furnished with protecting breastplates and girt with iron belts, so that you might have supposed them statues polished by the hand of Praxiteles, not men. Thin circles of iron plates, fitted to the curves of their bodies, completely covered their limbs; so that whichever way they had to move their members, their garment fitted, so skilfully were the joinings made.

Horse-archers

The word *sagittariorum* in the title of a cavalry unit denoted the men as being horse-archers. *Sagittarii* were primarily drawn from the areas which were famous for their skills with the bow, namely the Levant, Numidia, Thrace, Crete and Cyrenaica (Coulston 1985, 288–9).

Horse-archers were probably equipped with shafted weapons (spears etc.), particularly light horse-archers, who would otherwise have been very vulnerable if caught by the enemy. They did have the advantage over the heavy-armoured archers, in that they were extremely mobile and could more easily escape pursuit (Coulston 1985, 293–4).

During the first three centuries AD there is no evidence to suggest that shields were used. Vegetius stated that body armour was necessary because of the unsuitability of shields for archers (*Epitoma Rei Militaris* 1.20; 2.15). This situation changed, however, and by the sixth century Procopius describes horse-archers as being armed in the following manner (*History of the Wars* 1.1.12–16):

> the bowmen of the present time go into battle wearing corselets and fitted out with greaves which extend up to the knee. From the right side hang their arrows, from the other the sword. And there are some who have a spear also attached to them and, at the shoulders, a sort of small shield without a grip, such as to cover the region of the face and neck.

Light-armoured cavalry

Light-armoured cavalry could be equipped either with a lance and sword, or with lance, sword and javelins. Although these men did wear body armour, it did not cover as much of the body as that worn by the heavy-armoured cavalry, nor were the horses protected to the same extent. This gave the light cavalry greater mobility and versatility in battle, and a better chance of escape if pursued.

4 Recruitment

An army raised without proper regard to the choice of its recruits was never yet made good by length of time . . . (Vegetius *Epitoma Rei Militaris* 1.7).

Originally, auxiliary units were recruited from single provinces or tribes. Before AD 69, they were generally posted in, or near to the province from which they were raised. There were exceptions however: units from Illyricum were stationed away from their homeland as a result of the revolt in AD 6–9, and units recruited from areas which had been recently conquered, such as Britain, were transferred to other provinces (Dobson and Mann 1973, 193–4). After the mutiny of a sizeable number of the units stationed on the Rhine during the years AD 69–70, it was considered too dangerous to allow these units, most of which had been raised from a single tribe, to be stationed in their homeland. It was therefore decided that the native units should be replaced with troops drawn from outside the province, the same policy having been previously enforced on the Danube (Dobson and Mann 1973, 194).

Units, once established, were kept up to strength by localized recruitment from the area in which they were stationed. This system had obvious advantages for Rome; it meant that conscription may have become less necessary since presumably men would have been more willing to enlist if they knew that they were unlikely to be sent far from their homes. Furthermore, these soldiers would probably fight better in the defence of their own country, rather than an alien one to which they had been sent. There was, however, no guarantee that men would not be required to serve outside their homelands in the event of an emergency.

There were apparently some exceptions to the localized recruitment policy, the most notable being those men enlisted into the eastern bow-armed units, particularly those which were mounted (Dobson and Mann 1973, 194; Coulston 1985, 288). Furthermore, the desire to maintain good standards within the *alae* created mixed units of Gauls and Thracians, or Gauls and Pannonians, since during the first century AD the Gauls were considered to be the most skilful riders (Dobson and Mann 1973, 194). It may be that those units which required specialist skills recruited wherever possible a number of men from areas renowned for their ability in a specific field, so that a core of expertise existed within the unit, allowing others to benefit from their knowledge.

Conscription or volunteering

Men gained entry into the army either by conscription or by volunteering. Exactly how widespread the employment of conscription was a matter of debate. Obviously, men recruited voluntarily would have been preferable, but Brunt (1974, 90) believes that the state could not have relied on there being sufficient volunteers to fill the ranks, and would therefore have had to resort to compulsion on a larger scale than is sometimes believed. As noted by Brunt (1974, 90), throughout Rome's history both her citizens and her subjects had been legally liable to serve in the army. According to Ruffus (Brand 1968, 165 nos.50–1), men who evaded military service in wartime were condemned to slavery. If a parent removed a son from the army during wartime or disabled him in order to render him unfit for service, the punishment was exile and partial confiscation of property. In peacetime, however, the latter crime resulted in the offender being beaten with cudgels (Brunt 1974, 92). From the time of Hadrian, sophists, philosophers, doctors and *grammatici*, were, however, granted exemption from military service (*Digest* 27.1.6.8).

When large bodies of troops had to be recruited, due to either a war or a decrease in the number of men coming forward for enlistment, levies were made, particularly amongst subject peoples (Holder 1982, 46). Although compulsion was not always used in the execution of a levy, when it was it was called a *dilectus* (Brunt 1974, 103; Dobson and Mann 1973, 193). During the pre-Flavian period these were usually imposed upon areas which had been conquered (Holder 1980, 123). It is thought that tribes subjected to these levies would be required to supply a fixed number of men annually, from which the most suitable would be enlisted (Holder 1980, 123; Brunt 1974, 93). Where these *dilectus* were repeatedly undertaken, tribes understandably felt resentful. Such an instance is recorded by Tacitus (*Annals* 4.46) when referring to the Thracian revolt of AD 26: 'The cause of the insurrection, apart from the temper of the insurgents, was that they refused to tolerate the military levies and to devote the whole of their able-bodied manhood to the Roman service.' Conscription was always available as a method of enlisting recruits, but whenever possible, the Roman army would undoubtedly have preferred its soldiers to have volunteered since willing soldiers were presumably better soldiers.

It may be wondered what made a man voluntarily enlist into the Roman army for a minimum of 25 years. The reasons have probably differed little throughout history: it was a fairly steady job with a relatively good standard of living, and it probably offered a better chance of advancement than most occupations. Probably one of the primary incentives during the early Empire was the acquisition of Roman citizenship on completion of 25 years service. Juvenal suggested (*Satire* 16), however, that many men joined in order to terrorize civilians without fear of punishment. Another, much later, view of the incentives for enlistment is given by Florence Nightingale (1858):

> It has been said by officers enthusiastic in their profession that there are three causes which make a soldier enlist, viz, being out of work, in a state of intoxication, or, jilted by his sweetheart. Yet the incentives to enlistment, which we desire to multiply, can hardly be put . . . in this form, viz, more poverty, more drink, more faithless sweethearts.

Probatio

Once a man had decided upon a military career he had to undergo a long and protracted period of examination, called the *probatio*, before he gained entry on to a unit's records. There appear to have been different entry requirements for different army units. Thus, higher standards regarding height and ability were demanded of men wishing to join an *ala* than those expected of enlistees for a *cohors equitata*. Since the cavalry received more pay than the infantry (see pp.87–8), the latter unit enabled *pedites* with the desired abilities, but lacking in inches, the opportunity to become *equites* and increase their pay: whether a further height qualification distinguished the cavalry from the infantry within this unit is not known.

When an applicant was presented to the recruiting officer it appears to have been advisable for him to have come equipped with letters of reference regarding his character (Davies 1969c, 216–7; Watson 1981, 37–8). An example dating to the second century reads as follows (*P. Oxy.* 32):

> To Julius Domitius, *tribunus militum legionis*, from Aurelius, his *beneficarius*. I have once previously recommended my friend Theon to you, and now again, Sir, I ask you to look upon him as if he were me, as he is a man worthy of your regard. He has left his own family, property and business, and followed me, and through everything he has relieved me from worry. I therefore request an introduction for him to you. He can tell you everything about our business. Whatever he has said, he has done. I have a high regard for the man [several fragmentary lines]. May I wish you and your people, Sir, every happiness and success for many years to come. Look upon this letter, Sir, and imagine that I am talking with you.

There were a number of requirements that the applicant had to fulfil, and although Vegetius supplies us with the most detailed account of the recruitment procedure, he fails to mention the single most important factor which determined whether or not a man would be accepted into the army: free birth. Confirmation that free birth was a requisite for enlistment comes from the *Digest* (Marcianus *Rules* 2) where it is stated that slaves were forbidden to enter every kind of military service, under penalty of death. An interesting case is brought to light by two of Pliny's letters, which he wrote to Trajan during his governorship of Bithynia, requesting advice regarding an incident where two slaves had actually managed to reach their *probatio*, but had not yet been signed on to the books of a unit (*Letters* 10.29–30). The main problem lay in discovering who was at fault: if they were conscripts then the examiner was to blame; if they were sent as substitutes, then whoever offered them was at fault; if, however, they presented themselves as volunteers, then they themselves were guilty for not being truthful about their status. Unfortunately Trajan's replies have not survived, so the outcome of this case remains unknown.

There were other categories of men who were barred from enlisting. The military laws of Ruffus (Brand 1968, 149) state that any person who had been deported, committed adultery or any other public offence, could never serve in the army. Men sentenced to exile could receive the death penalty if they attempted to enrol.

According to Vegetius (*Epitoma Rei Militaris 1.4*), the ideal age for recruitment following, he states, ancient practice, was at the age of puberty. The reasons for this are obvious: instruction is more easily and lastingly absorbed, and the recruits have greater flexibility and endurance. Hadrian is reputed to have issued regulations on the age of recruits (*Scriptores Historiae Augustae* Hadrian 10.8), decreeing that no one was to enrol men earlier than physical maturity permitted, or later than 'common humanity allowed'. Both Dio (55.23.1) and Livy (22.11) imply that the maximum age for enlistment was usually 35. Furthermore, an analysis of approximately 500 legionary tombstones showed that 75 per cent of the men joined the army between the ages of 18 and 23 (Forni 1953, 26–7).

The height of the applicant was also important (Vegetius *Epitoma Rei Militaris* 1.5): 'We find the ancients fond of procuring the tallest men they could for the service, since the standard for the cavalry of the wings and for the infantry of the first legionary cohorts was fixed at six [Roman] feet, or at least five [Roman] feet ten inches.' (It is interesting to note that the British army of today stipulates the same height qualifications for men wanting to join the Household Cavalry (*pers. comm.* Sgt. M. Hardy)). Herodian writes of one soldier (6.8.1): 'In the army there was a man called Maximinus, from one of the semi-barbarian tribes of the interior of Thrace . . . As he grew to manhood, he was drafted into the army as a horseman because of his size and strength.' By the late Empire the minimum height qualification appears to have been reduced. Vegetius (*Epitoma Rei Militaris* 1.5), referring to the 'good old days', states that the sizes mentioned above might have been possible to maintain in the early Empire, when the military profession was a great deal more popular, but in his time standards had, through necessity, declined. He seems to attempt to console himself and his readers by stating that height is, however, not as important as strength. The Theodosian Code (7.13.3) demonstrates that by AD 367 the minimum height for a recruit had been lowered to five (Roman) feet seven inches. In all periods it must be wondered exactly how much emphasis was placed on men being within specified height limits: all armies like to present a uniform appearance, but at the end of the day the fighting ability of an army is more important than its attractiveness to the eye. During times of war and campaign, height qualifications would probably have been waived. It may be, however, that in certain units, such as the *equites legionis*, a greater effort may have been made to ensure that the men were of a reasonably similar size.

Vegetius gives advice on the physical qualities that the recruiting officer should look for in a potential enlistee (*Epitoma Rei Militaris* 1.6):

> The officer who is going to hold a levy, must pay particular attention to make his selection of the men who can prove to be suitable fighters, from their faces, eyes and the whole shape of their limbs. The quality not only of human beings but also of horses and dogs can be seen by many signs, as we are instructed in the writings of the experts. Therefore a young man who is to be selected to be a soldier, should have lively eyes, carry his head erect, his chest should be broad, his shoulders muscular, his arms strong, have long fingers, a modest belly, thin buttocks, and his feet and calves should be sinewy, not over-fat. When one finds these points in a recruit, less emphasis may be put on the height, as it is more important that the soldiers are brave rather than big.

All these requirements are the basic signs which would enable the recruiting officer to establish whether or not the candidate was physically capable and suitable for the army. The present British army employs the same criteria to discover if a recruit is prone to heavy weight gain, a problem which if serious, would prevent the man from joining the service. Certain physical disabilities would prevent a man from being accepted into the army. A document from Egypt (*P. Oxy.* 39) records that one man was disqualified from entrance due to his defective eyesight (though it is not certain whether he was being discharged from a military or a civil post: see Watson 1981, 41).

Some disabilities, however, did not prevent a man from enlisting, as is demonstrated by the *Digest* (49.16.4): 'One who was born with one testicle, or who has lost one, can lawfully serve in the army, in accordance with a rescript of the divine Imperial Trajan; for both the generals Sulla and Cotta are said to have been in this condition.'

A considerable amount of advice is offered by Vegetius regarding other factors for the recruiting officer to establish before a man is enlisted (*Epitoma Rei Militaris* 1.3). A prime concern was whether the applicant was from the town or the country. He believed that those from the latter were better qualified since they were accustomed to hard labour, inured to fatigue, untainted by luxuries and were prepared in some measure for a military life by their continual employment in farm work. When it was necessary to recruit from towns Vegetius suggested that such men should be treated harshly from the start, being forced to work on entrenchments, march in ranks, carry heavy weights, endure heat and dust, eat moderately and sleep in the open and in tents. Only when they had undergone these rigours should they be instructed in the use of arms.

Vegetius also believed that the background of the recruit was important (*Epitoma Rei Militaris* 1.7). He considered professions such as fishing, fowling and weaving, for instance, too womanly, advising that men in these trades be under no circumstances admitted to the army. On the other hand, smiths, carpenters, butchers and huntsmen were extremely suitable for the military profession. The recruiting officer also had to pay attention to the intelligence and mental state of the candidate. This was particularly necessary for those men wishing to secure positions of responsibility.

Once the applicant had successfully passed this stage of the selection process, he then had to undergo a further examination (Vegetius *Epitoma Rei Militaris* 1.8):

> The selected recruit must not receive the mark immediately, but must first be examined by exercise, to discover if he is really fit for such work. Both the quickness and strength required in this are thus shown, and whether he can learn the training in weapons, and whether he has a soldier's courage. For very many, although in outward appearance they seem suitable, are nevertheless proved by examination to be unsuited. Therefore the less suitable men must be rejected, and others of greater vigour must be selected in their place, as in every conflict it is not so much numbers as courage that is advantageous. Accordingly, instructions with weapons must be given in exercises each day to the recruits, who then receive the mark.

These instructions (see Chapter 6) lasted for a minimum of four months (Vegetius *Epitoma Rei Militaris* 2.5).

Once the enlistee had undergone his four months basic training, he then, according to Vegetius, received an indelible mark on his skin, was entered on the records and took the military oath (*Epitoma Rei Militaris* 2.5). There appears to be no evidence, however, for recruits being tattooed in the Principate (Davies 1969c, 218). Evidence from the end of the third century implies that soldiers received some form of identity disc, as is demonstrated by a document from North Africa, which records the minutes of a court hearing held in AD 295 (Davies 1969c, 218). The case concerned Maximilianus, who was being tried for refusing to become a soldier. The enquiry was presided over by the governor of the province, and the proconsul, Dio. The recruiting officer and defendant's father, Fabius Victor, and the *praepositus* of Caesariensis, Valesianus Quintianus, were called as witnesses:

> 12 March, AD 295, at Theveste, in the forum. Fabius Victor, together with Maximilianus, were brought before the court, and the prosecutor Pompeianus addressed the court. 'Fabius Victor has been appointed recruiting officer with Valesianus Quintianus, the *praepositus* of Caesariensis. Maximilianus, the son of Victor, is a good recruit, and since he has the qualities to be approved, I submit that he be measured.' Dio the proconsul said, 'What is your name?' Maximilianus replied, 'What reason have you for wanting to know my name? I cannot serve as a soldier, because I am a Christian.' Dio replied, 'Get him ready.' When he was being got ready, Maximilianus replied, 'I cannot serve as a soldier. I cannot do evil. I am a Christian.' Dio the proconsul replied, 'Let him be measured.' When he had been measured, his height was read out by equerry, 'He is five feet, ten inches.' Dio said to the equerry, 'Give him the *signaculum*.' Maximilianus resisted and replied, 'I do not do so. I cannot serve as a soldier. I am a Christian. I do not accept the *signaculum* of the secular world, and if you give me the *signaculum*, I will break it, because it has no validity. I cannot carry a piece of lead around my neck after the sign of my Lord.' Dio said, 'Remove his name.'

A solution to the problem may lie in the fact that Vegetius was interpreting the term *signaculum* literally, which would lead him to believe that the Roman army did actually tattoo their men with a permanent mark (Davies 1969c, 218). Alternatively, it is possible that although Vegetius was using early sources for his treatise, it was in his time current practice within the army for men to be tattooed (Jones 1987, 149), and therefore he assumed that the term had had the same meaning then also. By the sixth century AD tattooing appears to have been common amongst the military, as this quote from the doctor Aetius demonstrates (8.12): 'They call "tattoos" that which is inscribed on the face or some other part of the body, for example on the hands of soldiers, and they use the following ink. [The recipe follows.] Apply by pricking the places with needles, wiping away the blood, and rubbing in first juice of leek, and then the preparation.' Although Aetius mentions troops being branded on their hands, legal authorities indicate that tattoos could also be placed on the arms (*Codex Theodosianus* 9.40.2 = *Digest* 9.47.17).

Once the recruit had received the military mark (be it a tattoo or an identity disc), he would then take the military oath (*sacramentum*). During the Republic, in order to save time, this had been carried out in two stages: firstly, one man was chosen to recite the complete oath, a process which was called the *praeiuratio*, whereupon the remaining men would take turns in coming forward and taking the oath, by saying the phrase *idem in me* ('The same in my case'). It is believed that this procedure probably continued to be employed under the Empire (Watson 1981, 44). This time-saving service may have been reserved for use at the annual renewal of the oath, since presumably the numbers involved in a service for new recruits would have been considerably smaller, enabling each individual to recite the entire oath (Watson 1981, 49). Evidence for the wording of the military oath comes from Vegetius (*Epitoma Rei Militaris* 2.5), and although it is a Christianized *sacramentum*, it is not too dissimilar from the Republican version (see Watson 1981, 49):

> They swear by God, by Christ and by the Holy Ghost; and by the Majesty of the Emperor who, after God, should be the chief object of the love and veneration of mankind . . . The soldiers, therefore, swear they will obey the Emperor willingly and implicitly in all his commands, that they will never desert and will always be ready to sacrifice their lives for the Roman Empire.

In numeros referre

The recruit was now ready to be entered on the records of a unit (*in numeros referre*). In the eyes of the law, only now would the recruit be recognized as a soldier (*Digest* 39.1.42): 'An individual starts to have the right to make a will from the time when he has been entered on the records; before that time he does not have the right. Accordingly, men who are not yet on the records, even although they are selected recruits and travel at public expense, they are not yet soldiers. To be classified as soldiers, they must be entered on the records.' A copy of a letter dating from AD 103 records that the Prefect of Egypt had ordered the commanding officer of an auxiliary cohort, to place six approved recruits, on the books of his unit (*P. Oxy*. 1022):

> Copy.
> C Minicius Italus to Celsianus.
> Give instructions that the six recruits approved by me for the cohort under your command be entered on the records with effect from 19 February. I have appended their names and distinguishing-marks to this letter.

C. Veturius Gemellus	aged 21	no distinguishing mark.
C. Longinus Priscus	aged 22	scar on left eyebrow.
C. Julius Maximus	aged 25	no distinguishing mark.
[.] Julius Secundus	aged 20	no distinguishing mark.
C. Julius Saturninus	aged 23	scar on left hand.
M. Antonius Valens	aged 22	scar on right side of forehead.

> Received 24 February, AD 103, through Priscus, *singularis*.
>
> I, Avidius Arrianus, *cornicularius of Cohors III Ituraeorum*, state that the original letter is in the records office of the cohort.

As can be seen from the above document, all the soldiers had Roman names. It would appear that when a man was assigned to a unit stationed either in Egypt or Italy, he was given a new military name, aside from his native one. Evidence for this comes from a letter, written by a new recruit, stationed in Italy, to his father (*BGU* 423) in which he begins the letter with his birth name, Apion, and towards the end of the text writes that he is called Antonius Maximus.

This letter also states that Apion (Antonius Maximus) received three gold pieces for travelling money. This money, which was called the *viaticum*, would have been essential, since the recruit would have incurred many expenses during the time of his training period. There is some debate on whether different arms of the service received different amounts of money (Davies 1969c, 224). Using the available evidence, Watson (1981, 44) believes that there was probably a standard rate of 75 *denarii*, or three *aurei* (gold pieces).

As can be seen from the above, the Roman army took great care in the selection of its soldiers. There would always be, of course, some recruiting officers who would exploit their position, and who would, for whatever reason, enlist men unsuitable for military service.

5 Conditions of service

Pay

The pay scales for both the *auxilia* and the legions remain uncertain due mainly to the lack of evidence, though a number of scholars have attempted to reconstruct the pay scale for the *auxilia*, based on different fractions (one-third, two-thirds or five-sixths) of the legionaries pay (Domaszewski 1900; Brunt 1950; Watson 1959; Speidel 1973). Troops were divided into four classes in matters of pay: auxiliary infantry; cavalry in a *cohors equitata*; cavalry in an *ala*; and legionaries, and there were three pay scales: basic pay; pay-and-a-half (*sesquiplicarius*); and double pay (*duplicarius*). A further class, the *equites* of a legion, is added by Speidel (1973, 146). The legionaries are believed to have received the highest pay, although it has been suggested that the cavalrymen of an *ala* would have been paid the same or more (Speidel 1973). In the *auxilia*, the *alae* received the highest pay, with the *equites* of the mixed units receiving more than the *pedites*. A pay record (*stipendium*) of papyrus from AD 84 for a legionary soldier (Fink 1971, no.69), states that he was paid 297 *drachmae* (Spiedel 1973, 141–2), and a similar papyrus of AD 81 for two auxiliarymen, possibly cavalrymen of a *cohors equitata* since their *stipendia* include deductions for hay (Lewis and Reinhold 1966, 513–4; Fink 1971, no.68), records that they were paid 247½ *drachmae* (Speidel 1973, 142–3). The auxiliary total of 247½ is not, however, five-sixths of 297. This led Speidel to suggest that a 1 per cent deduction, possibly for an exchange fee for the conversion of *denarii* into *drachmae*, had been made before the amounts were credited to the men, giving totals of 300 and 250 respectively, making the auxiliary pay exactly five-sixths of the legionary (1973, 144).

The five-sixths theory has been questioned since it would mean that an auxiliary cavalryman would be paid the same as or more than a legionary (Breeze and Dobson 1987, 177). Such a situation, however, does not seem too improbable when it is considered that cavalrymen had extra demands made on their pay by the feeding and equipping of their horses.

A pay record on papyrus of AD 192 (Fink 1971, no.70), records the auxiliaries as receiving either 253 or 254 *denarii* a year. If, as suggested by Speidel (1973, 145), both the pay records of the auxiliaries referred to the *equites* of mixed units, then it is possible that auxiliaries received two-thirds of the pay of legionaries. Those who favour the one-third theory, do so because of its simplicity in constructing a pay scale, together with the belief, as stated above, that legionaries would have earned more than auxiliary cavalrymen in an *ala*.

The following table shows the figures for the three proposed pay scales in *denarii* per year, from Domitian (81–96) to Septimius Severus (193–211):

	Basic	*Sesquiplicarius*	*Duplicarius*
One-third			
miles cohortis	100	150	200
eques cohortis	150	225	300
eques alae	200	300	400
miles legionis	300	450	600
eques legionis	–	–	–
Two-thirds			
miles cohortis	200	300	400
eques cohortis	250	375	500
eques alae	300	450	600
miles legionis	300	450	600
eques legionis	350	525	700
Five-sixths			
miles cohortis	250	375	500
eques cohortis	300	450	600
eques alae	350	525	700
miles legionis	300	450	600
eques legionis	400	600	800

Soldiers received their pay not weekly, but three or four times a year (Breeze and Dobson 1987, 177). Before the men were given their pay, a number of deductions were made for items such as food, clothing, equipment, camp dinners, the burial club, which is only positively attested for the legions (Vegetius, *Epitoma Rei Militaris* 2.20), but presumed for the *auxilia*, and bedding. Cavalrymen had the extra burden of horse fodder and equipment. The money that was left was deposited in accounts for the soldiers, under the charge of the standard-bearers, allowing the men to save some of their pay if they so desired.

Rewards

Non-citizens were not entitled to receive individual awards, although whole units could be decorated for valour. These awards took the form of torques and the granting of citizenship, which was limited to the soldiers serving in the unit at the time. The *Ala Augusta Gallorum Petriana milliaria civium Romanorum bis torquata* received the torque twice (*bis torquata*) and the grant of citizenship (*civium Romanorum*).

Punishment and discipline

> No state can either be happy or secure that is remiss and negligent in the discipline of its troops. For it is not profusion of riches or excess of luxury that can influence our enemies to court or respect us. This can only be effected by fear of our arms. It is an observation of Cato that misconduct in the common affairs of life may be retrieved, but that is quite otherwise in war, where errors are fatal and without remedy, and are followed by immediate punishment. (Vegetius, *Epitoma Rei Militaris* 1.13.)

Punishment within the Roman army was governed by laws, and those ascribed to Ruffus are the most extensive (Brand 1968, 147–69). They demonstrate that both infantrymen and cavalrymen received the same punishments, except in the case of desertion to the enemy in peacetime (during wartime this was a capital offence), whereupon a cavalryman would only suffer a reduction in rank, whilst an infantryman would be dismissed from the army (Brand 1968, 167, no.58). Most crimes appear to have been allocated a specific punishment.

Capital punishment was reserved for treason; conspiring against commanders; insubordination towards an officer; striking an officer; inciting violence; wounding or killing a fellow soldier; fleeing from battle and breaking the lines; failing to execute a command during a battle; quitting the ramparts; entering the camp over the wall; abandonment of a commander; betrayal of a camp; feigning illness to avoid battle; giving information to the enemy; and desertion to the enemy in wartime.

The death penalty could be carried out in a number of ways. One of the most notorious is decimation, which entailed the execution of every tenth man, decided by lot, from soldiers who had been found guilty of cowardice in the presence of the enemy. The nine men who survived were sometimes forced to eat barley instead of wheat (Watson 1959, 119). Decimation was seldom used, however, and Tacitus describes it as a rare and old-fashioned penalty (*Annals* 3.21). An example where cavalrymen were dealt with in this manner is recorded by Ammianus (24.3.1–2):

> . . . the Persian leader called Surena had unexpectedly attacked three squadrons of our scouting cavalry, had killed a few of them, including one of their tribunes, and carried off a standard. At once roused to furious anger, Julian hurried forth with an armed force . . . and routed the marauders in shameful confusion; he cashiered the two surviving tribunes as inefficient and cowardly, and following the ancient laws, discharged and put to death ten of the soldiers who had fled from the field.

If an individual was found guilty of a capital offence, he could be hanged, beheaded, burned alive, or, in the case of desertion to the enemy, he could be thrown to wild animals in the arena, since by committing such a crime he was no longer considered to be a soldier (having been dishonourably discharged), or even a citizen, and thus was not protected by the law. In actuality, however, the death penalty was frequently not resorted to. Roman soldiers were a highly valuable resource, and in many cases consideration of rank, length of service, previous conduct, the nature and circumstances of the crime, and the age of the soldier (if he was young and this was his first offence, more tolerance might be shown), could enable the punishment to be reduced.

Non-capital offences (aside from those which by law warranted death, but where leniency had been shown and the penalty lessened) included permitting a standard to be captured by the enemy; retreating while the rampart was still intact; throwing away weapons during battle; stealing; and being absent without leave. There were a number of ways in which crimes such as these could be dealt with. Mutilation of the body was considered befitting in the case of rape, where the offender's nose was cut off, and for the stealing of pack animals the man might lose his hands. Another harsh, and more commonly employed punishment, was dishonourable discharge (*missio ignominiosa*), since it would mean that the man would receive none of the privileges to which he would normally have been entitled on leaving the army. Lesser penalties included reduction in rank, flogging, fines and deductions from pay.

Although these punishments appear harsh, it must be realized that what we may view as being too extreme today is not what would have been considered so in the period in question. Furthermore, as mentioned above, the sentence proscribed by law was mitigated whenever possible, and Ruffus (Brand 1968, 163 no.45) even writes that allowances should be made where drink is involved: 'Capital punishment shall be remitted in the case of soldiers who err and transgress on account of wine and drunkenness or other such licentiousness; but they must be transferred to another branch of the service.'

The military laws, therefore, were probably used with discretion by most, but there would always be a few ardent disciplinarians who would strictly abide by the book, or even decide that the laws were not harsh enough. One such man was Corbulo, who, according to Tacitus (*Annals* 11.18), had a man executed for putting his sword aside whilst digging a ditch! Instances such as this could have suffered from exaggeration, and it is probably fair to say that Roman military discipline was no more severe than was considered necessary, since recruits for the army would have been in short supply if execution had been quite so liberally applied as the laws would have us believe.

Diet

Archaeological, papyrological and literary evidence suggests that the diet of the Roman army was fairly well-balanced, nutritious and diverse. The standard fare eaten by soldiers stationed in forts was corn, cheese, bacon and vegetables, with sour-wine being the principal drink. This list was generally supplemented by various locally available foodstuffs, or specially purchased items bought by the soldiers, or supplied by friends or family at their request (see p.92). The most basic food was corn, which once ground, could be made into bread, porridge and soup (Davies 1971b, 125). According to Herodian (4.7.5), the Emperor Caracalla: 'ate the bread that was available; with his own hand he would grind his personal ration of corn, make it into a loaf, bake it in the ashes and eat it.'

Owing to the misinterpretation of statements by both Caesar (*Gallic War* 7.17) and Tacitus (*Annals* 14.24), it was previously believed (Parker 1958, 220) that the Romans refrained from eating meat whenever possible. Such an assumption, however, is clearly disproved on analysis of the animal bone evidence from forts (Davies 1971b, 126–8, Table I, Appendix 138–41; Johnson 1983, 195; Breeze and Dobson 1987, 189; Bowman 1974, 367). In the list of 33 forts given by Davies (1971b, Table I), the most common bones were ox, which were present at all 33, pig and red deer at 31, and sheep at 30. Other animals eaten included goat, roe deer, boar, hare and wild ox. Land was provided outside Roman forts (*territorium* or *prata*), on which the military or tenant farmers could graze livestock and grow crops (Johnson 1983, 195; Davies 1971b, 123). A fragmentary inscription from Chester-le-Street, England (*RIB* 1049) refers to the *territorium* of an unnamed *ala*. The keeping of livestock could also provide cheese and milk, and cheese presses have been found at a number of sites, including those from Longthorpe II, England (Dannell and Wild 1987, 69).

Vegetable remains have been recovered from many sites, including cabbage from Vindolanda, England, and peas and carrots from Vindonissa, Switzerland (Davies 1971b, 133). Pulses, particularly beans and lentils, are well attested for the army. A papyrus from Pselcis (Fink 1971, no.78; Johnson 1983, 196) records that an *eques* of a mixed unit received lentils, salt and vinegar, and an inscribed second-century pot-sherd records the *Ala Heracliana* being supplied with beans and lentils (Wilcken 1899, 1013; Davies 1971b, 133). Many varieties of grain were consumed, and the legionary fortress at Caerleon, Wales, produced the carbonized remains of cultivated and wild barley, rye, wheat, spelt, and cultivated and wild oats, although the latter may have been a weed.

The staple drink of the Roman army was sour-wine (*acetum*), which produced a drink called *posca* when watered down. Better quality wine (*vinum*) was available, but not as a basic item. Salt (*salaria*) would have been an essential item, not only for preserving meat and flavouring food, but also for consumption by the men during long marches and strenuous exercise in high temperatures. During experimental marches, in which the participants wore replica first- and fourth-century equipment, the problems that ensued from salt deficiency were recorded (Atkinson and Morgan 1987, 101–2): 'the legionary . . . suffered from bouts of nausea and dizziness after three to four hours on the march. Weight loss was excessive and during one particular 26 mile march on a very hot day seven pounds were shed! On this occasion also, temporary blindness and disorientation were experienced over a period of approximately 30 seconds.' It was therefore believed that the soldiers would either have carried a personal supply of salt and water, or would have had immediate access to these items (Atkinson and Morgan 1987, 102).

As stated above, the basic diet could be supplemented by a large range of foods. These could be obtained by the soldier himself, or he could ask friends or relatives to send them to him. Numerous letters written by auxiliaries on sherds of pottery were found at Wâdi Fawâkhir, Egypt (Guéraud 1942; Davies 1971b, 134–6), the majority of which are concerned with the acquisition of food. Items mentioned on these sherds include mustard, radishes, grapes, cabbages, oil, fish, onions and fodder for horses.

Of the supplementary commodities, seafood was very popular, particularly oysters, the shells of which have been found on numerous sites (Borgelin 1989, 33–4; Davies 1971b, 128–9). A private letter to a decurion on one of the Vindolanda writing tablets states that the sender had received 50 oysters from a friend (Bowman 1983, Tablet 6). Other types of seafood eaten included limpets, mussels, cockles, whelks and edible snails. Fish was also consumed, and Chesters on Hadrian's Wall produced evidence for perch, whilst sturgeon was eaten at the Saalburg, Germany, cod at Hod Hill, England, and pike at Butzbach, Germany (Davies 1971b, 129). Although the following evidence does not concern a cavalryman, it is interesting to note a letter on papyrus from a legionary to his father, explaining why he missed their meeting (*P. Mich.* 478, lines 8–13; Davies 1971b, 130): 'For it was at that time that so violent and dreadful an attack of fish poisoning made me ill, and for five days I was unable to drop you a line, not to speak of going to meet you. Not one of us was even able to leave the camp gate.'

Fish sauce was very popular within the Roman army. The most commonly used type throughout the Empire appears to have been *garum*, although *muria*, a fish sauce of inferior quality, may have been the variety which was more readily affordable for soldiers.

Poultry was also consumed, with chicken appearing to be the most popular (Davies 1971b, 130–1, Table III). The largest range of poultry remains comes from Valkenburg in the Netherlands, where chicken, several varieties of duck and goose, petrel, cormorant, heron, crane, crow and eagle were eaten (Davies 1971b, 130). Large numbers of egg shells were found in the barracks at Hofheim, Germany, and Vindonissa, Switzerland, suggesting that poultry was also kept for the production of eggs (Davies 1971b, 131).

There is abundant evidence for the eating of fruit and nuts, with the legionary fortress at Vindonissa, Switzerland, producing the widest range, including pears, cherries, apples, grapes, plums, peaches, hazelnuts, walnuts, chestnuts and beechnuts (Davies 1971b, 132).

As well as the low quality wine (*acetum*) which was standard issue, a greater choice was obtainable. An amphora handle from Mumrills, Scotland, had the words GLVK[VS (OINOS) scratched on it, and is therefore believed to have contained sweet wine (Davies 1971b, 131). Celtic beer (*cervesa*) was popular, particularly in the north European provinces. It was made from malted grain, probably wheat, or a grain known as *bracis* (Bowman 1983, 31).

On campaign, or during a siege, the diet of the Roman army was obviously less varied. Appian (3.3) gives a comparative description of the diet previously enjoyed by besieging troops, and the one which they had been reduced to: 'The soldiers were worn out by the continuous watch, lack of sleep, and the unaccustomed food of the country. They had no [vintage] wine, salt, sour wine or oil, but fed on wheat and barley, and large quantities of meat and hare boiled without salt, which upset their digestion.' Vegetius (*Epitoma Rei Militaris* 4.7) states that an army under siege should ensure that there are plentiful supplies of horse fodder, wine, fruit and cereals, and preserved meat, rather than live animals stored within the fort, since live animals would only place a further strain on supplies.

As noted by Davies (1971b, 137–8), probably the best testimony to the quality and quantity of the Roman military diet is that there is no recorded complaint about this aspect of army life.

Water supply, sanitation and hygiene

The supply of water to forts was obviously of the greatest importance. An abundance was required for drinking, cooking, the bath-house, latrines and workshops, and for watering the horses and baggage animals. It also had to be fresh, and as Vegetius advises (*Epitoma Rei Militaris* 1.22): 'Do not allow the army to use water that is unwholesome or marshy, as drinking bad water, just like poison, causes illnesses for the men.'

The choice of site was therefore determined, where feasible, by the availability of water, it being considered advantageous to incorporate a spring in the defences (Vegetius *Epitoma Rei Militaris* 4.10): '. . . perpetual springs within the walls are of the utmost advantage . . . [but] . . . where Nature has denied this convenience, wells must be sunk, however deep, till you come to water, which must be drawn up by ropes . . .' Forts where the water-table was fairly near to the surface were provided with wells, commonly found in the courtyard of the *principia* (headquarters building), as, for example, at Chesters on Hadrian's Wall (Bruce 1978, 113). Owing to

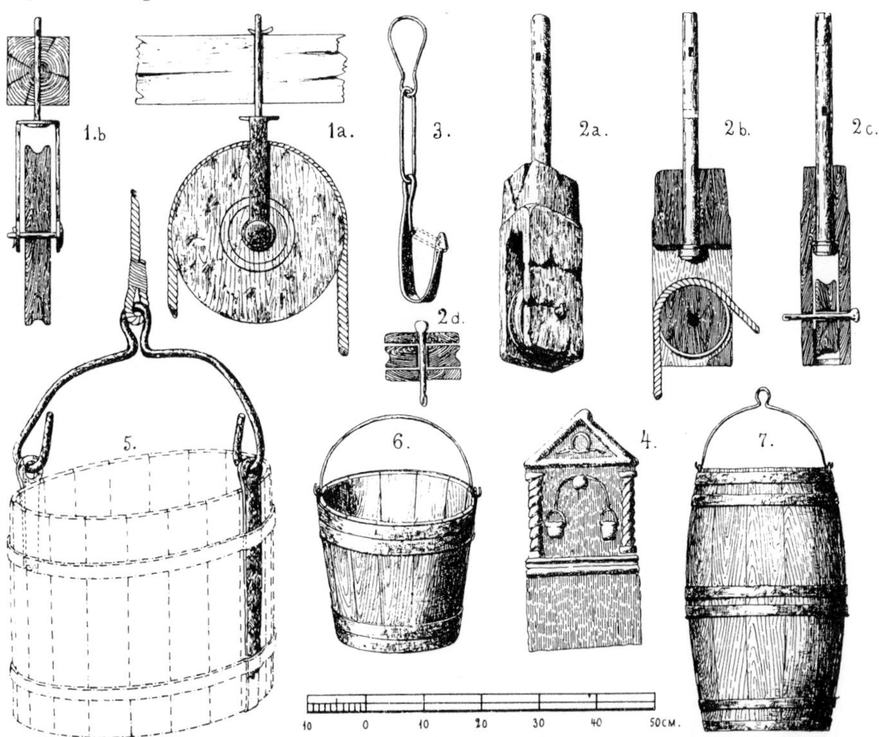

46 An illustration showing some of the objects recovered from the wells at Saalburg, Germany, including buckets, hoisting gear and fragments of rope. (From Jacobi 1897.)

the waterlogged condition of some of the wells at the Saalburg, Germany, wooden buckets, the rollers from hoisting gear, and fragments of rope were preserved (Fig.46) (Jacobi 1934; Johnson 1983, 202–3).

Where the water-table was too shallow to sink wells, or the fort was situated on bedrock, aqueducts or pipelines to a source outside the fort, and rainwater tanks, were employed (Johnson 1983, 204; for a list of Romano-British military aqueducts see Stephens 1985). Aqueducts are known to have existed at a number of sites, sometimes running large distances in order to maintain the correct levels. For example, the one which supplied Great Chesters on Hadrian's Wall brought water from the Haltwhistle Burn, which although only 3.5km (2¼ miles) away, required a route stretching 9.5km (6 miles) to be taken (Bruce 1978, 183; Johnson 1983, 206).

Epigraphic evidence can also provide information on the construction of aqueducts, since their repair is often recorded on inscriptions. Öhringen, Germany, produced a group of three altars (*CIL* XIII 11757–9), dedicated to the nymphs of the aqueduct, one of which read:

> To the everlasting nymphs, the Roman knight Caius Julius Rogatianus, prefect of the First Cohort of Belgians, bearing the titles Septimiana Gordiana, under the command of the governor . . . anus, has rebuilt the Gordian aqueduct, after it had been in disrepair for some time, through a new aqueduct over a distance of 5907 feet, because he wanted to feed the flowing waters into the commander's house and to the baths. It was dedicated on 4 December in the second consulship of the Emperor, our lord, Gordianus Augustus, and of Pompeianus.

Water tanks were probably always used in conjunction with some other method of water supply (Johnson 1983, 209). These large masonry tanks have been found at numerous sites, good examples coming from Housesteads and Corbridge. They are sometimes found in positions which suggest that they were collecting rainwater directly from the roofs of buildings, or were equipped with stone channels or pipes, allowing a constant stream of water to be maintained (Johnson 1983, 209).

As stated above, water was required for the latrines which were provided for the soldiers, with the officers possibly having a separate block solely for their use. In general they consist of a stone rectangular building, with a door on one side, and seating with wooden covers against three walls, under which runs a sewer. The positioning of the latrine block was important for its drainage, most being situated at the lowest corner of the site in the *intervallum* (Johnson 1983, 211). The latrines could be flushed out by a number of methods. The block at Housesteads on Hadrian's Wall was flushed by a channel, which was continually fed with water from a tank. The channel then went under the rampart, and discharged the waste at an

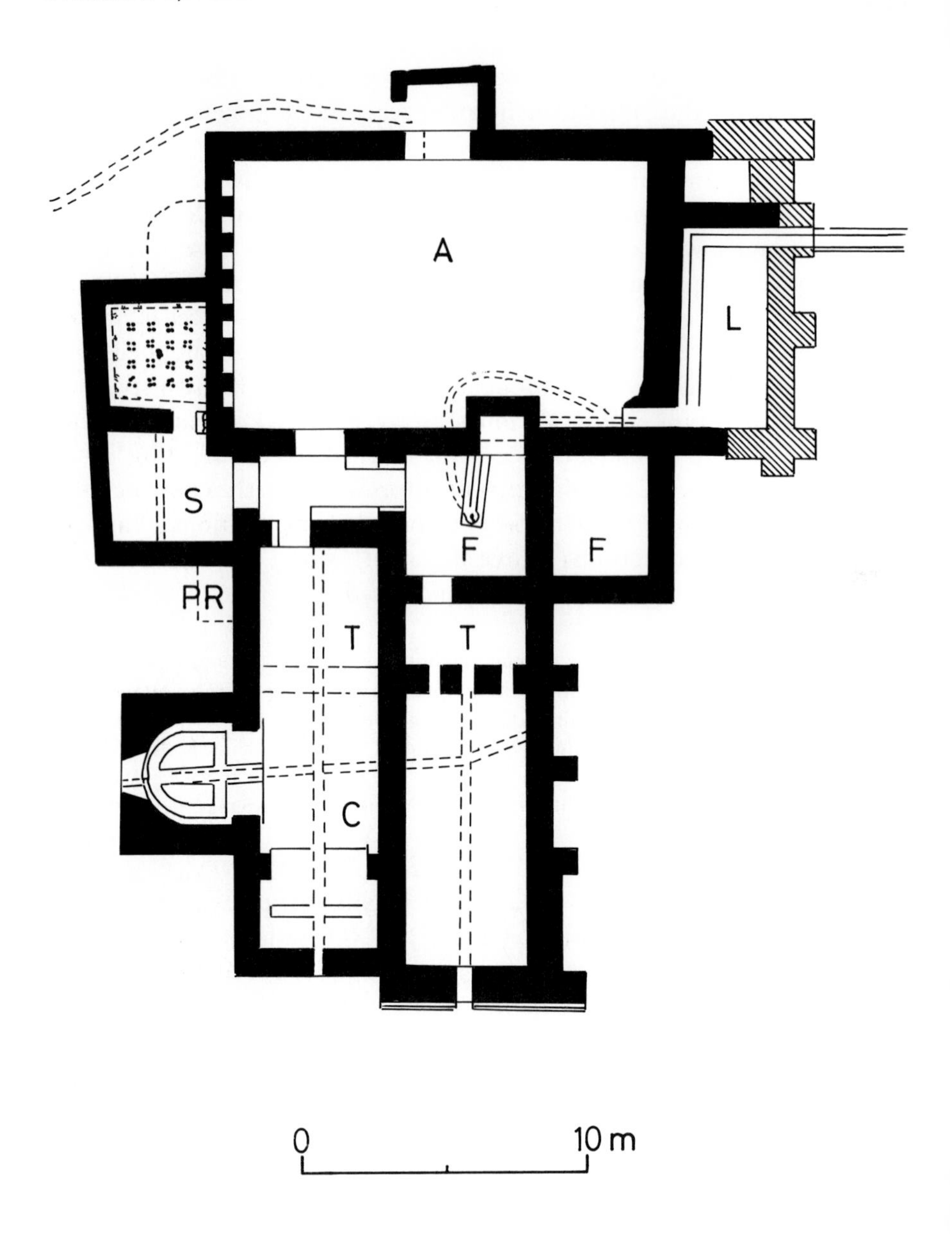

47 Plan of the bath-house at Chesters on Hadrian's Wall. Some bath-houses, such as Chesters, were supplied with more than one room of the same type. A: *Apodyterium* (changing room); F: *Frigidarium* (cold room); T: *Tepidarium* (warm room); C: *Caldarium* (hot room); S: *Sudatorium* (dry-heated room); L: *Laconicum* (dry-heated room); PR: *Praefurnia* (furnaces), (Redrawn by K.R. Dixon from Bruce 1978.)

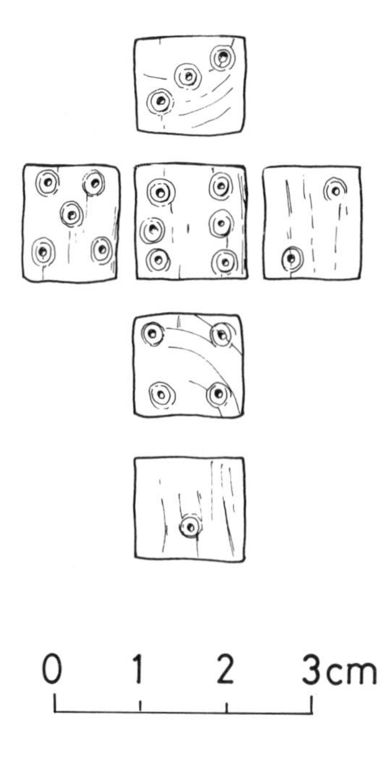

48 Bone die from Corbridge, England. (Redrawn by K.R. Dixon from Bishop and Dore 1989.)

unknown point down the hill (Simpson 1976; Smith 1976, 143; Bruce 1978, 148). If the latrines were incorporated into the bath-house, as at Bar Hill on the Antonine Wall, then the waste water from bathing was used for flushing (Johnson 1983, 213). Where no water system was available, such as at Hod Hill, England, it is believed that buckets would have been placed beneath the seats, the emptying of which would probably have been performed as a fatigue duty (Richmond 1968, 86–7).

Hygiene within the Roman army was of an exceptionally high standard. Every permanent fort was provided with a bath-house, which was built of stone and tile, and usually situated outside the walls. This was probably as a precaution against fire, which appears to have been the frequent cause of destruction, as is attested by inscriptions recording their repair (*RIB* 730; 791).

The Roman bath-house could consist of a number of elements (Fig.47). A changing room (*apodyterium*) was provided at the entrance of the bath-house. Finds of gaming pieces (Fig.48) and altars to the goddess Fortuna, imply that this area of the building was also used as a place for gambling. One of the walls of the *apodyterium* at Chesters had seven niches cut into it, and it is thought that these may have either served as lockers, or held altars or statues (Johnson 1983, 220). A series of steam baths followed, progressing in temperature from the cold room (*frigidarium*), to a warm room (*tepidarium*), and a hot room (*caldarium*). The bather then had his body coated in oil, whereupon a scraper (*strigil*) was used to remove the dirt (Fig.49). This was followed by a plunge into a cold bath. Some bath-houses were provided with a dry-heated room (*sudatorium* or *laconicum*) supplied with hot air by a furnace (*praefurnia*) which circulated the air under the floor that had been raised on pillars of tile or stone, and also through hollow wall tiles.

Medical care

A high standard of medical care appears to have existed in the Roman army. Vegetius (*Epitoma Rei Militaris* 3.2) states that: 'It is the constant duty of senior officers, and generals to seek diligently that sick soldiers should be brought back to health by suitable food and cured by the skills of the doctors.'

Evidence for medical posts amongst the army personnel comes from epigraphic and literary sources. The men who dealt with the dressing of wounds were known as *capsarii*, so called because of the round bandage box (*capsa*) which they carried. Their primary task in the field was to patch up the wounds, and get the soldiers to a hospital or a medical tent as quickly as possible. A scene on Trajan's Column (Fig.50) (Lepper and Frere 1988, Pl.XL, scene CIII) shows two soldiers, one sitting on a rock being attended to

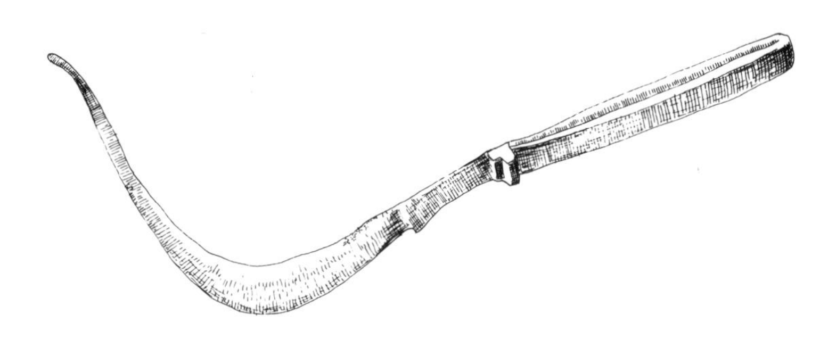

49 Bronze *strigil* measuring 25cm (10in) in length, from the bath-house of the legionary fortress at Caerleon. After a bather had gone through the sequence of baths his body was coated in oil, whereupon a *strigil* was used to remove the oil and the dirt. This example bears a Greek inscription which reads 'it washed you nicely'. (Redrawn by K.R. Dixon from Bédoyère 1989.)

50 Detail from Trajan's Column showing two soldiers; the one on the left is being aided by an orderly, whilst the man on the right is having a thigh wound bandaged by a *capsarius*. (Drawn by K.R. Dixon.)

by an orderly, and the other having a thigh wound bandaged by a *capsarius*.

Once the soldier had been brought to the hospital or medical tent, he was cared for by a *medicus* (Fig.51), who was a fully trained physician in overall command of all the medical staff (Davies 1970, 87). This is the most commonly attested medical post within the army, of which there were several grades. The *miles medicus* was the lowest ranking, the title *miles* implying that they were not officers (Davies 1969a, 87). The status of the *medicus ordinarius* is uncertain, although Davies believes that he would hold the rank of a centurion (1969a, 88–91).

Medical knowledge regarding the treatment of war wounds was clearly of a high standard, as is demonstrated by the medical work of Celsus. In one

51 [*Aesc*]VLAPIO / [*et*] SALVTI / [*pro salu*]TE ALAE VET/[*tonum*] C[*ivium*] R[*omanorum*] M[*arcus*] AVRE/[*lius* . . .]OCOMAS ME/[*dicus votum*] S[*olvit*] L[*ibens*] M[*erito*]
'To Aesculapius and Salus for the welfare of the Cavalry Regiment of Vettonians, Roman citizens, Marcus Aurelius . . . ocomas, doctor, willingly and deservedly fulfilled his vow.'
Part of a dedication slab to Aesculapius, erected by the *medicus* of an *ala*. From Binchester, County Durham (*RIB* 1028). (Redrawn by K.R. Dixon.)

section, he gives instructions on how to remove missiles (*De Medicina* 7.4.D5–C2):

> Missiles too, which have entered the body and become fixed within, are often very troublesome to extract. And some of the difficulties arise from their shape, some owing to the positions to which they have penetrated. Whatever the missile may be, it is extracted, either by the wound of entry, or through the spot towards which it is pointing. In the former case, the missile has already made a way for its withdrawal; in the latter the way out is made with the scalpel; for the flesh is cut through upon its point. But if the missile is not deeply seated, and lies in superficial tissue, or if it is certain that it has not crossed the line of large blood vessels or sinews, there is nothing better than to pull it out by the way it entered. But if the distance it has to be withdrawn is greater than that which remains to be

forced through, or if it has crossed the line of blood vessels and sinews, it is more convenient to lay open the rest of its course and so draw it out. For it will be more easily got at and more safely pulled out.

He also discusses how to prevent the haemorrhaging and inflammation of wounds (*De Medicina* 5.26.21–4), and methods of amputation (*De Medicina* 7.33.1–2).

Numerous examples of medical instruments have been found, with over 100 being discovered in the hospital (*valetudinarium*) of the legionary fortress at Neuss, Germany (Waterman 1970). The collection includes several types of spatula, probes, tweezers, scalpels, needles and spoons, together with a medical chest containing glass bottles for ointments. Another sizeable group, which included a lancing fork, forceps, scissors and leg splints, was found in the hospital of the legionary fortress at Aquincum (Hungary) (Szilágyi 1956, 69, Taf. 1).

Pharmaceutical knowledge in the army was sound, but empirical. The remains of medicinal plants have been found on military sites, and the remains of five were found inside the hospital at Neuss (Davies 1969a, 91). The antiscorbutic qualities of the *radix britannica* (thought to be the broad-leaved dock), were commented on by the Elder Pliny (*Natural History* 25.20–1), a use confirmed by the find of a medicine box lid inscribed with the words '*ex radice britanica* [sic]' (extract of the root of broad-leaved dock) (Davies 1969a, 92). Medicinal herbs may have been grown in hospital courtyards, which were laid out like gardens (Liversidge 1968, 329).

Temporary camps were equipped with a medical tent, which, according to Hyginus (*De Metatione Castrorum* 4), were positioned so that they would provide peace and quiet for those convalescing. Medical tents are mentioned in literature, and Dio (68.14.2) notes their presence during the Second Dacian War in AD 105: 'It was here that a cavalryman, who had been badly wounded, was carried from the battle, in the hope that he could be healed. When he discovered that he was incurable, he dashed from the tent (the shock had not yet affected him) and took his place again in the line, and died, after displaying great feats.'

There is little positive evidence for the existence of hospitals within auxiliary forts, although an inscription from Stojnik, Yugoslavia (*ILS* 9174 = *CIL* III 14537) attests a *valetudinarium*, presumably within the fort (*pers. comm.* J.C. Mann). Buildings which have been identified as hospitals appear to come in two basic plans: corridor and courtyard. An example of the former type was recognized at Corbridge, England (Fig.52), although doubt has now been cast on this interpretation since some believe the plan is more reminiscent of a workshop (*fabrica*) (Johnson 1983, 163–4). A hospital

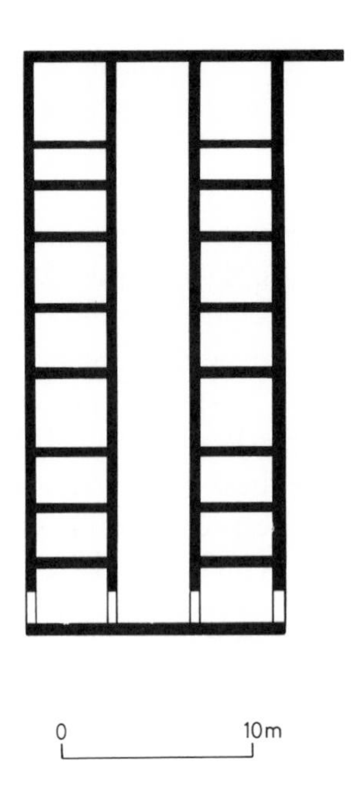

52 Plan of the supposed hospital of the corridor-type at Corbridge, Northumberland. Most now believe this building to be a workshop (*fabrica*) rather than a hospital. (Redrawn by J.R.A. Underwood from Johnson 1983.)

of the courtyard-type has been identified at Housesteads (Figs.53 and 54) (Charlesworth 1976). This example resembles a scaled-down and simplified version of a legionary hospital, of which several ground plans are known (Fig.55). It consists of four ranges of rooms or 'wards' surrounding the courtyard, a large room which has been interpreted as an operating theatre, a latrine and possibly a plunge bath.

The available evidence would, therefore, suggest that some auxiliary forts were provided with hospitals. If not, men whose condition was too serious or too specialized to be dealt with effectively by the medical staff present at the fort could be transferred to the nearest auxiliary or legionary hospital. As stated above, legionary *valetudinaria* were larger than their auxiliary counterparts, and may also have been better equipped to deal with certain complaints. The hospital at Inchtuthil (see Fig.55) is believed to have contained rooms which served as kitchens, baths, surgeries, mortuaries or accommodation for the doctors, although there is no associated evidence to be able to assign any of these functions definitely (Pitts and St Joseph 1985, 95).

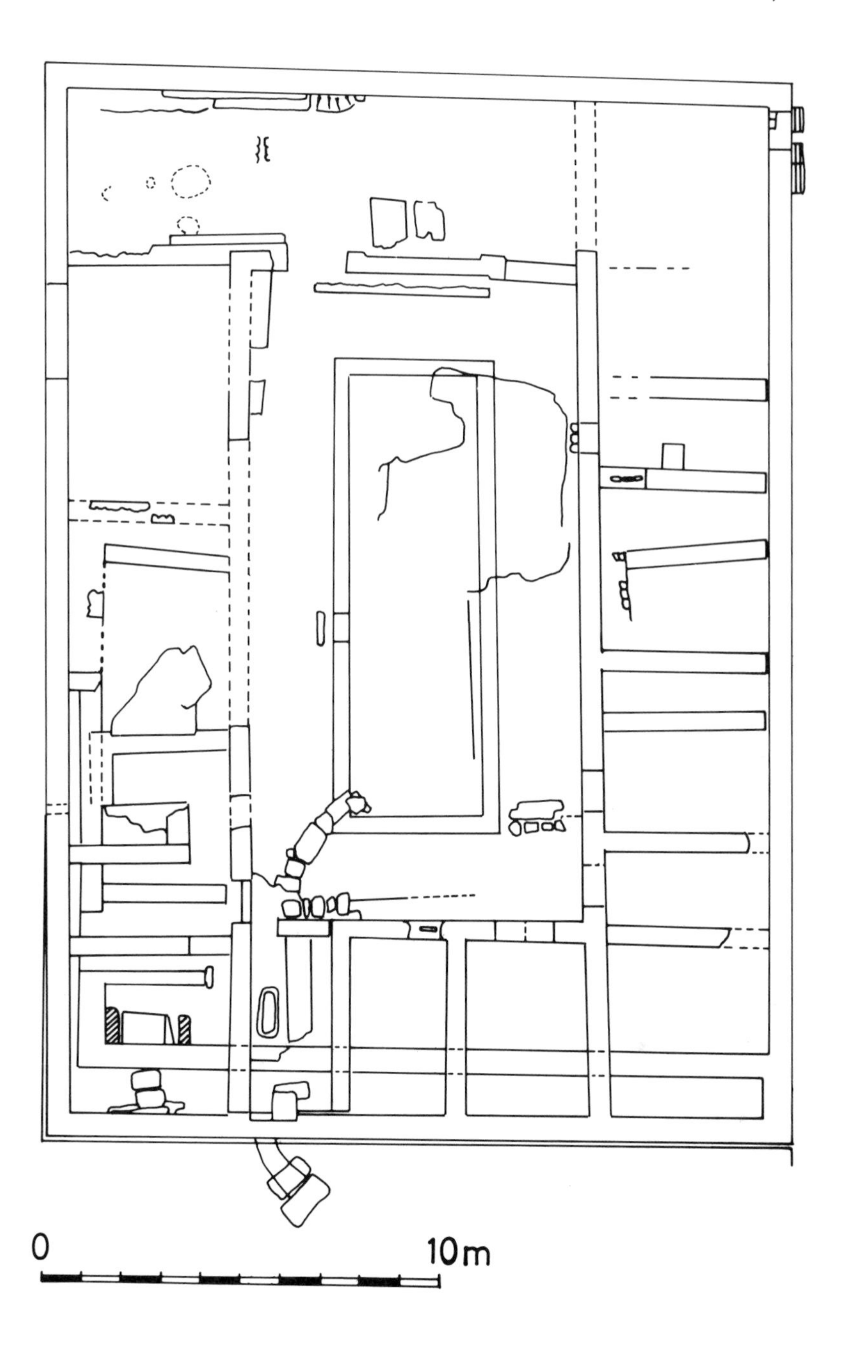

53 Plan of the building identified as a hospital at Housesteads, Hadrian's Wall. It is of the courtyard style. (Redrawn by K.R. Dixon from Charlesworth 1976.)

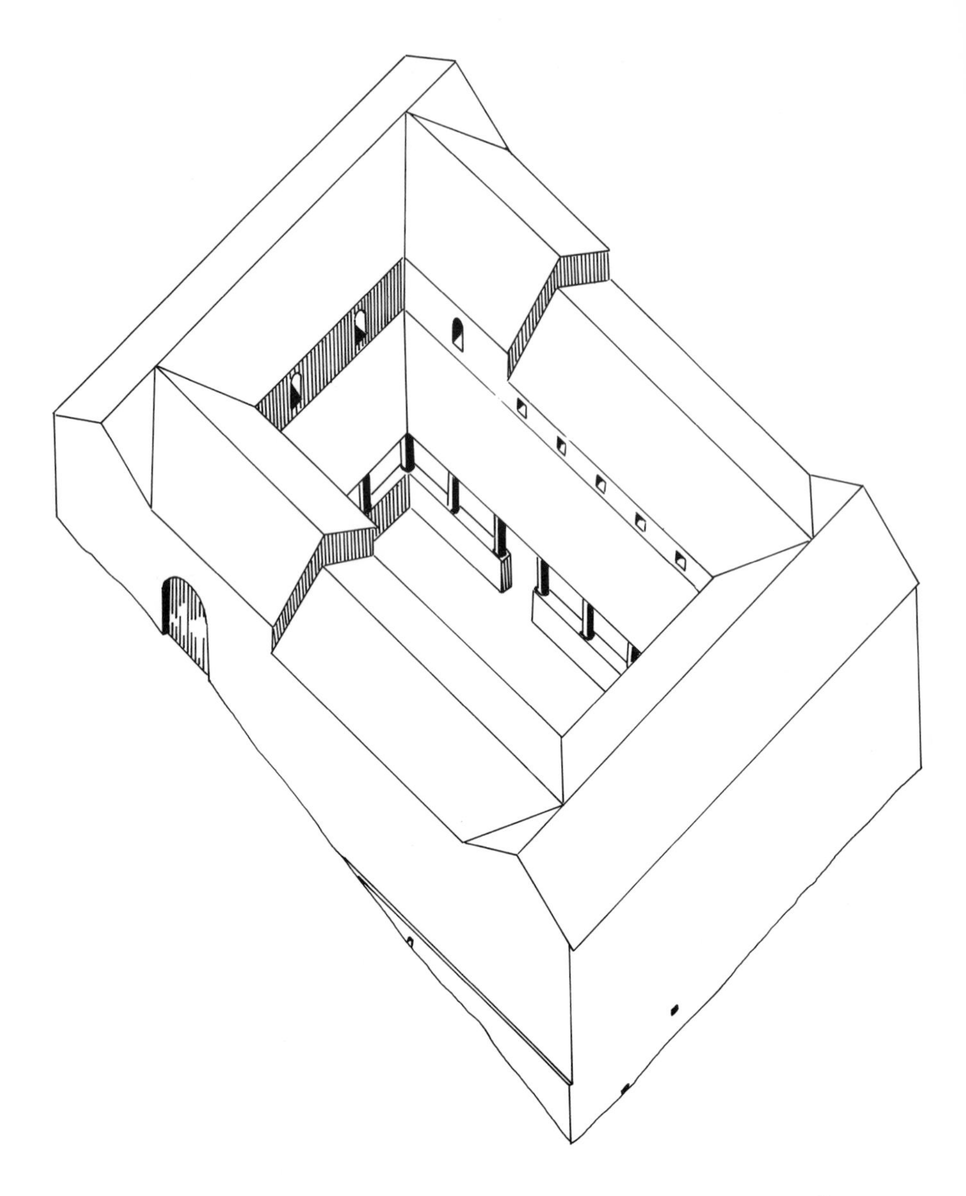

54 Reconstruction of the 'hospital' excavated at Housesteads, Hadrian's Wall (see Fig.53). (Redrawn by K.R. Dixon from Charlesworth 1976.)

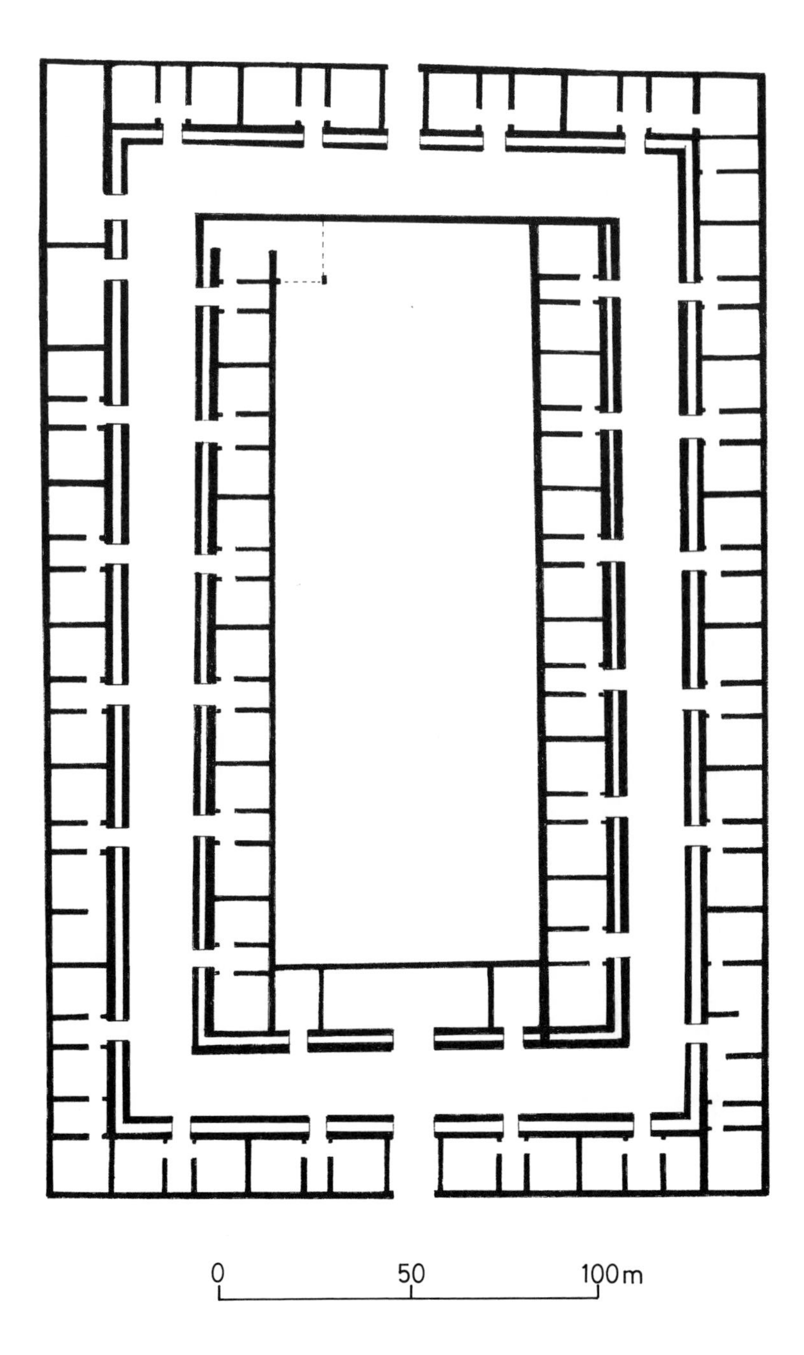

55 Plan of the hospital at the legionary fortress of Inchtuthil, Scotland. Note that the building identified as a hospital at Housesteads (Figs.53 and 54), resembles a scaled-down version of this example, which is also of the courtyard style. (Redrawn by K.R. Dixon from Pitts and St Joseph 1985).

There is both literary and archaeological evidence for sick soldiers receiving a special diet. Celsus (*De Medicina* 2.18–24) places all food into three categories, of which the first is the most nourishing, the second is an intermediate group, and the third is the most digestible. The foods listed in the last category were believed to be particularly suitable for invalids (Celsus *De Medicina* 2.18.4; 20.1–2; 24.1–3). The remains of these foodstuffs, which include shellfish, eggs, peas and lentils, have been found at a number of sites, the best example being Neuss, where the remains of all of these items were discovered in one of the rooms in the *valetudinarium* (Davies 1969a, 99).

Men who had suffered a serious illness would obviously have needed time to recover, and a document from Egypt, probably of Claudian date, records that several men from *Legio XXII Deiotariana* were sent to the coast to convalesce (*PSI* 1307 col.2,2).

The Roman army medical service was highly efficient and professional. Such a high standard was necessary for mercenary, if not humanitarian reasons; troops represented a considerable investment of time and money, and every possible precaution was taken in order to safeguard such a precious resource.

Death and burial

> Think of all those years lost by mothers and of the anxiety imposed on them while their sons are in the army. (Seneca, *Letter of Condolence to Marcia* 24).

Death whilst in service from combat, disease or natural causes, was an inescapable possibility, and the army therefore guaranteed every recruit, regardless of rank, a decent burial. Burial clubs are attested for the legions, and Vegetius states that a compulsory deduction was made from a soldier's pay (*Epitoma Rei Militaris* 2.20): 'There was, in addition, an eleventh bag in which the entire legion made a small contribution for a burial fund, so that if any of the soldiers died, the expenses for his burial were taken from this eleventh bag; this fund was kept in a basket in the custody of the standard bearers . . .'

Documentary evidence for burial clubs comes from pay-roll accounts, such as that of Proculus serving in Damascus (Fink 1971, no.68), who made an annual contribution of four *drachmae* to the fund (*ad signa*). The grant allocated on death was probably fixed at a standard rate, rather than being a direct reflection of the accumulated payments of the individual (Anderson 1984, 12–13). Such a provision would have been necessary in order to ensure that soldiers who had only recently joined the army and had met with an untimely death, would not have been penalized for their lack of opportunity to save enough money for their burial. Unfortunately, there is no evidence for the existence of burial clubs within the *auxilia*, although it is assumed that such an amenity would have been provided for this section of the army, and would not have been restricted to the legions.

Soldiers killed in battle were generally collectively cremated or buried under mounds near the scene of the conflict. If, however, a soldier died whilst in garrison, he would most likely be buried outside the fort in which he was stationed, since Roman law strictly forbade the burial of the dead within an inhabited area, be it a fort or a town (Anderson 1984, 11).

The Petty Knowes cemetery, situated outside the fort of High Rochester, England, has produced some interesting evidence (Charlton and Mitcheson 1984). Although no tombstones have been found in the vicinity of the burials, several examples have come from the surrounding area. These record a fort commander (*RIB* 1288), a common soldier (*RIB* 1292), a woman (*RIB* 1293), a freedman (*RIB* 1290) and the foster child of a tribune (*RIB* 1291). Thus, the cemetery does not appear to have been restricted to military personnel, allowing those connected with the garrison to use it also (Charlton and Mitcheson 1984, 19). A similar situation was found at Auchendavy on the Antonine Wall, where civilians are recorded on two tombstones from an otherwise military cemetery (Salway 1965, 159).

Most of the burials from the Petty Knowes cemetery consisted of small round mounds. One, however, retained two courses of stonework (Pl.16) (Bruce 1867, 330; Charlton and Mitcheson 1984, Pl.Ia), and may have been the final resting place of a unit commander. It was also noted that few possessions had been deposited in the graves, implying either that one or all of the garrisons had been too impoverished for personal possessions to have been left to the dead, or that it was '. . . the custom of the army to husband its resources for the use of the living' (Charlton and Mitcheson 1984, 18). It is possible that the soldiers at High Rochester made provision in their will for their equipment to be sold, rather than bequeathing it to a relative or comrade, or having it buried with them (Charlton and Mitcheson 1984, 18; Breeze 1976, 93–5).

From the reign of Augustus, all soldiers serving in the army had the right to leave a will (Anderson 1984, 13). The following example was written in AD 142 at Alexandria, Egypt (*Etud. Pap.* VI (1940), 1–20=*FIRA*, vol.III, no.47):

> Antonius Silvanus, cavalryman of the First Mauretanian Cohort of Thracians, prefect's orderly, of the troop of Valerius, made this last will and testament.
>
> My son, Marcus Antonius Satrianus [?], shall be the sole heir of all my military and household possessions, and all other persons are hereby disinherited. He shall formally enter upon the inheritance within the first hundred days; if he does not so enter, he shall be

disinherited. Then in second place my brother . . . Antonius R . . . shall be my heir, and he shall formally enter upon the inheritance within the next sixty days; if he does not become my heir, I give and bequeath to him 750 silver *denarii.*

I name Hierax son of Behex, *duplicarius*, of the same cohort, of the troop of Aebutius, trustee of my military estate to collect and deliver my property to Antonia Thermutha, mother of my heir above-named, so that she may conserve it until my son and heir has come of age and can receive it from her. To Hierex I give and bequeath 50 silver *denarii.* To Antonia Thermutha, mother of my heir above-named, I give and bequeath 500 silver *denarii.* To my prefect I give and bequeath 50 silver *denarii.* As for my slave Cronio, after my death, if he has performed all his duties properly and has turned over everything to my heir above-named or to my trustee, then I desire him to be free, and I desire the five-per cent manumission tax to be paid for him out of my estate.

Let no malice aforethought attend this last will and testament! For the purpose of making this will, Nemonius, *duplicarius*, of the troop of Marius, purchased the household and chattels; Marcus Julius Tiberinus, *sesquiplicarius*, of the troop of Valerius, acted as scales-holder; and Turbinius, standard-bearer of the troop of Proculus, acted as witness.

Last will and testament made at Alexandria on the coast of Egypt, in the imperial winter camp of Legion II Trajana Fortis and the Mauretanian Cohort, 27 March in the consulship of Rufinus and Quadratus.

I, the aforesaid Antonius Silvanus, verified the foregoing last will and testament of mine, and it was read aloud and I am satisfied with it as it stands.

[Witnesses:]
I, Nemonius . . . , *duplicarius*, of the troop of Marius, have affixed my seal.
[Seal of] Julius Tiberinus, *sesquiplicarius*, of the troop of Valerius.
[Seal of] Turbinius, cavalryman and standard-bearer of the troop of Proculus.
[Seal of] Valerius . . . Rufus, cavalryman and standard-bearer of the troop of . . .
I, Maximus, *duplicarius* . . . have affixed my seal.
[One signature illegible]
I, Antonius Sianus, have affixed my seal.

The phrase *ex testamento* inscribed on a tombstone records that it was erected by the heir or heirs of the deceased, according to the terms of the will, such as can be seen on an example from Mainz, belonging to Romanius, a 40-year-old cavalryman (see Pl.3). The army, like the civilian population, placed great importance on the remembrance of the dead by the living; and because the heir of the deceased gained in status by the deeds of his benefactor, tombstones were sometimes on a lavish scale.

Tombstones erected by the military give a biased view of burial within the army, since most of the surviving examples belong either to legionary and auxiliary officers, or to cavalrymen. Rank and wealth, therefore, are to a great extent reflected in funerary expenditure. It is true, however, that the elaboration and size of the tombstone and funeral, were ultimately the choice of the individual, who even if on a low pay scale, may have conscientiously saved money during his term of service, independently of the army burial club, placing more importance on death than his peers and superiors.

Marriage

Marriage is good for nothing in the military profession. (Napoleon, in Dewar 1990, 105).

The law banning soldiers up to the rank of centurion from forming legal marriages during their term of service is believed to have been imposed by Augustus (Campbell 1978, 154; Watson 1981, 133–4). This restriction was probably enforced to prevent the men's loyalty being split between the army and their families, particularly when there was a possibility that they would be posted away from their homeland. Uncertainty remains about the position of men who were legally married on entry into the army. It has been suggested that in such cases the marriage remained legal during service, and that any children born in this period were legitimate (Garnsey 1970, 47). Campbell, however, favours the view that such marriages were dissolved for the duration of the soldier's service, and that children produced within this time were bastards (1978, 155). He bases his belief on a group of second-century papyri from Egypt which contain the judgements of Roman officials on the marriage ban (Mitteis and Wilcken 1912). One of the officials, Rutilius Lupus, told a man who was legally married before he enlisted into the army, and whose wife had given birth to a son during his term of service, that 'he could not, while serving as a soldier, have a legitimate son' (Mitteis and Wilcken 1912, II.2, no.372, col.4). This ban was obviously unpopular with the men as it debarred children born during military service from inheriting their father's property since only legitimate offspring were entitled to this privilege.

The situation changed under Claudius, who, according to Dio (76.15.2), gave the rights of married men to soldiers (*conubium*), allowing any unofficial union during service to be made legal on their discharge from the army, and the children to become legitimate. The exact meaning of Dio's statement has been disputed, but it is believed that it was probably not referring to grants made by diploma to auxiliaries, but rather legionaries (*pers. comm.* J.C. Mann). What Claudius does appear to have done for the *auxilia*, however, is to stop the grant of citizenship ceasing with the death of the soldier, thus allowing it to continue with the children (*pers. comm.* J.C. Mann). Birth certificates of children born during service have been found. These were drawn up by soldiers to prove that their child had been born during service, and would therefore be entitled to citizenship on their father's discharge. The following example, dating to AD 127, comes from Egypt (*AE* 1937, no.112):

Marcus Lucretius Clemens, cavalryman in the troop of Silvanus in the First Cohort of Thracians, called the undersigned to witness and swore by Jupiter Best and Greatest and by the divinity of the deified Emperors and by the *genius* of the Emperor Caesar Trajanus Hadrian Augustus that while in military service he had become the father, by Octavia Tamustha, of a natural son, named Serenus, on 25 April in the year 11 of the Emperor Caesar Trajanus Hadrian Augustus; and he stated that he made this attestation on account of the restriction imposed by military service, so as to be able to have proof at his certification of [citizen] status after his honourable discharge that he [Serenus] is his natural son.

Done in the winter camp of the First Cohort of Thracians opposite Apollinopolis Magna in the Thebaid, on 1 May in the year above-stated.

[Witnesses]
Gaius Antonius Maximus, keeper of arms in the troop [?] of Lucius Farsuleius; Marius Antoninus, of the squadron of Rufus; Gaius Barga, soldier in the troop [?] of Lucius Farsuleius; Gaius Julius Marcellus, adjutant in . . . ; Titus Marsias Bammogalis[?] . . . ; Numerius Alexa son of Longus; Marcus Lucretius Clemens . . .

Discharge and retirement

Roman citizenship appears to have been awarded before the time of Tiberius, although under this particular Emperor it may have begun to be given after a fixed term of 25 years service. The system became fully developed during the reign of Claudius when the right of *conubium* was given in conjunction with the granting of citizenship (Mann and Roxan 1988, 344). The regularization of this grant resulted in the issuing of diplomas (a modern term), which consisted of a pair of bronze tablets, tied together with wire. These were distributed directly by the emperor and were inscribed on the front with a list of units stationed in the same province who also had men in their ranks who had served for 25 years, the recipient's name and that of the commanding officer, together with the date. A list of witnesses was engraved on the back. To prevent forgery, the text was duplicated on the inside of the plates, before it was tied and sealed, so that if there was any doubt of its authenticity, an official could check to see if the seal had been broken, and then inspect the details inscribed within. It is believed that these bronze diplomas were not automatically given to the soldiers, but were bought, if desired, by the men themselves (Mann and Roxan 1988, 342). They may only have been considered necessary by those soldiers who might need proof of their status and were moving away from their fort.

It is often assumed that diplomas were certificates of discharge (Webster 1985, 143), when in actuality they appear to have been issued to soldiers simply as verification of having served 25 years (Mann and Roxan 1988, 343). These were not certificates of honourable discharge (*honesta missio*), since they did not actually '. . . define the recipient as a veteran' (Mann and

Roxan 1988, 343). Additional certificates specifically recording discharge are known, and one wooden example from Egypt, belonging to a cavalryman, reads as follows (Mann and Roxan 1988, 341; *AE* 1906, 22 = *ILS* 9060 = *CIL* XVI, Appendix I):

> In the consulship of Manius Aviola and Pansa [AD 122], on the day before the nones of January [4 January], T. Haterius Nepos, the Prefect of Egypt, gave an honourable discharge to L. Valerius Noster, time-expired cavalryman of the *ala Vocontiorum*, from the troop formerly commanded by Gavius. [signature of prefect] I read that which is written above and gave an honourable discharge on 4 January.

Such documents were not standard issue to soldiers and would be acquired by men who needed proof of their status so that they could claim the privileges awarded to veterans. It is known, for example, that in Egypt an examination called the *epicrisis*, which was conducted by officials selected by the prefect, had to be endured by a veteran if he wished to settle in Egypt (Mann and Roxan 1988, 342). Soldiers may, therefore, have felt it prudent to have as much documentary evidence as possible to ensure a successful result. No similar examination is known outside of Egypt.

Honourable discharge could be granted to a soldier before he had completed his 25 years if he had been seriously wounded, or was considered too weak or ill to complete his term of service. This type of discharge (*causaria missio*) still allowed the man to gain the rewards he would have received had he completed his 25 years (Davies 1969c, 100). The privileges available on honourable discharge to an auxiliary did not include a grant of land or money, as it did for a legionary. They did, however, gain immunity from taxation and the opportunity to hold a municipal office, and of course, Roman citizenship.

Awards granted to non-citizen troops did change over time. In AD 140 children born during military service were no longer entitled to receive Roman citizenship, the grant being now limited only to those children conceived after discharge (Breeze and Dobson 1987, 194). It has been suggested that the reason behind this rule may have been to force sons born during their father's service to become soldiers themselves, it being the only way that they could become citizens (Breeze and Dobson 1987, 194). The situation changed again under Severus, who, according to Herodian (3.8.4–5):

> . . . gave a very large sum of money and many other privileges that they [the soldiers] had not had before; for he was the first to increase their pay and he also gave them permission to wear gold rings and to live in wedlock with their wives [?]. All these things are normally considered alien to military discipline and an efficient readiness for war. And Severus was certainly the first to undermine their tough and severe way of life, and their obedience in carrying out their tasks, and their discipline and respect for their officers, by teaching the troops to love money, and by introducing them to a life of ease.

This statement, together with documentary legal evidence (see Campbell 1978, 159–66) has been interpreted as implying that Severus lifted the ban on marriage during military service (Birley 1969, 63; Watson 1981, 137; Garnsey 1970). Such a move would have been very popular with the soldiers, and equates well with the advice Severus gave to his sons (Herodian 3.8.4): 'Live in harmony, enrich the troops and scorn everyone else.'

In AD 212 Caracalla, Severus' son, introduced the *Constitutio Antoniniana*, a law which granted Roman citizenship to all free people within the Roman Empire. Once this law was brought into being, the myriad of legal complications surrounding marriage were virtually eliminated, since it was more likely that both partners would be citizens.

1 A section of *P. Dur.* 100 showing the columns xxx to xxxii. This roster of *Cohors XX Palmyrenorum* consists of the remains of 44 columns, all written in the same handwriting except for a few amendments and annotations. Six centuries, five *turmae* and the *dromedarii* attached to the various centuries are listed in this document, dating from AD 219. (Photograph from Welles *et al.* 1959.)

2 Iron helmet of the second century from Heddernheim, Germany. Note the crossed reinforcing bars and the peak on the skull-piece, together with the large cheek-pieces which leave only the eyes, nose and mouth visible. (Courtesy of the Museum für Vor-und Frühgeschichte, Frankfurt, Germany.)

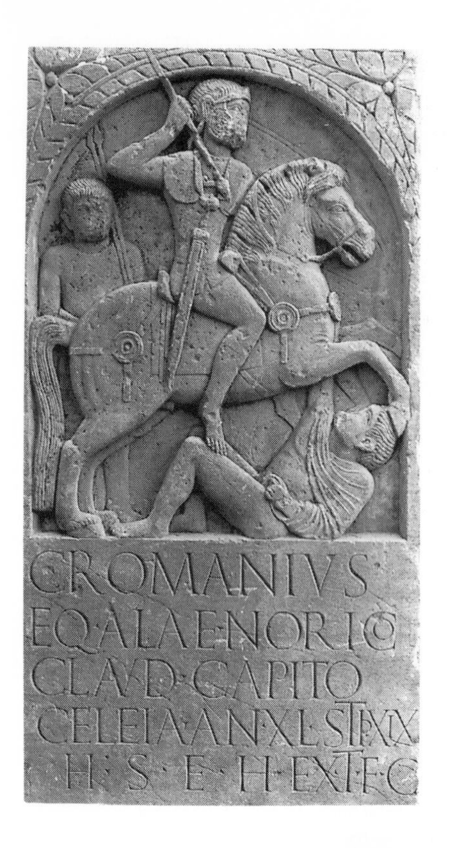

3 C[*aius*] *ROMANIVS* / *EQ*[*ues*] *ALAE NORICO*[*rum*] / *CLAVD*[*ia tribu*] *CAPITO* / *CELEIA AN*[*norum*] *XL STIP*[*endiorum*] *XIX* / *H*[*ic*] *S*[*itus*] *E*[*st*] *H*[*eres*] *EX* / *T*[*estamento*] *F*[*aciendum*] C[*uravit*]
'Gaius Romanius Capito, trooper of the *Ala Noricum,* from Celeia, Roman citizen of Tribus Claudia, 40 years old, of 19 years' service. Here lies buried. His heir had this erected according to the terms of his will.'

This tombstone, dating to the first century AD, provides evidence for the angle of the saddle horns, with the back pair hugging the rider's bottom, and those at the front protruding over the thighs. It is also notable for depicting the shoulder reinforcement hook-fastening on the mail shirt, resembling the example from Chessenard, France. (Courtesy of the Landesmuseum Mainz, Germany.)

4 A rather crudely carved tombstone from Chester depicting the longer style of mail shirt (*lorica squamata*), apparently worn by the cavalry from the third century onwards. (Courtesy of the Grosvenor Museum, Chester.)

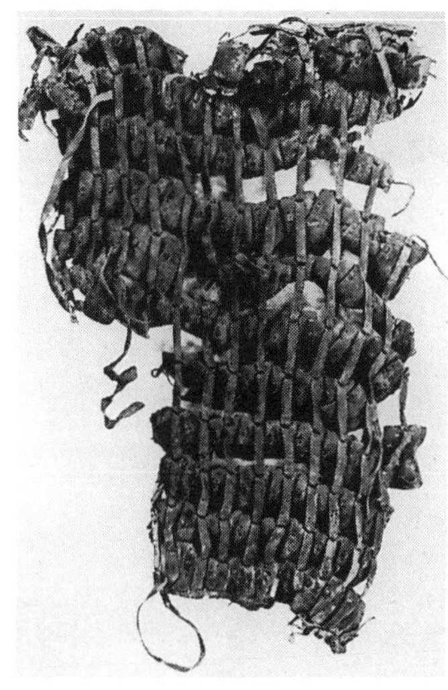

5 Lamellar thigh guards (*cuisses*) from Dura-Europos, Syria. Both guards are made from rawhide; one has been lacquered red and the other black. The lamellae have been laced together on the inner face in horizontal rows with hide, and joined vertically on the outer face with red leather laces. They would only have covered the outside of the rider's thighs. (Rostovtzeff *et al.* 1936.)

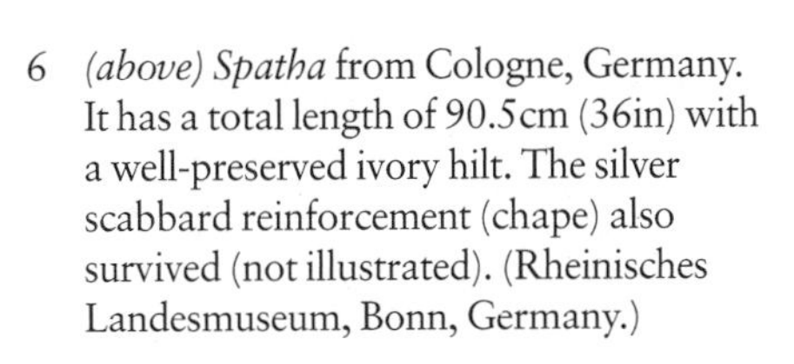

6 *(above) Spatha* from Cologne, Germany. It has a total length of 90.5cm (36in) with a well-preserved ivory hilt. The silver scabbard reinforcement (chape) also survived (not illustrated). (Rheinisches Landesmuseum, Bonn, Germany.)

7 The tail portions of at least two reed or cane arrows from Dura-Europos, Syria. The feathers (fletching) survive. Both of the feathered shafts were painted with black and red markings, thought to identify either their owner or a matching set. (Photograph from Rostovtzeff *et al.* 1936.)

8 Roman horn, possibly a *lituus* from Saalburg, Germany. It is thought that this type of horn may have been specifically employed by the cavalry (Dobson 1981, 237. Photograph courtesy of the Saalburgmuseum, Bad Homburg, Germany.)

9 *DIS MANIBVS FLAVINVS / EQ*[*ues*] *ALAE PETR*[*ianae*] *SIGNIFER / TVR*[*ma*] *CANDIDI AN*[*norum*] *XXV / STIP*[*endiorum*] *VII H*[*ic*] *S*[*itus Est*]
'To the spirits of the departed, Flavinus, trooper of *Ala Petriana*, standard-bearer, from the troop of Candidus, 25 years of age, of seven years' service. Here lies buried.'

Although this first-century AD tombstone is very worn, it is possible to gain some interesting information from it. Flavinus wears a helmet which is adorned with large upright feathers. Robinson suggested (1976, 3) that his helmet was possibly one of the highly-decorative masked examples which were worn during the *hippika gymnasia* (cavalry displays). In his right hand he carries a *signum* which appears to depict a head with rays radiating from it, possibly representing a deity sacred to the unit (Robinson 1976, 6). Other distinguishable features include a sword (*spatha*), oval shield, horse harness and trappings, and a fringed saddle cloth. (Photograph by J.R.A. Underwood courtesy of Hexham Abbey, Northumberland.)

10 Third-century AD dragon head from a standard found near the fort of Niederbieber, Germany. The head is hollow and open-mouthed, and is made of silvered bronze with the features picked out in gilt. Originally a pole would have been pushed through the hole in the lower jaw, and a long tube of material would have been attached to the collar of the head. When held on horseback, the air would have passed through the mouth, causing the material trail to stream out, giving the appearance of a living creature. (Photograph courtesy of Koblenz Museum, Germany.)

11 Photograph taken soon after the discovery of the scale bardings at Dura-Europos, Syria. It shows how the coat would have fitted on a horse's back. Note the hole where the saddle would have been. (From Rostovtzeff *et al.* 1936.)

12 A pair of first-century AD bronze eye-guards from Neuss, Germany. Although it was previously assumed that these loose eye-guards must have belonged to leather chamfrons, there is no direct evidence to substantiate this belief (Driel-Murray 1989, 291). (Courtesy of the Rheinisches Landesmuseum, Bonn, Germany.)

13 Silvered-bronze *phalera* from Doorwerth, the Netherlands. The decoration on this example is executed by a method called niello (*opus nigellum*), which involved incised designs being filled with a powder compound of silver sulphide. Once heated the compound hardens and the area can be polished, resulting in a smooth, shiny black finish, contrasting well with the silver background. The *phalera* is attached to the leather straps by a number of rings on the back (not illustrated). (Rijksmuseum van Oudheden, Leiden, the Netherlands. Photograph by J.R.A. Underwood.)

14 Silvered-bronze 'trifid' pendant and *phalera* with niello decoration from Doorwerth, the Netherlands. Note the two junction straps protruding from the top of the *phalera* for attachment to the leather straps of the harness. (Rijksmuseum van Oudheden. Leiden, Holland. Photograph by J.R.A. Underwood.)

15 Tombstone of Primigenius from Cologne, Germany. This tombstone is of a different style to those seen in previous figures and depicts the cavalryman walking behind the horse with the reins in his right hand. Primigenius' horse appears to be wearing its special sports equipment, worn during the *hippika gymnasia* (see Chapter 7). Note the trappings which adorn the harness, the triplet straps with their decorative plates close to the saddle, and the long fringed saddle-cloth with a shorter second cloth overlying it. (Courtesy of the Römisch-Germanisches Museum, Cologne.)

16 The most impressive burial monument in the Petty Knowes cemetery, situated outside the gates of the fort of High Rochester, England. Two courses of stonework remain and it is thought to have been the final resting place of a unit commander. (Courtesy of B. Charlton.)

17 Pair of bronze plates from Manching, Germany, which are believed to have been worn on the chest of a mail or scale shirt. Owing to their elaborate nature they may have been reserved for use during the *hippika gymnasia*. Note the two square-headed pins on the left plate. (Courtesy of the Prähistorische Staatssammlung, Munich.)

19 Pair of greaves reconstructed by H.R. Robinson. They are based on examples from the third-century AD Straubing find of sports equipment. (Photograph by J.R.A. Underwood, courtesy of the Museum of Antiquities, Newcastle upon Tyne.)

18 Bronze greave from Straubing. It is decorated with a relief of Mars wearing a Corinthian helmet, muscled cuirass, greaves and sword, and carrying a shield and spear. (Courtesy of Gäuboden-Museum, Straubing, Germany.)

20 Bronze sports helmet from Dobrosloveni, Romania, in the form of a woman's head, identified as such by the hair-style, diadem and the accessories worn in the hair (jewels, pendants etc.). (Courtesy of the Kunsthistorisches Museum, Antikensammlung, Vienna.)

21 Front view of an exceptionally fine silver-plated iron sports helmet from Emesa, Syria. Note the hinge placed centrally on the brow band and the oriental appearance of the face. (Courtesy of the National Museum, Damascus, Syria.)

22 Back view of the silver-plated iron sports helmet from Emesa, Syria (see P1.21). Note the exquisite scroll decoration running along the neck band. (Courtesy of the National Museum, Damascus, Syria.)

23 Bronze sports helmet of the first century AD from Ribchester, Lancashire. This helmet type is distinguished by the prominent peak which projects from a highly-decorated skull-piece. The skull-piece of this example depicts in high relief a battle between cavalrymen and infantrymen. Note the crest holder on the front of the skull-piece. (British Museum, London. Courtesy of the Trustees of the British Museum.)

24 Bronze sports helmet with silvered mask of the late second century AD from Pfrondorf, Germany. This style of helmet is distinguished by the hinged central area of the mask which covers the eyes, nose and mouth only. This particular example is in the form of a Medusa head, with the face being framed by hair intertwined with snakes. An eagle is perched on the brow. (Courtesy of the Landesmuseum, Stuttgart, Germany.)

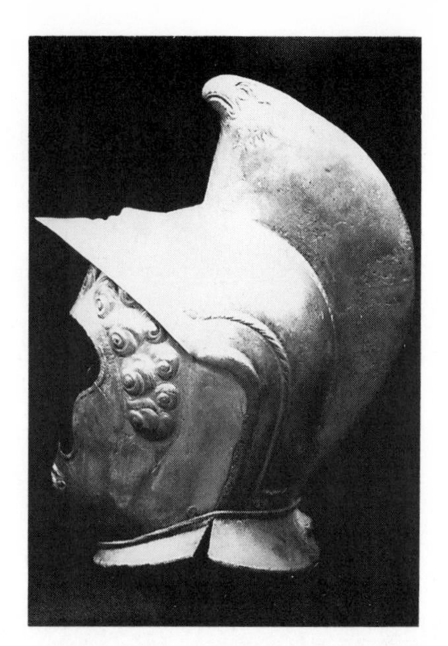

25 Reconstruction by H.R. Robinson of the late second to early third century AD bronze helmet from Heddernheim, Germany. The high crest on the skull-piece terminates in an eagle's head and the brow piece is engraved with a face. Note that only the central facial features would have been visible when worn. There is no evidence that this helmet was ever equipped with a small inner mask. Original in the Museum für Vor-und Frügeschichte, Frankfurt. (Photograph by J.R.A. Underwood, courtesy of the Museum of Antiquities, Newcastle upon Tyne.)

26 Iron face-mask from a sports helmet from Stuttgart-Bad Cannstatt, Germany. The group of helmets represented by this example was one of the most enduring forms, lasting from the first to the third centuries AD. They are characterized by depicting a youthful face with wavy hair on the skull-piece. (Courtesy of the Landesmuseum, Stuttgart, Germany.)

27 Bronze third-century sports helmet from Worthing, Norfolk. The crest on the skull-piece terminates in an eagle's head and the brow has an upturned peak. Sea-monsters are embossed on either side of the helmet. The remains of a broken hook on the brow indicate that originally a face-mask would have been attached (see Fig. 58). (Courtesy of the Castle Museum, Norwich.)

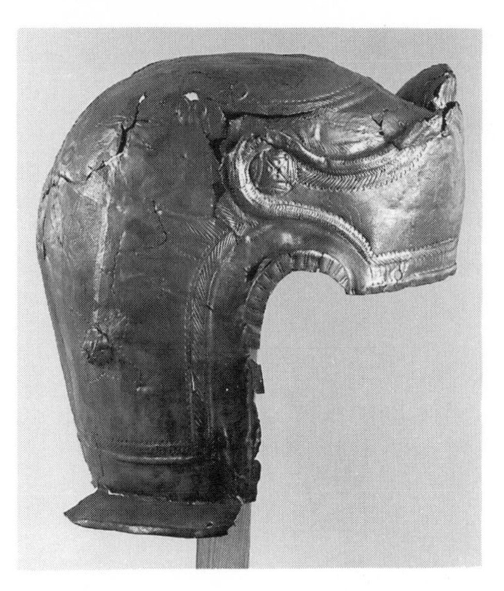

28 Bronze third-century sports helmet from Guisborough, Yorkshire. This group of helmets is distinguished by three rounded peaks on the brow band. The peaks on this example are bordered by snakes, whose heads meet at the centre of the brow. The central peak is engraved with Mars, whilst the outer two contain Victories. There are two bosses on the back of the helmet. One of the holes by which the right cheek-piece was attached can be seen just in front of the raised ear-guard. (Courtesy of the Trustees of the British Museum.)

29 Details of the tombstone of Genialis, from Cirencester, Gloucestershire. Note the peaked helmet which the rider wears and the elaborate trappings on the horse. It is believed that the equipment depicted on this tombstone may be that worn during the *hippika gymnasia*. (Photograph by K.R. Dixon, courtesy of Corinium Museum, Cirencester.)

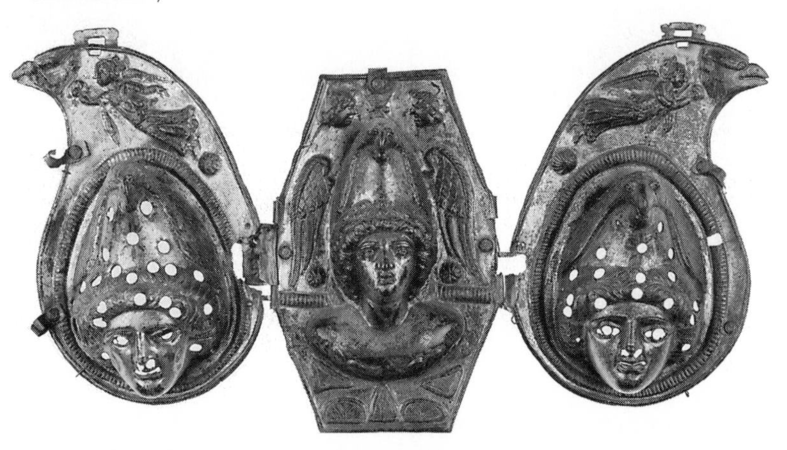

30 Bronze chamfron of the third century AD from Straubing, Germany. The central panel is adorned with a figure of Mars with a bust of Mars on the right panel and Minerva on the left. Note the elaborate eye-guards in the form of gorgons' heads. (Courtesy of Gäuboden-Museum, Straubing, Germany.)

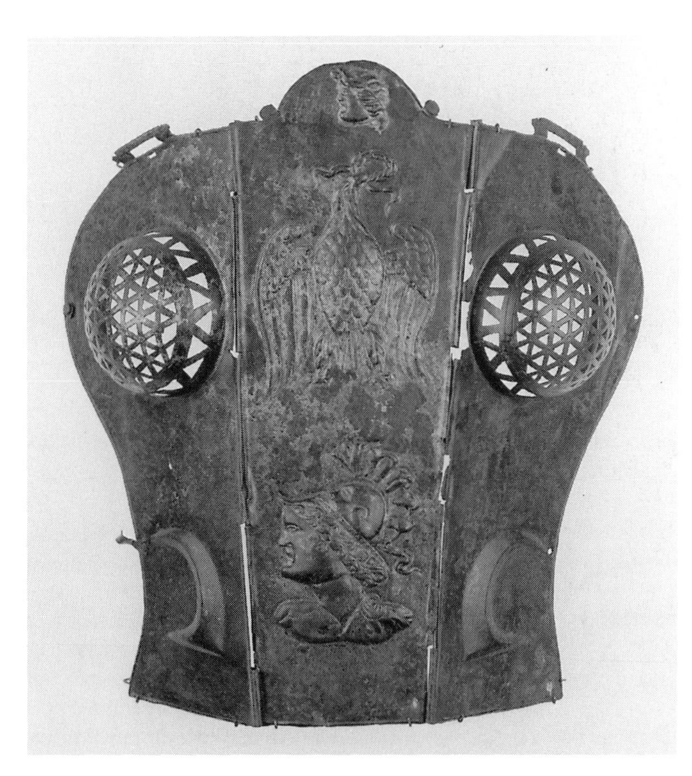

31 Bronze chamfron of the third century AD from Straubing, Germany. The central panel is adorned with an eagle and a bust of Mars. Each of the other two panels has a boar's tusk embossed on the lower portion. Note the openwork eye-guards. (Courtesy of the Gäuboden-Museum, Straubing, Germany.)

32 Bronze eye-guards with central plate, third century AD in date, from Straubing, Germany. The central panel is decorated with a figure of a Minerva, flanked by two snakes. The frames of the two openwork eye-pieces are decorated with a figure of Victory and a lion. (Courtesy of Gäuboden-Museum, Straubing, Germany.)

33 Two bronze openwork eye-guards, which appear to have been directly attached to the bridle. (Courtesy of the Mittelrheinisches Landesmuseum, Mainz, Germany.)

34 *(left)* Reconstruction of a medallion from Bonn by H.R. Robinson. It is uncertain whether these highly-decorated discs adorned the chests of horses during the *hippika gymnasia* or whether they were shield bosses for shields also used in these displays. This example contains a bust of Ceres and was silvered-bronze. (Photograph by J.R.A. Underwood, courtesy of the Museum of Antiquities, Newcastle upon Tyne.)

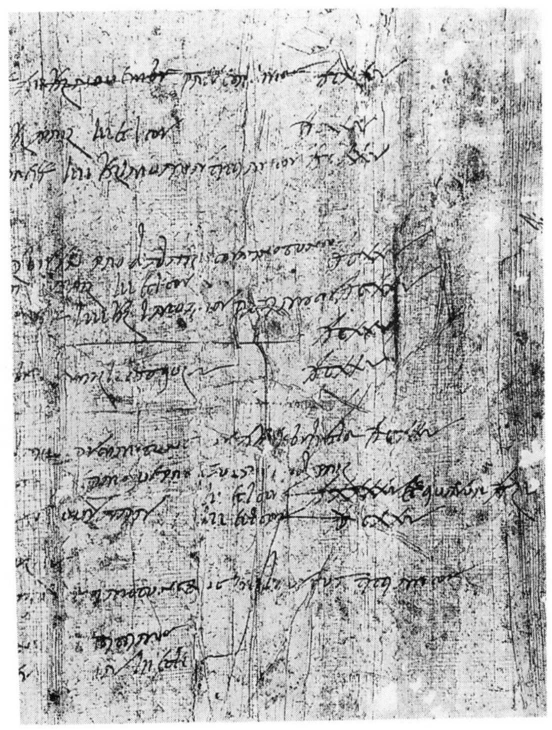

35 List of men and mounts of *Cohors XX Palmyrenorum* from Dura-Europos (*P.Dur.* 97, right-hand side). The names of soldiers are followed by descriptions of their horses, giving each animal's age, its colour and distinctive markings. If the soldier had lost his horse the entry by his name read '*amisit eq[uum]*'. The purpose of this list remains unknown; there are few parallels from elsewhere in the Roman Empire, so it cannot be proved that such lists of men and mounts were regularly drawn up for each army unit. This may have been a special case, compiled to outline the need for remounts within the cohort. (Photograph from Welles *et al.* 1959.)

6 Training

Training embraces two slightly different concepts, one arising from the other. Firstly, horses and riders must be taught all the basic skills, and following this the secondary implication of training is that of practice and exercise to maintain the skills once learned. A horse must first be trained to accept a rider on his back and to obey commands which are conveyed to him in a variety of ways. A new recruit must be trained to ride not just one horse but to perform all the required manoeuvres on any horse. In other words he must be trained in horsemanship. Thereafter, beyond the initial training, horses and soldiers must keep their skills up to standard by continual drill and exercises in the field, as Vegetius pointed out (*Epitoma Rei Militaris* 2.23): 'The very essence of an art consists in constant practice.' Quite apart from the training and subsequent practice, horses must be regularly exercised if they are to be kept in fit condition and ready for action (see p.218ff).

The men

> The courage of a soldier is heightened by his knowledge of his profession, and he only wants an opportunity to execute what he is convinced he has been perfectly taught. Vegetius (*Epitoma Rei Militaris* 1.1).

It is believed that a large percentage of men who joined the army became, initially at least, infantrymen (Gilliam 1965, 80). The situation may have differed with regard to the *alae*, into which some men were possibly directly enlisted (Gilliam 1965, 79–80). In either case, however, all recruits, before they could be enrolled on the books of a unit, had to undergo a minimum of four months' basic training (Vegetius, *Epitoma Rei Militaris* 2.5). According to Vegetius (*Epitoma Rei Militaris* 1.8), during this period the recruit is tested

> . . . by exercise, to discover if he really is fit for such work. Both the quickness and strength required in this are thus shown, and whether he can learn the training in weapons, and

whether he has a soldier's courage. For very many, although in outward appearance they seem suitable, are nevertheless proved by examination to be unsuited. Therefore the less suitable men must be rejected, and others of greater vigour must be selected in their place, as in every conflict it is not so much numbers as courage that is advantageous. Accordingly, instructions with weapons must be given in exercises each day to the recruits . . .

Vegetius (*Epitoma Rei Militaris* 1.4) lists the various exercises included in the basic training:

A recruit must have time to learn everything. For the art of weapons – whether you wish to train a cavalryman, foot-archer or infantryman – must not seem small or light, to teach them all the whole range of arms drill and movements, not to desert their posts, to keep their ranks, to throw their weapons with great force and accuracy, to dig ditches, to plant a palisade with skill, to handle their shield and deflect the oncoming weapons of the enemy by holding it at an angle, to avoid a blow with skill and deliver one with bravery.

Additional training was also given in swimming (Vegetius *Epitoma Rei Militaris* 1.10): 'During the summer months every recruit without exception must learn to swim . . . It is of the greatest advantage that not only the infantry but also the cavalry and even the horses and the soldiers' servants (who are called *galiarii*) should be exercised in swimming, in order that they might not be inexperienced in the case of any necessity.' There are several recorded instances of cavalrymen fording rivers on horseback, or dismounting and swimming alongside their mounts (Tacitus *Annals* 14.29; *Histories* 4.12; Herodian 7.2.6–7; 8.4.3; Ammianus Marcellinus 24.2.8.); and Tacitus, referring to Agricola crossing to Anglesey from Britain, remarks upon the skill of the British in such a situation (*Agricola* 18):

His plans had been hastily formed and so, as was natural, he had no ships on the spot; yet the resourcefulness and determination of the general bridged the straits. For after unloading all the baggage he picked a body of native auxiliaries who knew the fords, and had that facility in swimming which belongs to their nation, and by means of which they can control simultaneously their own movements, their weapons, and their horses . . .

Probably the best display of skill given in water, is that recorded on the epitaph of Soranus, an *eques* of a mixed unit (*CIL* III 3676 = *ILS* 2558):

I am the man who, once very well known to the banks in Pannonia, brave and foremost among one thousand Batavians, was able with Hadrian as my judge, to swim the wide waters of the deep Danube in full battle kit. From my bow I fired an arrow, and while it quivered still in the air and was falling back, with a second arrow I hit and broke it. No Roman or foreigner has ever managed to better this feat, no soldier with a javelin, no Parthian with a bow. Here I lie, here I have immortalized my deeds on an ever-mindful stone, which will see if anyone after me will rival my deeds. I set a precedent for myself in being the first to achieve such feats.

Basic infantry training was essential for cavalrymen since they were sometimes required to dismount because of the nature of the terrain (Frontinus *Stratagems* 2.3.23; Tacitus *Agricola* 37), or the unsuitability of the situation to the employment of cavalry, such as the instance recorded by Procopius (*History of the Wars* 1.18.43–9): 'There he himself [Belisarius] gave up his horse and commanded all his men to do the same thing and on foot with the others to fight off the oncoming enemy . . . Then the Romans turned their backs to the river so that no movement to surround them might be executed by the enemy [the Persians], and as best they could under the circumstances were defending themselves against their assailants.' There was also the obvious danger of a cavalryman having his horse killed or injured during battle, or the soldier himself receiving a wound which necessitated him fighting on foot. It can reasonably be assumed that dismounted cavalry would have been at a disadvantage against trained infantrymen, not only because of their lack of relevant experience, but also due to the unsuitability of their equipment, which was not generally geared towards close quarter fighting. This opinion is expressed by Caesar, who cites with some surprise an example of dismounted cavalry actually beating infantry, implying that such victories were indeed rare occurrences (*Spanish War* 15):

> With nearly all armies what normally happens in a cavalry battle is this: when a cavalryman is once dismounted and closes in with an infantryman to engage him, he is not by any means regarded as a match for the latter. However, it turned out quite otherwise in this battle. When picked light-armed infantry took our cavalry by surprise by coming forward to engage them, and when this manoeuvre was observed in the course of the fighting, quite a number of our horsemen dismounted. As a result, in a short time our cavalry began to fight an infantry action, to such good purpose that they dealt death right up close to the rampart.

Whether or not cavalrymen continued to receive infantry drill once they had completed the compulsory minimum of four months' basic training is uncertain. There does, however, appear to be no sound reason why the Roman army would not have considered such instruction a prudent measure, since it could only have improved the rider's chance of survival in battle, and made him a more adaptable soldier.

Basic training over, the cavalry recruit would then be instructed in the rudiments of riding, or if he already possessed some experience, he would probably proceed directly to tuition on the use of weapons on horseback, and the field manoeuvres used within the army.

The men were trained by various specialist instructors called *exercitatores* and a *magister campi*. Herodian (6.8.1–2) states that Maximinus, who had begun his career as a cavalryman, was made an instructor because of his military experience, and was put '. . . in charge of all the recruits to give them military training and turn them out fit for battle.'

The horses given to 'green' recruits would possibly have been previously trained in the fundamental skills by rough-riders. Such a system would seem only sensible, allowing the novice rider to become accustomed to being in the saddle, without the pressure of dealing with an untrained mount, which, according to one modern British cavalry officer, was the most frightening ordeal he had endured (from the BBC documentary series *In the Highest Tradition* by Ian Woolridge).

The first step in the programme of basic instruction would be how to sit on the horse. Xenophon (*Art of Horsemanship* 7.5–7) states that the rider should be seated

> . . . as though he were standing upright with his legs astride. For thus he will get a better grip of his horse with his thighs, and the erect position will enable him, if need be, to throw his spear and deliver a blow on horseback with more force.
>
> The lower leg including the foot must hang lax and easy from the knee down. For if he keeps his leg stiff and should strike it against anything, he may break it, whereas a loose leg will recoil, whatever it encounters, without disturbing the position of the thigh at all. The rider must also accustom himself to keeping his body above the hips as loose as possible, for thus he will be able to stand more fatigue and will be less liable to come off when he is pulled or pushed.

The recruit was also instructed in the correct ways to mount and dismount (Vegetius, *Epitoma Rei Militaris* 1.18):

> The ancients strictly obliged both the veteran soldiers and recruits to a constant practice of vaulting . . . They had wooden horses for that purpose placed in winter under cover and in summer in the field. The young soldiers were taught to vault on them at first without arms, afterwards completely armed. And such was their attention to this exercise that they were accustomed to mount and dismount on either side indifferently with their drawn swords or lances in their hands. By assiduous practice in the leisure of peace, their cavalry was brought to such perfection of discipline that they mounted their horses in an instant even amidst the confusion of sudden and unexpected alarms.

Furthermore, according to Arrian (*Ars Tactica* 43): '. . . they demonstrate [in displays] how a man wearing his armour can leap on to a horse when it is running.' Such proficiency is all the more impressive when it is remembered that such feats were performed without the aid of stirrups.

The rider then had to learn how to use the reins and his legs to control the movements of the horse. These exercises may have been carried out in a ring (*gyrus*), an example of which has been tentatively identified at The Lunt, Coventry (Fig.56). At this stage the rider may have had the added security of the horse being held on a lunge rein by a trainer.

Once the trooper had mastered the ability to make the horse obey his instructions, and to turn in any direction at any speed, he was ready to be

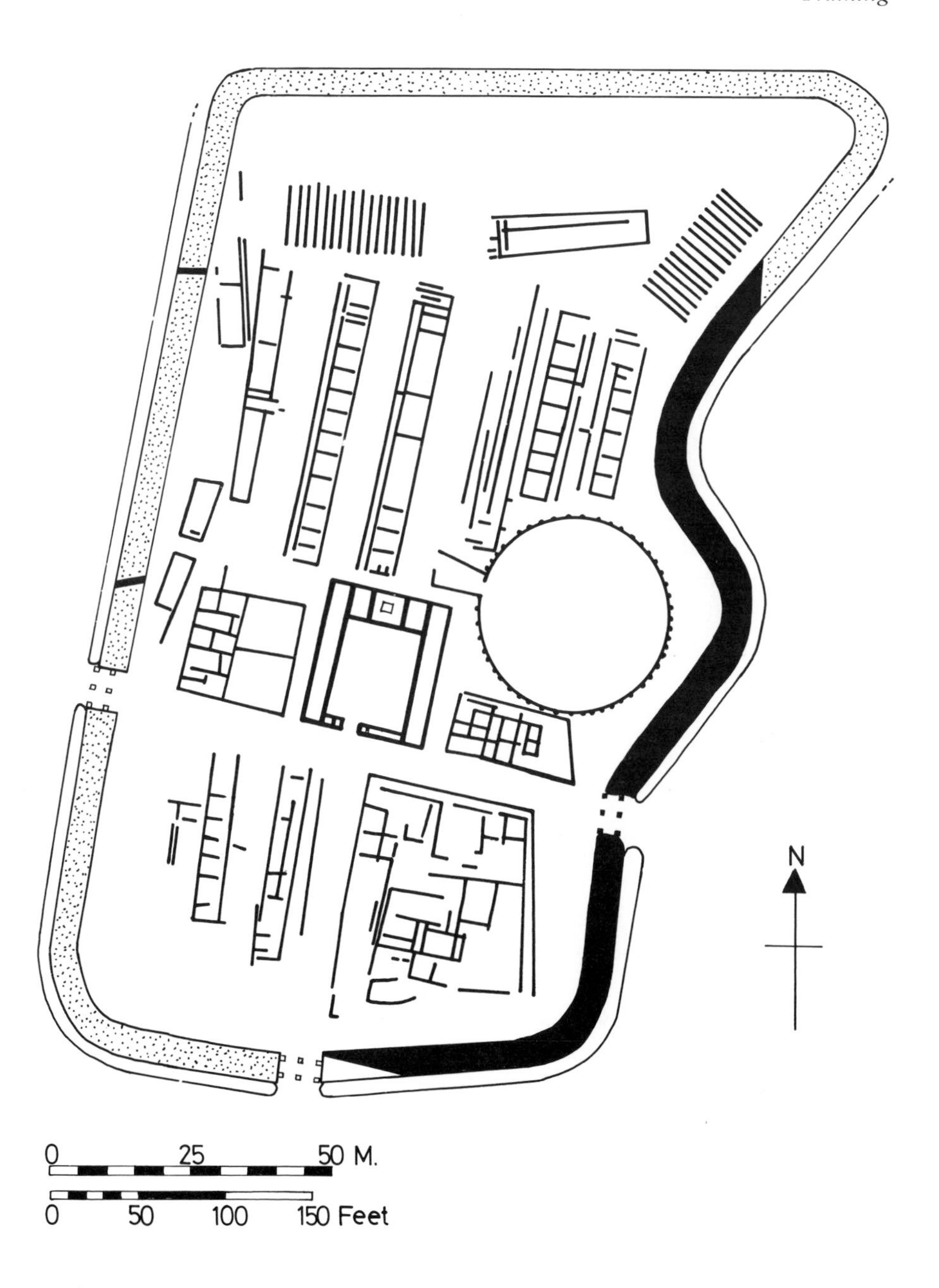

56 Plan of The Lunt fort at Baginton near Coventry, showing the circular structure which has been interpreted as a *gyrus* for training horses. (Redrawn by G. Stobbs from Hobley 1969.)

taught how to make the horse jump obstacles and ride over uneven terrain and still remain in the saddle. Xenophon stresses the importance of this aspect of the training (*Art of Horsemanship* 8.1.): 'As the horse will frequently have to gallop down hill and up hill and along a slope, and as he will have to leap over, and to leap out, and to jump down at various times, the rider must teach and practise both himself and his horse in all these things.' There is evidence to suggest that equal consideration was placed on this exercise by the Roman army. Onasander, in his book on generalship (10.6.) states that: 'Similarly, the commander should exercise the cavalry; he should arrange practice battles including pursuits, hand-to-hand struggles, and skirmishes; these manoeuvres should be held on the plains and around the base of the hills as far as possible in broken country, as it is impossible to gallop at full speed either uphill or downhill.' Arrian (*Ars Tactica* 44) also comments that: '. . . their horses practice jumping across a trench and over a wall . . .'. Disused hillforts have been proposed as an ideal area to practise on, with the ramparts and ditches providing excellent training in controlling the horse in all of the above aspects (Davies 1968a, 90–4), and it is possible that an area of the hillfort at Hod Hill (which also had a Roman fort incorporated into its defences) was used for such activities. It is perhaps interesting to note that it was felt by some men of rank in the British cavalry of the nineteenth century that insufficient training was given to troopers on rough ground. Nolan (1853, 162) stated that: '. . . we must have a great deal more out-of-door work. The soldiers ought to practise their various exercises in the open field.' This change of policy away from the riding school, was also favoured by the Duke of Cambridge, Inspector General of Cavalry, who suggested that greater emphasis should be placed on open air training, including the leaping of ditches and the jumping of hurdles (Wylly 1908, 354).

The recruit would now advance to the use of weapons on horseback. This was bound to cause problems for the trooper, as it necessitated him controlling the horse with only one hand, and probably eventually by just his legs, since both his hands would be employed in holding his shield and lance/sword or a bow. Initial training, however, may have been performed on foot or on a wooden horse.

According to Vegetius (*Epitoma Rei Militaris* 1.11–12) special practice equipment was used during training: 'They gave their recruits round bucklers woven with willows, twice as heavy as those used on real service, and wooden swords double the weight of the common ones . . . their reason for exercising recruits with arms of such a weight at first was, that when they came to carry the common ones, which were so much lighter, the difference might enable them to act with greater security and alacrity in time of action.'

No practice weapons have been positively identified, although Davies (1968b, 91) suggested that a rectangular object from Dura-Europos, consisting of wooden rods held together with leather, may have been a practice shield.

The sword drill for infantrymen, in which each soldier practised his blows against a wooden post, was described by Vegetius (*Epitoma Rei Militaris* 1.11–12). Cavalrymen may also have been trained in such a manner in order that they would gain the suppleness of wrist required. The sword drill for a cavalryman in the British army was probably not too dissimilar to that used by the Roman army, and is therefore worthy of inclusion (Moyse-Bartlett 1971, 84):

> Particular attention was paid to the position and balance of his [the rider's] body as he learnt to control his weapon in attack and defence. The six offensive cuts, diagonals down and up, horizontal right and left was increased to seven. They taught the recruit to apply the edge of the blade at the correct angle to prevent it from turning in the hand. The cuts were complimented by seven defensive guards, designed to protect both horse and rider.

The muscles used to hold a sword are ones which most people employ generally in daily life, although obviously not in such an intense manner. This does not, however, apply to those used to hold a shield, which requires the employment of muscles rarely developed by most people (*pers. comm.* G. Minney), and although it is true to say that the Romans lived in a more manually-based society than ours, the use of double-weight shields must initially have caused the recruit a great deal of stiffness and pain.

The double weight principle was also applied to javelins (Vegetius, *Epitoma Rei Militaris* 1.15): '. . . the recruits . . . were furnished with javelins of greater weight than common, which they were taught to throw at the same post [as that used for sword drill]. And the masters at arms were very careful to instruct them how to cast them with proper aim and force. This practice strengthens the arm and makes the soldier a good marksman.'

The men in horse-archer units were probably drawn from peoples renowned for their skill in this field, since the effective use of a bow on horseback '. . . virtually required the archer to be "born in the saddle"' (Coulston 1985, 288). Maurice (*Strategikon* 1.1.) states that an archer

> . . . should be trained to shoot rapidly on foot, either in the Roman or the Persian manner. Speed is important in shaking the arrow loose and discharging it with force. This is essential and should also be practised while mounted. In fact, even when the arrow is well aimed, firing slowly is useless. He should practise shooting rapidly on foot from a certain distance at a spear or some other target. He should also shoot rapidly mounted on his horse at a run, to the front, the rear, the right, the left. He should practise leaping on to the horse. On horseback at a run he should fire one or two arrows rapidly and put the strung

> bow in its case, if it is wide enough, or in a half-case designed for this purpose, and then he should grab the spear which he has been carrying on his back. With the strung bow in its case, he should hold the spear in his hand, then quickly replace it on his back, and grab the bow. It is a good idea for the soldiers to practise all this while mounted, on the march in their own country. For such exercises do not interfere with marching and do not wear out the horses.

Unlike other cavalrymen, the horse-archer, once he had dropped the reins, could not control the animal by his legs, since in order to perform his shots it was necessary for him to twist a great deal, forcing him to continually press his knees against the horse's flanks. If the horse responded to these nudges everytime, the archer would never have been able to keep to a straight course. It was therefore essential for him to train his horse to ignore such leg movements. Control, therefore, may have been exercised through a similar system to that used by Islamic horse-archers. It consisted of a strap (*musta'ãn*), which was attached to the ends of the reins and secured to the ring-finger of the archer's right hand (Latham and Paterson 1979, 82). This enabled him to recover the reins quickly after releasing his arrow.

Once the basic skills had been learned, a continual programme of advanced training was undertaken, so that accuracy of aim and blow, and a greater confidence on horseback could be achieved. Xenophon advocated hunting as an excellent form of training (*Art of Horsemanship* 8.10.): 'Since it is necessary that the rider should have a firm seat when riding at top speed over all sorts of country, and should be able to use his weapons properly on horseback, the practice of horsemanship by hunting is to be recommended where the country is suitable and big game is to be found.' Since this form of training also provided supplements to the military diet (Davies 1971b, 128), it may have been one of the more popular forms of target practice, as is demonstrated by an inscription from County Durham (*RIB* 1041), which reads: 'To Unconquerable Silvanus Gaius Tetius Veturius Micianus, prefect of the Sebosian Cavalry Regiment, on fulfilment of his vow willingly set this up for taking a wild boar of remarkable fineness which many of his predecessors had been unable to bag.'

Where conditions were unsuitable for hunting, Xenophon (*Art of Horsemanship* 8.10–11) recommends that

> . . . it is a good method of training for two riders to work together thus: one flies on his horse over all kinds of ground and retreats, reversing his spear so that it points backwards, while the other pursues, having buttons [a knob that fitted onto the tip of weapons, akin to those used by modern fencer's on their foils, in order to render any strikes harmless to the opponent] on his javelins and holding his spear in the same position, and when he gets within javelin shot, tries to hit the fugitive with the blunted weapons, and if he gets near enough to use his spear, strikes his captive with it.

One of the main methods of training cavalry and improving their standard of performance is by displays and tournaments, a practice that has been employed by many, if not all, armies throughout the ages. The Roman army was no exception to this rule, having an event known as the *hippika gymnasia* in which the riders wore special sports equipment of extraordinary elaborateness. These displays will be discussed fully in Chapter 7 and are recorded by Arrian in detail in his *Ars Tactica*. They consisted of the cavalrymen performing many complex manoeuvres and difficult feats of skill with weapons. One such manoeuvre, the 'Cantabrian' gallop, demonstrates clearly the types of skills the cavalry were expected to master and is worth quoting here (Arrian, *Ars Tactica* 40):

> It is done as follows: the defensive formation of cavalry protected by their armour, is arrayed on the left of the platform . . . except for the two horsemen who receive the direct 'fire'. They charge from the right . . . and wheel to the right, but whilst they are still charging, another charge develops on the left and wheels into a circle. These horsemen . . . use . . . full-length spears, without iron tips, but heavy enough to be cumbersome for the throwers, and not without danger to the men who form the target. For this reason they have orders not to aim at the helmet, and not to throw the spear at the horse, but before the horseman wheels and exposes any part of his side, or his back becomes exposed as he turns, to aim at the shield and hit it as hard as possible with the spear. The precision of this exercise depends on the man who has gone into this 'Cantabrian' circle, coming as near as he can to those riding past him and scoring a bull on the shield, his spear either thudding on the shield or piercing right through it. The second man picks off the second in the other line, and the third man his opposite number, and so on. The noise is, of course, terrific, and the countermovement appears elegant in such a manoeuvre, and one side gains practice in marksmanship and violence in throwing, while the other side gains practice in safely guarding against an assault.

All the manoeuvres performed in the *hippika gymnasia* would have developed skills extremely valuable to possess in battle, and by using displays as a means of perfecting them, the men would also get some enjoyment and satisfaction out of becoming proficient in these moves.

Some men would become not just competent riders, but horsemen. Examples of horsemanship are numerous in the literary sources, one of the best instances being that recorded by Procopius about the Gothic leader Totila (*History of the Wars* 8.31.19–21), who so enthralled the Roman army by his antics on horseback that they forgot about the battle:

> And he himself [Totila], sitting upon a very large horse, began to perform the dance under arms skilfully between the armies. For he wheeled his horse round in a circle and then turned him again to the other side and so made him run round and round. And as he rode he hurled his javelin into the air and caught it again as it quivered above him, then passed it rapidly from hand to hand, shifting it with consumate skill, and he gloried in his practice in such matters, falling back on his shoulders, spreading his legs and leaning from side to side, like one who has been instructed with precision in the art of dancing from childhood. By these tactics he wore away the whole early part of the day.

Another example comes from Josephus (*Jewish War* 6.2.8.160–3.):

> . . . a trooper from one of the cohorts, named Pedanius – when the Jews were at last repulsed and being driven down into the ravine – urging his horse at top speed along their flank, snatched up one of the flying foe, a youth of sturdy frame and in full armour, grasping him by the ankle; so far did he stoop from his horse, when at the gallop, and such muscular strength of arm and body, along with consummate horsemanship, did he display.

As mentioned above (p.118), where possible the troops were exercised outdoors, either in the surrounding countryside or on the parade ground, one of which was placed outside every auxiliary fort (Johnson 1985, 215). This consisted of a levelled area of land, with a raised platform (*tribunal*) on one side, from which the commander reviewed his troops. The parade grounds of several forts are known. The example at Hardknott, England, which was artificially levelled, measures approximately 165 by 90m (540 by 300ft), and still retains the stone *tribunal* standing to a height of 6m (20ft).

A number of altars dedicated to the mothers of the parade ground (*matres campestres*) have been found in the vicinity of forts, and are believed to indicate the site of a shrine or temple on the parade ground (Davies 1968a, 75). These deities are of Gallic origin, and they appear to have been worshipped exclusively by horsemen (Davies 1968a, 73; Birley 1976, 108). A number of examples of these altars have been found in Britain, including one from Benwell, England (*RIB* 1334), which reads: 'To the three Mother Goddesses of the Parade Ground and to the Genius of the First Cavalry Regiment of Asturian Spaniards styled . . . Gordian's Own Terentius Agrippa, prefect, restored this temple from ground-level.'

Once the weather became too inclement for the men to train outdoors, they carried out their drill under cover (Vegetius *Epitoma Rei Militaris* 2.23): 'To continue this drill without interruption during the winter, they erected for the cavalry riding schools covered with tiles or shingles, and if they were not to be procured with reeds, rushes or thatch.' There is both archaeological and epigraphic evidence for the existence of these exercise halls (*basilica equestris exercitatoria*). During the third century, the *principia* at Haltonchesters on Hadrian's Wall was extended, some believe, to house a riding school for *Ala I Pannoniorum Sabiniana* (Davies 1968a, 75; 1974, 21). An inscription recording the building of a cavalry exercise hall was found at Netherby (see Fig.20; *RIB* 978):

> For the Emperor Caesar Marcus Aurelius Severus Alexander Pius Felix Augustus, *pontifex maximus*, with tribunician power, consul, father of his country, the First Aelian Cohort of Spaniards, one thousand strong, part-mounted, devoted to his Deity and majesty, built a cavalry drill-hall, long since begun from the ground, and completed it, under the charge of Marius Valerianus, Emperor's propraetorian legate, under the

direction of Marcus Aurelius Salvius, tribune of this cohort in the consulship of our Lord the Emperor Severus Alexander Pius Felix Augustus.

Every precaution was therefore taken to ensure that the men could train daily, and not have their routine broken by the weather conditions. According to Vegetius (*Epitoma Rei Militaris* 1.1), constant training was essential, and he believed it to be one of the main factors which contributed to Rome's acquisition of an empire: 'Victory in war does not depend entirely upon numbers or mere courage; only skill and discipline will insure it. We find that the Romans owed the conquest of the world to no other cause than continual military training, exact observance of discipline in their camps and unwearied cultivation of the other arts of war.'

The horses

Clearly the training of both horse and rider should be carried out simultaneously, but before the new cavalry mount was assigned to the new recruit the two may have undergone some initial and separate training already. In the modern British army, horses are not usually assigned to troopers immediately, but they are first trained by rough-riders whose task it is to school the horses in the basic skills that will be required of them. This is equivalent to a test, and occasionally some horses fail and have to be rejected. There is no firm evidence that the Romans used a similar system, but this may be the kind of procedure implied by the term *probatio* which is used of the inspection of remounts (see p.149–50).

Each horse would probably be judged individually, depending upon its age and experience. In some instances, the horses obtained for the Roman army may already have been through some sort of training programme, in which case they would be used to being ridden and would need only specific instruction for army purposes. Other horses may not have been schooled at all, and would need to be trained from the beginning. The amount of time this would take would vary from horse to horse, depending upon his character. 'No hard and fast rule can be made as to how long it should take to train a young horse. Peculiarities of breed, temperament, climate, age and condition will cause variation, and horses with weak points in their conformation will take longer to train than well-shaped horses' (War Office 1937b, 117). Horses are like people and display a variety of temperaments; some are bad-tempered or over-enthusiastic, with minds of their own, others are stupid, lazy or easily bored. Yet others are good-natured, well-dispositioned and enjoy their work, making it possible for the rider and mount to develop a rapport and trust which can only be beneficial (Moyse-Bartlett 1971, 82).

The question of who carried out the initial training of a horse and where this was done are bound up with the supply of remounts to the army, and unfortunately there is little evidence to clarify the problem. It has been suggested that the circular structure called the *gyrus* at The Lunt near Coventry was used for training horses and riders, and if this is correct it could imply that there were central depots for the training of horses which would then be sent out to the units which needed them; training would then continue within that unit. This system, or one like it, may have been used to keep up the supplies of remounts to units in the provinces. Horses obtained by various means and from various locations could be brought to the central depot or depots, inspected and given some training, and then allocated to the *alae* and *cohortes*. Troopers who were already experienced would be able to continue the schooling of their remounts. It is less certain whether each unit would train its own recruits or whether these would also assemble at a training depot for their initial instruction, before joining their units.

It has to be acknowledged that the slow, patient, humane methods of training young horses advocated by modern authorities in numerous publications probably had no bearing whatever on the practices of the Roman army. It is probable that the average rider was as sentimental and sensitive about the sufferings of an animal as his modern counterpart is sentimental about the clanking of an engine which is about to seize up. More importance would be attached to the necessity of carrying out the various tasks the cavalry was asked to perform, and both training and subsequent usage would be bent to that end. Blücher declared that it was worth losing a few hundred horses from exhaustion if the outcome of his plans was successful (Yorck von Wartenburg 1902, vol.I, 214). It is likely that this attitude was prevalent in the Roman army as well, and probably extended to the methods used in training horses. In the nineteenth century, Nolan (1853, 158–9) listed the faults in training British cavalry remounts and proposed an alternative, more humane, system based on his own experience. Whether or not he was correct is not the point at issue; training of remounts was not carried out for the benefit of horses, but for that of the army. The view that this should be achieved in the shortest possible time and with the minimum of effort may have been quite acceptable in some of the Roman provinces, resulting in what would now be termed cruelty to the horses.

The training programme for a British cavalry horse in 1937 was divided into three stages, each of about 17 weeks' duration. Lessons were not to last for more than an hour and a half, and the horses had one day off every week. In the first stage the horse was merely led about, and not saddled until roughly the sixth week. After about eight weeks, someone would 'back' the horse to get him used to carrying the weight of a man. The other exercises would continue all the time as the horse was lunged or made to trot round on long reins (War Office 1937b, 117–19). At this stage the rider did not take any part in training the horse; all control remained with the trainer, and the rider simply acted as a passenger (Hardman 1976, 115). Hobley (1974, 374) envisaged that the so-called *gyrus* at The Lunt (see Fig.56) would have been used to train horses on the lunge rein, where they would be made to trot in circles in both directions, learning obedience to the trainer's voice. This is quite possible and cannot be decisively proved or disproved. The US cavalry trained new horses and riders in the 'Bullring' at Jefferson Barracks in the nineteenth century. This was a circular structure 18.5m (60ft) in diameter, located in the riding hall. It should be noted, however, that it was more often used for punishing defaulters, who were made to run round it at triple time for half an hour (Rickey 1972, 44). The Lunt remains unexplained except by guesswork. At other forts, if training of remounts was carried out, it may have been done in meadows where the only archaeological trace would be post-holes from the fencing which may have surrounded the training area.

When the horse was used to carrying the weight of a man, the second stage of training could begin. By now the rider would take control, directing the horse by rein and leg movements, concentrating on turning movements, jumping, cantering and slow gallop. The use of weapons would not be undertaken until the first two stages were satisfactorily completed. In the third stage of training, sword and lance work would begin, and cross-country riding to accustom both horse and rider to the tasks they would be asked to carry out as part of normal duties.

The optimum results which were desired from the training of a cavalry horse were listed in the War Office manual (1937b, 134):

> A properly trained remount should fill the following qualifications: stand still for mounting and dismounting; lead well; be as well balanced as his make and shape will allow; be obedient to the correct aids; be able to passage, rein back, halt and do a figure of eight correctly, and be capable of being ridden with one hand; turn about actively on his haunches; be a good jumper over all kinds of obstacles and a safe performer over all kinds of country; be steady on parade and be accustomed to traffic, gunfire and unusual sights and sounds; go alone in company at any pace required without pulling and pull up quickly and smartly when required; be trained to the use of weapons; leave the ranks quietly and without fuss.

There are several passages in this list which could have been written by Xenophon.

7 The *hippika gymnasia*

Wherever there are troops and leisure for it, there should be an attempt at military display. (Sir Winston Churchill, in Dewar 1990, 63).

Many armies, if not all, have indulged in the performance of tournaments and displays, since they not only provide the troops with entertainment, but, more importantly, they are also an excellent method of improving the men's battle skills and morale. The *hippika gymnasia* was the tournament of the Roman cavalry which took place on the parade ground situated outside of the fort. The participating riders and their mounts wore and used special equipment. Many books refer to these items as 'parade equipment'. In this book, however, the term 'sports equipment' is used. This decision was taken on the basis of the definition of these terms given by Bishop (1990) as follows: 'Parade equipment' was a soldier's entire kit which was worn during static inspection parades; all of this kit *could* be worn in combat. 'Sports equipment', on the other hand, included highly decorative items, designed specifically for display; although some of these items could conceivably have been worn in combat, it seems highly unlikely that they would have been. The latter term is, on this definition, applied to the following items, divided into two sections, one set for the men and one set for the horses.

Equipment: the men

Clothing

Arrian states (*Ars Tactica* 34) that: 'Instead of breastplates they [the cavalry] wear close-fitting Cimmeriand tunics [leather jerkins] embroidered with scarlet, red, blue/hyacinth or other colours.' This may have been the mode of dress during the second century, but by the third century it appears that the men were possibly wearing some form of armour, since a number of ornately embossed bronze breast plates have been found (Robinson 1975, 161). The plates, which have rivet holes along their outside edges, have an average length of 15cm (6in) and a width of 7.9cm (3in). They are curved on

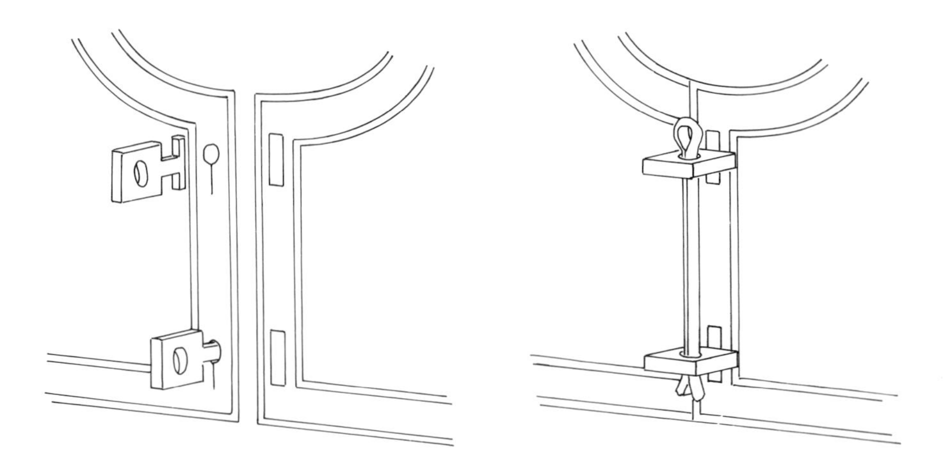

57 Diagram to show how the plates shown in Pl.17 were fastened. The square-headed pins on the left plate were pushed through the slots on the right plate. Once through the slots, the heads of the pins were turned and a rod was driven through the holes in the pin-heads in order to prevent the pins from slipping out of the slots when in use. (Redrawn by J.R.A. Underwood from Garbsch 1978.)

the upper edge to fit the wearer's neck (Pl.17 and Fig.57). It is possible that these plates were attached to leather shirts, but Robinson (1975, 161), on the basis of a plate from Pfünz, Germany, which has a rivet holding a scale on the underside, believes that they were mounted on *loricae squamatae* (see pp.38ff).

A further item of clothing that Arrian mentions being worn by the cavalrymen is trousers (*Ars Tactica* 34): 'About their legs they wear trousers, not loosely fitting like those of the Parthians and Armenians, but drawn tight about the legs.' The type of trousers described by Arrian is well attested on monumental and sepulchral reliefs, although those worn in displays may have been more ornate and brightly coloured than those for daily wear.

Greaves

Although Arrian does not mention greaves having being worn in the *hippika gymnasia*, a number of very ornate examples have been recovered from various sites, in particular the five bronze guards, including a pair, from the Straubing hoard of sports equipment (Pl.18) (Keim and Klumbach 1951, 19–23, Taf.14–8; Garbsch 1978, 9–12 Abb.4, 48–9, B9–14, Taf.3). All the known examples consist of a leg guard with a hinged cap for the knee, with two or three opposing pairs of rings on the leg piece, and one on the knee, through which straps would be passed in order to secure the greave to the leg.

The greaves vary in both the quality and quantity of the decoration (Pl.19). Three of the greaves and one knee guard from Straubing can be positively identified as having being worn by cavalrymen, since the inscriptions on the back refer to *turmae* (Keim and Klumbach 1951, 20–2, Taf.16; Garbsch 1978, 48–9, B10–12; Macmullen 1960, 34 no.24–6, 36 no.44).

Javelins

According to Arrian (*Ars Tactica* 34) the javelins used in the *hippika gymnasia* were '. . . made without iron, and while they might injure the eyes of the horses, they fall harmlessly on their sides, particularly since the sides are for the most part protected by the horse's armour'.

No examples of these weapons have been found, presumably because of their organic nature, but they may have been similar to those used for training (see pp.118–19).

Helmets

The elaborate masked helmets which were worn during the *hippika gymnasia* are described by Arrian (*Ars Tactica* 34):

> The horsemen enter fully armed and those of distinguished station or superior in horsemanship wear gilded helmets of iron or bronze, to draw to themselves the gaze of the spectators. Unlike the helmets made for active service, these do not cover the heads and cheeks only but are made to fit all round the faces of the riders with apertures for the eyes, so as to give protection to the eyes without interfering with vision. From the helmets hang yellow plumes – a matter of decor as much as of utility. As the horses move forward, the slightest breeze adds to the beauty of these plumes.

Large numbers of these helmets have been recovered, the majority coming from territories once under Roman rule. Both males and females are represented, possibly in order for some of the riders to take the role of Amazons in a mock battle (Robinson 1975, 124). Female helmets can be recognized by the hair-style and by the use of diadems, ribbons and jewels (Pl.20). A number of these sports helmets, both male and female, appear to depict the faces of orientals, such as the example from Emesa, Syria (Pls.21 and 22) (Garbsch 1978, 20, 63, 04, Taf.17, 03–4).

Little evidence exists for crest holders on sports helmets, although some are provided with loops above the brow, such as the example from Ribchester (Pl.23). One of the helmets from Newstead in Scotland also had a plume tube riveted onto the left side of the skull-piece (Curle 1911, 170, Pl.XXIX).

Two different methods were employed in attaching the mask to the skull-

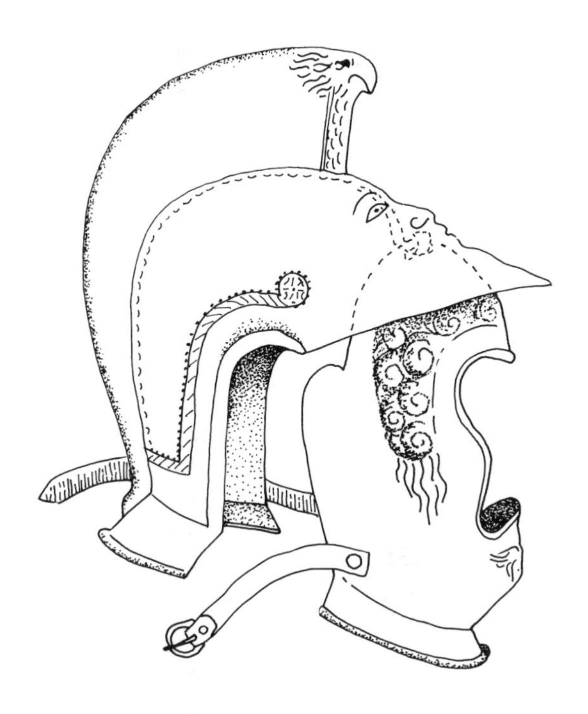

58 Drawing based on a helmet from Heddernheim, Germany (see Pl.25), showing a particular method of attaching the partial face-mask. A slot was cut in the top of face-mask and this was then placed over a hook fixed to the underside of the helmet skull. The two sections were then secured at the neck by a leather strap. (Redrawn by K.R. Dixon from Robinson 1975.)

piece. One common way was to hinge either the full face mask (See Pls.21 and 22), or one covering only the eyes, nose and mouth (Pl.24), to the centre of the brow head. The second method (Fig.58) entailed a slot being cut centrally at the top of the mask, which was then slipped over a hook protruding from the underside of the skull-piece. Leather straps riveted to the lower edges of the mask, and buckling on one side of the neck, kept the two parts of the helmet closed when in use. As stated above by Arrian, not all cavalry sports helmets were provided with masks, and Robinson suggests that the example from Heddernheim, Germany (Pl.25), was of this type (1975, 129 Pl.376–7).

More than one typology based on stylistic and constructional variants exists, and the following descriptions of the main groups is a synthesis of those produced by Robinson (1975, 107–35) and Garbsch (1978). One type, which was in use from the first century to the late second century AD, consists of a face mask attached by a horizontally placed hinge in the centre of the brow to a skull-piece in the form of a highly decorated helmet, such as the silver-plated iron example from Emesa, Syria (See Pls. 21 and 22; Garbsch 1978, 20, 63, 04, Taf.17, 03–4).

Helmets distinguished by prominent peaks projecting from the rim of richly embossed skull-pieces only appear in the late first century and the early second century AD. The bronze helmet of this style from Ribchester (see Pl.23) depicts a battle between cavalrymen and infantrymen on the skull-piece (Robinson 1975, 112 Pl.310–13; Garbsch 1978, 21, 58, II, Taf.12, II).

The most enduring type of sports helmet, with examples dating from the first to the third centuries AD, takes the form of a head with a youthful face, with embossed wavy hair on the skull-piece, rather than an ornate representation of a helmet. This group is the largest, with Germany contributing the greatest number (Pl.26).

During the late second and the early third centuries, some helmets appear to have retained the surrounds of the face but not the central features (Robinson 1975, 129). An example of this type comes from Heddernheim, Germany (See Pl.25). The skull-piece has a tall crest which finishes in the head of an eagle, below which, on the brow, is an embossed face, giving the impression of a Greek helmet when viewed at a certain angle (Garbsch 1978, 21–2, 72, 053, Taf.29; Robinson 1975, 129 Pl.376–7). Variants on this style are those helmets, such as a bronze example from Worthing, England (Pl.27) (Garbsch 1978, 21–2, 74, 061, Taf.30, 01; Toynbee and Clarke 1948, 20–6, Pl.II–IV), which have crests, but mythological creatures replace the embossed face on the skull-piece. Furthermore, they are provided with face masks.

The last major group, which dates from the third century, has three rounded peaks on the brow band, and the helmet is fitted with cheek-pieces but not a mask (Pl.28).

Sculptural evidence for sports helmets, indeed sports equipment in general, is on the whole scarce. The first-century tombstone of Genialis from Cirencester (Pl.29) (*RIB* 109), clearly depicts a peaked helmet of the type found at Ribchester (see Pl.23), but owing to the damaged nature of Genialis' face, it is unfortunately impossible to know if it was provided with a mask.

Shields

Arrian states that cavalry in a display (*Ars Tactica* 34): '. . . carry oblong shields of a lighter type than those used in action, since both agility and smart turn-out are the objects of the exercise and they embellish them to give a pleasant appearance.' No examples of this type of sports shield have been found, although the Dura-Europos examples give some idea of how elaborately decorated and brightly coloured they might have been (Rostovtzeff *et al.* 1939, 326–69, Figs.83–4, Pls.XLI–VI).

Standards

According to Arrian (*Ars Tactica* 35), during the *hippika gymnasia* both Roman and Scythian standards were carried. He described the latter as follows:

> The Scythian standards are made like snakes, hanging from the pike-poles and of proportionate length. They are made by sewing together scraps of dyed cloth, and look like serpents from head to tail so as to be a more impressive sight. When the horses are standing still, these contrivances look no more than a variegated patchwork hanging down, but when the horses are urged forward the wind fills them and they swell out, so that they look remarkably like live creatures, and even hiss in the breeze which the brisk movement sends through them.

The head of one of these dragon standards was found near the fort of Niederbieber, Germany (See Pl.10) (Garbsch 1978, 88, Taf.48).

Equipment: the horses

Bardings

A passage in the *Ars Tactica* (34), already quoted, implies that some form of barding was worn by the horses during a *hippika gymnasia*: '. . . they [the javelins] fall harmlessly on their [the horses] sides, particularly since the sides are for the most part protected by the horse's armour'.

The only known examples of bardings are the three in scale armour from Dura-Europos (see Pl.11 and Fig.30; and pp.61–3) (Rostovtzeff *et al.* 1936, 440–9, Pls.XXI–II). It is possible, however, that the horse-coats spoken of by Arrian were made of leather or linen, and thus their chance of survival in the archaeological record would be greatly reduced. If such materials were used, they would have given the person responsible for their decoration great scope for the application of colourful and elaborate designs, which would have been in keeping with the other ornate equipment used in these displays.

Chamfrons

> The horses have frontlets carefully made to measure . . . (Arrian, *Ars Tactica* 34).

Chamfrons are the protective head covers worn by horses. They could be made either of leather or metal (usually bronze). The most complete examples from Britain were found at Newstead, Scotland (Curle 1911, 153–

5, Pl.xxi; 1913, 400–5, Fig.11–12), and Vindolanda, England (see Fig.34; Driel-Murray 1989, 283–90, Fig.5–6). These two chamfrons are virtually identical in style, comprising a leather mask, with two circular holes for the eyes, two ear-flaps, and an overall design executed in metal studs. Stitch-holes indicate that originally a name-plate, *tabula ansata*, probably of leather, had been sewn onto the frontlet just below the eye-holes (see Fig.34 for an example).

It has been suggested that the metal eye-guards which have been found on numerous sites (See Pl.12), would have belonged to these leather chamfrons. Direct evidence is lacking, however, with the possible exception of one of the Vindolanda chamfrons, which shows signs of damage around the eye-holes, possibly caused by the attachment of guards (Driel-Murray 1989, 291).

Two distinct groups of metal chamfrons can be recognized. The first group consists of those chamfrons which are constructed in three high-relief hinged panels, with 'built-in' eye-guards on the two side-panels, giving a similar coverage area to those executed in leather. These eye-guards could take the form of heads (Pl.30), or an openwork design (Pl.31).

The chamfrons belonging to the second group comprise a central plate, to which is hinged two eye-guards (Pls.32 and 33).

Medallions

A number of large circular metal medallions have been found (Pl.34). Exactly what function they served is uncertain, but their extremely elaborate nature implies that they were probably worn in the *hippika gymnasia*. Most believe that they were either worn by the horses at the front of the chest, or formed elaborate shield bosses for the men (Garbsch 1978, 12–13). Both of these suggestions may be correct, since it is possible that not all of the examples served the same purpose.

The manoeuvres

Our knowledge of the manoeuvres executed in the *hippika gymnasia* is based upon Arrian, who describes these displays fully in his *Ars Tactica*. On entering the parade ground the cavalry, according to Arrian (*Ars Tactica* 36), rode to the left of the tribunal and halted in close formation, with their shields covering both their own and their horse's backs, forming a mounted *testudo*. The line then divided in half, one to receive the javelin fire, and one to charge. Two fully armoured riders stood in front of those facing the fire. The aim of the exercise was to test the accuracy of the men throwing, who had to try and hit the armour of the two troopers standing in front, who were in turn tested on their ability to protect themselves with their shields. Whilst this was happening, some of the men in the *testudo* rode out from the line, and tried to hit the assailants as they rode past. Arrian (*Ars Tactica* 37) then writes:

> It is at this point that good horsemanship is especially needed to be able simultaneously to throw at those who are charging in and to give one's right hand side the protection of the shield. When riding parallel to his target, the rider must swivel himself to the right in order to throw; when making a complete about-turn, he must throw in the manner called, in the Gallic tongue *petrinos*, which is the most difficult of all. For he must turn right round as far as the tenderness of the sides will allow, to face the horse's tail, so as to throw backwards as straight as possible, and having done so, he must quickly turn forward again and bring his shield to cover his back, since if he turns without getting protection, he exposes a vulnerable target to the enemy.

The same exercise was then repeated on the other side of the tribunal, and then once more on each side, finishing with another display of skill at arms:

> . . . and on making the second charge from the left, they do not simply wheel right, ride past the platform and take their leave, but the quickest of them keep one javelin each in reserve and the very best keep two each. And as they approach the platform on their ride past, they suddenly put their horses into a turn, and whilst still on the turn, throw slantwise at the far boundary of the parade ground . . . When those who have reserved two come up, they slightly incline the head on the right side under the shield as far as they can, turn round and throw the remaining dart backwards [i.e. the opposite direction in which the horse is moving]. (*Ars Tactica* 39).

They then performed the 'Cantabrian' gallop (see p.121), during which some of the cavalry gave a demonstration in continuous throwing (*Ars Tactica* 40), which entailed the men attempting to discharge as many darts, as far as they could, before they left the parade area. Arrian states (*Ars Tactica* 40) that fifteen was considered to be good, but praise indeed went to those who managed to raise the number to twenty. Demonstrations in marksmanship then followed: 'Each man carries one lance, and before he gets near the platform, he must whirl his lance with all his might, and, as soon as it reverberates, throw it, taking aim at the target which has been set up . . . on the left of the platform.' (*Ars Tactica* 41).

The display concluded in the following manner:

> They advance first with pikes levelled in defensive style, then as though they were overtaking a fleeing enemy. Others, as if against another enemy, as their horses turn, swing their shields over their heads to a position behind them and turn their pikes as though meeting an enemy's assault. This manoeuvre is called, in Gallic *toloutegon*. Also they draw their swords and make a variety of strokes, best calculated to overtake an enemy in flight, to kill a man already down, or to achieve any success by a quick movement (along) from the flanks. Nor is this all: they demonstrate in as great a variety as possible, the number of shapes and forms which can be given to the act of leaping on a

> horse. Finally they demonstrate how a man wearing his armour can leap on to a horse when it is running. Some call this the 'wayfarer's jump'. (*Ars Tactica* 43).

After witnessing such a performance by an *ala* in AD 218 at Lambaesis, North Africa, Hadrian is recorded to have commented:

> You did everything in orderly fashion. You filled the field with manoeuvres. Your javelin hurling was not without grace, although you used javelins which are short and stiff. Several of you hurled your lances equally well. And your mounting was smart just now and lively yesterday. If there were anything lacking I should notice it; if there were anything conspicuously bad, I should point it out. But you pleased me uniformly throughout the whole exercise . . . Your prefect evidently looks after you carefully. I bestow upon you a largess . . . (*CIL* VIII, 2532 and 18042 = Dessau 2487 and 9133–5).

The above descriptions of the manoeuvres executed during the *hippika gymnasia* clearly show the usefulness of these events as training. All the exercises undertaken would stand the rider in good stead during actual combat and would enable him to gain greater confidence on horseback, since the moves required the cavalryman to be in total control of his mount.

8 The employment of cavalry in peacetime and wartime

Peacetime

> Soldiers in peace are like chimneys in summer. (William Cecil (Lord Burghley) in Dewar 1990, 203).

As Vegetius notes, constant drill during peacetime was of the greatest importance (*Epitoma Rei Militaris* 2.23):

> In short, both legionary and auxiliary troops should continually be drilled in cutting wood, carrying burdens, crossing ditches, swimming in the sea or in rivers, marching full step and even running with their arms and baggage so that inured to labour in peace, they may find it not difficult in war. For, as the well trained soldier is eager for action, so does the untaught fear it. In war discipline is superior to strength; but if that discipline is neglected, there is no longer any difference between the soldier and the peasant.

Aside from the rigorous drilling that all soldiers underwent, the cavalry also performed many other duties during peacetime, of both a military and a civilian nature.

Military duties

Different units within the army were employed in various roles during peacetime. The majority of evidence for the duties undertaken by mixed units comes from papyri, such as the *pridianum* of *Cohors I Hispanorum Veterana quingenaria equitata*, which has been dated to *c.*AD 105 (*Ch LA* 219; Fink 1971, n.63, 217–27; Davies 1971a, 757). This particular report states that some cavalrymen were sent across the Erar (possibly a river), to obtain horses; others were on garrison duty; a decurion was serving as a guard to the governor; a number of *equites* were on a scouting assignment and a decurion was overseeing some grain ships. Two duty rosters of *Cohors XX Palmyrenorum* dating to *c.*AD 219 and 222 provide further information (*P. Dur.* 100 and 101; Fink 1971, n.1 and 2, 18–81; Davies 1971a, 758–9). Yet again their tasks included garrison duty, scouting, relaying messages and dispatches between bases, escort duty and serving as guards to the governor. Few of these duties were undertaken exclusively by the *equites*, with the possible exception of carrying messages (Davies 1971a, 758), the majority being performed in association with the infantry.

During the third century AD each of the four outpost forts north of Hadrian's Wall were occupied by a *cohors milliaria equitata*. One reason for their popularity may have lain in their ability to provide small forces of both infantry and cavalry, enabling them to deal with small-scale frontier disturbances. If larger forces were required, the men of more than one fort could be combined: the cavalry contingent of two milliary *ala* combined produced the equivalent of an *ala*.

Military deployments also provided greater security for the civilian population. The two duty rosters of *Cohors XX Palmyrenorum* mentioned above (Fink 1971, n.1 and 2), record a number of men as being on garrison duty. Such posts were necessary, not only as military installations, but also to keep in check brigandage throughout the provinces and in districts where prosperity had attracted crime. In a military context, posts were stationed at points of strategic importance, or where there was a perceived threat from hostile peoples.

Although the *singulares* were primarily employed as bodyguards to the Emperor or the governors, they did undertake a number of other duties. A papyrus from Egypt (Fink 1971, n.87) records them being employed to carry documents from the headquarters of the province to another unit. There is also some evidence to suggest that they provided a communications system, both internally and externally of the province, for the governors. An example of this may be indicated by the stationing of an *eques ex officio singulariorum* 400km (250 miles) from the governor's headquarters in Mauretania Caesariensis (*CIL* VIII.9763; Davies 1976, 140). The offices of *stator* and *stationarius* are attested within the *singulares* (*CIL* III.12356; *AE* 250), both of which were associated with police or communications work (Davies 1976, 141). *Singulares* might therefore have been used to police the routes of communication and the *stationes* of the Imperial post (*cursus publicus*) (Davies 1976, 141).

Civilian duties

The Roman army provided the Empire with a large body of highly trained men who were capable of dealing with most policing tasks. It was their duty to suppress crime and to quell public disorders. All these tasks would usually have been undertaken by mixed forces of infantry and cavalry, but mounted troops were occasionally considered to be more suitable, especially when dealing with angry mobs and large unruly crowds, a modern parallel being the presence of mounted police at football matches. Josephus records numerous examples where mixed forces were used to quell public disturbances (*Jewish Wars* 2.236; 2.258–260; 2.261–332), but one of the most detailed accounts comes from Herodian, who describes a disturbance under Commodus (1.12.6–9):

> Then suddenly, without any warning to the people, the whole Imperial cavalry appeared on the scene, fully armed at Cleander's orders, charging and cutting down anyone they came across. The mob, without weapons and on foot, could not stand up to the armed horsemen. They turned and ran for the city. Some were just cut down by the swords of the soldiers and trampled under foot by the horses, but many others died in the crush of the crowd [and the horsemen] as they stumbled on top of each other. The cavalry were unchecked in their pursuit right up to the city gates, slaughtering those who fell without mercy. But when the people that had stayed behind in the city saw the horror of what had happened, they locked the doors of their houses and climbed on to the roofs, from where they pelted the horsemen with stones and tiles. The horsemen began to get a spell of their own treatment... Under the steady hail of stones the horses stepped on the rolling pebbles and slipped, throwing off their riders.

Wartime

> Cavalry ought to be at once the eye, the feeler, and the feeder of an army. With good cavalry an army is in comparative security, and in a condition to march into and subsist upon an enemy's country. It reaps the fruits of victory, covers a retreat, and retrieves a disaster. (Nolan 1853, 61).

This was stated rather more succintly by Napoleon: 'Cavalry is useful before, during and after the battle.' The cavalry undertook all those roles which required mobility and speed. In most countries they provided the only available means by which actions could be carried out quickly, and, on land, the fastest and most efficient way of gaining vital information concerning enemy movements. During a campaign, there were a number of duties which had to be constantly performed by the cavalry.

Foraging

> An army unsupplied with grain and other necessary provisions risks being vanquished without striking a blow. (Vegetius *Epitoma Rei Militaris* 3.26).

Vegetius discusses at length the importance of ensuring adequate supplies for an army campaigning in hostile territory (*Epitoma Rei Militaris* 3.3): 'Famine makes greater havoc in an army than the enemy, and is more terrible than the sword. Time and opportunity may help to retrieve other misfortunes, but where forage and provisions have not been carefully provided, the evil is without remedy. The main and principal point in war is to secure plenty of provisions and to weaken or destroy the enemy by famine.' Such a policy was adopted by Caesar against Petreius and Afranius during the Civil War in Spain (*Civil Wars* 1.72):

> Caesar had entertained the hope that, having cut off his adversaries from their food supply, he would be able to finish the business without exposing his men to fighting or bloodshed. Why should he lose any of his men even in a successful battle? Why should he suffer soldiers who had served him so well to be wounded? Why, in a word, should he make trial of fortune? Especially as it was as much the duty of a commander to win by policy as by the sword.

The task of foraging was obviously well suited to the cavalry, since if they were suddenly sighted by the enemy they could make a hasty retreat. Occasionally, however, the cavalry were caught unawares, as is recorded by Caesar (*Spanish War* 26), who describes how a number of his cavalry were killed while collecting wood in an olive grove.

Dispatch riders

At all times throughout a campaign messages would need to be carried from one area to another in order to inform officers of the current situation, or to instigate the movement of troops. The cavalry were obviously ideal for ensuring that instructions and information reached their destination as quickly as possible. Josephus (*Jewish War* 3.10.6.503–4), records how a cavalryman was sent by Titus to his father Vespasian, to tell him that the city of Tarichaeae had been captured.

Reconnaissance

> Time spent on reconnaissance is seldom wasted. (*British Army Field Service Regulations*, 1912, in Dewar 1990, 187).

Whilst the army was marching through enemy territory it was essential for the cavalry to scout ahead and on the flanks, in order to prevent the troops being caught unawares, for, as Vegetius states (*Epitoma Rei Militaris* 3.6):

> It is asserted by those who have made the profession their study that an army is exposed to more danger on marches than in battles. In an engagement the men are properly armed, they see their enemies before them and are prepared to fight. But on a march the soldier is less on his guard, has not his arms always ready and is thrown into disorder by a sudden attack or ambush. A general, therefore, cannot be too careful and diligent in taking necessary precautions to prevent a surprise on the march and in making proper dispositions to repulse the enemy, in case of such event, without loss.

According to Ammianus (24.1.2): 'He [Julian] . . . arranged to have 1500 mounted scouts riding a little ahead of the army. Who advancing with caution on both flanks, as well as in front, kept watch that no sudden attack be made.'

Scouts could also be used to survey the area through which the army was to march to locate the safest and easiest route to take; such use is recorded by

Tacitus (*Histories* 3.52) who tells how Antonius and the other Flavian commanders sent their cavalry on ahead to reconnoitre throughout Umbria, in order to find the safest way to approach the Apennines. If the only route available was not passable in its discovered state, then a body of cavalry and infantry could be sent in advance to clear or level the road (Josephus *Jewish War* 3.7.3.141–2).

Before a siege was undertaken, it was essential that a reconnaissance of the city or fortification was carried out. Extremely valuable information could be gained, as is demonstrated by a passage from Caesar's *Gallic War* (3.25), in which he relates how a party of cavalry which had moved round the enemy's camp, were able to inform Crassus that it was not fortified with the same care on the rear side. Josephus (*Jewish War* 5.2.1.52) tells of one instance when Titus, during a reconnaissance of Jerusalem '. . . with some 600 picked horsemen . . . rode forward to reconnoitre the city's strength and to test the mettle of the Jews'. It is interesting to note that on both occasions when Titus is personally engaged in reconnaissance (Josephus *Jewish War* 5.2.1.52; 5.6.2.259), he takes 'picked' cavalrymen. This suggests that the troopers were not necessarily all drawn from the same unit, and were specifically chosen for the task, presumably because of their experience and reliability.

Outpost duty

> Outposts have a double object: to watch over the safety of the army, and to observe the movements of the enemy. (Nolan 1853, 259).

Once the army had set up camp, outposts had to be established so that any movements the enemy made could be quickly reported back to the commander and the relevant course of action taken. As noted by Nolan (1853, 260): 'Men cannot stand ready under arms day and night to resist an attack . . . thus every position . . . is surrounded by a chain of guards to protect it from surprise, and to give rest and security to the occupants.'

The nature of the terrain dictated the type of troops selected for the duty, although in virtually all cases they would be lightly armed. In open country cavalry would be employed, whilst broken ground would require the use of infantry. If the terrain was a combination of the two, then mounted troops would patrol the front and the flanks, so that in the event of approaching danger they could gallop back to the infantry outposts, giving them time to head back to the security of the camp (Nolan 1853, 261).

Outpost duty was obviously open to risks, as is demonstrated by a quote from Caesar (*Spanish War* 10): 'When a few of our horsemen on outpost duty were discovered by the enemy, who were in greater strength, they were driven from their post, and three of them were killed.'

Ammianus records an instance when the soldiers failed to execute their duty (18.7.1–3):

> For about 700 horsemen, belonging to two squadrons who had recently been sent to the aid of Mesopotamia from Illyricum, a spiritless and cowardly lot, were keeping guard in those parts. And dreading a night attack, they withdrew to a distance from the public roads at evening, when all the paths ought to be better guarded. This was observed by the Persians, and about 20,000 of them . . . passed by the horsemen unobserved, while these were overcome with wine and sleep, and hid themselves with arms behind some high mounds near Amida.

As Xenophon noted (*Cavalry Commander* 4.10–12), outposts could also be used to ambush enemy troops:

> When it is necessary to keep a look out, I am all in favour of the plan of having hidden outposts and guards to protect your friends and snares to trap the enemy . . . Besides, if you conceal your outposts, you will have the chance of luring the enemy into an ambush by placing a few guards in the open to screen the hidden men. Occasionally, too, a cunning trap may be laid by posting a second body of exposed guards behind the men in hiding; for this plan may prove as deceptive to the enemy as the one just referred to.

The battlefield

> The nature of the ground is often of more consequence than courage. (Vegetius *Epitoma Rei Militaris* 3.26).

The nature of the terrain played a vital role in an engagement since it dictated the types of troops which would achieve the best results. Vegetius discusses this subject in detail (*Epitoma Rei Militaris* 3.13):

> Good generals are acutely aware that victory depends much on the nature of the field of battle. When you intend to engage, endeavour to draw the chief advantage from your position. The highest ground is reckoned the best. Weapons thrown from a height strike with greater force: and the party above their antagonists can repulse and bear them down with greater impetuosity, while they who struggle with the ascent have both the ground and the enemy to contend with.
>
> There is, however, this difference: if you depend on your foot against the enemy's horse, you must chose a rough, unequal and mountainous situation. But if, on the contrary, you expect your cavalry to act with advantage against the enemy's infantry, your ground must indeed be higher, but level and open, without any obstructions such as woods or morasses.

The perfect terrain for the employment of cavalry was encountered by Caesar (*Spanish War* 29): 'Moreover, with a level plain like that and a calm, sunny day, it was a tempting situation for cavalry – a wonderful, longed-for and well-nigh heaven-sent opportunity for engaging battle.'

It was, of course, not always possible for an army to choose the battle site, and ancient authors record many instances where the Roman army suffered heavy losses due to the unsuitability of the terrain, a good example being the engagement against the Jews in the pass of Beth-Horon (*Jewish War* 2.19.8.548–9): 'Here, while the infantry were hard put to it to defend themselves, the cavalry were in still greater jeopardy; to advance in order down the road under the hail of darts was impossible, to charge up the slopes was impracticable for horse; on either side were precipices and ravines, down which they slipped and were hurled to destruction; there was no room for flight, no conceivable means of defence.'

One method by which the cavalry could eliminate the problems caused by unsuitable terrain was to dismount, as is illustrated by an episode which Frontinus records (*Stratagems* 2.23): 'The Emperor Caesar Augustus Germanicus [Domitian], when the Chatti, by fleeing into the forests, again and again interfered with the course of a cavalry engagement, commanded his men, as soon as they should reach the enemy's baggage-train, to dismount and fight on foot. By this means he made sure that his success should not be blocked by any difficulties of terrain.'

The employment of the different types of cavalry in battle

The heavy-armoured cavalry

> 'When the men pursued,' they declared, 'there was no escaping them, and when they fled, there was no taking them; and strange missiles are the precursors of their appearance, which pierce through every obstacle before one sees who sent them; and as for the armour of their mail-clad horsemen, some of it is made to force its way through everything, and some of it to give way to nothing.' (Plutarch *Lives: Crassus* 18.3–4).

Clibanarii and *cataphractarii*, when armed with the *contus*, would have been employed as 'shock' cavalry in battle, being a formidable sight when seen by the opposing infantry line charging towards them, and with skill pinning them down sufficiently for the light horse-archers to try and sweep round the flanks.

The effectiveness of 'shock' tactics was reliant on the heavy-armoured cavalry fighting and manoeuvring in close order, otherwise the power of their charge, which formed an almost impregnable wall, would be broken, leaving the individual riders in a vulnerable position owing to their lack of mobility. Heavy-armoured cavalry could also be equipped with a bow as well as a lance. In such instances, the bow would be used initially to inflict panic through heavy losses on the enemy (if they were not similarly equipped), who in such a state would more easily crumble at the sight of a charging mass of lancers (Coulston 1986, 68). If, however, the enemy were comparable in armament, then an archery duel would be fought before both armies resorted to using the *contus*.

The effectiveness of heavy-armoured cavalry in general, has always been disputed. Nolan (1853, 64), stated that heavy cavalry 'are calculated only to show an imposing front in the line of battle, and their history proves them to be more formidable in appearance than in reality.' He then outlined the reasons for this (1853, 68–9):

> If a heavy-armed horseman gallops and exerts himself only for a few minutes, the horse is beat by the weight, and the rider is exhausted in supporting himself and his armour in the saddle . . . : such a man is at the mercy of any light horseman that may turn upon him.
>
> Speed is more than weight: in proportion as you increase weight you decrease speed, and take from your cavalry that impetus which ought to be its principal element.

There were obvious disadvantages to this type of cavalry, particularly the tiring affect of the armour on man and horse, as was noted during the battle of Argentoratum (Strasburg) between the Romans and the Alamanni in AD 357 (Ammianus 16.12.37–8): 'our cavalry, which held the right wing, unexpectedly broke ranks and fled . . . Now that had happened for the reason that while the order of their lines was being re-established, the cavalry in coat-of-mail, seeing their leader slightly wounded and one of their companions slipping over the neck of his horse, which had collapsed under the weight of his armour, scattered in whatever direction they could . . .' In the same battle, however, Ammianus states (16.12.21–2) that the only way the enemy could defeat heavy-armoured cavalry was by sending infantry amidst their cavalry where they could creep about low and unseen, and by piercing the horse's side throw its unsuspecting rider headlong, enabling him to be slain with little trouble.

The lack of mobility of heavy-armoured cavalry, particularly against light cavalry, was undeniable, but as Speidel noted (1984, 154), if they had been the utter failure that some tend to believe, would they really have remained in use in the Roman army from the second to the sixth century? There is no doubt of the impact that *clibanarii* and *cataphractarii* had on their opponents, and the fact that the Romans felt it necessary to adopt this type of cavalry, implies that they were considered to be a worthwhile addition to the army.

Light-armoured cavalry

Light-armoured cavalry, who were sometimes equipped with a bow (see below) were considered to be the most versatile and the most useful of all the styles of mounted troops. They were usually positioned on the flanks of an army, from where they could try to harrass, and hopefully, encircle the enemy's wings.

This type of cavalry was particularly well suited to skirmishing, making constant sallies against the enemy in order to exhaust the infantry and force them to be continually on their guard. Unlike the heavy-armoured cavalry, whose role it was to charge an army directly, the light-armoured mounted troops were specifically equipped to wear down an enemy through persistence. As will be seen, they served many functions which the heavy cavalry were ill-equipped to cope with.

Horse-archers

Horse-archers could be either heavy- or light-armoured. The light horse-archers had greater mobility than the heavy-armoured bow-armed *cataphractarii* and *clibanarii*, which enabled them to be employed in a skirmishing role against both infantry and cavalry. They could also be used to feign flight and draw the enemy out in pursuit to make them more vulnerable.

Their main role in battle was to demoralize and disorganize the enemy, by inflicting heavy losses from a distance. By the sixth century AD, bow-armed cavalry were extensively employed. If both armies were similarly equipped with mounted archers, the battle would initially take the form of an archery duel. If, however, the enemy could not reply in kind, then horse-archers could inflict great carnage, as is demonstrated by a passage from Procopius, when describing the superiority of the Romans over the Goths (*History of the Wars* 5.27.27–8):

> Practically all the Romans and their allies, the Huns, are good mounted bowmen, but not a man among the Goths has had practice in this branch, for their horsemen are accustomed to use only spears and swords, while their bowmen enter battle on foot and under cover of the heavy-armed men. So the horsemen, unless the engagement is at close quarters, have no means of defending themselves against opponents who use the bow, and therefore can easily be reached by the arrows and destroyed; and as for the foot-soldiers, they can never be strong enough to make sallies against men on horseback.

Order of battle

Instructions on the correct positioning of the cavalry for battle, are given by Vegetius (*Epitoma Rei Militaris* 3.16):

> The line of infantry being formed, the cavalry are drawn up on the wings. The heavy horse, that is, those with *loricae*, and troopers armed with lances, should join the infantry. The light cavalry, consisting of the archers and those who have no *loricae*, should be placed at a greater distance. The best and heaviest horse are to cover the flanks of the foot, and the light horse are posted as above mentioned to surround and disorder the enemy's wings. A general should know what part of his own cavalry is most proper to oppose any particular squadrons or troops of the enemy. For from some causes not to be accounted for, some particular units fight better against others . . .
>
> If your cavalry is not equal to the enemy's it is proper, after the ancient custom, to intermingle it with light infantry armed with small shields and trained to this kind of

> service. By observing this method, even though the flower of the enemy's cavalry should attack you, they will never be able to cope with this mixed disposition.

In addition to those men positioned in the lines, there would have been some held in reserve (Vegetius *Epitoma Rei Militaris* 3.17):

> The method of having bodies of reserves in rear of the army, composed of choice infantry and cavalry . . . is very judicious and of great consequence towards the gaining of a battle. Some should be posted in rear of the wings and some near the centre, to be ready to fly immediately to the assistance of any part of the line which is hard pressed, to prevent it being pierced, to supply vacancies made therein during the action and thereby to keep up the courage of their fellow soldiers and check the impetuosity of the enemy.

As Arrian states (Dent 1974, 572), men might also be held in reserve in order to provide protection for the commander: 'Certain squadrons of *equites singulares* . . . and two hundred picked infantry from the legions, the regular headquarters guard, and the officers of the legionary mounted companies will escort the commander. They will constitute a special reserve to deal with unforeseen circumstances.'

Cavalry in action

> Cavalry is essentially an attacking, not a defensive force . . . The cavalry soldier that deliberates is lost. (Marshman 1876, 182).

Cavalry is only an effective arm when it is offensively employed, since once it is forced to become defensive, and is confined in a restricted area, it loses its main advantages of mobility and speed, a point clearly illustrated by this passage from Caesar (*Spanish War* 23):

> And so, in their too eager anxiety to carry destruction within the area of the latter's defence position, they were cut off by enemy squadrons and light-armed troops. Had not their gallantry been of the highest order, they would have been captured alive; for they were, moreover, hemmed in so tightly by the emplacements of the camp as to make it well nigh impossible for a horseman to defend himself in the restricted space.

When cavalry were employed in an offensive role, especially in a charge, they were capable of devastating results. This manoeuvre, however, required certain conditions and a great deal of skill and timing in order for it to be successful. Advice on how to execute a charge is given by Nolan (1853, 279, 281–2):

> The charge must be decided promptly, and executed vigorously; always met, and carried out at speed . . . No distance can be laid down at which to charge, it depends on so many different circumstances. When the ground is favourable and your horses in good condition, you can strike into a gallop sooner; but the burst, the charge itself, must always be reserved till within 50 yards, for in that distance no horse, however bad, can be left behind, nor is there time to scatter, and they fall upon the enemy with the greatest effect.

Cavalry charges were likely to stand a greater chance of success if the enemy had already been demoralized and depleted by light horse-archers, since most writers on military matters agree that well disciplined, determined infantry, could rarely be defeated by this manoeuvre (Nolan 1853, 292–314; Coulston 1986, 68; Strachan 1985, 64–5). One of the main reasons for this is that horses, whenever possible, will avoid a direct collision with an obstacle, and thus when they are confronted by a wall of unyielding spearpoints they will instinctively try to wheel away from them. Only if the infantry has lost its nerve, and the courage needed to hold fast has gone, will the charge be able to break the line and scatter the men in disarray.

Arrian gives advice on how to repel a cavalry charge (Dent 1974, 572):

> If, however, he does persist, and charge home on our heavy infantry centre, then the second and third ranks of the legions will close up on the front, until they are actually touching, so as physically to support them under the shock of impact; thus the attacking horsemen will be confronted with an unbroken and immovable hedge of spearpoints at the level of a horse's chest. Spearmen in the fourth rank will thrust at them, and those of the fifth and following will throw their spears overhand. By this means we cannot fail to repulse the enemy and force him to retire in disorder with heavy losses.

There are numerous instances cited by the ancient authors which vindicate this belief, including this very detailed account from Procopius (*History of the Wars* 1.18.44–8):

> Then the Romans turned their backs to the river so that no movement to surround them might be executed by the enemy, and as best they could under the circumstances were defending themselves against their assailants. And again the battle became fierce, although the two sides were not evenly matched in strength; for foot-soldiers, and a very few of them, were fighting against the whole Persian cavalry. Nevertheless the enemy were not able either to rout them or in any other way to overpower them. For standing shoulder to shoulder they kept themselves constantly massed in a small space, and they formed with their shields a rigid, unyielding barricade, so that they shot at the Persians more conveniently than they were shot at by them. Many a time after giving up, the Persians would advance against them determined to break up and destroy their line, but they always retired again from the assault unsuccessful. For their horses, annoyed by the clashing of the shields, reared up and made confusion for themselves and their riders.

If the cavalry were repulsed by the infantry lines, they then had to perform the difficult task of wheeling their horses round with enough control to allow them to return to their army in an orderly manner. Failure by the cavalry to execute such a manoeuvre successfully could have disastrous consequences (Procopius *History of the Wars* 7.32.16–19):

> But when shortly they reached their own infantry, their misfortune was doubled and trebled. For they did not come to them in an orderly retreat, as with the purpose of recovering their breath and renewing the fight with their assistance, as is customary; indeed they had no intention either of throwing back their pursuers by a massed attack or

> of undertaking a counter pursuit or any other military manoeuvre, but they arrived in such disorder that some of the men were actually destroyed by the onrushing cavalry. Consequently the infantry did not open intervals to receive them, but they all began to flee precipitately with the cavalry, and in the rout they kept killing each other just as in a battle at night.

When the cavalry engaged in close-quarter fighting with infantry, their height advantage would become a very effective means of slashing at the heads and backs of their opponents, although, of course, they themselves would be vulnerable to leg wounds. If, however, they were engaged with enemy cavalry, the wounds incurred would be of a different nature, and the battle itself must have been absolute mayhem, with horses rearing and throwing their riders on to the ground, where they would stand little chance of escaping the hooves of the other mounts. The report of a cavalry officer who fought at the Battle of Balaclava, although comparative, paints a graphic picture of the sheer horror and confusion that was presumably present at all such fights (Warner 1977, 102–3):

> I can't say I saw the man who hit me, we were all in a crowd cutting and hacking at each other, and I did not know till some time after that I was touched when my wrist got stiff, then I found the cut through my coat, it was only bruised for a few days . . . The wounds our long swords made were terrible, heads nearly cut off apparently at a stroke, and a great number must have died who got away. Our corporal who was killed was nearly cut to pieces, his left arm nearly severed in four places, I suppose there must have been a good many at him at once, as he was very strong and a good swordsman. All the Russians seem to cut at the left wrist, so many men lost fingers, and got their hands cut.

One method by which the cavalry could draw the enemy out from their defensive or static positions, making them a more vulnerable target, was to feign a retreat. This tactic was usually performed by light-armoured cavalry, who were obviously the most suitable for this task since it required great speed and mobility, ensuring that the men were not caught by the enemy. An example of this tactic is recorded by Josephus (*Jewish War* 4.1.8.60): 'The craft of Placidus, however, won the day; for when the Jews opened hostilities he feigned flight and having drawn his pursuers far into the plain, suddenly wheeled his cavalry round and routed them.'

Vegetius warns of the dangers of pursuing a retreating enemy without due caution (*Epitoma Rei Militaris* 3.22): 'A rash and inconsiderate pursuit exposes an army to the greatest danger possible, that of falling into ambuscades and the hands of troops ready for their reception. For as the temerity of an army is increased and their caution lessened by the pursuit of a flying enemy, this is the most favourable opportunity for such snares. The greater the security, the greater the danger.'

After the battle

The retreat

> However skilful the manoeuvres, a retreat will always weaken the morale of an army . . . retreats cost always more men and material than the most bloody engagements, with this difference, that in a battle the enemy's loss is nearly equal to your own, whereas in a retreat the loss is on your side only. (Napoleon, *Military Maxims*, Chandler 1987, 57 n.6)

In the event of a retreat, the primary role of the cavalry was to cover the rear of the fleeing infantry, and where possible, to distract the enemy's attention from this vulnerable target. Vegetius suggests ways in which a commander may attempt to rescue his men's morale in such a situation (*Epitoma Rei Militaris* 3.22):

> In the first place your men must not imagine that you retire to decline an action, but believe your retreat an artifice to draw the enemy into an ambuscade or a more advantageous position where you may easier defeat them in case they follow you. For troops who perceive that their general despairs of success are prone to flight. You must be cautious lest the enemy should discover your retreat and immediately fall upon you. To avoid this danger the cavalry are generally posted in front of the infantry to conceal their motions and retreat from the enemy.

The rout

> It is the business of the cavalry to follow up the victory, and to prevent the enemy from rallying. (Napoleon, *Military Maxims*, in Chandler 1987, 73 n.51).

After an enemy had been defeated, it was usually the cavalry's task to prevent the opponents from rallying, and to harry their retreat from the field. The full horror of being pursued by cavalrymen, armed with swords and javelins, is graphically described by Josephus (*Jewish War* 3.2.2.16–18):

> For, once their [the Jews'] front ranks were broken by the cavalry, a rout ensued, and, the fugitives falling foul of those in their rear who were pressing forward to the wall, they became their own enemies, until at length the whole body, succumbing to the cavalry charges, were dispersed throughout the plain. This was extensive and wholly adapted to cavalry manoeuvres, a circumstance which materially assisted the Romans and caused great carnage among the Jews. For the cavalry headed off and turned the fugitives, broke through the crowds huddled together in flight, slaughtering them in masses, and, in whatever direction parties of them fled, the Romans closed them in and, galloping round them, found them an easy mark for their javelins.

If an army was deficient in its mounted arm, the opportunity to achieve a decisive victory was often lost, as is demonstrated by an incident during Caesar's invasion of Britain (*Gallic War* 4.26): 'The moment our men stood firm on dry land, they charged with all their comrades close behind, and put the enemy to rout; but they could not pursue very far, because the cavalry had not been able to hold on their course and make the island [Britain]. Thus one thing was lacking to complete the wonted success of Caesar.'

9 Military records and the supply of horses

Records

From the Republic onwards the Roman army kept detailed records of its personnel, their dates of enlistment and their current locations on specific duties. According to Appian (*Civil War* 3.7), when Mark Antony wanted to know the names of troublesome men in his army, the military tribunes could produce these from their files, 'for it is customary in Roman armies to keep at all times a record of the character of each man'.

Several papyri, principally those from Dura-Europos in Syria, reveal that records were also kept of the horses of an individual unit. It is reasonable to suppose that this practice was uniform throughout the Empire, though the methods used to record information may have differed from province to province. At Dura, three of the surviving texts (*P. Dur.* 56) probably formed part of a roll of letters sent from the provincial governor to the commander of *Cohors XX Palmyrenorum*, assigning mounts to named horsemen. The letters seem to have been pasted end-to-end, possibly in the order that they were received. The roll may have been concerned solely with the matter of assigning horses, rather than a mixture of different types of records. Since there were about 240 *equites* in a normal cohort, and 650 *equites* in the five *turmae* of *Cohors XX Palmyrenorum* (Fink 1971, no.1), a separate file of letters all concerned with one subject would be justifiable (Gilliam 1950, 172, n.5). Another roll was labelled with a docket *epistulae equorum* (*P. Dur.* 130A).

There was probably a standard format for the files on assigning mounts as the letters contain the instruction *in acta ut mos refer*, 'enter in the records according to the usual procedure' (*P. Dur.* 56.A.7–8; 56.C.6; 58.4). The language used in AD 208 (*P. Dur.* 56) had not changed some thirty to forty years later (*P. Dur.* 58), and this again argues for some standardization at least within the unit in question if not over the whole province (Pl.35) (Davies 1969b, 436).

Another papyrus (*P. Dur.* 97) lists some of the men of the cohort together with their horses and may have been compiled using the information in the original letters assigning the mounts to each man. Both the letters and the list of horses detail the age, colour, distinguishing marks and brands, if any, of each horse. The order of the list seems to have been determined by the cavalrymen, and it may be that all the men were from one *turma*, arranged by their date of enlistment, which was the normal method used in other military records. But there is insufficient evidence to be certain of this since the beginning of the roll has not been preserved and this is where there may have been information as to whose *turma* it was. No details are given about the men save for their names, and the document seems to have been drawn up purely for the purpose of listing horses. Where a horse had been lost, this was noted next to the man's name, usually with the date of the loss appended. One entry reads *Malchus Gora amisit equum*, 'Malchus Gora, lost his horse'. No date appears in this entry but dates are given for the others.

The list of horses, present or missing, may have been compiled for the cohort's files, or there may have been two copies, one of which was forwarded to the provincial headquarters as part of a requisition for replacements for horses lost. Unfortunately this cannot be proved, and even if it could it is still not possible to be certain that this was a regular procedure used in all mounted units throughout the Empire, or whether this particular list was drawn up at Dura in especially straitened circumstances due to several losses in minor skirmishes. Since the letters assigning mounts specify for which soldier the horse was destined, the submission of a list naming the men who had lost their horses may have been the approved method of requisitioning remounts. The most direct method would certainly have been to send in a list of names from the *amisit equum* entries, while keeping the complete list in the cohort files. But this is not definitely known to be the case, and there is not enough corroborative evidence from other records either from Syria itself or from other provinces.

The provision of remounts seems to have been supervised by the provincial government, and it is likely that the responsibility for all military horses rested with the governor himself. One of his duties was to prevent the removal from the province of any military horse, as attested by a law quoted in the *Digest* (49.16.12). It dates originally from the second century and was reiterated by the jurist Macer: *equum militarem extra provinciam duci non permittere*.

It is clear from the military records that horses intended for the army were inspected before being passed on to their units, just as recruits were subjected to an initial *probatio* before they were assigned to their cohorts. The terms used to describe both men and horses were the same. In AD 103 the

Prefect of Egypt assigned to one of the cohorts 'six recruits approved by me', *tirones sex probatos a me* (*P. Oxy*. 1022). This is echoed in one of the Dura letters, where a four-year-old horse, reddish in colour, was approved by the governor: *ecum* [sic] *quadrimum rus[seum] . . . probatum a me* (*P. Dur*. 56A).

Although it is stated that the horse was approved by the governor, this need not mean that he carried out a personal inspection of each animal. Presumably he could delegate the tasks of procuring and examining horses to subordinate officials on his staff (Gilliam 1950, 175 no.20). It is not known whether there was a permanent body of men who were assigned to this on a full-time basis. The inspection of a horse would require specialist knowledge and it would have been unwise simply to employ anyone who happened to be available unless he was of proven worth. There would most likely have been men specifically appointed for this purpose. In the later Empire officials known as *stratores*, under the supervision of an *archistrator*, were responsible for remounts (Rostovtzeff 1957, 705 no.40) (see also pp.157f.), and Ammianus relates how the *strator* Constantianus was sent to Sardinia to inspect horses (29.3.5).

At times when there was an urgent need for mounts, it may have been the accepted procedure to ask soldiers to inspect horses, especially if the available mounts were from areas close to their forts. This may be the reason why one of the men from *Cohors XX Palmyrenorum* was listed in the rosters as absent on this duty, *ad equum prob[andum]* (*P. Dur*. 100.38.18). This man, Saedus (son of ?) Magdaeus, had served for twenty-six years in the cohort and should by then have been a good judge of horses (Gilliam, in Welles 1959, 41). In another papyrus (*P. Dur*. 66 PP 12) there appears to be some evidence of a soldier taking individual action in relation to this, but it is not known if these instances were special measures because of a great urgency for remounts, or whether the procedure was normal. It is possible that a soldier would be asked to accompany a higher-ranking member of the provincial government who would then take responsibility for assigning the horse or horses once the soldier had carried out his inspection and given a favourable verdict. Gilliam (1950, 200–1) suggested that some officials may have been given authority to inspect mounts in their areas. As he points out, three types of official apart from the governor approved horses for the Palmyrene cohort at Dura, all high-ranking men; of these one was the provincial procurator (*P. Dur*. 97, 15; 17) and another the *Dux* (*P. Dur*. 97, 21; 23; 24) who was based at Dura and responsible for the defence of the lower Euphrates frontier. These officials may have had to issue their letters assigning mounts through the office of the governor instead of acting independently, but this is not clear. They performed these duties over a period of four years, which suggests that it was a regular occurrence and not an emergency measure (Gilliam 1950, 201).

Besides the term *probatus* the words *aestimatus* and *signatus* appear in the records concerning horses. These are possibly not exactly synonymous with each other but may not denote widely divergent procedures. *Aestimatus* (*P. Dur.* 97, 15) may simply be an alternative to *probatus*, but it could also mean that the horse had been inspected and judged sound but had not undergone the standard test, whatever that may have been. *Signatus* (*P. Dur.* 97, 21; 23) may be more precise. Gilliam (1950, 202) thought it meant that the horse had been marked in some way, indicating that it had been officially approved. It may denote that the horse had been branded, just as *signaculum* with relevance to soldiers may mean that they had been tattooed. Davies (1969b, 447) suggested that *signatus* distinguished a secondary stage after *probatio*, during which the horse underwent its initial training, and if the performance was up to standard it would be 'certified' or *signatus*. Whatever its meaning, *signatus* does not occur in the records as often as *probatus*, and it may merely indicate that a horse had been received and 'signed for' by the official concerned, in each case the *Dux*, not the governor. But *probatus* was also used of the *Dux* so the distinction was not necessarily made on account of his office.

The horse was probably regarded as part of the soldier's equipment, for which money was stopped from his pay. 125 *denarii* seems to have been the standard amount charged to the soldiers for horses in the Dura records. The list of mounts (*P. Dur.* 97) was written by one clerk and the columns of figures denoting the amounts charged for the horses were added by a different person. In one instance he made a mistake by writing the amount next to the name of a man who had lost his horse and the figure was sponged out (*P. Dur.* 97, 13; Gilliam 1950, 205). It is not known how the 125 *denarii* related to the market value of horses; it was presumably a figure set by the military authorities and not the actual price of the animal. Gilliam (1950, 180–1) states that it is higher than prices of horses in Egypt, but lower than the probably excessive prices of AD 367 and 401 in the *Codex Theodosianus* (11.1.29; 17.1 and 2). But comparison between provinces is not especially helpful and mid-third century prices probably bear no relation to later values when inflation had set in.

The amount of 125 *denarii* varies only slightly in the records, and seems to have been fairly constant for many years. A hundred-and-something *denarii* (the exact figure is not clear) was the price of a horse in AD 139 (Fink 1971, 75). In AD 208, two soldiers each paid 125 *denarii*, and in the Dura list of AD 251, nine of the ten horses were charged at the same price. For some reason which is hard to discern, one of the horses in this list was treated differently (*P. Dur.* 97, 16). The amount is divided into two parts, which if added together total 100 *denarii*; the entry reads *XXXXV et [e] quaesus LV*, '45 and 55 *denarii* from the treasury'. Perhaps the soldier paid 45 *denarii* and the treasury paid the rest, but it is not clear why the amount was only 100 *denarii* in total instead of 125, and whether 'from the treasury' means that the rest of the money came from either regimental funds or from the provincial headquarters. This must remain an unexplained special case, since there is insufficient information to throw any light on it.

If the market price of horses had suddenly risen it is to be expected that the military authorities would have to extract more from the soldiers to cover the expense, but the machinery for buying horses is imperfectly understood. It may be that the 125 *denarii* was all that was paid to the vendor under the terms of military requisitions, but it is much more likely that the provincial government paid for the horses at their market value and there was probably a fund set aside for this. It is not known if the 125 *denarii* stopped from the soldiers' pay was returned to the provincial coffers, and it is equally uncertain whether the soldier paid for the first cavalry mount or received it free on being made a cavalryman. Nor is it clear whether he then paid for every new mount whatever the circumstances in which it had been lost, including either in battle or from disease, neither of which can always be attributed to negligence. When the soldier left the service he may have been able to keep his horse, but it is likely that since horses were always urgently needed in the army, the age and condition of the animal having been taken into account, the horse may have been given to someone else. In this case, when he retired, a soldier may have been refunded the amount he had paid for the horse; or if he did not have to pay for the first one, he may have had to surrender his mount as a matter of course. In some instances the horses belonging to men who had died or been killed in battle were possibly redistributed among the ranks as replacements.

It is possible that there were always some men without horses in Roman cavalry units. Horse strength was probably never exactly equal to the numbers of men, and even if on occasions the required quantity was achieved or even exceeded, the numbers of animals unfit for work and soon to be sold or otherwise disposed of would always have to be taken into consideration. In a strength report of the Canadian North West Mounted Police for 1878, for instance, the number of horses was not sufficient for the numbers of men and wagons at each post, and of the ones which were listed some were too young and some were ready for disposal, so that the effective horse strength was very much less than the already inadequate paper strength (Turner 1950, 425 and 428). This sort of situation could well have applied to some Roman units.

It is not certain whether spare horses were kept at forts ready for immediate use whenever a horse was lost. Although it might be expected that this would be the case, the papyrological evidence seems to argue against it. Horses were assigned to the men at Dura from a central authority, if not from a central pool stock, and this would seem to indicate that it was not provincial policy to maintain reservoirs of horses at each fort, unless of course the situation at Dura was so bad that the cohort had already used up its spare horses and was down to rock-bottom levels. Unfortunately it is unknown whether the papyrological evidence represents normal everyday circumstances or whether the procedures were irregular and unusual, and applicable only to one province at one time.

As Gilliam remarked, if the Dura list of mounts was representative of the state of the entire cohort, it was not well prepared for action, since seven out of 20 men were without horses (1950, 196, no.110). On closer analysis, the situation could possibly have been even more serious. The list dates from AD 251, and of the 13 surviving horses, five had been assigned in that same year (Gilliam 1950, 197 no.117).

Horse losses

There were various probable reasons for horse losses, ranging from occasional outright neglect, through outbreaks of disease sometimes of epidemic proportions, to accidents and of course slaughter in combat. Horse wastage caused through neglect can sometimes be attributed to ignorance and lack of training on the part of the men. It is unnecessary and unacceptable but it is an incontrovertible fact that it happened. With some notable exceptions, the French cavalrymen of the eighteenth and nineteenth centuries did not look after their mounts as good horsemen should. It was said that during the Napoleonic wars it was possible to smell the sore backs of their horses from a considerable distance. The situation was repeated in 1918, when virtually every horse belonging to the French cavalry at Damascus had a sore back. This stemmed from the fact they carried such an enormous amount of kit which, though very neatly stowed, made taking the saddle off and putting it back a very laborious procedure. Consequently the horses were hardly ever unsaddled and the men compounded the situation by remaining in the saddle while halted (Preston 1921, 319). Neglect was not confined to sore backs. In 1812 when the French cavalry was marching to Moscow, thousands of animals died of colic because they were allowed to graze freely and unsupervised at nights on green grain and clover, whereas the Germans and Poles in Napoleon's army cut forage and fed their horses regularly and properly (Elting 1988, 319). Similar problems were faced by all armies, and Roman units probably differed widely in their treatment of horses. Ultimately everything depends on the attitudes of the soldiers, and more particularly on the officers and their knowledge of horses, their ability to train the men and to enforce the regulations which they themselves must lay down. Some officers in later armies were absolutely meticulous, such as General Sebastiani of Napoleon's 2nd Cavalry Corps, whose horse inspections were called 'pitiless' by one of his officers, Rilliet. But as this officer came to realize, the strict enforcement of rules was vital, since 'cavalry can only survive by paying attention to details which have to do with care of horses' (Johnson 1978, 120). Sentiment probably played little part in this. Even inanimate motor transport and other machinery require maintenance; what is necessary is efficiency based on knowledge, both of which are sometimes sadly lacking.

Horse deaths from diseases would be common. It is doubtful if the facts of contagion were understood by the Romans, and the practice of isolating sick animals was probably rarely adopted. Some treatments specified by the ancient authors would have been effective, but others would have been positively detrimental if not lethal, and there were probably many deaths which nowadays would not be inevitable. During campaigns some of the Roman cavalry may have been out of action or may have had to fight on foot. Such occurrences were not uncommon in later armies. At the Battle of Blenheim for instance, 1200 French dragoons fought on foot because their horses had died of disease (Cowles 1983, 224). In the Roman army, as in any other, there were probably injuries which could have been avoided. There were possibly some accidents during training and exercising, resulting in broken legs or other damage which could not be healed. In France between 1914 and 1918 the majority of the cases for surgical treatment were due to kicks from other horses. Those which sustained fractures in this way had to be destroyed (Blenkinsop and Rainey 1925, 548–9). Hip injuries were also quite common and were caused by insufficient care and attention in leading horses through gateways when a horse was turned too sharply or allowed to become restive. Loose fencing posts, wires and jagged timbers also caused injuries (Blenkinsop and Rainey 1925, 633–5). By far the most common complaint was damage to, or diseases of, the feet (Blenkinsop and Rainey 1925, 360, 556–8, 634, 658–9), and the maxim 'no foot, no horse' assuredly applies to all armies at all periods.

Theft should not be discounted as a reason for horse losses in the Roman army though numbers are impossible to estimate. Josephus relates how some of Titus' troops consistently had their horses stolen (*Jewish War* 6.152–3). It is likely that on some occasions horses stampeded and escaped. Success in recovering these may have been only partial, as both US Cavalry and the North West Mounted Police records attest. Some horses escaped by stampeding in France in 1914 (Blenkinsop and Rainey 1925, 658). The standard form for 'Returns of casualties in horses' during the First World War was divided into the following sections: sick with units; died or killed; destroyed; and missing; indicating that the latter case was accepted as unavoidable loss. In April 1917 in operations around Gaza, 317 horses and mules were killed, 10 died of disease or exhaustion, 30 had to be destroyed and 80 were listed as missing (Blenkinsop and Rainey 1925, 44; 186). Gilliam (1950, 197–8) suggested that at Dura the most likely explanation for the loss of horses would be the continuous border skirmishes and raids, and possibly internal disorders which the cohort was called upon to suppress. According to Gilliam's argument, these events would be too unimportant to merit attention from the chroniclers. But there is no real evidence that this was the case, and even if it were, there would also be horse losses from the other aforementioned causes. Unfortunately the papyrus records merely state that a horse had been lost and do not indicate the cause. The normal wear and tear on a unit's horses is difficult to estimate, but it must be borne in mind that not all losses were necessarily sustained from enemy action.

Whatever the 'normal' losses sustained by army units stationed on the frontiers, in war they would naturally be increased on all counts. The likelihood of accidents would probably be greater and the spread of contagious diseases exacerbated by congregating animals in large groups. In some cases cold and wet weather compounded by bad feeding may have been responsible for a considerable number of horse deaths, especially on active service. In later times, bad weather and lack of supplies certainly played a great part in reducing horse numbers. In the United States during the plains campaigns in the winter of 1868–9, Sheridan was forced to use some of his cavalry as infantry because of horse deaths, and in March 1869 Custer lost 276 horses in three days (Utley 1973, 152–3; 158–9). In other cases, lack of both constant vigilance and adequate preparation was responsible for reduced horse numbers. For instance, in 1805 the Austrian government found itself in the situation of going to war against Napoleon with an estimated 37,000 cavalry without mounts (Fournier 1914 Vol.1, 358 no.1).

In the Roman army, shortages of horses perhaps did not reach such disastrous proportions but instances are recorded where cavalry operated without horses because none were available. Octavian had 500 cavalry without mounts at Tauromenium when he was attacked by Sextus Pompey (Appian, *Civil War* 5.110). Jones (1973, 646) quotes a letter of Synesius relating how the *Dux* Cerialis took command of a unit of mounted archers and sold all the horses, so 'they became just archers'.

Remounts

Provision of remounts would ideally operate on two levels, one on a provincial basis to cope with the day-to-day administrative needs of the units stationed in a province, and the other on a completely different, Empire-wide level when major wars were being fought. In normal circumstances a provincial unit could probably still remain operational without its full complement of horses as it was perhaps possible to wait until sick or injured horses were fully recovered. These animals would remain on the rosters and so would not need replacing. Only dead animals and those to be destroyed would be struck from the records, thereby creating a need for remounts. In warfare, injured horses, and those which had gone lame or were simply too debilitated to continue, could well be eventually nursed back to health, but once out of action they would need to be replaced just as urgently as dead animals if the various units were to remain in operation. The needs of an army on active campaign and those of a provincial army policing and controlling its own territory are quite different.

Replacement would not be a simple matter of finding, receiving and allocating the horses, for they would not be trained for the Roman cavalry. A similar problem was faced by later armies in times of shortages. In 1812, after the march to Moscow, the French replaced 64,000 horses by purchase, requisition and donation, but of these only the 4000 transferred from the gendarmerie had been properly schooled (Johnson 1989, 122). In the Boer War, which wasted horses by the thousand, any remounts became very difficult to obtain, and *trained* remounts were impossible to find, and the cavalry virtually ceased to exist (Pakenham 1979, 327–8). One of the problems was a lack of veterinary supplies, so that severely exhausted and debilitated horses which could have been saved were simply shot (Tylden 1965, 30). In the First World War horses that were returned to the front having convalesced were much preferred to unseasoned remounts (Blenkinsop and Rainey 1925, 189).

Very little is known about how the Romans obtained remounts for their troops, either within the provinces or during wars. There was probably some central organization and a well established bureaucracy in each province, in preference to a system that left everything to individual unit commanders, which would probably have resulted in great inequality of horse provision. It is assumed from the military records that since the governor and other high officials were involved in the provision of horses for the army, the remount service must have operated at a provincial level, and indeed it would make sense to combine the resources of the province and organize the supply of animals (including both cavalry mounts and baggage mules) under some form of central control. It is possible that the term *equisio*, or *equiso*, denotes someone who had responsibility for obtaining or checking supplies of horses. The governor's *equisio* at Vindolanda may have been more than just his personal groom. The *equisiones* of the inscription found near Aquincum were attached to *Legio II Adiutrix* (*CIL* III 13370) and their function is unknown.

In the late Empire, the officials called *stratores* under an *archistrator* (Rostovtzeff 1957, 705 n.40), and commanded by the *comes stabuli* were responsible for the levy of horses for the court and the cavalry (Jones 1973, 373). Instructions about remounts were issued to *stratores* in the *Codex Theodosianus* (6.31.1). During the Principate, legionary legates and provincial governors numbered *stratores* among their staff. These have been interpreted as grooms or stable masters, and also as guards since they were commanded in one case by a legionary centurion who was also in charge of the *singulares* (*CIL* XIII 8203 = *ILS* 2418; Speidel 1974, 544). This argument about their function is not conclusive: a legionary centurion would be quite capable of commanding two batches of men performing different tasks. Besides it is not certain how many *stratores* would be included under his command. It is possible that *stratores* were few in number and that they were connected with the remount service. It has to be conceded that there is no proof of their main functions, and it is only in the later history of the Empire that *stratores* were definitely linked with the provision of horses.

In Britain, a *strator consularis* who died at Irchester (Fig.59) (*RIB* 233) has been linked with the remount service or more specifically with horse breeding. A possible *strator* from Dover (only the first two letters, ST, are

59 The tombstone of Anicius Saturninus, described as *Strator Consularis* (*RIB* 233). It has been suggested that Anicius may have been an official employed in the remount service to the army, and there may have been a horse-breeding centre at Irchester. (Redrawn by K.R. Dixon.)

extant on the inscription) was translated as 'transport officer' (*Britannia* 8, 1977, 427). This is a modern interpretation not based on any evidence, but it is perhaps more descriptive than 'groom', which can be misleading. The officer may have been concerned not so much with stable management and the welfare of horses, as with ensuring that there were some horses to be managed.

The British Army *Remount Manual* (War Office, 1937a), greatly influenced by the experiences of the First World War, distinguished between two types of remount depots, one a base depot behind the lines and the other on the lines of communication, known as an advanced remount depot. It was stipulated that two separate routes should be established for the transport of base remount horses to the front and for horses being returned from the front to the separate veterinary establishments, so as to avoid infection. Spare horses were to be returned to the remount depots to be reallocated.

The Roman organization was probably not so sophisticated. It is not certain whether there would have been a ready stock of remounts on campaigns, nor whether sick, injured and exhausted horses were cared for and returned to the army once they had recovered. Practice probably varied according to availability of animals and staff. The Emperor Maurice stated the necessity of keeping reserve horses with the army, but they should be left in camp and not taken to the battle lines unless this was unavoidable, when they should be positioned behind the second or support line with the baggage (*Strategikon* 4.8; 5.2).

Supply of horses

Several means of obtaining horses would have been available. Sometimes horses were received *en masse*, for instance after the conclusion of a war the terms of a treaty might stipulate that the defeated enemy must provide horses. The 5500 Sarmatians raised by Marcus Aurelius and sent to Britain no doubt provided their own mounts (Dio 71.16). When the Quadi sued for peace in AD 169–70 large numbers of horses and cattle were given to the Romans (Dio 72.11). Special methods could be adopted to obtain horses in times of war. Germanicus accepted weapons and horses from Italy and the provinces of Spain and Gaul to make up the losses of the campaigns of AD 15 (Tacitus *Annals* 1.71). In AD 69 civilians who sided with Vitellius voluntarily offered horses (Tacitus *Histories* 1.57). One of the least expensive means of keeping up horse numbers in warfare was to capture some of the enemy's. Scipio gained gold, silver, ivory and horses in this way (Appian *Roman History* 8.4.23). This method of obtaining horses was employed by most armies throughout history. Napoleon wrote in his Order of the Day to the Army of Italy on 9 May 1796 that 'the sole valid prizes are horses captured in battle' (Howard 1961, 112).

It is unknown how the Roman administration dealt with the sudden influx of large numbers of horses raised in these different ways. The animals may have been distributed immediately to the units which needed them, or kept at a few central depots as reserves. Much would depend on the conduct of the war and the particular needs of the troops, and on efficient paperwork by the army clerks to collate the information on where the horses were needed most.

When a large number of horses were received all at once, some measures would have to be taken for the receipt and inspection of the new mounts, entering them in official records, and feeding and housing them temporarily until they were eventually allocated to various units. On campaigns, such depots would probably be temporary and leave little archaeological trace. Post and rail fencing and picket lines may have been used to control the horses, either outside permanent forts to which the animals could be delivered, or at temporary depots set up for the purpose. There would probably be a need to divide the animals into groups. Some may have been rejected on physical or other grounds, though it could be argued that if it was a treaty arrangement unsuitable horses would not have been accepted since it would contravene the terms. Some, if not all, of the horses would need at least rudimentary schooling for the cavalry, and it is unknown whether this was carried out by the army staff when the horses were received or by the soldiers of the units to which the horses were allocated.

The provision of horses by treaty arrangement at the end of a war was probably at best an arbitrary and variable method of supply. It is true that some treaties stipulated that a certain number of animals and/or men should be provided annually, but others simply demanded a single contribution. Commodus concluded peace with the Quadi and Marcomanni in AD 180 on this basis, when he raised a large number of troops immediately, but also relieved the tribes of an annual contribution thereafter (Dio 72.2). The Roman army would probably need an additional and more regular source of supply to ensure provision of horses to all units during their normal operational duties and not all provinces would have been able to rely upon a supply of animals by treaty arrangements.

Requisitioning was another method whereby the army could keep its horse numbers up to the required level. When circumstances demanded it, this may have been temporarily brought into operation in certain provinces all through the history of the Empire. The requisition of horses may be the reason why an unknown number of cavalrymen were absent from their unit on campaign in Dacia at some time between AD 100 and 105. They had left the province across the Erar (possibly a river), to collect horses (Fink 1971, n.63). Sometimes requisitioning may have been of an unofficial and probably unrecorded nature. According to Tylden, the first priority of an unmounted soldier is to steal a horse (1965, 24). The Napoleonic French cavalry occasionally augmented its horse numbers in this way, as infantry, sutlers and camp followers eagerly 'picked up' horses as they found them (Elting 1988, 316).

In the fourth and fifth centuries AD official requisitioning of horses became common, as is shown by the *Codex Theodosianus* (6.31; 11.17 and 18). Tax payments of horses were commuted into money payments, probably because the system was unsatisfactory. Provincials supplied horses which were unsuitable, and persuaded the officials to accept them by means of bribes, so that army authorities probably received mounts which they could not use. Instead of producing a horse, provincials were to contribute specified equivalents in cash, as stipulated in the *Codex* (6.31).

It was probably not adequate to rely totally on the process of requisitioning during the period of the Empire and there must have been times when the system broke down altogether when supplies were exhausted. Tacitus (*Annals* 2.5) describes just such a situation in Gaul. It is reasonable to expect that in each province the Romans made some efforts to breed horses for the army (Davies 1969b, 453–4; Applebaum 1972, 218) but very little is known of Imperial stud farms and horse breeding for military purposes until the late Empire, when there were stud farms in Thrace and eastern Asia Minor where horses were bred for the army (Jones 1973, 671; Rostovtzeff 1957, 647–8 n.92). With regard to the early Empire, the ancient authors were much more concerned with horses for the circus and the races, rather than the army, and although Varro listed the best horse-rearing areas of the late Republic (*De Re Rustica* 2.7.1 and 6) and Columella devotes several chapters to horse breeding in general (*De Re Rustica* 6.27 to 29), there is little specific information on cavalry horses and where or how they may have been obtained.

As has been mentioned, in Britain the presence of a *strator consularis* at Irchester (*RIB* 233) has sometimes been linked with horse breeding, but there is no proof. Likewise there is no evidence to support Richmond's suggestion that the Sarmatians at Ribchester undertook horse breeding in the area when they retired from the army (1945, 22–3). Yet at the same time, as Davis has pointed out in connection with medieval war-horses, if an army requires large numbers of horses, it cannot simply wait for natural developments to provide them, and eventually some form of breeding programme must be instituted (1983, 5). Furthermore, Major General

Rimington who had observed the hardiness of the Boer ponies as against the unsuitability of the imported English mounts, always maintained that the most suitable horses for use in any country were those which were native to that country (Rogers 1959, 230). Selective breeding from the animals that were available would be a reasonable method by which to ensure supplies of cavalry mounts, and this was possibly instituted in most provinces. Nobis (1973, 250) in examining the skeletons and teeth of 31 horses at Krefeld-Gellep, concluded that the larger horses had been bred from selected smaller ones, and this procedure was already in operation in the first century since the horses were probably killed in the Batavian revolt of AD 69.

If the army regularly took steps to breed many of their own mounts there would presumably be military stud farms in the best locations for horse rearing, where there was a plentiful supply of fodder. As Hyland (1990, 76–7) points out, horses withdrawn from military service because of injuries or other causes, would still have been useful for breeding purposes. It may have been a regular practice to use retired military horses in this way. As an alternative to military stud farms there may have been civilian contractors who undertook to supply horses to the army, subject to inspection by the military authorities but relieving them of the administration of breeding centres. But it has to be admitted that there is not a shred of evidence for this. As Tylden points out (1965, 12), breeders (whether civilian or military) need civilian outlets where horses unsuitable for the army can be sold, since in breeding horses it is not possible to achieve a hundred per cent success rate.

In addition to breeding from specially selected native ponies, it would be reasonable to suppose that the Romans also imported horses into certain provinces to improve the stock, at least at first. There is not much proof of this, however, despite Azzaroli's assertion that it was so (1985, 155; 172). The literary evidence does not provide sufficient detail, save that Caesar stated that in contrast to the Gauls, the Germans did not import horses to upgrade their herds (*Gallic War* 1.48). Skeletal evidence is too sparse in most provinces to draw any conclusions about the origins and breeds of the horses used by the cavalry. As Azzaroli points out (1985, 162) the development of horse breeds is not as easy to trace as it is in other animals, such as dogs, and the size and build of a horse is not always indicative of breed. At Newstead, Ewart distinguished between unimproved native British breeds and larger slender-limbed ponies 'built on the lines of the smaller breeds of modern Arabs'. These he thought may have been brought to Britain from Gaul, where the native breeds may have been improved by cross-breeding with Spanish or North African types (Curle 1911, 362–71).

It is not known if there was a deliberate policy of importing horses into various provinces, either for the purposes of breeding from them, or simply as remounts. But it is quite likely that the military authorities in each province at least aimed for self-sufficiency in the provision of horses, even if they did not always achieve it.

As Gilliam points out (1950, 177 n.32) the military records from Dura do not specify the nationality of the horses and it is to be expected that they all came from Syria. In contrast, in Rome itself racehorses were recorded by their name and nationality because horses would be imported from all over the Empire. A Cappadocian horse is mentioned at Dura (*P. Dur.* 56c) but this could be taken as an indication of breed rather than place of origin and so does not necessarily mean that the horse had been imported into the province; it could have been bred in Syria.

Within most provinces suitable horses may have been purchased at all times on the open market, even if the army also undertook to breed from a selection of native horses, because mounts of good quality should not be missed and because demand may sometimes have exceeded supply. One reason for employing high-ranking officials to take responsibility for approving horses, apart from the absolute necessity of ensuring that they were physically sound, may have been to establish a fair price so that neither party was cheated and to avoid legal wrangling. Horse dealers in all periods have hardly been regarded as the most honest members of the community.

The horses arrived at Dura all year round, possibly as and when they were needed, and it does not seem that there were deliveries of horses in batches, say at half-yearly or annual intervals (Gilliam 1950, 173 n.8). If the remount service was able to provide horses when demand arose, this may indeed imply the existence of central depots whence stock could be drawn at any time, but it is not known how long the men who received mounts at Dura had been without horses. It seems less likely, however, that the remount service would wait for requests to be sent to them and then despatch someone to look for the requisite number of horses from whatever source they could be found to fill the gaps. The process was probably continuous, and the most sensible way of ensuring supplies would be to maintain a pool stock at a central depot or several depots if the province was a large one. These would be situated in the best areas for forage and supplies, not necessarily hard by the frontiers or the forts themselves. It is possible that in some instances breeding centres and remount depots may have been linked, staffed by government officials and/or soldiers seconded to these areas, who were responsible for the initial training of young horses and remounts obtained from a variety of sources. In Britain The Lunt at Baginton near Coventry is a likely candidate, though this is conjectural. The association of the site with the training of horses is probable, but its use as a remount depot as well is only a possibility.

10 Roman cavalry mounts

The ideal horse

Much of what the ancient authors have to say about the ideal qualities of a horse appertains to racers and chariot horses rather than to cavalry mounts, but at least it was recognized that different characteristics were necessary in horses intended for different purposes. Varro (*De Re Rustica* 2.7.15) lists the qualities of horses to be used for warfare, transport, breeding and the circus, and Vegetius (*Ars Mulomedicinae* 3.6.2) divides horses into three categories: for war, the circus and for riding, with the best types for each category. As Varro points out, all horses should not be judged and valued by the same standards.

Latin authors list the points to look for in any horse. Virgil (*Georgics* 3.74–90) describes an extremely noble steed, high stepping, brave, with a high neck, clean-cut head, short belly, plump back and a well-muscled chest, and a thick mane falling to the right. Columella (*De Re Rustica* 29.1–4) agrees with this description, adding that the ideal horse should have wide nostrils and straight legs. All this makes sense in a military context. Open nostrils denote better air intake (Hyland 1990, 6) and therefore stamina, straight legs mean that there should be no strain on the joints, and a broad chest indicates better respiration and more strength. If a horse's mane falls to the right, it leaves the left side of the neck free and more sensitive to instructions which the rider wishes to convey with his left hand, while his right hand holds his weapon.

By far the best advice on military horses is to be found in Xenophon (*Art of Horsemanship* 1.2–17). He recommends that inspection should begin with the feet and work up, listing the common faults with hooves and legs and the problems which cause lameness; Xenophon laid great emphasis on speed in a horse.

When the Roman military authorities inspected horses they would of course rely upon their experience to select the mounts most suitable for their purpose. The responsibility for this could not be delegated to men without knowledge of either the army or of horses. Shortage of suitable men in Mesopotamia in 1916 led to the purchase of many animals that were either too young or too ill to be used, features which were obvious at a glance to trained and experienced veterinary officers but not to the men who had been sent to buy them (Blenkinsop and Rainey 1925, 298). It is quite likely that such wastage also occurred in the Roman army because of lack of personnel.

As mentioned above it is unfortunately not possible to discern precisely the different breeds of horses from skeletal evidence (Azzaroli 1985, 162). The shape of the skull and the coarseness or fineness of the limbs provide clues as to appearance and broad general type. From bone evidence, Ewart was able to divide the Newstead horses into 'broad-browed big-boned ponies . . . from 11.2 hands to 12.2 hands', slender-limbed ponies of the 'Celtic' type, just a little larger, and 14-hands horses of the Libyan variety 'built on the lines of the finer kinds of desert Arabs' (in Curle 1911, 368).

The horses on most Roman tombstones and sculptures were not intended to be faithful portrayals of particular breeds, and though it might be possible to draw some vague generalizations about the characteristics of the animals, artistic representations are at best an unreliable guide. Likewise the idealized horses of noble equestrian statues and those depicted on monuments such as Trajan's Column. It has been pointed out that there are different types of horses on this last monument which are intended to represent 'an awareness of different horse types' (Davison 1989, 146). The Roman cavalrymen ride horses with heavy bodies and light legs, with light manes and a high-set tail; the Moorish cavalry horses have concave heads and rounded noses, long necks and flowing manes. The enemy, Sarmatians and Dacians, ride smaller horses.

But whilst the differences in appearance may represent the sculptors' intentions to distinguish breeds, the portrayals are not perhaps to be taken as the literal truth. They could be artistic but stylized stereotypes employed as indicators of the different kinds of troops which took part in the wars.

Vegetius (*Ars Mulomedicinae* 3.6.2) listed horses by their country of origin, which is not exactly the same as breed, and since he was writing in the fourth century the list is not necessarily indicative of the types of horses used by the Romans in the preceding three centuries. Sources of supply and centres of breeding may not have remained constant over such a long period. Nor is it possible to assert that the horses that Vegetius mentions were imported in large numbers from their countries of origin. Though this may have been the case it is equally possible that the named types of horses were bred within the Empire as well, from stock brought in some time in the past.

Of the favoured breeds, the Numidian or Libyan horses were generally most admired, at least in the early Empire. These terms, together with the more general 'African', probably all refer to the same breed (Hyland 1990, 11). Aelian (*De Animalia* 3.2) says that the Libyan horses 'are exceedingly swift and know little or nothing of fatigue; they are slim and not well fleshed but are fitted to endure the scanty attention paid to them by their masters'. Appian has nothing but praise for the Numidian horses (*Roman History* 8.2.11; 8.7.41; 8.14.100) and Frontinus describes how the Numidian auxiliaries in Quintus Minucius' army took the enemy by surprise in 192 BC, by pretending to be bad horsemen until they spied their chance and suddenly dashed through the lines, wreaking havoc as they went. Thus fine appearance in a war-horse is not always necessary; it is performance that counts.

Size of horses

Paulo ante vesperam visus est Firmus, equo celsiori insidens. 'A little before evening, Firmus was seen, mounted on a tall horse' (Ammianus 29.5.48). This quotation raises the question as to what, in AD 373, constituted a tall horse? It would be extremely useful if the size of Roman cavalry horses could be established since it affects everything to do with them, including harness, stabling, their mobility and their uses in peace and war.

In order to estimate the size of horses, historians and archaeologists are limited by the evidence available to them. It is unfortunate that the military records concerning cavalry horses in which age, colour and distinguishing marks are so meticulously recorded, provide no clues as to horse sizes. This negative evidence can be used to support two contradictory arguments: either that some effort was made within each unit or indeed each province to obtain horses of a standard height, in which case there would be no need to record these details in the descriptions of each horse; or that within certain limits, rigid adherence to a standard size was not considered an important factor, and there was considerable variation. Analogy with modern practice favours the first possibility; the skeletal evidence from Roman sites favours the second.

On the subject of horse size, ancient literature is not much more helpful in that it provides little more than adjectival descriptions such as the one quoted above, which do not help very much without some more precise yardstick. For instance, Caesar considered the horses of his German allies unsuitable, and he remounted the tribesmen on horses taken from the military tribunes and re-enlisted veterans (*Gallic War* 7.65). Previously he had described the horses of the Germans as *prava atque deformia*, 'crooked and mis-shapen', but he admitted they were strong and efficient (*Gallic War* 4.2). In some translations this description is rendered as small and ugly.

Prava 'crooked' could easily be a mistake for *parva* 'small', and it is quite likely that the horses were not very tall, since Caesar describes how the German horsemen were accompanied by footmen who ran with the cavalry, supporting themselves by holding on to the manes of the horses and so keeping pace with them (*Gallic War* 1.48). This suggests, but does not prove, that the horses were small, and this may be the reason why Caesar found them unsuitable. If this is so, how small was small to a general of the late Roman Republic? What was the quality which Caesar looked for in a horse and why did the German ones not come up to his standard? Without reliable statistics, literature can do no more than provide hints.

The same can be said of artistic and sculptural representations of horses. It is difficult to ignore the vast quantity of sculpture from all over the Empire and from all periods of its history, but it is also fraught with hazard to place too great a reliance upon such a source of information and to endow it with any accuracy, because there are so many problems. It is possible for instance that the size of the horses in some sculpture was deliberately scaled down to emphasize the importance of the rest of the scene (Coulston 1986, 62). The horses in most sculptures whilst not reduced to mere stylization are not portraits of specific animals, and some of the more crude or unskilled representations are hardly to be taken seriously. It may be possible to assert that some of the horses in Roman art probably represented a reasonably acceptable norm to a Roman observer, in that they would have appeared neither impossibly small nor impossibly large, but within these two vague parameters there is room for considerable variation. Davison (1989, 146) suggests that the horses of the Roman auxiliaries shown on Trajan's Column represent the typical ideal cavalry mount of an average size of about 14 hands. But it is questionable whether these sculptures depict an accurate record of the horses or merely an idealized and ennobled view of them, and more important, it is questionable whether ideal appearance and average size had any relevance to the daily life of a Roman cavalry unit, which would operate not with ideals and averages, but with actualities, and would adapt accordingly.

The most reliable guide to the size of Roman horses is the evidence to be deduced from the bones of animals discovered on various sites, but even this is not straightforward and without its problems. It is only rarely that entire skeletons are discovered that can provide accurate statistics of horse sizes. For the most part, size has to be estimated from the relevant long bones of partial skeletons, and in many excavation reports measurements are not given, so that it is not always possible to draw definite conclusions about size and build of the animals (Luff 1982, 136).

In the past it was thought that the excavated remains of horses from

Roman sites seemed to fall into three groups, consisting of small, medium and large animals. Ewart divided the Newstead horses into three categories, one of 14 hands and over, a medium range of 12–13 hands and a smaller one of under about 12 hands (1911, 362–77). The Corbridge remains also seemed to fit into similar categories (Meek and Grey 1911, 84).

The threefold division of horse sizes noted at Newstead and Corbridge was not repeated at Krefeld-Gellep, where many Roman horses were found over an extended period of excavation. These are dated to sometime in the first century, since one of them lay underneath a layer of burnt debris of second-century date, and the excavator suggested that the horses belonged to the scene of the last stand of the Batavian auxiliaries in their revolt against Rome in AD 69 (Pirling 1978, 138). Of the 31 horses from Krefeld described by Nobis only two were of 11.2 and 12.2 hands high. The rest varied from 13.2 to 15.1 hands high. Larger horses, one 'approaching modern size', were found at Dormagen (Müller 1979a, 73), and a horse of 15.3 hands high was found at Frocester Court Villa in Britain.

Where measurements such as these have been obtained, it is perfectly true that the archaeological record so far supports the average size of the horses of Trajan's Column, as interpreted by Davison. 'The excavated data . . . seems to suggest an average height of around 14 hands' (Bishop 1988, 111). But it must be remembered that averages are calculated from a range of sizes, and in reality the skeletal remains of horses so far discovered show that the size of the animals ranged from just over 10 hands to 15 hands and more. The use of averages can be misleading and it is but a short step to the declaration that the Romans all rode cavalry horses of about 14 to 14.2 hands, which is not sufficiently precise.

In connection with the Krefeld-Gellep horses, Nobis suggested that the smaller ones may have belonged to the Batavians and the larger ones to the Romans but this cannot be proved (1973, 250). There is a constant desire on the part of most authors to classify the smaller horses as something other than cavalry mounts, possibly because the use of such small mounts detracts from the dignified and noble view of the Roman army that has unconsciously been built up and absorbed. A formula has evolved that explains away the incontrovertible skeletal evidence: small beast equals baggage animal, larger beast equals cavalry mount, very large beast equals officer's mount. This may of course be entirely accurate but it is not based on solid proof, so it remains a matter of personal opinion and conjecture.

It is worth noting in relation to baggage animals that at Gergovia Caesar gave his muleteers helmets and mounted them on baggage mules so that they would look like cavalry (*Gallic War* 7.45). If there was a very marked difference between the relative sizes of baggage animals and cavalry mounts, this would have fooled no one. Ewart identified an ass at Newstead which he estimated 'measured about 13 hands at the withers' (in Curle 1911, 371), so it would seem that some baggage animals were the same size as some horses.

Vegetius (*Epitoma Rei Militaris* 1.5) recommends that cavalrymen should all measure six Roman feet, but he was describing the ideal situation and not necessarily what was the case either in his time or indeed at any time in the past. In fact Vegetius himself ends his next paragraph, on the ideal physical characteristics of soldiers, by suggesting that if most of the necessary attributes are present, then there need not be such emphasis on height, because it is more important that soldiers should be brave, rather than tall (*Epitoma Rei Militaris* 1.6). In the late Roman Empire, regulations were laid down concerning the size and age of horses for the army: 'Our provincials shall know that in the horses that they offer certain requirements as to shape, stature and age must be observed' (*Codex Theodosianus* 6.31). Unfortunately the optimum standards are not actually listed. The next clauses are revealing, in that it is clear that the officials appointed to receive horses as tax payments had been taking bribes to accept animals which were probably sub-standard. This illustrates the fact that whenever recommendations and regulations such as these have to be issued, it can sometimes indicate that the desired results are very far from those actually existing at the time of writing. Sometimes both men and horses may have been shorter than the ideal recommendations, depending on availability and the current wastage rate. In optimum situations of course it would be possible to filter out all but the very best of available recruits and mounts.

In 1799 Lord Amherst issued a general order relating to the British cavalry, which among other things advocated the policy of 'well sizing the men to their horses, when fit for the ranks, and not taking them from them afterwards on account of either growing a little' (Rogers 1977, 79). The British cavalry of the eighteenth century patently did not use ponies of 11 hands or so, but the purpose of this comparison is to illustrate the possibility that the Romans may have had to adapt on occasion to the availability of men and animals, matching men with suitable horses. Modern practice is to select and purchase horses of similar size and appearance, bred especially with the cavalry service in mind, and where possible in certain circumstances the Romans may have adopted the same principles, for instance for the Emperor's bodyguard and entourage, and for that of a provincial governor perhaps, where fine appearance would be important. But for campaigns and on active service where needs were urgent and resources stretched there may have been occasions when anything answering to the loose description 'horse' may have sufficed, which may account for the use of two-year-old horses at Krefeld and Dura (below pp.173–4). Certainly in later historical periods when horses were in short supply, armies took whatever they could find within certain limits, for instance in September 1806 Napoleon was so short of horses, and prices in France were so high, that he authorized the purchase of horses in Germany and he relaxed the minimum height regulations as well (Johnson 1978, 43). In 1813, though enough saddle horses were provided for the French cavalry they were mostly small animals (Elting 1988, 319). There would naturally be a lower limit beyond which a horse was not acceptable for military purposes, even in hard-pressed times of war when standards may have lapsed.

It is not entirely out of the question that horses smaller than the average were sometimes ridden by cavalrymen. Davis (1989, 21) relates how an eleventh-century Norman, Richard son of Asclettin, was reputed to have ridden a horse so small that his feet touched the ground, which implies that small stature of a horse does not prevent its use as a mount, at least temporarily, and such a situation is possibly represented by the use of animals of around 11 hands in the Roman army. Perhaps significantly, the small animals that have been found were probably casualties of war or at least some kind of fighting. It has been argued (see p.178) that burial was not the normal method of horse disposal, except in circumstances where there was neither opportunity nor time to do anything else. The small skeletons may represent the use of horses which in normal circumstances would have been rejected, and which if they were still alive when the action was over would have been replaced as soon as better and larger animals became available. It is interesting to note that in Judaea during the First World War 'owing to the chronic shortage of horses in the country, those details of regiments who did not usually accompany their units into action were, in 1917, given donkeys to ride'. There were about half a dozen in each cavalry regiment and they were replaced gradually by captured Arab ponies, though some of them were used right through the war and kept up with the horses on long fast marches, carrying the same amount of kit (Preston 1921, 326–8).

At the other end of the scale, the horses of 15 hands and more were probably always among the largest, and it may be that the Romans did not strive to breed taller animals than this. Naturally the size of a horse and the tasks it is capable of performing are related, but height is not always as significant as build, and chest measurement can be a better indication of stamina, as Major General Rimington pointed out in *Our Cavalry* in 1912 (quoted in Rogers 1959, 229). Rimington thought that the 'natural' size for a horse was 14–15 hands and anything larger than this produced by artificial forced growth was not necessarily more efficient. It is clear that horses of over 15 hands would carry more weight in a charge than those of only 14 hands, but it would cost more to feed and care for them (Rogers 1959, 229).

There can be no doubt from the number of recorded instances of outstanding performance and descriptions of their sterling qualities that certain breeds of horses of 13 to 14 hands are hardy and reliable and their size in no way inhibits their carrying capacity. This is a theme that occurs again and again in modern literature, usually accompanied by examples of physical prowess and stamina, the most common being Captain Nolan's description of the Persian horse of 14.3 hands which carried a trooper and his kit, a total weight of 22½ stone, over 800 miles without losing condition (Nolan 1853, 334).

Regulations for the British cavalry of 1729 tried to limit the size of horses to 15.2 hands, but these regulations were possibly ignored, since the Duke of Cumberland reiterated them in 1746, declaring that horses should not exceed 15 hands and should be bought at five years old to prevent the excuse that they had grown (Rogers 1959, 99–101). Frederick the Great weeded out the large horses in his army and limited their height to 15.3 hands, because he wanted swift, mobile cavalry and anything larger was too slow (Rogers 1977, 78).

By 1900 the Boer War had revealed that the horses brought out from England were no match for the smaller Boer horses, and in that year Sir Walter Gilbey wrote a book on small horses in warfare, in which he pointed out the 'peculiar suitability of small horses for certain campaigning work which demands staying power, hardiness and independence of high feeding'. There follows a description of the performance of different breeds of small horse in various parts of the world, ending with the recommendation that a new breed of 14-hands' ponies should be developed by crossing native English types with Arab sires 'to achieve that soundness of constitution and limb which are such conspicuous traits in the Eastern horse' (1900, 40).

Two questions which need to be asked but probably cannot be satisfactorily answered are: whether the horses of a *cohors equitata* were smaller than those of an *ala*; and whether horse size increased with the passage of time during the Empire.

There is no firm evidence to support or refute the suggestion that there was a difference in size between the horses of the cohorts and the *alae*. It has not been possible to determine whether the skeletons of horses found at various sites belonged to an *ala* or a cohort, and indeed in some cases it is not even certain if they were military horses, so there are no statistics from which to draw any conclusion. Some authors have inferred that the *cohortes equitatae* were not so well mounted as the *alae*, and that this probably meant that their horses were smaller. This is usually based firstly on Hadrian's *Adlocutio* to the Numidian army (*CIL* VIII 18042 = *ILS* 2487) in which he makes a distinction between the two types of unit, and secondly on comparisons with the light cavalry of the eighteenth-century European armies, in which generally speaking the horses were smaller than those of the first line or heavy cavalry.

Contrary to the interpretation often put upon it, Hadrian's speech to the Numidian army does not provide irrefutable evidence that the horses of a *cohors equitata* were smaller than those of an *ala*. It is merely stated that 'the appearance and quality of the horses is in keeping with the level of pay'. Whether the terms appearance and quality were meant to embrace size as well as performance, turn-out and decoration is a matter of opinion.

The validity of comparisons between the horses of the *cohortes equitatae* and those of the light cavalry of the later European armies is debatable. Davies (1971a, 756; 761) argued that the horsemen of the *cohortes equitatae* were trained in the same way as those of the *alae* but were employed as 'second line cavalry', responsible for policing, escort duties and maintaining communications, thus acting in a supporting capacity to the first line cavalry, or *alae*. This he illustrated by analogy with a work of Marshal Saxe written in 1732, in which it was recommended that the horses of the heavy cavalry should be not less than 15 hands and those of the light cavalry between 13.2 and 14 hands. This distinction between the two kinds of cavalry and the respective size of their horses is found in the eighteenth-century British army and that of Frederick the Great, among many other examples.

With regard to the Roman cavalry however, the terms 'heavy' and 'light' can be misleading. Insufficient evidence is available about how the *alae* and *cohortes equitatae* were used, and it is not even known if the two kinds of cavalry were indeed divided into two broad classes. They may have been exactly the same in the eyes of the Romans, and more likely different regiments may have been used in different ways regardless of their titles.

The usefulness of units of light horse using smaller animals than the heavy cavalry is amply demonstrated from comparatively recent historical experience, but whether this also applied to the Romans must remain conjectural. The evidence concerning the horses does not permit a firm conclusion, and whilst it is probable that the duties of the two kinds of cavalry units differed, the size of their horses may not have been so markedly divergent, and the *cohortes equitatae* and *alae* cannot be classified as light and heavy cavalry in the modern sense.

In discussing the horses from the Roman site of Chelmsford, Luff (1982, 204) suggests that over the first four centuries of the Roman Empire the size of horses increased, though it is not possible to ascertain whether this came about because of selective cross-breeding from native stock or by imports of larger animals. Breeding larger horses from specially selected native stock would have been a sensible method of operation (if somewhat slow), for the army to adopt in each province. Nobis suggests that this was the case at Krefeld-Gellep where by comparing the skeletons and especially the teeth of 31 horses he concluded that the larger animals owed their origin to selective cross-breeding from the smaller ones (1973, 250). Azzaroli (1985, 155; 172) contends that wherever the Romans extended their Empire they introduced larger horses, but he insists that since this occurs quite rapidly it is too quick to be the result of selective upbreeding from native Iron Age stocks. Most of these native horses were small as a result of poor breeding conditions, and the Romans, Azzaroli suggests, must have imported larger horses, probably from Gaul or Spain. Unfortunately references and details of how this was undertaken are lacking.

The suggested gradual increase in horse sizes during the Empire is a process which cannot be traced or proved without a representative selection of complete horse skeletons from the relevant periods. In any case the crucial factor would be build, that is to say overall skeletal structure allied with adequate muscling (*pers. comm.* A. Hyland) not necessarily height alone, and as has already been mentioned, much depends upon the breed of horse as well.

The Dura bardings or trappers dating from the mid-third century would not seem to be designed for particularly massive horses, and in estimating the space necessary for horses when the army is drawn up in ranks, the Emperor Maurice allowed three Roman feet by eight feet for each horse (*Strategikon* 9.5), which does not suggest that the horses were of enormous stature. Instead of breeding to gain ever increased height, in the late Empire the Romans may have concentrated on stockier horses which could carry the weight of men, equipment and armour.

As Azzaroli pointed out, it is an over-simplification to project backwards into antiquity the modern distinction between heavy occidental or 'cold-blooded' horses and light oriental 'hot-blooded' breeds (1985, 170). There were some occidental breeds which were not at all heavy and conversely not all oriental breeds were light. Azzaroli concluded that breeds of heavier build were developed independently. The Persians developed the heavy Nisean breed, but Azzaroli maintains that there was probably no direct Persian influence on Roman horse breeding for the first two to three centuries of the Empire. By the fourth century, however, in Vegetius' day 'Persian' horses, which may or may not be the same as the Nisean breed, were much praised. They were especially famous for their comfortable gait which made them ideally suitable as riding horses. They may also have been used by the army as war-horses, but Vegetius does not mention them in his list of breeds most suited to battles, the chief of which were the Huns or Hunnisci with strong limbs and bodies longer than they were tall. This suggests once more that ever increased height was not an overriding criterion for the Roman army, but that build and strong back and legs were far more important.

Age of horses

In modern practice it is not considered advisable to begin training or exercising a horse until it is two or three years old because until then the leg bones are not properly formed and considerable damage can be done by putting too much strain on them too soon (Hardman 1976, 104). Columella (*De Re Rustica* 6.29.4) recommended that there should be no severe exercise until a horse was at least four: 'At two years of age a horse is suitable to be trained for domestic purposes; but if it is to be trained for racing it should have completed three years, and provided that it is entered for this kind of effort only after its fourth year.' Varro (*De Re Rustica* 2.7.13) also recommends that breaking a horse should not commence until it is three years old, even though 'some breeders claim that a young horse can be broken at eighteen months'. A three-year-old, Varro says, is growing most rapidly and putting on muscle.

The available information concerning the ages of Roman cavalry horses indicates that the animals ranged from two years old to over 20 years. Two horses at Lauriacum were under three years old, and three horses died at Krefeld-Gellep before the age of four (Nobis 1973, 232). These mounts had presumably not been in service very long. A two-year-old horse was purchased at Dura for a soldier of *Cohors XX Palmyrenorum* in AD 245, and was still in service in AD 251, aged eight (*P. Dur.* 97). The large majority of the Krefeld-Gellep horses (14 out of a total of 27) were aged between four and seven years old, but it is not known how old they were when they were purchased or requisitioned nor how long they had been in army service. Nine of the 27 were aged between eight and 13 years old and one was over 20. At Dura, four two-year-olds were purchased, one in AD 208 (*P. Dur.* 56) and three more at some time before AD 251 (*P. Dur.* 97). The rest of those listed for *Cohors XX Palmyrenorum* probably varied in age and were simply listed as *aequatus* (or *aequata* if they were mares). Gilliam (1950, 199) argued that this term refers to the fact that the horses' teeth were no longer of any use in determining their ages. By the time a horse is seven years old, the formative changes in its teeth have already taken place and thereafter it is not possible to age the horse accurately (Hyland 1990, 45–6; 82). If Gilliam's suggestion is correct then *aequatus* denotes a horse of seven years old or more. The word appears in the military records in the place where it would be expected to find the age of the horse, and conversely where the age *is* specified *aequatus* never appears and seems always to have been used instead of a term for age in years. Two of the mares purchased at this indeterminate age in AD 245 and 249 respectively, were both still in service in AD 251, and would by then be at least 13 and nine years old, most probably even older.

In optimum circumstances the army would perhaps buy horses at four or five years old and retire them at roughly 17–18 years. Age is an advantage in a horse when it is required to perform hard work. Young horses are not capable of prolonged and severe muscular efforts. But on the other hand, older horses do not recuperate so quickly, and exposure to wet and cold and unfavourable management is better borne by younger animals. In the First World War it was found that the best horses with greatest resilience were those aged five to 12, and thereafter the rate of recuperation began to slow down (Blenkinsop and Rainey 1925, 65).

The length of service of Roman cavalry horses is not sufficiently documented. But for comparison the Marquess of Anglesey in the nineteenth century reckoned on 12 years of use on average from each horse for the British cavalry, allowing for the time it would take to train it. In peacetime, the early-nineteenth-century British army bought its horses on the open market, choosing three-year-olds, whereas most dealers preferred four-year-olds. This meant that the army got first pick of the available animals (Anglesey 1973, 107; Tylden 1965, 21). These young horses would not be put to immediate work. The use of horses under three years old at Lauriacum and the two-year-olds at Krefeld-Gellep in the first century AD and Dura in the third may indicate that there was a chronic shortage of horses, at least at the times and places concerned. In times of peace there may have been some provinces where supply of horses exceeded demand, but this was probably rare. The army would have used vast numbers of animals as cavalry mounts and for transport, and provision of replacements would have been a full-time task. Losses in action, as at Krefeld-Gellep and possibly on the frontier at Dura, probably exacerbated a situation already precarious.

Name and brands

None of the horses in the military records appear to have been given names, at least not on any official basis, and it is not known whether the soldiers commonly referred to their horses by name. Gilliam (1950, 177 n.32) thinks that the horses probably had names (Fig.60), and outside military circles, race horses and chariot horses certainly did. Toynbee (1973, 178–9) gives a

60 Representations of horses showing brand marks. The positions of the brands correspond quite closely to notes on such marks in the Dura papyrus records, as interpreted by Gilliam. (Redrawn by G. Stobbs from Klumbach 1952.)

long list of such names compiled from literature and from mosaics depicting named horses. The most common of these are from Africa showing horses tethered in courtyards or tied to trees, with their names picked out above them in mosaic tiles (Vigneron 1968, pl.9; Toynbee 1948, pl.4 and 5; Hyland 1990, pls.25 and 26).

Horses and cattle were often branded in the Roman Empire, but it is not known if military units used this method of identifying horses. Strabo (5.1.9) recounts a tale in which a man branded all his horses with the sign of a wolf, and Virgil (*Georgics* 3.158) describes the branding of cattle with the owner's mark and a sign for the breed, possibly a mark signifying its parentage but this is not clear (White 1970, 287). The mark of ownership was possibly applied to horses as well, and may account for the fact that some of the horses in the military records were already branded, sometimes in two places, when they were brought into the army. The positions of the brands were carefully noted in abbreviated form, and the abbreviations have been interpreted by Gilliam (*P. Dur.* 97 and commentary). Some horses were unbranded, and this was probably expressed by the initials *s.n.* for *s[ine] n[ota]*, literally 'without mark' or brand. The initials *n.f.a.d.* probably meant *n[ota] f[emore] a[rmo] d[extro]*, brands on the right thigh and shoulder, or *s[inistro]* if they were on the left side. The positions of these brands accord well with the pictorial representations of brand marks on horses collected together by Klumbach (1952) where the majority of horses were marked with a cross in a circle, a Maltese cross or star-shaped brands, mostly on the right side though occasionally on the left.

The term *signatus* as used in the military records has been taken to indicate that some horses were branded, but the irregular occurrence of the word rather weighs against this, because it would seem that whatever was meant by *signatus*, it was not a standard practice. This term was differently interpreted by Davies (1969b, 447) (see above p.151), who maintained that the army did not have a policy of branding horses, but that perhaps identity discs were placed around their necks. For this latter suggestion there is no evidence at all, and if the army needed to identify its horses, the best method would surely be to add another brand mark to the ones the horse already carried. An identity disc could be removed much more easily by a thief; brands can be altered but this is more difficult and more readily detectable. The practice may have depended upon provincial custom or even on the individual unit's policy. The absence of any written record of branding by the military authorities signifies absolutely nothing. If it was never done, then naturally it would not be mentioned, but if it was common or standard practice then equally this would not need to be put down in the records; it would be taken as read.

Gelding

It is not possible to ascertain from skeletal remains whether or not horses have been gelded. The practice in the Roman army may have varied according to time and place and was most likely dependent upon the breed of horse. The evidence suggests that in general the Romans did not geld cavalry horses, but may have done so in certain cases, and on occasions may have bought horses which had already been gelded. The military records do not contain any details about this, and merely specify the gender of the horse.

Both Strabo (*Geography* 7.4.8) and Ammianus (17.12.3) describe how the Sarmatian horses, small in stature but spirited and difficult to manage, were gelded to make them more docile, and Ammianus added that this ensured that they did not become unruly at the sight of mares or give away the position of the troops lying in ambush by excited neighing. These passages from Strabo and Ammianus could imply that the Romans thought gelding was unusual. Varro (*De Re Rustica* 2.7.15) seems to imply that military horses were ungelded when he states that for the most part the army needed spirited horses, whereas the more docile geldings were necessary for road service (*in viis*). There are several extant sculptures which show ungelded cavalry horses, including the groups on Trajan's Column, and more specifically on the Marcus Column, where the horses of the Emperor's bodyguard are portrayed as stallions (Davison 1989, 146). Further, on some cavalry tombstones there is no room for doubt that the horses depicted are entires.

The customary objection to the use of stallions and mares together is that the practice would lead to fighting between rival horses and cause far too much trouble. But this very much depends upon the temperament of individual horses, and as much as anything upon individual handling (*pers. comm.* A. Hyland). Sometimes mares can be just as vicious and troublesome as stallions if they take a dislike to each other. In defence of mares, it may be worth noting that Wellington in the Peninsular War requested mares in preference to horses (i.e. geldings) because they could bear the work better (Brereton 1976, 77). The Romans used mares and male horses in the same units, as is attested by the Dura papyri (*P. Dur.* 97) and sometimes they would probably be stabled together, as at Dormagen (see p.193). Whether there were any problems arising from this and whether they were solved by gelding some of the stallions is not recorded. It is likely that each horse was treated as an individual and its tolerance for other horses could have been accommodated by altering its position on the line of march, in picket lines and in stables. Gelding was probably not employed as a routine procedure for the purpose of making horses manageable, but it may have been carried out occasionally where other remedies had failed (Hyland 1990, 81). At certain times and in certain places gelding may have been subject to the vagaries of fashion, about which archaeology can tell us little. In the fourth century AD, for instance, Gallic geldings fetched high prices and were much valued (Luff 1982, 204). But this may have only applied in civilian contexts and army practice may have differed.

Disposal

When a cavalry horse was to be disposed of it is possible that it had to be inspected by some government official just as it was when it was received, to ensure that in this case there was no question of corruption on the part of the army commanders who could and sometimes did make a profit from selling horses. There is admittedly no evidence for such inspections, but it would be consistent with Roman efficiency and bureaucracy. During the First World War, army veterinary surgeons had to inspect and give their authority for disposal of animals (Blenkinsop and Rainey 1925, 568). A number of horses were sold to agriculturalists as farm horses, and some were sold for meat to civilian traders. But these livestock formed only a small proportion of the horses disposed of, the majority of which were already dead, either from disease or injuries which necessitated their destruction.

In the Roman army the number of horses in any province where there were mounted units would have been extremely high. The number of skeletons or even individual horse bones so far discovered is not at all representative of the numbers that must have been disposed of during the history of the Empire. Burial of cavalry mounts was probably not a feature of the regular disposal process, and the entire or partial skeletons which have been found up to now, at Newstead, Krefeld-Gellep, Lauriacum and so on, were possibly buried only because there was not enough time to carry out the usual methods of disposal, and burial was probably the only rapid alternative which could be employed on the spot, preferable to leaving decaying corpses. The horses killed at these and other sites were probably casualties of war buried during a clearing-up process after hostilities had ceased in that locality.

In more mundane circumstances, disposal was probably more orderly. It is likely that a horse's usefulness did not cease once it was dead. Pennant on his travels in the eighteenth century reported that he had seen 'a stupendous number of horse bones' near Stanwix (Birley 1961, 206) which led to the suggestion that there may have been a knacker's yard there. This must remain unproven, but there probably was a regular method of horse and

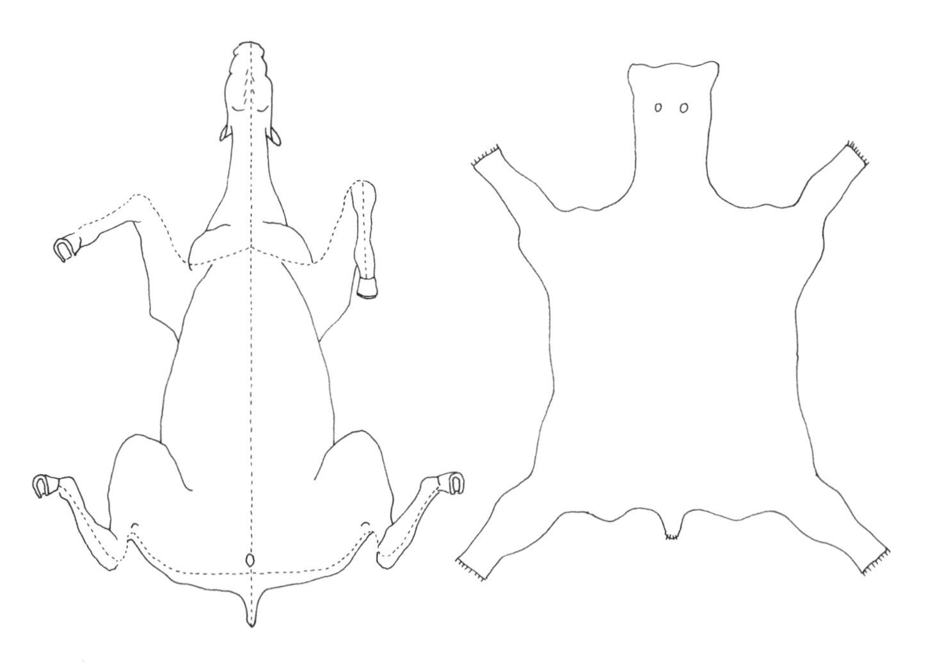

61 Instructions issued to army veterinary establishments during the First World War on how to skin a horse. Where possible, disposal of horses was thorough and would leave no trace of bone, hoof or hide. (Redrawn by K.R. Dixon from Blenkinsop and Rainey 1925.)

mule disposal at each cavalry fort, a process which may have been carried out at sites some distance removed from the forts themselves. On 3 March 1917 the War Office Veterinary Department issued instructions for 'dealing economically with hides and carcasses of army horses and mules' (Fig.61). Among other things the hair of mane and tail was cut off, washed and stored, and the hides were removed and sold to civilian markets; the Romans must also have found ample use for both commodities. Fat was rendered down and sometimes used by the veterinary service, or sold for soap manufacture. Bones were boiled to extract oil, and then sold, or if they had to be buried would 'retain their commercial value for years'. Meat was either sold as animal food or to civilian markets, or buried along with the entrails (Blenkinsop and Rainey 1925, 684–91; 719–21).

At the fortress of Longthorpe butchery marks were found on horse bones, indicating that the animals had been used for meat. It may be significant that few bones were found in the fortress itself but many more were found on the industrial site outside it (Dannell and Wild 1987, 68; 187). In France in the First World War, horse carcass processing plants were established, run by army personnel on industrial lines, at eight centres, including Le Havre, Rouen and Calais (Blenkinsop and Rainey 1925, 684–5). There may have been Roman versions of these plants situated outside most forts. They may have been some distance from the military establishments and thus beyond the limits of most excavations.

Horse meat was probably not given to Roman soldiers, but civilians may have bought it and it may have been fed to slaves. The Canadian North West Mounted Police occasionally fed it to their huskies, and apart from its sale as animal food during the First World War, permission was obtained to feed prisoners on it (Blenkinsop and Rainey 1925, 685). The archaeological trace of the truly vast numbers of horses consumed in the First World War would be minimal and though the comparison of the methods of disposal may not be valid for the Roman Empire, it is at least likely that the Roman army exploited their horses to the utmost, even after the death of the animals, and this would be compatible with the lack of archaeological evidence for cavalry horses.

11 Stables and grooming

Stables

The provision of stables within Roman forts is taken for granted, but it has not yet been proved conclusively that all the horses of mounted units were stabled inside their forts. Study of many forts is considerably limited by lack of definite information as to the size and type of garrison, so that in some cases it is not possible to say whether there were any mounted troops present at all. Even when it can be established that the occupying unit was an *ala* or an equitate cohort, there is still uncertainty about the exact numbers of horses involved. Furthermore, there are very few Roman forts where the entire area has been excavated, and so most authors have to rely on conjecture, usually designed to prove that on grounds of spacing there would have been room for however many animals the excavator thought there should have been in the unit in question. This mostly depends in turn on the tentative identification of one or two buildings as stables, followed by the expectation, without proof, that similar blocks existed in unexcavated areas of the fort.

Estimates of the number of horses in a unit vary because it is impossible firstly to assess how many men there would be in each *turma*, and secondly how many horses each officer would own. Furthermore there is no information about whether remounts were kept at the fort. Hyginus (*De Metatione Castrorum* 16) says that decurions would have two extra horses, and *duplicarii* and *sesquiplicarii* one extra each, but the exact number of men in each *turma* is not established beyond doubt. Curle (1911, 75) suggested a total of 544 horses for an *ala* of 480 men. Simpson and Richmond (1941, 30–3) thought that a *turma* comprised 30 men, and that there would be 35 horses per *turma* allowing for Hyginus' figures of three for the decurion and two each for the junior officers. More recently, Frere and St Joseph (1974, 28 n.49) assumed a total of 36 horses per *turma*. This reckoning, not based on any solid facts, would give a minimum of 864 horses for a milliary *ala*, 576 for a quingenary *ala*, and 280 and 136 for a milliary cohort and a quingenary cohort respectively (Johnson 1983, 320 n.181). It must be stressed that these figures are entirely theoretical.

The dimensions of a stable, or an individual stall, not unnaturally depend on the size of the horse. Modern practice allows 3 × 1.8m (10 × 6ft) for a stall for a hunter with a space 2.4m (8ft) behind, or 4.8m (16ft) between a double row of horses. Thus each horse is allowed about 5.5sq.m or 60 sq.ft (Ewer 1982, 166–9). The British army veterinary service on the western front during the First World War allowed 3 × 1.7m (10 × 5.5ft) for each horse, and in the hotter climates of Egypt and Palestine individual stalls were 3.6 × 1.5m (12 × 5ft) (Blenkinsop and Rainey 1925, 268; 586). Military stables in Germany around the turn of the century ranged from 9 to 10.5m (*c.* 29$\frac{1}{2}$ to 34ft) wide, accommodating two rows of horses and a middle alleyway. In Austria at the same period a double row of horses occupied a width of roughly 9.5m (30ft), allowing for three equal divisions of 3.16m (10ft) for the central gangway and each horse (Fabricius 1937, 47–8).

The estimated space for each horse in the presumed Roman military stables is usually rather less than these recommended dimensions, but the capacities of many Roman stables are based for the most part on hypothetical calculations and not on established fact. One exception to this generalization is Dormagen, where sufficiently large areas of the stables were excavated to be certain about the dimensions of some of the compartments in each block. Individual cubicles or boxes were typically *c.* 3–3.5m × 3.5–4m (10–11$\frac{1}{2}$ft × 11$\frac{1}{2}$–13ft). But the number of horses per cubicle is not definitely known, so the space allocation must be estimated. The excavator suggested that there were two to three horses per cubicle (Müller 1979a, 48), so the space available for each animal could have varied from *c.* 4–5sq.m (*c.* 43–54sq.ft) to *c.* 6–7sq.m (*c.* 64–75sq.ft). Probably the true figure lies somewhere between the two extremes, and may have been approximately the same as the modern allowance for a hunter.

The estimate of three horses per cubicle may not be unreasonable, for the skeletons of three horses were found in a farm stable measuring 3.1m (10ft) wide at the Roman villa of Boscoreale, Italy (Applebaum 1972, 149). This allows each horse a space only 1m wide, which seems far too small by modern standards, and the fact that three horses were found in a civilian stable should not perhaps be applied as a standard by which to judge military establishments. But there is possible confirmation for this very narrow spacing from other civilian stables at Tebessa in Algeria and other sites in Roman North Africa. The use of these buildings is not absolutely certain, but the stone troughs found inside all of them may be correctly interpreted as mangers, though they could just as easily have been storage bins for agricultural produce (Davison 1989, 142). In a large aisled building at Tebessa the space between the mid-points of each trough is 1m. This resembles very closely the 1m spacing of the possible mangers set into the walls, three to a room, at the late Roman fort of Qasr Bshir in central Jordan. The same arrangements were also noted at the military post at Umm el-Jimal (Parker 1987, 475–6). The ground-floor rooms of the Byzantine fort at Timgad were found complete with mangers set into the walls and some of the tethering rings still *in situ*, and 'the distance between the mangers is only a little more than Tebessa' (Davison 1989, 142). Although it is tempting to see in all this a uniform Roman approach to the method of stabling horses, it is not certain that the civilian and military buildings just listed were all used as stables. On the subject of the large building at Tebessa, Gsell (1901, 286) says that overall there would be no hesitation in interpreting the building as a vast stable, but then goes on to express doubt due to the very close spacing of the horses and their probable difficulty of entering the compartments, which statement also applies to the rooms at Timgad and Qasr Bshir.

At other forts there is less information about the internal arrangements of the stable buildings and the size of individual stalls or boxes, so the space allocation is usually reconstructed by a combination of few facts and much intelligent guesswork. For instance, the suggested allowance at Benwell was 4.7sq.m (51sq.ft) for the larger compartments and only 3.2sq.m (35sq.ft) for the smaller. At Ilkley 4.3sq.m (47sq.ft) per horse was allowed in the stables of the first fort, while at Halton 3.2sq.m (35sq.ft), and Carzield 2.7sq.m (30sq.ft), seem to be far too small. This very meagre space allowance is usually excused on the grounds that the horses were probably only very small, possibly 12–13 hands at the most, and they would therefore fit comfortably into the calculated areas. But there are two objections, firstly that the horses may not all have been so small, and secondly, there is no definite proof that animals were accommodated in the way in which the excavators suggested. Davison (1989, 481–3) usefully summarizes theoretical space allowances of stables in Roman forts.

In Britain it seems fairly certain that there were stables at Hod Hill, but this site is not without its problems and it is perhaps not typical of arrangements in other forts which were built later and occupied for a much longer time. None the less the Hod Hill stables 'are in danger of becoming accepted as the Roman norm' (Wells 1977, 660). They always feature in any discussion on stables because they are the only certain British examples. More recently, buildings were identified as stables at Usk; they contained soakaway pits, which may indicate that they indeed housed cavalry horses, but this is not yet certain (see p.193).

At Hod Hill (Fig.62) six rectangular blocks were identified as stables, and in two of them internal partitions were traced. Two categories of compartments were noted, the smaller 3.36 × 3.66m (11 × 12ft), possibly accommodating a single row of three animals with a 1.8m (6ft) alley behind them, and the larger, 3.36 × 5.49m (11 × 18ft), with six horses in two rows of three each, with a 1.8m (6ft) alley between them, which arrangement should accommodate a total of 252 horses. It was concluded from the worn and stained patches on the floor of one of the rooms that the animals had been tethered to the cross-walls and not the outer walls (Richmond 1968, 83). The internal arrangements of the stable blocks at Dormagen support this conclusion (Müller 1979a, Pls.50 and 52) and the theoretical reconstructions of stables at Künzing (Schönberger 1975, 58; 63) and Krefeld-Gellep (Pirling 1986, 18) both adopt this plan. At Künzing, Schönberger suggested that the horses were tethered to the cross-walls, but the hypothetical arrangements allow the horses much more room than Richmond's calculations (see Figs 67 and 69–71).

Wells (1977, 661) raised two points for consideration about these reconstructions. Concerning Hod Hill he noted that the distance over the centre points of the worn patches on the floor was only about 1m (3ft), which implies that the animals were quite small, probably not much more than 10 hands, and it has been suggested that the stables may have been for baggage animals (Johnson 1983, 180). If so, it is permissible to wonder why baggage animals were stabled and not the cavalry horses, unless these were housed in the other four buildings where internal partitions were not traced. It is not impossible that in some instances, both baggage mules and cavalry horses were stabled together, as they sometimes were in the US cavalry. The pack-mules of Troop 'B', Fourth US Cavalry, were stabled and corralled together with the horses 'so that they soon became attached to them and indifferent to others, therefore easy to herd' (Cabaniss 1890, 248–9).

Wells' second objection surrounded the seemingly complicated method of tethering horses to the cross-walls of a building (1977, 663). He was writing before the report on the excavations at Dormagen were published (Müller 1979b), where the layout of the stalls indicated that this was indeed the method by which animals were tethered at this fort, possibly two or three to a stall. But Wells' point is still valid, in that a much better method of stabling horses is to tether them down the length of a building. This is simpler, takes up less space and facilitates access for feeding and cleaning. Partitions between individual animals are not always necessary if horses are tied up in rows (Frere and St Joseph 1974, 27 n.48). Known kickers can be accommodated in individual stalls (War Office 1904, 12; Wells 1977, 664). Xenophon (*Cavalry Commander* 1.4; 14; 15) recommends that kickers and vicious animals should be rejected, because 'such animals do more damage

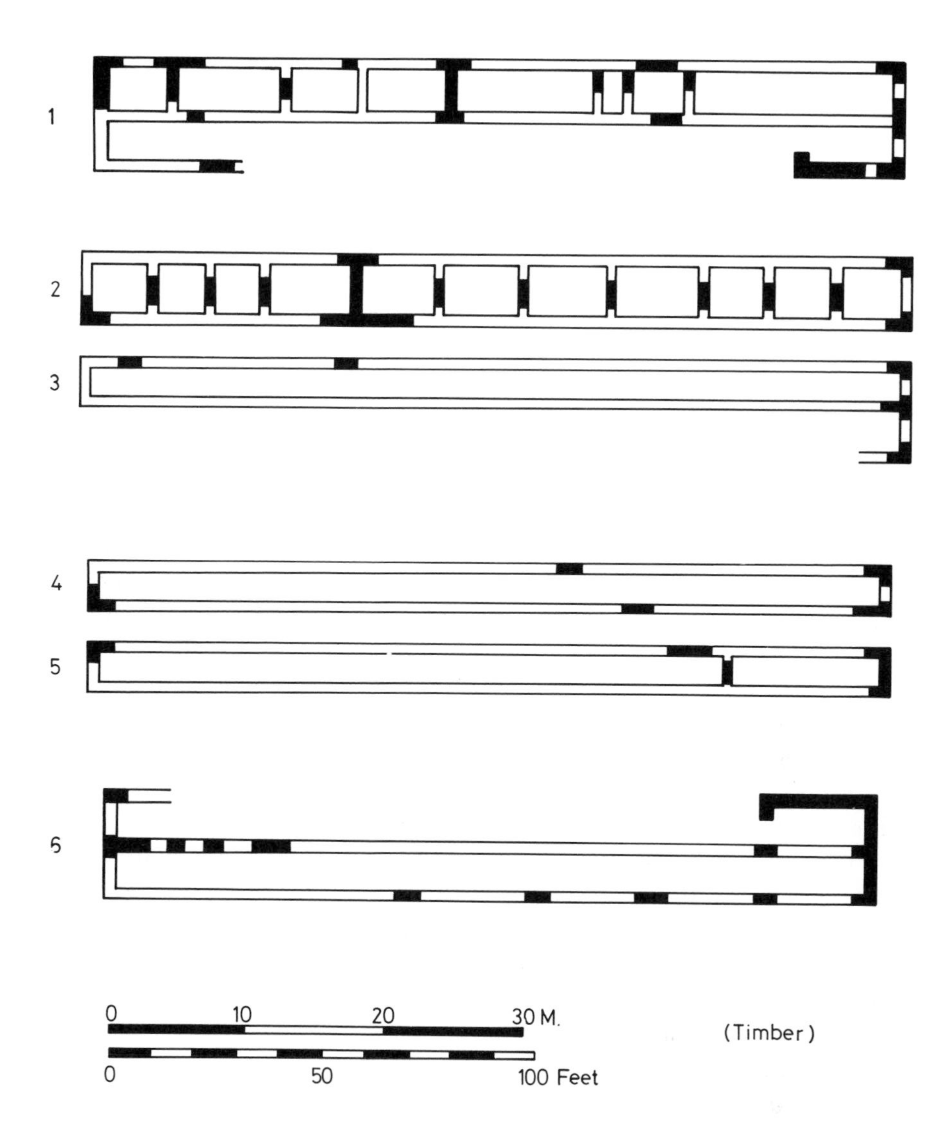

62 The six rectangular blocks at Hod Hill interpreted as stables. From the evidence of the stained patches on the floor in one of the blocks, it was suggested that the animals were tethered to the cross-walls of the building. Similar arrangements were used at Dormagen (Figs.70 and 71). (Redrawn by G. Stobbs from Richmond 1968.)

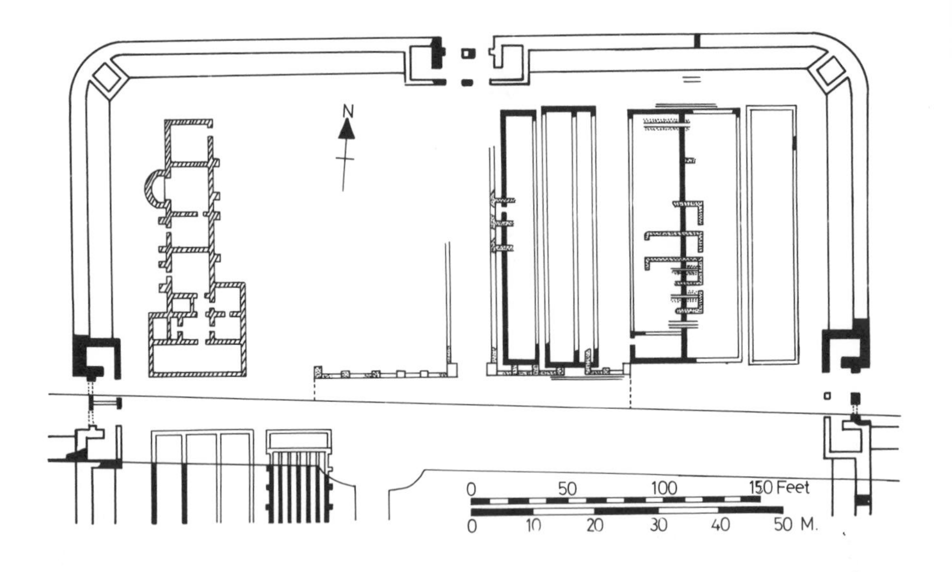

63 The fort at Halton Chesters showing the location of the so-called stable block in the north-east corner. (Redrawn by G. Stobbs from Simpson and Richmond 1937.)

than the enemy'. But there would need to be a plentiful supply of horses before all kickers would be rejected, and most armies were forced to tolerate them for at least some of the time.

Two rows of horses tethered down the length of a building was the method envisaged at Niederbieber, where two blocks were identified, one 30m (98ft) long and the other not fully excavated but possibly over 70m (229ft) long. These buildings seem not to have had internal divisions, but as mentioned above this is not always necessary. The two blocks at Niederbieber could have accommodated up to 120 horses (Fabricius 1937, 47–8). Unfortunately it still cannot be ascertained if all the horses of the occupying unit were stabled inside the fort. Niederbieber is very large (5.2ha or 13 acres) and would presumably have held a correspondingly large number of men. The garrison seems to have been a mixed one of *exploratores* and a *numerus Brittonum*, and it is not certain how many of these would have been mounted.

Besides those at Hod Hill, the most frequently quoted examples of stables in Roman forts in Britain include Halton (Fig.63) and Benwell on Hadrian's Wall, Brough-on-Noe, and Ilkley. At some forts the presence of drains and/or water tanks has been used to support the identification of stable blocks. Drains ran across the building at Halton (Fig.64) (Simpson and Richmond 1937, 164) and down the length of another at Brough-on-Noe (Jones and

Wild 1968, 92). Water tanks are not unknown in Roman forts, but at Gellygaer (Ward 1903, 69–70) and Benwell (Simpson and Richmond 1941, 14) they were linked with stable buildings and the presence of horses. The absence of any internal partitions in a building at Wallsend suggests that it may have been a stable rather than a barrack block.

At most sites the major problem is that it has not been possible to recover the entire plan of the putative stables, and so none of the dimensions are based on more than careful calculation. The identification of a stable at Benwell rests on three factors. Firstly, it is known that an *ala quingenaria* was stationed there, which means that accommodation would have been

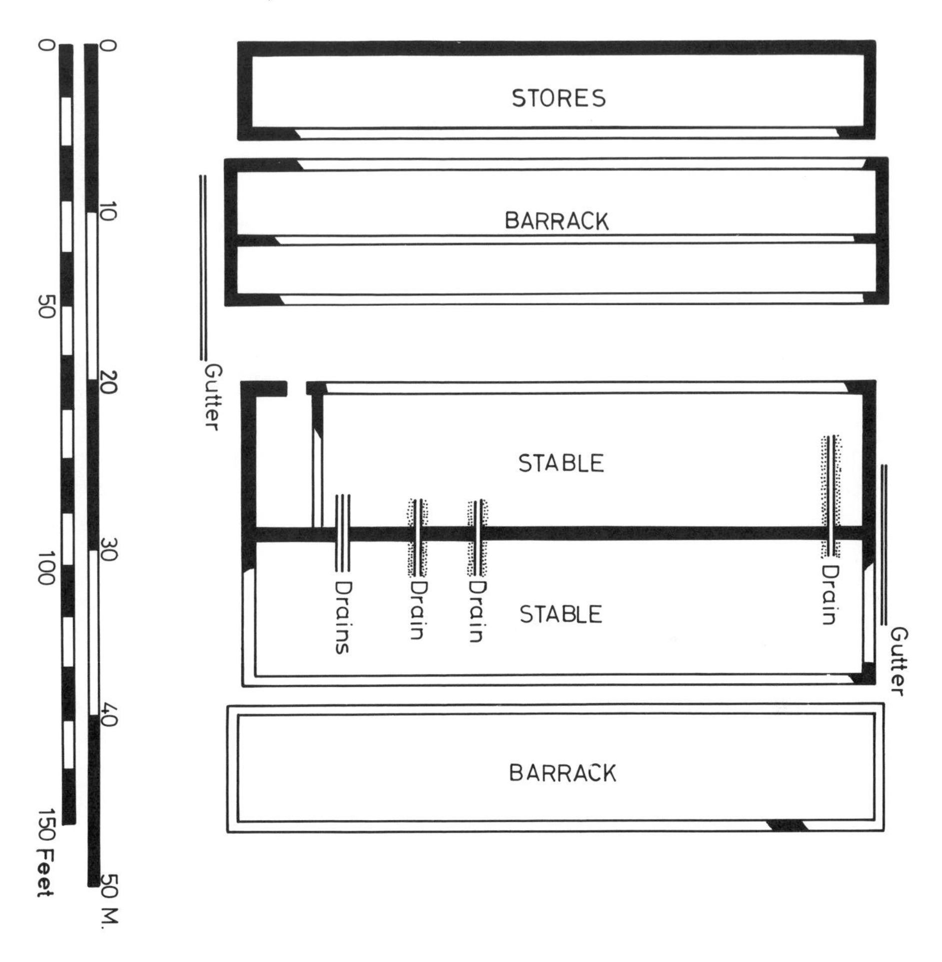

64 Plan of the buildings at Halton Chesters interpreted as stables. The lack of internal partitions and the presence of drains suggested to the excavators that these buildings were not used as barracks and may instead have accommodated horses. (Redrawn by G. Stobbs from Simpson and Richmond 1937.)

needed for about 500 horses. There was then an interruption when a milliary equitate cohort with an unknown but large number of horses, took its place for a while (Simpson and Richmond 1941, 4). Secondly, the excavators sought a comparison with the buildings which they themselves had identified as stables at Halton, where in the third century 'the stabling was . . . built in groups of ten compartments each measuring 10ft × 25ft and furnished with a central drain' (Simpson and Richmond 1941, 31; 1937, 164–71). Thirdly, the elaborate water storage system with two filter tanks, comparable to the settling chambers of civil aqueducts, was related to the presence of horses inside the fort (Simpson and Richmond 1941, 16). Unfortunately so little of the stable building was recovered that it is impossible to be absolutely certain of its function. It was calculated that there would have been ten divisions, as at Halton, each measuring 3.6m × 9.1m (12ft × 30ft) and holding seven horses. This is only just feasible and not proven.

The case for Brough-on-Noe seems stronger and has met with wide acceptance. Here, a drain ran along the length of the building and then turned at right angles to emerge underneath the wall (Fig.65). Two horses'

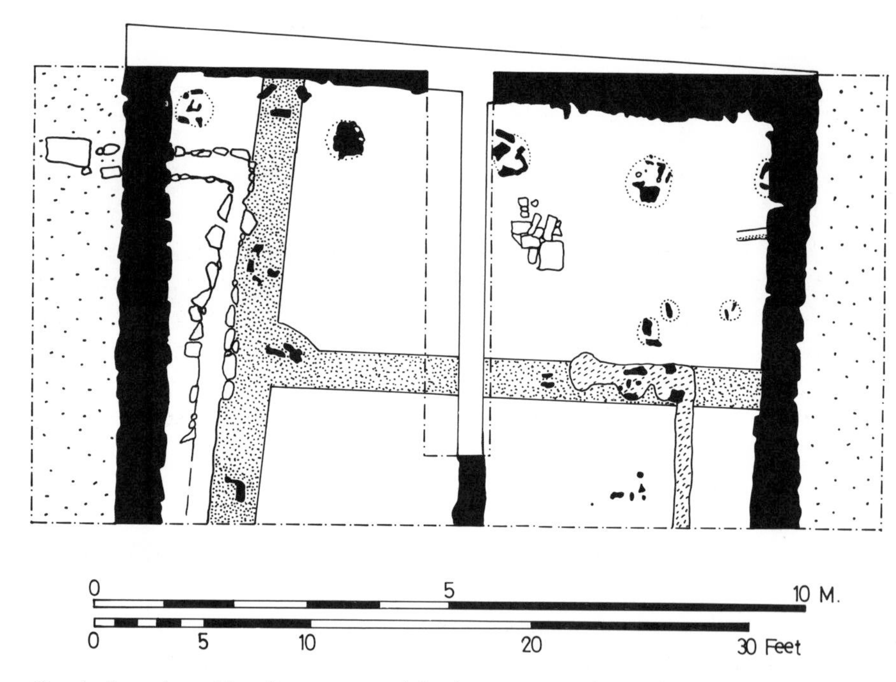

65 At Brough-on-Noe the presence of the drain running down the length of the building and passing underneath the outer wall was taken as support for the suggestion that this building was a stable. (Redrawn by G. Stobbs from Jones and Wild 1968.)

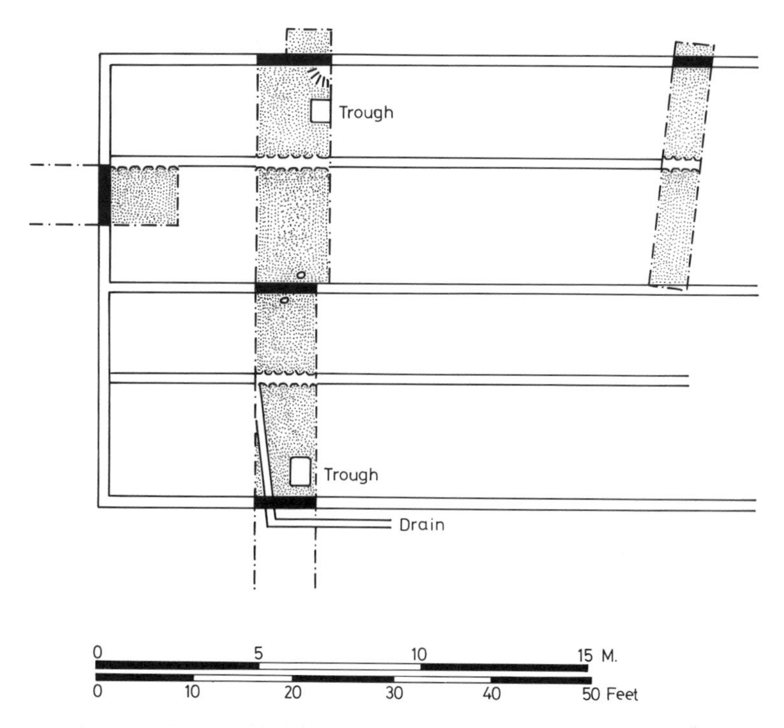

66 The stable block at Ilkley showing the position of troughs and drains. The absence of internal partitions indicates that these buildings were not used as barracks. (Redrawn by G. Stobbs from Hartley 1966.)

teeth and manure were found in it (Jones and Wild 1968, 92). But it is not quite correct to describe the drain as parallel to the stable wall as some have done (Wells 1977, 663; Johnson 1983, 177). On the published plan it runs slightly at an angle and could very easily belong to the outer edge of a building on a different alignment which preceded the so-called stable. Furthermore where the drain turns to go out under the wall it seems to form a T-junction with a deeper and possibly older channel (Jones and Wild 1968, Pl.IIIa). These niggling doubts, coupled with the fact that once again the entire building could not be excavated, would seem to suggest that at least a note of caution should be adopted before accepting the designation of stable.

The fort at Ilkley was occupied in the first century and in the Antonine and Severan eras. A building in the first fort which Hartley identified as a stable (Fig.66) had no drain in it, but it was suggested that timber guttering may have been used, which would leave no archaeological trace (Hartley 1966, 32; 71 n.29). The building had a longitudinal partition dividing it into 'an open area 20ft 9in. wide on its west side and a section 9ft wide along the east side, subdivided by cross-walls' (Hartley 1966, 31). This is an unusual arrangement which suggests that the building was not a barrack, but it does not automatically imply that it was a stable.

The stable of the later periods seems more certain. 'Identification of the function of the building rests on the central drain of each half, on the flushing arrangements for them and on the presence of troughs or mangers and tethering posts' (Hartley 1966, 37). But again the whole building was not fully excavated and its total length is unknown, and so the number of horses accommodated in it must be a matter for speculation. More importantly, it is still not clear whether all the unit's horses were stabled inside the fort.

Other forts where it is thought that there might have been stables include Carzield (Birley and Richmond 1939, 161), Newstead (Curle 1911, 70) and Bearsden. It is not certain if any cavalry were present at this last fort, but it is possible that some cavalrymen were outposted to Bearsden from the nearby fort at Castlehill, and a building resembling the Ilkley stable was discovered (Breeze 1979, 23; Hartley 1973, 6–7).

Two forts which have caused some problems are Bainbridge and Gellygaer, where stables have been tentatively identified despite the fact that the garrisons were probably all infantry. At Bainbridge a building with a central drain was found, which may have been a stable for baggage animals. Each unit would require such animals, but it is not known how many and 'stabling for these animals has never been satisfactorily identified' (Breeze and Dobson 1974, 18 n.6). Richmond suggested that this was also the solution for the stable at Gellygaer, but Hartley disagrees (1966, 31 n.23), suggesting that the unit at Gellygaer was in fact an equitate cohort and that the stable is a genuine one for cavalry horses. This is perhaps less likely in view of the small size of the fort. It is possible that the building under discussion was a *fabrica*: the water tank at the end of the block could have served some industrial purpose, and its presence is not necessarily associated with horses.

The fort at Niederbieber in the Roman province of Upper Germany, has already been discussed in brief (p.186). The reconstruction of the stable blocks at Künzing (Fig.67) while ingenious in the allocation of space for horses, and also for stable guards and storage for fodder, remains a hypothetical case which has not been proven. The buildings in question may have been used as stables but so little of the internal area was excavated that the arrangements cannot be definitely established. In Lower Germany the case of Valkenburg (Fig.68), where the stable had an internal drain and a trough outside, seems a little more certain (Johnson 1983, 178–9). But the

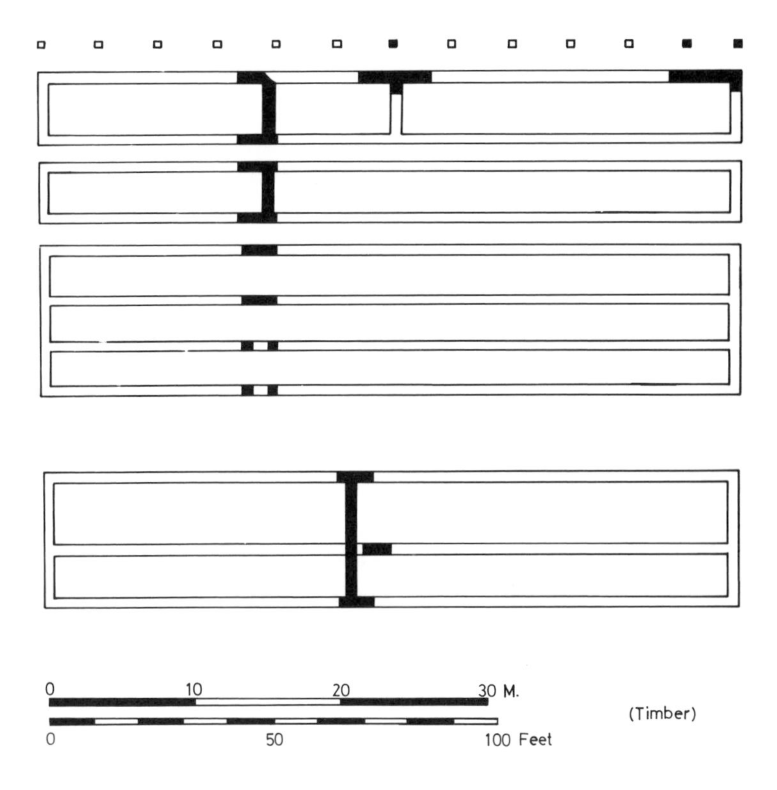

67 Plan of the stable blocks at Künzing. (Redrawn by G. Stobbs from Schönberger 1975.)

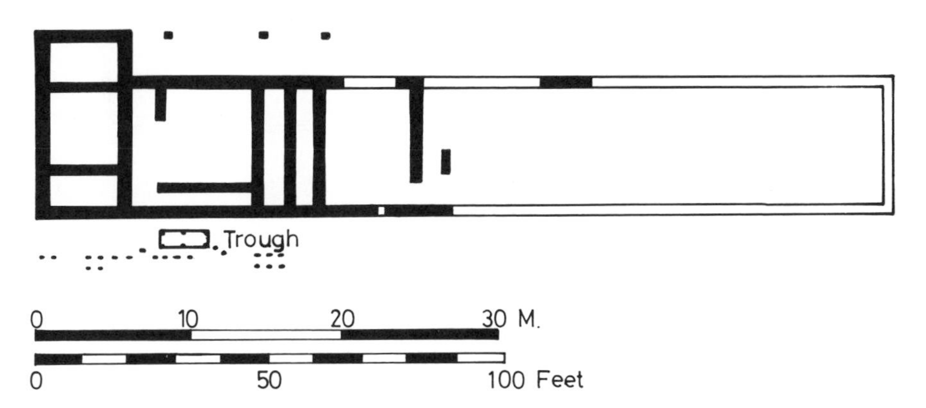

68 The presence of a trough outside this building in the first fort at Valkenburg may indicate that horses were accommodated here. But since water would be necessary for many different purposes, the presence of troughs does not automatically prove that the buildings associated with them were stables. (Redrawn by G. Stobbs from Johnson 1983.)

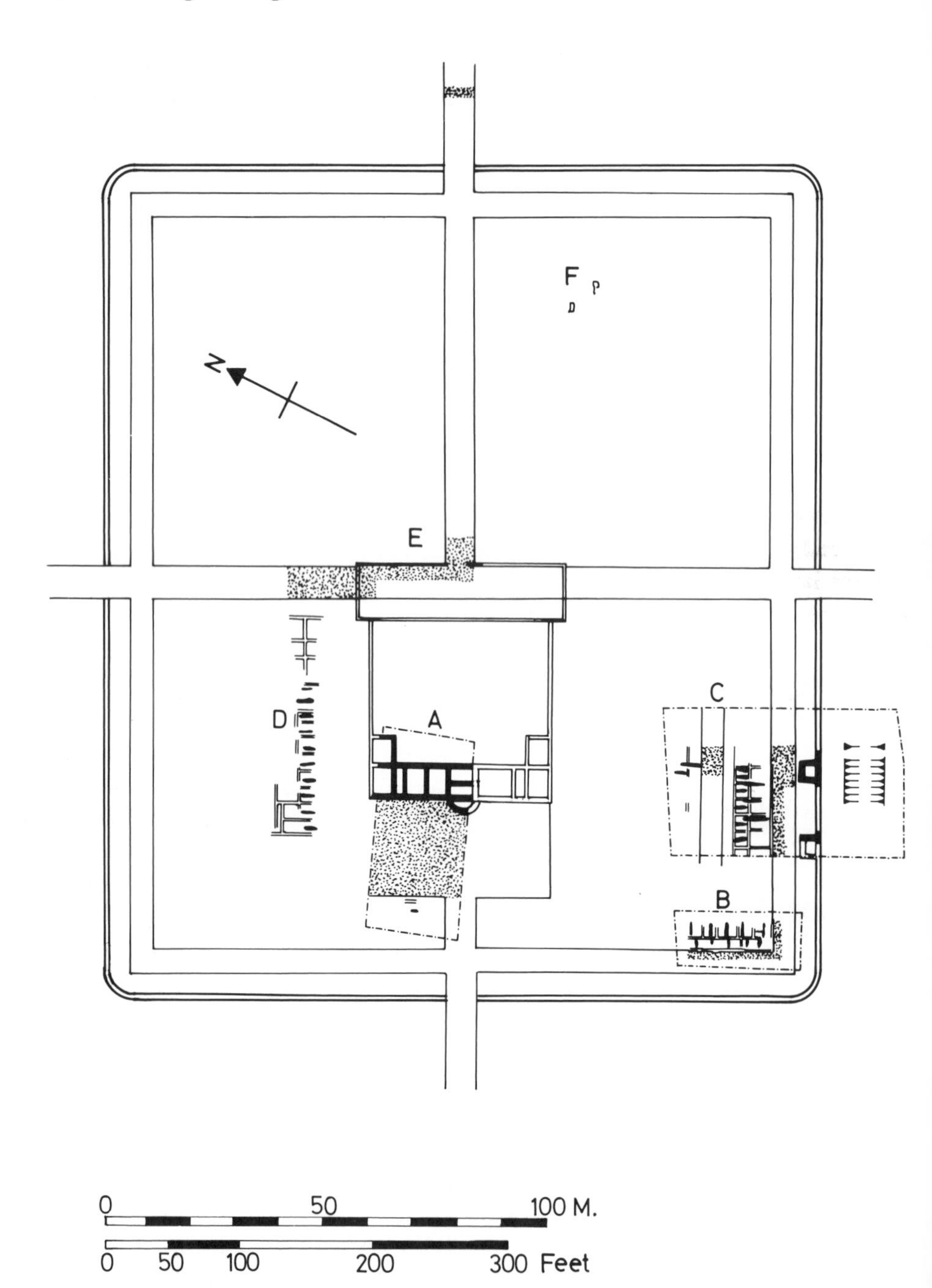

69 Site plan of Dormagen showing the location of the stable blocks labelled B, C, and D. (Redrawn by G. Stobbs from Müller 1979a.)

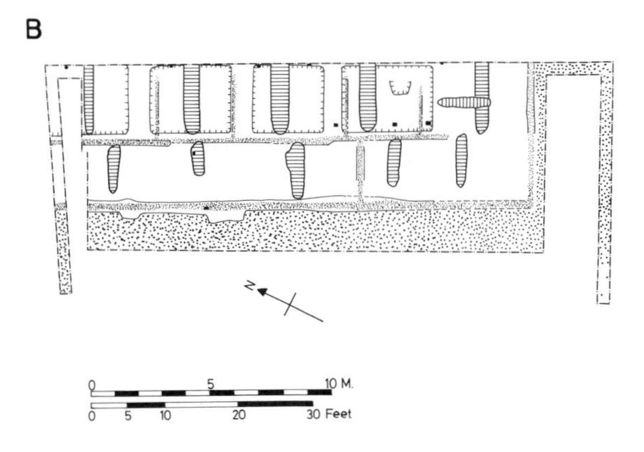

70 Area B at Dormagen, showing the soakaway pits running across the width of the individual rooms. Chemical analysis of the contents of these pits revealed the presence of animal dung and urine. (Redrawn by G. Stobbs from Müller 1979a.)

fort where the existence of stables seems irrefutable is Dormagen (Figs.69 and 70).

This fort lies between Neuss and Cologne on the Rhine in Lower Germany. It was built in timber *c.* AD 80–90, and reconstructed in stone about the middle of the second century, probably when the *Ala Noricorum* arrived there (Müller 1979a, 36). In different areas of the fort four separate stable blocks were discovered, three of which possibly accommodated both men and horses under one roof. The building in area C (Fig.71) of the fort was divided longitudinally, and the presence of hearths in the cubicles on one side, and soakaway pits dug into the floors of the stalls on the other, indicate that the troopers lived in one half of the block and their horses in the other.

The soakaway pits were roughly 3m (10ft) long and *c.* 0.6–0.9m (2–3ft) wide, sunk about 0.6m (2ft) deep. Chemical analysis of the soil from the infill of the pits confirmed that it contained a much higher proportion of phosphate and nitrogen than the surrounding earth (Müller 1979a, 129 ff.), which indicates the presence of animal dung and urine. The position of the soakaway pits relative to the walls varied slightly; in some stalls they were close to the rear wall but in most they were placed more centrally. The latter, Müller suggested, were intended for male horses, and the former, fewer in number, were for mares, such an arrangement taking cognizance of the different directions in which horses pass urine (Müller 1979a, 48). Buildings of a very similar type have been found at Usk, where in one barrack block rooms with hearths back on to cubicles with pits dug across them. Phosphate analysis of the contents of the pits is awaited.

The Dormagen stables are the most convincing so far, but once again it is not certain if there was enough accommodation for all the horses of the *ala* and it is worth repeating that no fort has yet been excavated where it can be stated unequivocally that all the horses of any unit were stabled inside. It has been suggested that some horses were kept outside forts (Johnson 1983, 176). The corral system of the US cavalry has been quoted as a possible parallel (Wells 1977, 662). Very few of the forts of the American frontier were surrounded by defences, and some of the animals, cattle as well as horses, were kept outside. Direct attacks on forts were rare, but Indians were ever vigilant for an opportunity to run off a fort's herds (Utley 1973, 81–2), and sometimes they succeeded (Rickey 1972, 208; 278). Horses occasionally simply took fright and stampeded (Rickey 1972, 172). The problems facing cavalry units of the Roman army were conceivably not much different. Horse-thieves were presumably equally at home in peaceful areas as in war zones, and if horses were kept outside they would probably need to be guarded all the time.

In the European climate it is to be expected that some kind of stabling would need to be provided in the winter months. But whilst oriental hot bloods cannot stand outside in a north European winter, native horses that have evolved to cope with the climate can do so (*pers. comm.* A. Hyland) and strictly speaking the best possible environment for horses is to be kept outside all year round. When kept indoors they need a great deal of care and attention if they are to remain fit and healthy (White 1970, 290–1). It is absolutely essential to keep the floors of stables dry to preserve the horses' feet, and grooming is very important. The stables must be regularly cleaned, or respiratory and other troubles will soon develop. On the other hand, horses can survive extreme winter conditions in the open air if they are properly looked after and provided with wind-breaks or rudimentary shelter. A horse's natural winter coat will provide considerable protection from the elements. For instance, in the First World War, some unit commanders ignored the standard regulations to clip their animals in November, so that their horses' coats grew thick and were waterproofed by the grease in the hair. The choice had to be made between clipping to avoid the spread of mange, and not clipping to afford some protection against the winter conditions. In the quagmire of the Somme in 1917 clipping had to be abandoned (Blenkinsop and Rainey 1925, 380). Grooming was confined to 'scraping off the mud with canteen knives and rubbing down with hay or straw'. The horses subjected to this treatment mostly survived; the clipped ones died in their hundreds (Brereton 1976, 128).

These circumstances were of course extreme, and were made worse by bad feeding. In more peaceful circumstances horses would survive the

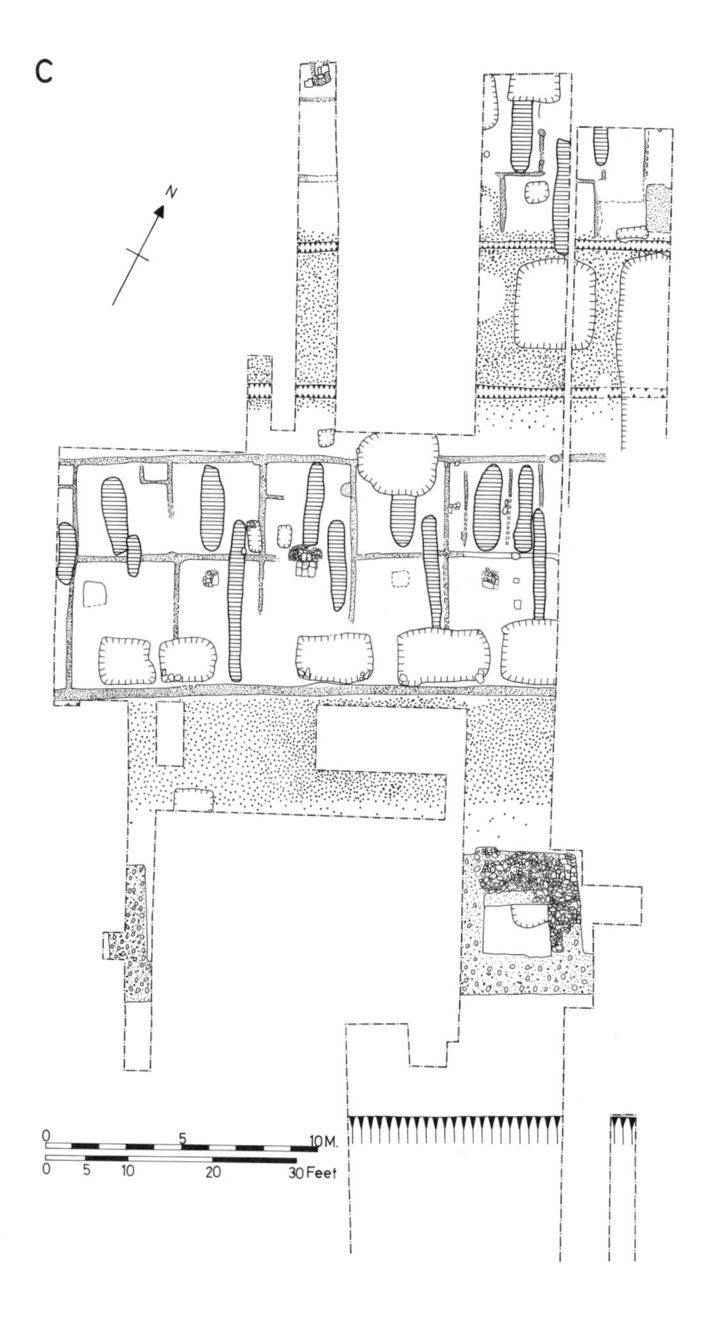

71 The excavation of the buildings of area C at Dormagen revealed evidence that men and horses may have lived together under one roof. In the cubicles along one side of the building, hearths were set into the floors, while on the other side of the block there were soakaway pits dug into the floors. (Redrawn by G. Stobbs from Müller 1979a.)

winter in the open if fed and looked after adequately. Shelter need not consist of buildings or even temporary lean-to sheds and the like; blankets can fulfil the purpose just as well. A recent suggestion is that at some forts the horses may have been sheltered in the *intervallum* area. At Petronell for instance this measures 9m (29ft) wide, and a substantial drain runs round the *via sagularis*, two factors which may indicate that horses were kept there on occasions (Davison 1989, 132). It would not be practical to use this area constantly, and whilst it would be one way of solving the problem of night-time security and ensuring access to each horse if necessary in an emergency, there would probably not be enough space for all the animals even in the whole of the *intervallum* area. The presence of drainage alone is not always indicative of the presence of horses; it can sometimes mean that there was a need to carry off surplus rainwater and nothing more. Even if this was the solution at Petronell, the principle cannot be applied to all forts, since in some buildings encroached on the *intervallum* area. During the day, whether they were stabled or picketed, those horses which were not working or being exercised were probably turned out. Frere and St Joseph (1974, 7 n.48) suggested that horses could be let out to graze in meadows around forts on a rota system, but it is only a suggestion.

Most of the evidence for the lands surrounding forts concerns legionary fortresses. Each legion controlled a large *territorium* and grew a percentage of its own food. *Prata* (meadows) are mentioned on inscriptions, for instance in Spain, *Legio IIII Macedonica* set up boundary stones between their own meadows and the fields of the neighbouring civilian areas (*ILS* 2454; 2455). Auxiliary units controlled agricultural land and meadows as well, as another inscription shows, recording the boundary between the meadowlands of *Cohors III Gallorum* and the *civitas Biduniensum* (*ILS* 5969). As Macmullen (1963, 9) points out, sickles and scythes were found at Newstead and other Roman forts. The Newstead examples had been repaired, which suggests that they were used repeatedly (Curle 1911, 283–4). Tacitus (*Annals* 13.54) mentions 'fields left empty for the use of the soldiers' indicating that agriculture was a normal undertaking.

The limits of the lands farmed by the army cannot always be so precisely defined. They probably lay some considerable distance from the fort and certainly beyond the bounds of the *vici*. Much of the land immediately outside a Roman auxiliary fort was usually taken up by civilian settlers, but the civil settlements or *vici* were often clustered together in close proximity to the fort itself, and fields may have existed further away from the dwellings and cemeteries. Besides, it does seem that *vici* were planned for by the military and confined to certain predetermined areas around forts (Sommer 1984, 14), leaving plenty of space for meadows and fields, which sometimes

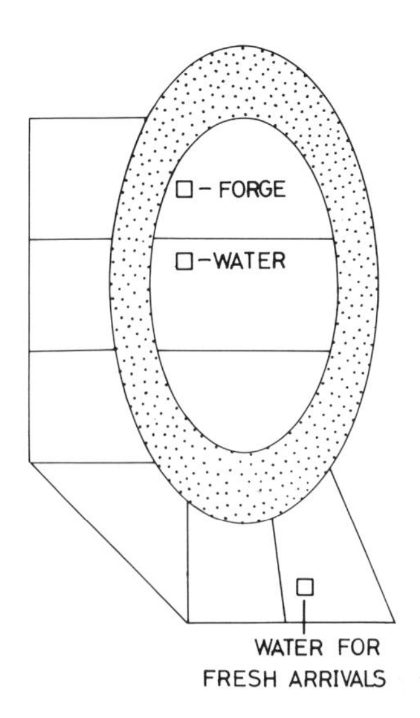

72 Diagram of a 'kraal' system from the War Office *Remount Manual* (1937). Horses were kept in paddocks around an oval track used for exercising groups of animals from one paddock at a time. The size of the 'kraal' varied according to circumstances, but the length of the track was usually between 400 and 600 yards. (Drawn by J.R.A. Underwood.)

were extensive: an estimated 3444ha (8500 acres) around the fortress of Xanten for instance (Higham 1989, 161). Provision of grazing lands would therefore not have presented too many problems, and it should have been possible to rotate the use of meadows to prevent them from becoming unusable. Four thousand horses were originally accommodated on 1215ha (3000 acres) of the grasslands of Gournay-en-Bray during the First World War. With the approach of winter the number of horses was reduced to 1200, because the grass disappeared and the pasture was too cut up to be of use. A system of open sheds and kraals communicating with an exercise track, supported by the use of the available pasture, became the norm for depots for convalescent horses in France, each designed to hold 1200 horses, staffed by three officers and 128 men (Blenkinsop and Rainey 1925, 629).

Grazing animals are not immediately available for work, and at times it may have been necessary to exercise closer control over some groups of horses to which more immediate access was necessary, or which needed to be kept under observation.

An alternative method of managing horses, if they are not to be allowed to graze freely, is the corral or paddock system. The 1937 *Remount Manual* published by the War Office describes a 'kraal' for controlling large numbers of horses (Fig.72). It is pointed out that picket lines involve great labour, whereas the kraal system saves on manpower, is suitable for any number of horses, can be improvised in existing fields or set up in any suitable open area and the horses can be kept fit for work with little or no grooming. A railed oval track is used for exercising the horses, the size dependent on the number of animals, with paddocks around it containing horses of varying classes and degrees of fitness. The occupants of each paddock are let on to the track for about half an hour, at least twice a day. 'It will be noticed how very few attendants are thus required for a very large number of horses, . . . [and] an observer . . . can see all the horse from a Kraal as they pass him' (*Remount Manual* (1937) Appendix II section 5).

If this kind of system was in use at Roman forts it would be difficult to trace archaeologically. Most excavations do not go beyond the fort ditches or the buildings of a *vicus*. A possible contender is Stanwix, which held a milliary *ala*. During the excavations outside the fort at Tarraby Lane lines of post-holes were discovered; these were taken to indicate 'high post-and-rail fences' which would be most suitable for controlling horses (Smith 1978, 28–31; 37). Such a use for these posts is by no means definite, but remains a strong possibility.

At Benwell it is just possible that an annexe outside the fort was used for horses. Breeze and Dobson (1969, 47) pointed out that the fort is too small for an *ala* and all its horses, and Sommer thought that the ditches discovered by Petch in 1928 could define an annexe, though he questioned why one should be needed when the Vallum could in part have served that purpose (1984, 17).

In warmer climates horses could be kept outside forts more successfully, and it is possible that they were picketed around fort perimeters. There would be very little archaeological trace of picket lines.

The arrangements for the security of grazing animals or horse-lines are not known. The nearest parallel is from Hunt's *Pridianum*, where an unknown number of soldiers and *sesquiplicarii* may have been 'on guard over draft animals' (Fink 1971 n.63, 227), but the phrase is extremely vague, because the animals could merely be in transit, not grazing. Josephus (*Jewish War* 6.152–3) recounts Titus' severe punishment of a trooper to set an example to the men who continually let their mounts graze while foraging and just as continuously lost them to the Jews who ran them off. After the punishment 'they no longer let them graze, but went forth on their errands clinging to them as though man and beast were inseparable'. Occasional opportunities such as this for letting horses graze does not solve the problem of how the animals were organized within forts.

It is thus hard to be certain about exactly where Roman cavalry horses were housed, if at all, but it is possible that a dual system of stables and corrals was employed. At some forts, stables may have been provided for the officers' horses, and those animals which were ill or in need of special care and attention, possibly including those recently returned from work or being prepared to do some work. The rest of the horses may have been kept outside, sometimes in corrals where they could be exercised, or where possible allowed to graze, perhaps by rota. Those not in corrals may have been picketed at nights. Insufficient work has been done to verify or disprove this suggestion. The amount of territory involved would be very large, to avoid exhaustion of the ground, among other reasons, and this would be well beyond the confines of most excavations. A compromise conclusion perhaps, but it is not at odds with the evidence. The US cavalry employed such a dual system (*contra* Wells 1977, 662, who said that stables were not part of the normal layout). Plans of forts in Arizona drawn in 1877 by Major-General Irving Macdowell plainly show stables as well as corrals (Brandes 1960, 11; 37; 49; 54; 71; 79). If the corrals were for cattle instead of horses they were usually labelled 'Q.M.' and listed as part of the Quartermaster's stores. At Fort Buchanan, Arizona, a corral was built to take all the horses of the unit stationed there (Brandes 1960, 22). On the other hand 'stable guard' was a daily duty, and in 1878 a group of soldiers petitioned Congress about their mundane existence of constant drudgery, instead of military action. They complained about building 'quarters, stables and storehouses', and 'policing quarters and stables' (Utley 1973, 83–4). These soldiers seemed to be drearily certain that stables existed in at least one fort.

Whether they were stabled or corralled, horses would require daily care and attention. Naturally they would have to be watered and fed, and it would make sense to keep them in good health and condition. Unfortunately the details of such necessary routines are virtually unknown. The military records that do exist provide valuable information about the day-to-day activities of soldiers but to date there is very little known about the arrangements for looking after a unit's horses.

Comparison with more recent army practice may not be valid in all aspects, but since horses and their basic needs probably have not changed much, the basic principles remain the same, subject to regional and chronological variations. Wherever and whenever stables were in use, daily or at least regular cleaning and mucking out would be necessary. In the US cavalry and the British army special clothing was sometimes worn for grooming and for cleaning the stables, and at morning stables, when stalls were cleaned and horses fed and groomed, in some units all men helped muck out before they commenced grooming (War Office 1899, 7). In the Roman army it is not known whether men were detailed to do this on a rota system, or even whether each man would look after his own horse. The Romans possibly did not wear special clothing for stable duty, but unlike some of the forts of the American West, Roman forts were provided with bath-houses, so there was no lack of hygiene for the men who may have performed such duties.

It has been suggested that a soldier at Dura-Europos was given this task in *c.*AD 219. The duty roster of *Cohors XX Palmyrenorum* at Dura lists the men of the unit and their allotted tasks. One J. Maximus has the entry '*ras* . . .' by his name (*P. Dur.* 101.33.9), the meaning of which is unknown (Welles 1959, 357). It may be shorthand for *rastrum*, a rake or a toothed hoe, with which Maximus had been detailed to muck out the stables, as Johnson has suggested (1983, 179–80). But *rastrum* is used by Latin authors principally in an agricultural or horticultural context, and it is just as feasible that Maximus had been sent to hoe a field or garden, so whilst it may be possible to link this evidence with stables it has to be admitted that it is not absolutely certain. If *ras* . . . was the abbreviation used to denote stable duty, it is surprising that it does not occur more often in the rosters. Presumably mucking out the stables would require more than just one man, and it is more likely that each trooper looked after his own horse, mucking out the stable himself.

It is not known what happened to the manure after it was removed from the stables. There would have been middens somewhere around each fort, used perhaps like ordinary farmyard middens on cultivated fields. In Egypt during the First World War manure was sold to civilians, and when supply exceeded demand it was incinerated. Sometimes it was dried in the sun and spread on the exercise track, where it prevented the horses from ingesting sand, and so protected them from contracting sand-colic (Blenkinsop and Rainey 1925, 173). In wetter climates, of course, this procedure could not be followed, but it was probably not an insurmountable problem. Nineteenth-century horse-cab companies based in towns and cities were not brought to a halt by an inability to dispose of manure, all the more remarkable when it is realized that some London stables were arranged in two storeys.

In the Roman army, as in any other, much of the stable routine would be concerned with keeping the floors dry, as has been mentioned. Xenophon (*Art of Horsemanship* 4.3) recommended that sloping floors should be used as these would carry off excess wet, and they should be paved with small stones so that they would not be slippery. Columella (*De Re Rustica* 6.30.2) maintains that floors can be kept dry if they are made of 'boards of hard wood, or if the ground is carefully cleaned from time to time and chaff thrown over it'. As White points out (1970, 290) this is not totally effective since the boards would rot. But replacement would be simple enough. In

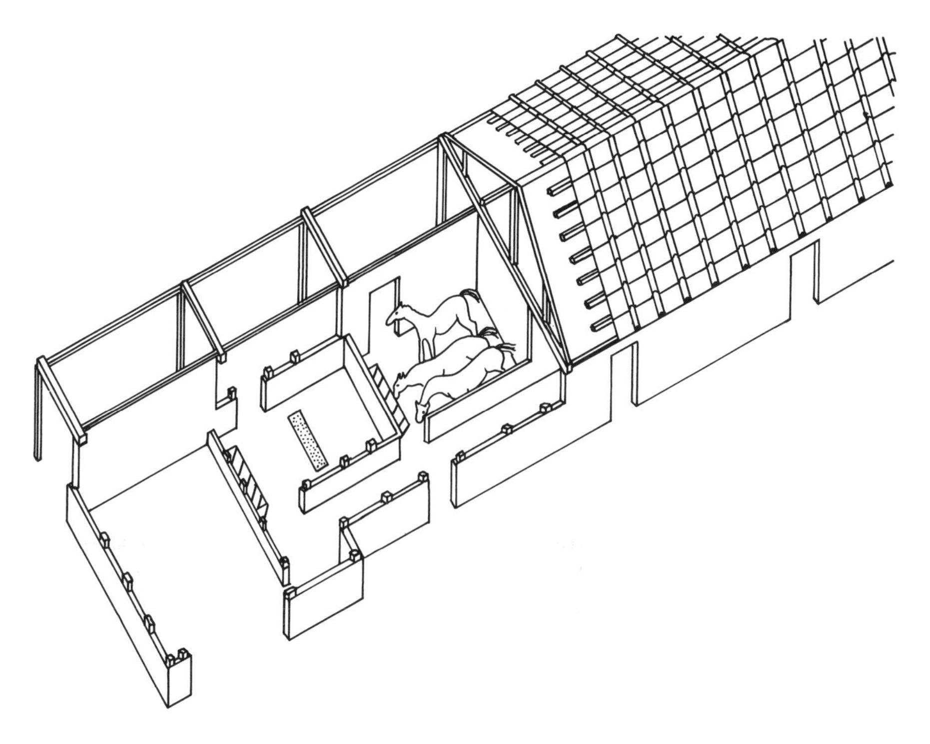

73 Reconstruction of the stables at Krefeld-Gellep, showing how the horses may have been housed. Evidence from Dormagen (Fig.71) shows that horses may have been tethered to the cross-walls of the stable building rather than in two lines down the outer walls. (Redrawn by G. Stobbs after Pirling 1986.)

England and some parts of Europe up to the beginning of the twentieth century, floorboards were used consisting of removable planks which could be taken out and washed, or replaced when necessary (Hayes 1947, 143). The soakaway pits at Dormagen may have been covered with boards (Müller 1979a, 48).

If horses are kept in stables, bedding is necessary to prevent injuries when the horse lies down, and to absorb the manure and moisture. A wooden floor is much kinder to the animals than a hard one of small cobbles such as Xenophon suggests, but bedding is still necessary even on floorboards. The most absorbent material is peat moss, which the Romans would have probably obtained for no payment. It is portable, stackable, prevents the horse eating his bed and is fire proof. In the nineteenth century it was thought that peat moss caused thrush and rotted a horse's feet, and for these reasons its use was discontinued in British cavalry stables (Hayes 1947, 170; Timmis 1929, 180). Sawdust may have been used by the Romans for horses' bedding when it was available, and presumably straw was also used. There would be little archaeological evidence of any of this if it was regularly removed, nor of the sort of wicker dung-skep which was sometimes used in more modern British stables to clear soiled bedding and manure (Hayes 1947, 177).

The air inside a stable can never be as pure as that outside, but the ideal to aim for it is to keep a horse in an environment as near as possible to the natural outdoor conditions. Ventilation is very important and one means of achieving this is to build stables quite high, allowing for a freer circulation than low ceilinged buildings. Russian cavalry horses were so housed and despite very low temperatures they thrived. The French cavalry, on the other hand, suffered losses until *c.* 1836 when stables were enlarged, when deaths were reduced (Hayes 1947, 133). The artist's reconstruction of the stables at Krefeld-Gellep (Fig.73), with the horses situated in the centre of a building with aisles on either side, would appear to be badly ventilated, and if these were truly the arrangements whereby horses were accommodated, some of them possibly did not survive it. The example of the French cavalry just quoted illustrates that the military did not always avoid mistakes.

Grooming

The artificial conditions imposed on horses by stabling them and making them work create the need for grooming. In the wild state, a horse needs to exercise only in so far as he must continually find food, and his coat grows long in winter to provide protection against the elements. But stints of hard work, which are not natural to a horse, followed by periods of idleness and regular feeding when the horse does not have to exert himself, mean that the natural cleansing process of the skin stops, escape of secretions is reduced and health suffers. The extent to which horses should be groomed depends on how they are housed. In the open, much depends upon climate, food supply and the existing condition of the animals. Unclipped horses with long coats could survive out of doors all year round, and they would not need grooming unless for the sake of appearance. A long coat diminishes slightly the horse's capacity for fast work; sweat is more profuse and difficult to dry off, which increases the risk of chills, but thorough grooming to remove grease reduces the ability to withstand cold. In India a compromise was sometimes adopted, whereby unclipped horses were groomed, but kept outside covered with blankets in very low temperatures (Hayes 1947, 197). Though there is no information it is possible that some similar methods were adopted by the Romans in the colder European climates; but blankets are not proof against wet weather. Deep grooming in cold and wet conditions would not be advisable. As an alternative, it is probable that straw wisps were used to rub horses down, or that they were rubbed by hand, which makes the coat glossy without irritating the skin (Hayes 1947, 199).

Stabled horses would need to be groomed thoroughly on a regular basis. Columella (*De Re Rustica* 6.30.1) recommended that the body of a horse should be cleaned every day, but he provided no details on procedure or equipment. He merely indicated that the horse's back should be rubbed by hand; this would stimulate the blood supply pressed out by carrying a load, whether it be man or baggage, and also the best way of judging the condition of a horse's coat is by running the bare hand over it. If a horse is falling sick, the first signs always show in his coat.

Accommodation for grooms has been looked for in one or two forts, for instance at Hod Hill where Richmond identified grooms' quarters, specifically at both ends of one stable block in each pair (1968, 83). But the function of these rooms was not definitely established, and remains unproved. At Ilkley, the presence of some sherds of pottery in the stable block was explained by the possibility that grooms lived in the building (Hartley 1966, 37).

It need not be the case that certain men in each unit were appointed specifically as grooms, even in the wider sense of 'stablemaster', and not simply men detailed to look after the welfare of a number of horses. A better explanation for the presence of the pottery sherds at Ilkley is that there would most likely have been a stable guard, night and day, organized on a rota system. The US cavalry mounted guard on stables 24 hours a day; these were usually called stable police (Rickey 1972, 94; 96; 172; Utley 1973, 83–4). British army practice recommended posting guard on stables while the men were away (War Office 1904, 12). These regulations included picket lines as well as stables: 'horse-lines or stables are in the charge of line sentries or stablemen. These men come on duty to relieve the night stable piquet sentries . . . Their meals will be brought to them by the room orderlies' (War Office 1899, 9). The pottery found at Ilkley need not imply that grooms lived in the building; guards may have had their meals there while on duty, but these would be ordinary soldiers who lived in the barracks. The reconstruction of the stables at Künzing allowed space for 'Stallwachen', or guards, rather than for grooms (Schönberger 1975, 59; 63).

The question of who performed the grooming will possibly never be properly answered. Tarruttienus Paternus, a Roman jurist of the second century AD whose writings survive only in fragments, mentions *stratores*, often translated as grooms, in a list of legionary specialists (*Digest* 50.6.7). It is a misleading translation which should not be taken to imply that the legions and possibly the *auxilia* detailed certain men to care for the horses. Legionary legates and provincial governors commonly had at their disposal a corps of *stratores* who 'cannot have been stable boys' (Speidel 1974, 541).

In regular armies of more recent times, the enlisted men were responsible for grooming their own horses. The practice helps to foster good relations between man and animal, essential if the two are to work together, and it keeps the men occupied. Those men who were detailed to other duties during stable hours delegated their responsibilities to someone else, who could easily feed and groom two horses. In the British army men were instructed and supervised by an officer while grooming their mounts, or at least this was the ideal to be aimed for (War Office 1899, 6–10; 1904, 11). In the Roman army there is evidence that specific horses were issued to named soldiers (*P. Dur* 97) and it is likely that each animal was the soldier's responsibility until its death or eventual replacement. He would feed it and perhaps groom it himself, or if he possessed a slave he would see to it that these tasks were adequately performed by his servant.

It is known from epigraphic evidence that some Roman soldiers owned slaves; this may not have applied to all the enlisted men, but on many cavalrymen's tombstones there is a figure shown beside that of the deceased which can be interpreted as a slave, and in some cases soldiers set up tombs to their slaves. In the ancient sources there is frequent mention of a class of people called *calones*, which means servants, and is sometimes translated as grooms (Ammianus 22.2.8; Caesar *Gallic War* 2.24; *Civil Wars* 1.52). These men probably attended to the needs of the horses as well as those of their masters.

In any army the best way of ensuring that necessary duties are carried out is to stipulate the hours for performing them and for officers to supervise the proceedings, instead of leaving everything to the discretion of the men. The amount of attention paid to each horse would depend on the time spent on other work or exercises and it is likely that in the Roman army most peacetime routines were performed according to a schedule as far as possible, with times laid down for watering, feeding, exercising and grooming. The most important times for grooming would be when horses returned from work, when it would be necessary to examine backs for sores, dry the coat, possibly with a straw wisp, and clean out the feet. Even a thorough grooming of a stabled horse should not take too long. The British army manual on stable management states that the dirtiest horse can be cleaned in an hour if the groom works with a will, and at grooming times no horse was passed as clean until it had been inspected by an officer (War Office 1904, 10–11).

In the Roman army it is possible that the officers of each *turma* were responsible for the supervision of stable duties, picket lines and grooming. A decurion and his subordinate officers would have been responsible for about 30 to 50 horses, or possibly more if remounts were kept at the fort, but an experienced officer ought to have been well enough acquainted with each animal to know its habits and idiosyncracies, and to be able to notice immediately any signs that it was losing condition or that its rider was neglecting it. Inevitably, probably not all units maintained optimum standards and there were perhaps instances of unnecessary animal wastage caused through bad management or ignorance. But the very longevity of the Roman army must bear some relation to its standard of efficiency, and it would be totally at odds with the highly disciplined and mostly successful performance of the army if troopers rode broken-down, neglected horses. Besides, the fine workmanship and elaborate designs of Roman sports armour and horse trappings indicate that there was a keen sense of pride in appearance among all units, most especially in the cavalry, and this would include not just the cavalrymen but also would extend to the horses. It is difficult to imagine that such expensive and beautiful trappings were put straight on to an unkempt horse, brought at a moment's notice from stable or field. On ceremonial occasions at least, if not at regular times, it is to be expected that a great deal of time and effort would be spent on grooming.

Little is known of the equipment for grooming from either civilian or military contexts. Xenophon speaks in the vaguest terms of 'grooming implements', which he does not describe, because ancient readers would no doubt know quite well what he meant. He suggests that no instrument except the hand should touch the horse's back, and that the horse's head should be washed, 'for, as it is bony, to clean it with wood or iron would hurt the horse' (*Art of Horsemanship* 5.5). Brushes were most likely made of wood and fitted with a webbing strap like modern examples, and these would only rarely survive. It is possible that remains of such items would be interpreted as sandals, unless they were found almost complete with unmistakable bristles still attached (*pers. comm.* L. Allason-Jones). Hartley (1966, 37) suggests that a broken *strigil* found in the stables at Ilkley may have been used for grooming. It could have been used as a sweat scraper or for removing mud from horses' legs. In many cases, wisps of straw were probably used for rubbing down horses, and this practice would not be archaeologically detectable.

12 Water and food supply

Water supply

Water storage tanks, wells and aqueducts are known at several forts, but not all of these forts necessarily held mounted units. Water is necessary for a variety of purposes, besides the obvious drinking and bathing, so it cannot be stated that the tanks at Benwell, Brough-on-Noe or Gellygaer necessarily supplied horses. But it is amply demonstrated that the Romans took considerable care over the provision of water, and therefore the supply of drinking water for cavalry horses and baggage animals would not have been a problem, save in circumstances of severe drought and at some times on campaigns.

Archaeological evidence has shown that there was a piped water supply at the legionary fortress at Chester, where lead pipes were found stamped with the name of the governor Cn. Julius Agricola and dated to AD 79. An inscription from Öhringen, Germany, records a 'new aqueduct' in AD 241, providing water for the *praetorium* and the baths (*ILS* 9179b). Excavation reports of Roman forts in Germany nearly always pay some attention to the water supply, even if only to consider where the best source may have lain. At Künzing, Schönberger investigated the water provision fully and published a hypothetical plan of the fort's supply system (1975, 83). Despite this it is still not known how the water reached the horses at any Roman fort. Although consumption would vary according to climate and the amount of work done each day, each horse would have to be watered two or three times a day to provide the necessary average of six to eight gallons which each would consume. Twice a day may have been sufficient, as was found by an experiment carried out during the Sinai desert campaign in the First World War. Horses of the same type and of equal condition were selected and divided into two groups, one watered three times a day and the other watered twice. The latter group improved in condition more rapidly than those watered three times a day, and when the amount of water consumed was measured, it was discovered that horses watered twice a day consumed more than those watered three times (Preston 1921, 315). Common sense dictates that troughs must have been provided, but it is difficult to prove that water tanks inside forts were specifically intended for horses. In most forts, there would have been little room to water large numbers of horses directly at the tanks, but there was probably no need to do so. It is likely that the only animals kept inside forts during the day were convalescent horses and officers' mounts, which could be taken to drinking troughs by rota. In circumstances where a horse could not be led to water troughs, buckets may have been used, which is of course extremely labour intensive and time consuming.

It is possible that in most instances horses were watered at rivers, since nearly all forts were situated close to such a water supply. If this was the case, the same routine may have been adopted both at the fort and also on field service, when rivers and streams provided the only source of supply. Horses may have been taken to water *turma* by *turma*, supervised by an officer. The War Office in 1904 recommended that horses be taken unit by unit 'at stated intervals, to avoid confusion at the watering place . . . No man should take more than two horses to water. The practice of sending four or five horses tied together under one man is objectionable; it must result in several horses not getting sufficient water' (War Office 1904, 20). There follows a recommendation that the watering place should have a sound bank and bottom, with wide approaches and exits, so that movement is not hindered. Where banks are steep, ramps should be provided, one for horses arriving, placed upstream, and one for them to leave by, placed downstream.

All of the above naturally describes ideal circumstances which would not always occur when an army was on campaign. But the Romans were nothing if not practical and sufficiently regimented to have operated along the lines described. A late source, Maurice's *Strategikon*, shows that by the end of the sixth century some thought had been given to the problems of the water supply, presumably based on earlier experience. Maurice describes how to store water in earthenware jars or in barrels, pierced so that water can run into another container to be poured back into the jars, to keep it constantly fresh (*Strategikon* 10.4). In another chapter (11.22) he suggests that if there is only a small or narrow stream available, it is much better to water the horses from buckets. This would, however, take a long time to execute and may have hindered progress considerably. The Desert Mounted Corps in Judaea during the First World War faced this problem. Sometimes even when the wells had plenty of water in them, the time taken to raise it meant that units had to move on before horses had had their fill, and on some occasions the horses tolerated and survived extreme conditions. One battery of the corps rode and fought for nine consecutive days, during which horses were watered only three times (Preston 1921, 314–15).

Food supply

A horse in its natural habitat, living on grass, will eat most of the time; it requires food in small amounts frequently throughout the day, so that it is better to feed a stabled horse about three or four times a day rather than only once or twice (Edwards and Geddes 1973, 140). Grass alone, even when supplemented by hay in the winter months, is not sufficient for working horses since it will not keep them in hard condition. To achieve this, extra food, usually cereals, must be given, and equally important, horses must be regularly exercised as well.

Xenophon (*Cavalry Commander* 1.3) emphasized the importance of sufficient food for horses so that they would be able to perform as well as required and he recommended that the government authorities should reject horses which could not keep up with the rest, so that their owners would be induced to feed them properly. All of this suggests that Xenophon wished to outline the drawbacks in the system whereby there was no standing army. In his day individual citizens were responsible for their own animals' welfare, and there was no central authority to enforce regulations and see that they were carried out.

Correct feeding for any horse is essential if it is to be kept fit and healthy, and to a certain extent this depends upon the characteristics and temperament of each animal; horses, like humans, are subject to personal preferences. This means that each horse must be constantly supervised in case it begins to lose condition, a fact recognized by the British army: 'in every stable there are horses which require individual attention' (War Office 1904, 6). It was recommended that officers should take especial care at feeding times to ensure that each horse was receiving enough food and water. The feeding times were properly regimented, one man being sent ten minutes before the stated time to collect feeds for his section. A report was made to the senior officer that feeds were ready and then the order 'Feed' was sounded. 'If this is not done it is not possible to tell with certainty that all the horses have been fed' (War Office 1899, 10).

The quantity of food necessary to sustain each horse depends upon its size and the amount of work it is to perform. The ratio of cereals to hay can be varied, provided that the horse always receives adequate food-value to sustain the amount of work it is doing. Generally speaking, modern horses are fed more hay and less cereal when they are not working; when in work, horses require less roughage, so the quantities of hay can be reduced, but they require more protein and 'energy' foods, so the cereal ration should be increased (Ewer 1982, 118). Oats, barley and maize are the most commonly used modern cereals, but barley is fattening, and usually slightly less barley or maize is given compared to oats.

In the eighteenth century, British army cavalry horses were allowed a daily forage ration of 5.4kg (12lbs) of oats and 4.5kg (10lbs) of hay (Rogers 1977, 47). By 1904 these quantities had changed in proportion to each other, and each horse was allowed 5.4kg (12lbs) of hay, 4.5kg (10lbs) of oats and 3.6kg (8lbs) of straw, divided into three feeds, or better still where conditions permitted, four feeds a day. In addition, chaff was mixed with feeds, and bran mash, sometimes with linseed, was given once a week, the recommended times being Saturday evenings. Chaff 'prevents horses from bolting their food unchewed' (War Office 1904, 8).

Chaff was probably also given to Roman cavalry horses mixed with their feeds. Columella, writing in the first century AD, mentions chaff, albeit as a commodity to strew on floors of stables (*De Re Rustica* 6.30.2). It is reasonable to suppose that it was also used as a foodstuff and that Roman horses were fed on a mixture of chaff and cereal produce. In the later Roman Empire soldiers in some areas had to collect their own hay and chaff within a radius of 32km (20 miles) around their forts, with the balance made up from government storehouses. In late Roman Egypt provision of chaff was taken seriously and officials were sent to collect it (Jones 1973, 629; 1262 no.46).

As an essential commodity for maintenance of health in cattle as well as horses, and indeed in humans, salt was widely used in the Empire. Columella describes how in the early days of Rome it was thrown on to the stones around cattle pens for cows to lick, but by his own day, rock salt was provided in pastures, which is much less wasteful.

A variety of fodder crops were listed by the Roman agricultural writers, but, naturally, not all of these could be grown all over the Empire because of differences in soils and climate. The fodder crops that Cato listed are quite limited when compared to those of later writers (White 1970, 202). At some time in the first century BC medic clover (lucern or alfalfa) reached Italy; Varro included it in his list of fodder crops, and Columella enumerates all its splendid qualities ending with the statement that the yield from one *iugerum* of it provides enough to feed three horses for a year (*De Re Rustica* 2.10.25). A mixed crop of barley, vetch and legumes, called *farrago* is mentioned by Pliny (*Natural History* 18.142), Columella (*De Re Rustica* 2.10.31), and Varro (*De Re Rustica* 1.31.4–5) who says it is good for purging horses in the spring.

All the above authors are concerned with civilian farming practice, specifically that of Italy itself, so it is not possible to say how much of the information which they provide can be applied to the Roman army. The evidence for cereal rations issued to the cavalry is not abundant. Polybius' account is the main written source (6.39.12–14), but he described the military procedures of the Republic. There was no standing army at this time and the conditions obtaining at later periods in the history of the Empire were different.

Polybius distinguished between the Roman cavalrymen and those of the allies. The men were issued with wheat and the horses were fed on barley, and the rations were two *medimni* of wheat and seven of barley per month for the Roman cavalryman, and one and one-third *medimni* of wheat and five of barley for the allied cavalryman. This distinction cannot necessarily be applied to the cavalry troops of the Imperial Roman army, so it is not really certain how valid these figures would be for the cohorts and *alae* of the Empire.

Furthermore there are problems about the exact quantities of the rations which Polybius noted. He wrote in Greek, which means that he had first to translate the Latin terms into their equivalent measures in his own language. The conversion from ancient Greek to modern equivalent weights varies quite considerably. For instance Brereton's interpretation (1976, 20) was that each horse was allowed ten and a half bushels of barley per month, which gives a ration of 9kg (20lbs) per day – an extremely large amount, which may not be correct. Walker (1973, 340) translated the Greek terms back into Latin and then into English, and decided that since the Roman *eques* was expected to maintain three horses and one attendant, the rations must have been divided accordingly. He arrived at a figure of 1.5kg (3½lbs) of barley per day for each horse, which is probably more realistic. This does seem quite low compared to modern standards, but the protein content of ancient cereals was higher than that of modern produce, so that this amount was quite adequate. Hyland (1990, 91) estimated that each horse would consume 4.5kg (10lbs) of hay and 1.5kg (3½lbs) of grain per day.

The evidence found in two military papyri seems to support these estimates. In AD 187 a *duplicarius* of the *ala Heracliana* at Coptos, Egypt, received 20,000 *artabai* of barley as the year's supply for the horses of his unit. Walker links this to a sixth-century papyrus (*P. Oxy*. 2046) which gives the daily ration per horse of one tenth of an *artaba*. On this scale, the 20,000 *artabai* for the *ala* at Coptos 'would be sufficient to feed 548 horses for 365 days' (1973, 340).

These figures may perhaps be entirely accurate, but it is possible that there was considerable variation in the quantity and quality of food issued to cavalry horses in different provinces and also at different times in the history of the Empire. A comparison of sixth-century with second-century figures may be misleading in the absence of firm evidence, even when the mathematical calculations seem to be compatible. The information contained in the surviving military papyri mostly concerns the eastern provinces, and this may not be readily applicable to those of the west. Some breeds of horses are hardier than others, and can endure long stints of hard work on food which would be inadequate for less tolerant breeds. It is unlikely that all the horses used by the Romans were exactly the same throughout the Empire; consequently it is to be expected perhaps that there should be some variation also in their care and management. The amounts of food given to horses and the type of grain used were presumably determined by the availability of crops and the local agricultural systems. Imports were not out of the question, of course. A papyrus of AD 100–5 from Moesia (Hunt's *Pridianum*) shows that men from *Cohors I Hispanorum Veterana* had gone to Gaul for clothing and grain, and other men were 'at the grain ships' (Fink 1971, no.63).

The papyri from Egypt and Dura-Europos indicate that barley formed the basis of the cereal ration for the cavalry horses in the east. Where names and ranks are available from the Dura rosters they show that cavalrymen were sent to procure barley, a task usually noted in the records as *ad hordeum*, which means literally 'to the barley', abbreviated to *ad hord* or *ad hor*. In AD 219 Julius Antoninus was sent on this errand (*P. Dur.* 100.33.26), and three years later it was the turn of Aelius Licinnius (*P. Dur.* 101.36.18). Both men were *duplicarii* (Welles 1959, 41). A record written in Greek in 225 shows that a decurion and a cavalryman were given money for the purchase of barley (*P. Dur.* 129) and in 233 an unknown number of soldiers and cavalrymen were sent for barley with more men detailed to arrange transport or escort for it (*P. Dur.* 82). Unfortunately it is not stated where the grain came from nor how far it would have to be transported; the military authorities would not need to note down such details since it would be well known where the soldiers had gone. The records were concerned only with the names and numbers of men absent for whatever reason.

In Britain hulled barley has been found in a burnt deposit dated to AD 90–130, from south-west of the fortress at Caerleon (Applebaum 1972, 109) and grains of barley were recovered from the latrine at Bearsden (Breeze 1982a, 149). But the Roman cavalry horses in Britain may have been fed on other cereals. Recently, it has been suggested that the Roman military presence in Britain perhaps stimulated the demand for oats (Haselgrove 1982, 83). Oats form a very hardy crop, well suited to the wetter and colder climate of the Highland zones, and the first-century writer Columella recommended oats as a fodder-crop. It may be significant that oats were found at the forts of Castlecary and Birrens, where in each case a part-mounted unit was stationed (Applebaum 1972, 109). Oats were grown in the south of Britain from about the end of the first century AD; at Verulamium oats and other cereals were found stratified in early second-century levels. The evidence indicates that oats were used in civilian as well as military contexts, and it is likely that in the Roman period oats formed part of the diet of humans as well as horses, just as they do today. But it is not clear whether cultivation of oats was enforced by military requisitions, or whether some natives, sensitive to a ready-made market, took the opportunity to meet the demands of the army on a voluntary basis.

Besides oats and/or barley a horse needs regular supplies of hay. Most of the evidence for how this was obtained comes once again from Egyptian papyri, two of which concern the *Ala Veterana Gallica*. Serenus, of the *turma* of Donacianus in this unit, addressed a receipt to the hay contractors (*conductores faenarii*) for hay for the whole *turma* in June AD 130 (Fink 1971, no.80). The *conductores* may have been civilians, as were the sutlers contracted to supply the eighteenth-century British army. Civilians sometimes provided wood and hay for the US Cavalry too (Rickey 1972, 91). Fink suggests, however, that the *conductores faenarii* were probably military personnel.

In another papyrus dated to AD 179, a group of cavalrymen wrote receipts in soldiers' mis-spelt Greek for their hay money (25 *denarii*) for the year (Fink 1971, no.76). These two pieces of evidence would seem to contradict each other; in the first papyrus one man receives the hay for a whole *turma*; and in the second, money is issued to individual soldiers. There is no evidence as to how the hay was paid for, but it would be sensible to pay for the whole amount for the *turma*, whereas it would seem rather unwieldy for each cavalryman to procure and pay for his own supplies of hay. It is possible that the procedure was comparable to the reimbursements made to the cavalrymen of the British army in the eighteenth century. They were allowed a forage ration for 365 days of the year, but when their horses were sent out to grass, the money saved on the unused forage was paid to each soldier (Rogers 1977, 47). A large proportion of the Roman cavalry receipts for hay money dated to January AD 179, and the amount is always the same, 25 *denarii*. It seems that this money was not spent immediately on hay, since one man asked that it should be paid directly to his brother to pay off a debt. If cavalrymen were allowed to spend their hay money on whatever they liked, there could be no guarantee that they could afford to replace the 25 *denarii* from their own pockets, and therefore no guarantee that the horses would receive their rations, which seems to be a very unmilitary approach to the matter. A much better system is for one or two men to arrange the hay supply corporately for the whole *turma*, which was perhaps the normal procedure, and to reimburse the men who took their horses to grass.

Most of the soldiers state in their receipts that they are leaving for a variety of places. Some of them merely say that they are going to the country (*boukolia*) (Fink 1971, no.76: 6, 16, 18, 24, 27, 33, 36, 42, 45). This Greek word can mean not just country but also grazing or pasture. Six of the men say that they are bound for Scenas Mandras, the Greek version of Scenae Mandrorum (Fink 1971, no.76: 9, 17, 21, 31, 35, 37), situated on the eastern bank of the Nile roughly opposite Memphis. The modern Egyptian name for Scenae Mandrorum is Helwan, which means sweet, as applied to sweet pasture, and the Greek *mandra* means cattle pens or grazing lands. Other places mentioned as the destinations of the various soldiers include Arsinoë, Aphrodito[polis] and Mariotis, on Lake Meroë in the Fayum. These places are situated in fertile grasslands that could have been used by the Romans for grazing cavalry horses, and grass would have been plentiful from November to April. The greater part of the men left at different dates throughout January, and smaller groups left in February and March. They belonged to different *turmae*, so there was possibly a rota system to release a few men at a time from each *turma*, so that not too many soldiers were absent all at once from each troop.

In other provinces it may not have been necessary to arrange for cavalrymen to take their horses to specified grasslands and it may instead have been possible for horses to graze close to their home-base. The possibility that meadows existed near to some Roman forts has already been mentioned. Whether the horses were kept in picket-lines, corrals or stables inside forts, those which were not working may have been turned out to grass each day during the spring and summer months. The quartermaster sergeant of a troop of the Fourth Cavalry in Arizona in the mid 1880s described how the cavalry horses and the baggage mules were all turned out together each day. Elsewhere he stated that when called out in the night, the cavalrymen could be ready to move much more quickly than in the daytime, because there were no animals to be brought in (Cabaniss 1890, 248; 250), which implies that they were rounded up and corralled or stabled each night. The same system may have been in operation at some Roman forts, wherever the military situation and the climate allowed animals out to grass during the day. At night they may have been brought back to corrals or stables, which would require fewer men to guard them.

There is admittedly not much evidence for this during the early Empire. Most of the available information dates from the fourth century and concerns the eastern provinces. In AD 362 a ruling was made that no fodder should be issued to cavalry horses until 1 August each year, which may imply that in spring and early summer horses were at grass. By the end of July the grazing would have dried up in the eastern provinces, and thereafter fodder would be necessary (Jones 1973, 629). Somewhat later, at the turn of the fourth and fifth centuries, a rather frantic series of regulations was issued in an attempt to limit the encroachments made by the army on the pasturelands of various cities (*Codex Theodosianus* 7.7.3–5). These depredations may have been caused by the mobile field army rather than the static frontier troops. At least some of the units on the frontiers, the *limitanei*, had permanent pastures attached to their forts (Jones 1973, 629) and there is no reason to think that this was a new development of the late Empire with no antecedents in the early Empire; presumably Roman cavalry horses were put out to pasture whenever and wherever it was available.

Very little is known about how often or in what manner the feeds reached the horses in the Roman army, and practically nothing is known about how and where the grain and fodder were stored. Mangers existed in civilian stables, and Vegetius (*Ars Mulomedicinae* 1.56.3–5) says that cleanliness is important and that where more than one horse is to eat out of it, the manger should be divided into sections so that each horse eats only its own rations and does not steal those of another animal. The troughs at Tebessa have already been mentioned, and the possible mangers built into the wall at Qasr Bshir may have had wooden linings or racks set into them to hold the feeds (see p.183). At Tiddis (Castellum Tidditanorum) in Numidia a manger was cut out of the rock in a stable building in the fort (Vigneron 1968, Pl.6a). A late Roman fortlet on the *limes Palaestinae*, probably garrisoned by a detachment of *Cohors I Flavia equitata*, contained a stone manger in one of the rooms opening on to the courtyard (Gichon 1971, 195).

Hay would have to be put into racks or nets, which Vegetius suggests should not be too high nor too low. If horses were fed outside there would be considerable wastage of food in windy climates. The British army solved this problem in Egypt by netting the hay and issuing extra-large nose-bags to each horse (Blenkinsop and Rainey 1925, 62; 169).

The question of storage is probably unanswerable. Cavalry forts do not seem to contain more granaries than forts occupied by infantry, neither can it be stated that the granaries of cavalry forts are consistently larger than those of infantry forts, so the simple and logical conclusion that the grain for the horses was stored alongside that for the men cannot be substantiated. In most cases, the total floor area of the granaries is unknown, and there is no information as to whether the grain was stored in bins or in sacks, or how high it could be stacked if in the latter. In addition, the number of men and horses in each unit is not established and the ration scales are not understood (Gentry 1976; Manning 1975, 117–18). Thus there are too many imponderables to be certain of anything. A possible alternative is that within cavalry forts different buildings were used for storing horse feeds and they simply have not been recognized. It is notoriously difficult to establish the usage of a building by purely archaeological methods. Food for animals may have been kept outside forts, but this too is very difficult to substantiate. Where stables were in use there may have been storage lofts, but this is only conjecture. Schönberger (1975, 59; 63) allowed space in the reconstruction of the Künzing stables for storage of fodder, but this is not based on fact.

It has been estimated that the horses of a single *ala* would eat their way through more than 600 tons of barley in a year (Davies 1974, 318). After the harvest this quantity of barley would have to be kept clean and dry. Each unit may have used more than one source of supply, and the evidence furnished by the papyri suggests that in some cases soldiers were sent at intervals to collect or buy barley (p.211), so that the quantities in store at any one time may not have been impossibly large. But if all the hay for the entire year was received all at once, as might be implied by the papyrus of June AD 130 issued by the *Ala Veterana Gallica* (Fink 1971, no.80) (p.212) it would occupy a very large area. Haystacks are not impractical and will keep dry if properly thatched, but they are not safe because of the risk of spontaneous combustion and even attempts at arson, which may have been a risk if stacks were outside forts. There are more unusual dangers, too; Ammianus (23.2.8) records how in AD 363 soldiers at Batnae started to take hay from a stack which resulted in it falling down and killing fifty of them. The hay intended for army units may not have been brought directly to the forts for storage; at Fort Bowie in Arizona, occupied from 1862 to 1894, the hay camps were 13km (8 miles) away (Brandes 1960, 19). Space allocation in Roman forts is not fully understood, and it may be worth quoting Captain Hinde's notes on *Discipline of the Light Horse* written in 1778, where he recommended that food should not be kept in stables but looked after in the men's rooms (Rogers 1959, 125). This still implies some central store whence rations could be drawn at intervals, but at Roman forts supplies for horses may not have been kept within the walls. The problem of storage may one day be solved as more excavations take place; in the meantime it can be pointed out that at many Roman forts there are buildings of unknown purpose, sometimes labelled 'stores' for want of any better description.

The provisioning of a standing army, as opposed to armies on campaign, requires tremendous organization and depends upon 'carrying capacity and the stability of the economic system on which the food supply is based' (Groenman-van Waateringe 1989, 99). The volume of rations for horses needs emphasis if only to highlight the administration which of necessity lay behind it to ensure the regularity of supplies. A single military unit may have been able to provision itself adequately from its surrounding area, but in several provinces fully or partially occupied forts lay in quite close proximity to each other, thereby creating potential pressure on the resources of the region. But a stable and regular supply system, utilizing the resources of the entire province and even those of other provinces, could operate smoothly in normal circumstances and monitored to guard against times of dearth. The problems facing armies on campaign and the later mobile armies were naturally quite different. Normal sources of supply could not be used; food and fodder would have to be found wherever the army was, and on occasions the entire resources of an area could be wiped out at one stroke.

It is the availability of food and water which perhaps more than anything else limits the activities of cavalry. Sometimes it is transport which fails even though supplies are available. For this reason Caesar stayed in winter quarters as he did not think that supplies could be carried (*Gallic War* 7.10). Although horsemen can naturally move faster and cover greater distances over a period of a few days, infantry can often march further in the end (Rickey 1972, 245). Much depends on the ability of the horse to survive on short rations and some breeds suffer more than others in this respect. Even when the food offered to them is wholesome or at least adequate, some horses do not readily adapt to a change of diet. In the Peninsular War, Wellington's horses died in their hundreds for lack of suitable forage. They were accustomed to oats in England and would not eat the grain, mostly rye or Indian corn, which could be obtained for them. Indian hay was spurned by the horses of the Western Front during the First World War, and even though they were hungry, they would not eat it because it was not the sort of crop they were used to (Blenkinsop and Rainey 1925, 191–2).

Some of the horses used by the Romans were perhaps more accommodating. Appian praises the splendid qualities of the Numidian horses in two passages: 'the Numidians' horses never even taste grain. They feed on grass alone and drink but rarely' (*Roman History* 8.2.11). And later he repeats that the Numidians used small swift horses which lived on grass when they could find nothing else and could bear both hunger and thirst when necessary (*Roman History* 8.14.100).

The vulnerability of horses with regard to their feeding and watering was always a factor that could be exploited by resourceful commanders to weaken the enemy. Caesar relates how at one stage during the Civil War Pompey, being reliant upon supplies of food and fodder brought by sea, had to resort to feeding his horses on leaves of trees and pounded roots of reeds (*Civil War* 3.58). It is not recorded how the horses responded to this. In a similar situation Caesar himself was forced to hug the coastline and was cut off from corn and fodder by the troops of Petreius. The veteran cavalrymen, well used to this sort of thing, 'collected seaweed from the beach, washed it in fresh water, and by giving this to their hungry beasts, kept them alive' (*African War* 24). Seaweed is used as an additive to horse feed today.

Caesar's commentaries are full of references to the corn supply and rations for both animals and men; at the siege of Alesia he ordered the men to have 30 days' fodder ration and likewise 30 days' corn for themselves, *pabulum frumentumque* (*Gallic War* 7.74). Maurice's *Strategikon* emphasizes the importance of collecting enough fodder in advance in case the horses cannot be taken out to graze, or worse still in the event of a defeat, when the army would be unable to gather fodder unhindered (7.1.7; 13; 7.2.10).

In the late Empire, *capitus* was the term used for fodder for the horses, and it was the equivalent of *annona* or rations for the men. These rations were collected in each province and brought to the State granaries to be distributed to the army by government officials. There was, theoretically at least, tighter control than previously over the supply of fodder, and also of corn for the men. The *capitus* consisted mostly of barley and troops had to gather their own hay to supplement the rations (Jones 1973, 629). The military encroachment on civil grazing lands has already been mentioned (see p.196). There was still room for corruption in the supposedly tightened system. It appeared that officers could divert the supplies intended for the men and horses. In AD 381, according to one of the *Orations* of Libanius (2.37.9), soldiers were going hungry and without boots, and the horses were being starved because the officers had sold the rations of food and clothing (Jones 1973, 646).

13 Welfare

Exercise

In addition to proper feeding and adequate care and attention, regular exercise is just as important, indeed essential, for a horse's welfare. The military manuals of the late nineteenth and early twentieth centuries emphasize the importance of keeping horses in 'hard condition', which 'is the result of sufficient and judicious feeding coupled with properly regulated work. Troop horses suffer as much from insufficiency of regular exercise as from excess of work' (War Office 1904, 6). Cooped up in the mountains of Judaea in 1918 British cavalry horses could not be exercised because of the terrain and lack of staff and consequently they suffered loss of condition. The same problem in the Balkan campaign was solved by turning the horses out during the day along with the mules and allowing them to roam at will. It was found that they digested their rations much better because they were exercising by wandering in search of grazing all day, and 'they were punctual, almost to the minute, in filing back to their own lines at feed times' (Blenkinsop and Rainey 1925, 228; 279–80).

The build up to this ideal hard condition should be gradual. Horses that have been sick or out to grass or just idle for a time cannot be expected to survive sudden hard and fast work. 'Many cases of foot diseases, laminitis and sprained tendons are caused by horses that have been resting being given a hard or fast day without proper preparation' (War Office 1904, 6). Once the horses are in hard condition they can stand up to the rigours of campaigning or normal hard and continuous work much better than those that have not been regularly exercised. For instance, it was found during the First World War that the horses taken from the cab companies survived longer than most other animals because they were used to hard work and had been properly looked after.

The efficiency and sometimes the safety of a cavalryman depends on the condition of his horse (Nolan 1853, 61; War Office 1904, 5). Fitness cannot be achieved without exercise; expertise in handling and manoeuvring a horse cannot be achieved without constant practice, so the two processes can often be combined. Xenophon recommends that horses should be ridden up and down hills, over all kinds of terrain, and taught to leap ditches so that when circumstances demand these abilities in battle, the horse and rider will be well practised (*Cavalry Commander* 1.5; *Art of Horsemanship* 8.1–11).

The employment of Roman cavalry horses and the amount of exercise they were given would be inextricably bound up with the daily routine and special duties of the units to which they belonged. The military papyri provide much useful information about the daily life of Roman units, but because of the uncertain nature of some of the abbreviations contained in them this information can be problematical. One such abbreviation is found in the Dura papyri (*P. Dur.* 100; 101; 116) and may refer to exercising horses. It is significant that the notations refer only to cavalrymen and not to the infantry of *Cohors XX Palmyrenorum*. The duties of these *equites*, between two and four from different *turmae*, are variously described as *ad m. ambul.*, *ad man. ambul.*, *m. ambul.* or *m. amb.*, all of which presumably refer to the same task.

The initial *m.* or *man.* is not understood. Gilliam (in Welles 1959, 41) suggested that it might be a place name. The abbreviation *ambul* is presumably short for *ambulare*, which Vegetius (*Epitoma Rei Militaris* 1.27) uses to describe training exercises or route marches which he recommends should be organized regularly for both infantry and cavalry. There is no evidence that the men so listed at Dura were all sent off together, nor who commanded them if this was so, nor how long the exercise would last. But it is likely that a group of men, a few from each *turma* so as not to reduce the overall efficiency of the unit, would be sent on exercises to keep the horses in condition and the horsemanship of the men up to standard.

At any one time some of the horses of an *ala* or equitate cohort may have been resting, since no horse can work at a constant fast pace all year round. It is likely that especially in winter, the horses were brought up to condition on a rotation system, so that there would always be a supply of fit horses for any work that had to be done and for any emergencies which did not require the turn out of the entire unit. Stabling may have been used on a rotational basis for the mounts kept in peak condition and ready for action at a moment's notice (Hyland 1990, 96–7). Very serious emergencies would probably entail the use of all the horses whether they were in good condition or not.

Any horses that were resting could be kept on a maintenance routine and given enough food and exercise to ensure their well-being. The animals to be brought into hard condition would need to be exercised and worked more,

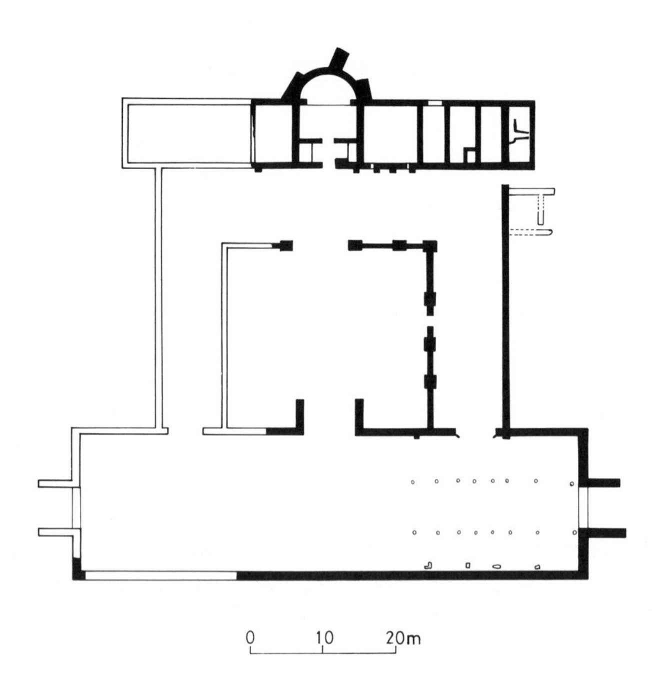

74 Plan of the *principia* and forehall at Aalen. (Redrawn by G. Stobbs from *ORL*.)

and consequently would need proper feeding commensurate with their activities. Underfeeding horses while trying to make them fit is a waste of time and is inefficient. In modern practice it takes about one month to achieve fitness after a period of rest, and three months to achieve peak condition.

The presence of forehalls in front of the headquarters buildings at some forts gives rise to the possibility that some of the cavalry exercised under cover at least during the winter. Most of these forehalls, sometimes called *Exerzierhalle* in German, are associated with cavalry units. At Aalen (Fig.74) for instance, where a huge forehall was built in front of the *principia*, stamped tiles attest to the presence of the *Ala II Flavia milliaria*, and at Künzing there was a forehall from about AD 90 and *Cohors III Thracum c.R. equitata* occupied the fort in the late first and early second centuries.

The forehall was usually built across the whole width of the street in front of the *principia* and often projected beyond the headquarters building on either side. There were usually wide entrances in the two short sides as well as in the long façade, where there was sometimes an elaborate porch. In general the halls seem to have been roofed, since roof tiles have been found in some of them, and in some instances the building was linked to others in the vicinity, forming an impressive architectural setting around the *principia* (Johnson 1983, 120–1).

The use of such buildings as drill-halls and for exercising cavalry horses is not proved beyond doubt but two pieces of evidence suggest that this may have been the case. Vegetius (*Epitoma Rei Militaris* 2.23) refers to roofed porticoes or riding halls in which the cavalry exercised during the winter, and large open halls in which infantry could be drilled in bad weather. He does not specifically state that these halls were attached to the *principia*, nor even that they were always inside the forts. The second piece of evidence comes from Netherby, where an inscription records the building in AD 222 of a *basilica equestris exercitatoria* by *Cohors I Aelia Hispanorum milliaria equitata* (Fig.75) (*RIB* 978). This inscription, however, was not necessarily associated with the *principia*. It was found in 1762 reused as a drain cover, so it is quite likely that the cavalry drill hall was a separate building. Another inscription from Lancaster (*RIB* 605) records the rebuilding of a bath-house and a basilica which had 'fallen down through age' (*vetustate conlabsum*), and yet another from Lanchester associates bath-house and basilica,

75 Inscription (*RIB* 978) from Netherby attesting the building of a cavalry drill hall (*basilica equestris exercitatoria*) in AD 222; the word *basilica* is spelt *baselica* (line 5). It is not certain where the drill hall was situated. The inscription was reused as a cover for a drain, which need not have been anywhere near the original building commemorated. (Redrawn by K.R. Dixon.)

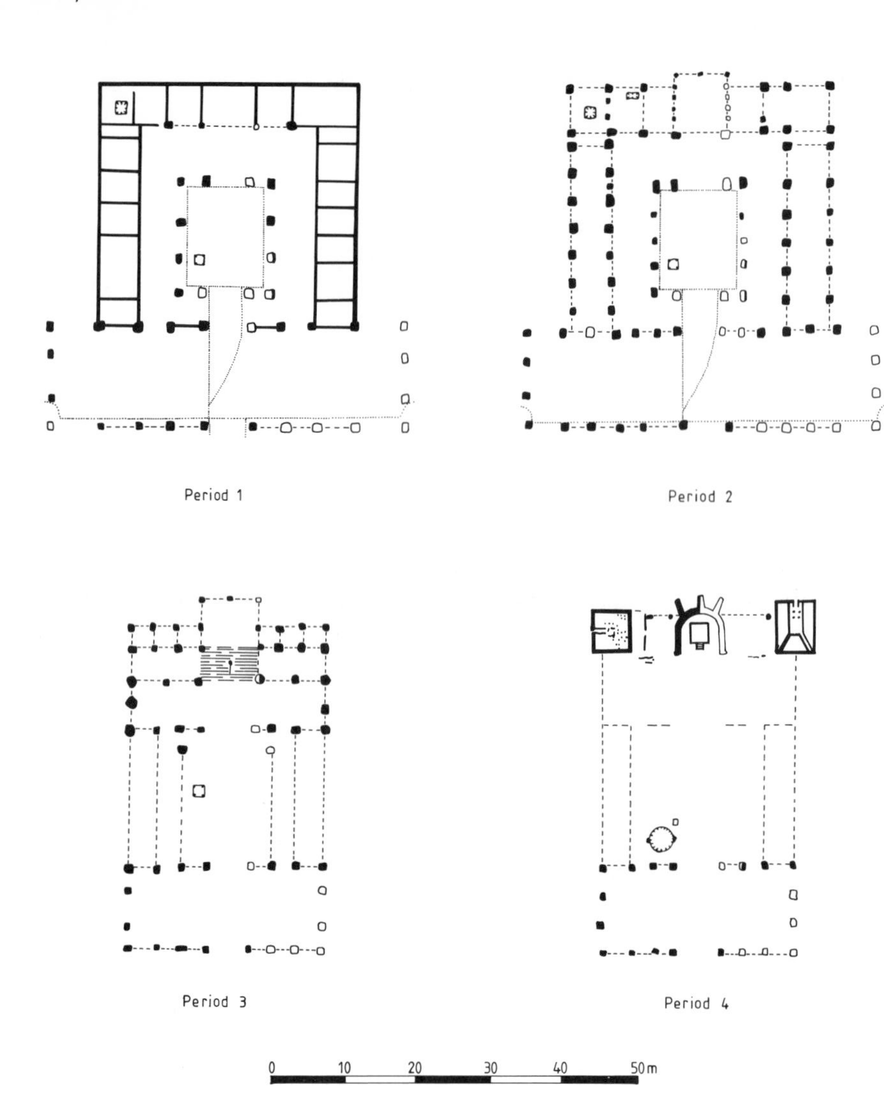

76 Plans showing the successive stages of development of the forehall of the *principia* at Künzing which was reduced in size in its later phases. (Drawn by G. Stobbs from Schönberger.)

balneum cum basilica (*RIB* 1091). Since the word *basilica* simply means hall there is no evidence that in the last two cases the buildings had anything to do with exercising cavalry horses, although the association is sometimes made. The unit at Lancaster was the *Ala Sebosiana* (*RIB* 605) and another inscription from Lanchester (*RIB* 1276) shows that the unit there was an equitate cohort. Whilst this strengthens the case that the *basilicae* were cavalry exercise halls, it must be borne in mind that when attached to a bath-house, they could provide an exercise area for the men instead.

The passage from Vegetius and the inscription from Netherby attest that in some forts buildings existed for the purpose of exercising horses and practising drill, but as yet there is nothing that irrefutably links them with the forehalls attached to headquarters buildings. These forehalls may have fulfilled some other purpose, and some of them may have been built because they were fashionable and impressive. The *basilicae* for which there is some evidence may have been separate buildings.

One objection to this use of forehalls attached to headquarters buildings as indoor riding schools is that they were erected in front of the buildings where all the daily administration would be carried out and therefore one of the busiest areas (Figs 76 and 77). It does not seem that there was any other entrance to the headquarters buildings except through the forehall, so that for anyone with business to transact in the *principia*, the experience would have been akin to crossing the Spanish riding school in Vienna on each inward and outward journey.

Furthermore, though the majority of forehalls so far known have been found in cavalry forts, at least two have been found in infantry forts. One is at Murrhardt and the other at Hesselbach (Fig.78), a *numerus* fort of 0.6ha ($1\frac{1}{2}$ acres), where the forehall is too small for any possibility of exercising horses in it. It is likely that more infantry forts possessed a *principia* with a forehall but these have not been found. Some of the forehalls were of timber, even though the *principiae* were built of stone, and it is quite possible that in some excavations the traces of such structures have been missed, especially if the excavation did not extend across the *via principalis* to pick up remains of the façade. The use of such forehalls as riding schools or drill halls must remain an unproven theory, until perhaps an inscription is found clearly associated with such a building, definitely attesting its purpose.

Veterinary evidence

In ancient literature veterinary medicine was often included in treatises on agriculture. The association with agriculture naturally meant that there should be great emphasis on the ailments and treatments of draught

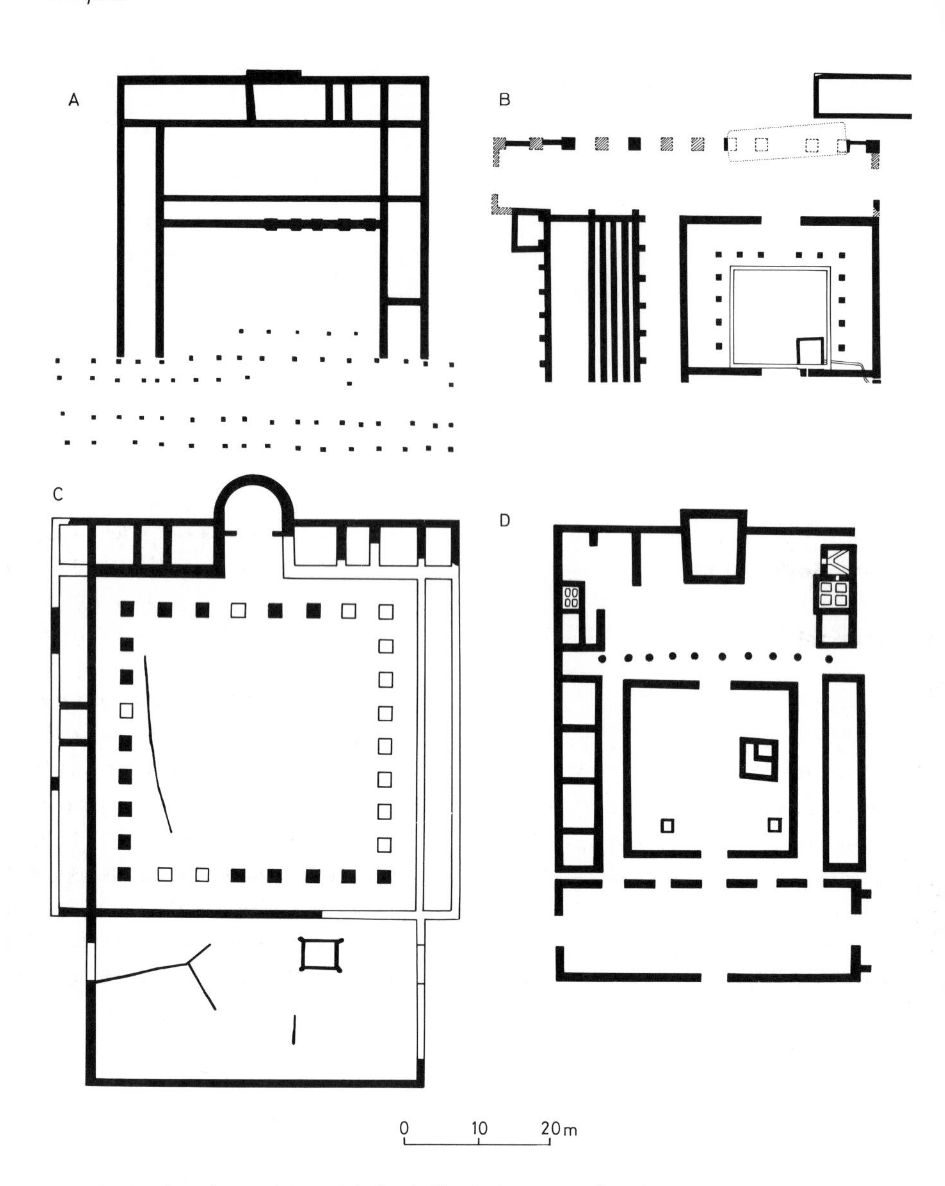

77 Examples of *principiae* with forehalls. A: Zugmantel with a stone *principia*; B: Wallsend; C: Niederbieber; D: Saalburg. (Redrawn by G. Stobbs.)

animals. The word *veterinarius* derives from *veho* which means to draw or pull, and which is the origin of the modern word 'vehicle'. Much of the information on farm animals in general is to be found in the works of the Carthaginian Mago, about whom very little is known. The original date of his work is not established but it is thought that it was translated into Latin sometimes after 146 BC, when Carthage fell (White 1970, 18).

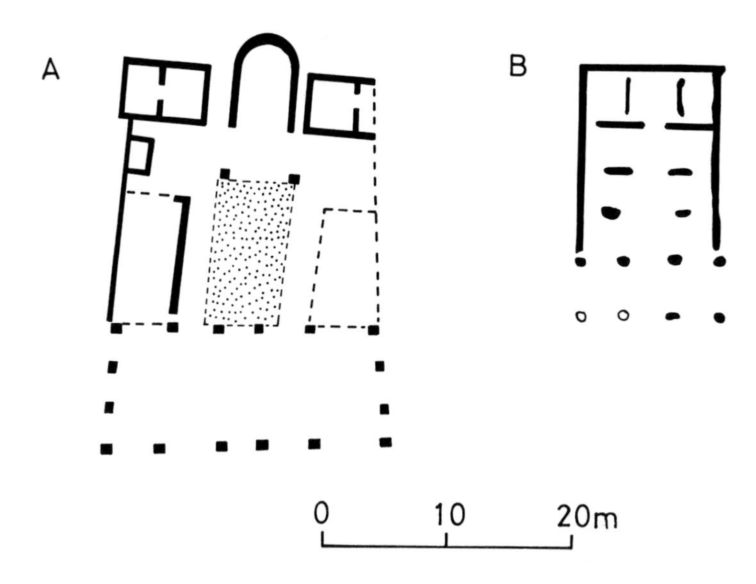

78 Plans of the timber forehalls attached to the headquarters buildings of the small forts at Kapersburg (A) and Hesselbach (B). These forehalls are much too small to allow the exercising of horses in them. (Drawn by G. Stobbs.)

Though Cato, Varro and Columella all devote sections of their works on agriculture to veterinary medicine, it is Columella whose writings are most plagiarized or copied by later authors. Pelagonius, for instance, in his mid-fourth-century work *Commenta artis medicinae veterinariae* used at least seventeen passages of Columella's work almost verbatim. Later in the fourth century, Vegetius produced a work of synthesis of all that he could find in Latin about the treatment of horses. This is the *Ars Mulomedicinae*, written by a man who was not necessarily a veterinarian himself, but who knew and loved horses and was concerned that the low status of veterinary medicine meant that the profession did not attract intelligent and capable men (Walker 1973, 303).

Evaluation of the efficacy or otherwise of the catalogue of treatments and remedies listed by the ancient authors is more properly the task of a veterinarian or horse specialist, and will not be attempted here. Vigneron and Walker, among others, have usefully summarized the ancient authors' works and commented on the relevant passages. More recently Ann Hyland (1990) has employed her deep knowledge of horses to describe their treatment in the Roman world in general.

The evolution of specialists in equine medicine seems to have begun quite early in Greece where they were called *hippiatroi*. The Romans do not seem to have had a term for this. A variety of titles is known from the Roman world. The term *veterinarius* is used consistently by Columella and this shows that the word can stand alone, but it is also found as *medicus veterinarius*, and other titles such as *medicus pecuarius* are known. A more common title is *mulomedicus*, used by Vegetius throughout his *Ars Mulomedicinae*, and it is also found in the *Codex Theodosianus* and Diocletian's *Edict*. The *Digest* uses the term *veterinarius* but the source is a second-century text.

Three inscriptions are known, all from Rome, attesting to the use of *mulomedici* (*CIL* VI 9611; 9612; 9613), and on a tombstone from Gaul a *mulomedicus* is depicted carrying a hipposandal (Fig.79)(Vigneron 1968, Pl.10b). These men were all civilians; likewise the *mulophysicus* from Britain (Wright 1977, 281). In military contexts the evidence is slight. A *medicus veterinarius* is recorded for the First Praetorian Cohort in Rome (*ILS* 9071), and a Greek inscription declares that Gaius Aufidius was *hippiatros* of *Cohors I Thebaeorum* (*IGR* 1.1373). *Veterinarii* are among the *immunes* of a legion listed in the *Digest* (50.6.7). The use of all the different terms probably represents a lack of precision rather than a narrow specialization in one particular field (Walker 1973, 314).

All Roman army units would require personnel to look after their animals. Baggage and draught animals and herds of cattle, were possibly in the care of a *medicus pecuarius* or staff with similar titles. *Veterinarii* have not unreasonably been associated with the *veterinarium* of Hyginus (*De Metatione Castrorum* 4) with the result that excavators have looked for such an area inside forts to identify as the veterinary hospital, or at least the place where treatment took place. Walker (1973, 313) disputes this idea and assigns the *veterinarium* to the draught and baggage animals, stationed in the middle of the camp for better protection while the army was on the march. Very little is known about where sick and wounded animals might have been treated in permanent forts. It may have been feasible to carry out examinations and some treatment in picket lines or stables, but more serious cases would require a separate area, so it is to be expected that sick animals would be brought to an established point inside or outside the fort. This area would ideally be roofed to afford protection from the weather. Columella (*De Re Rustica* 6.19) describes stocks and their dimensions for the restraint of horses while undergoing treatment, but so far no indisputable evidence for such an arrangement has come to light in Roman forts. In some forts where it is known that cavalry were present but the stable accommodation seems very limited, it is possible that the building or buildings so identified, particularly those without visible traces of partitions such as at Wallsend, may have been reserved for the treatment of horses and for their care whilst convalescing.

79 Tombstone from Roman Gaul showing a civilian *mulomedicus* carrying a hipposandal. (Redrawn by G. Stobbs from Vigneron 1968.)

Many questions about *medici veterinarii*, *hippiatroi* and the like in the Roman army cannot be answered on present evidence. For instance it is unknown how many of them there would be in each unit, so that no estimate can be made of how many horses each man would be responsible for. The epigraphic evidence suggests that the two men mentioned above whose army units are listed (see p.226) were permanently attached to those units and would be paid as soldiers belonging to their respective cohorts, though it is not known what rank they held. It has been suggested that *medici* in the

Roman army held a special rank, possibly equivalent to that of a centurion, but this may not apply to *medici veterinarii*. In recognition of their specialist knowledge and to facilitate their work among other ranks, it could be argued that officer status would be necessary. It is possible that there was only one veterinary 'officer' for each cohort or *ala* assisted by a staff of lower ranking soldiers, but this is to use modern parallels to an extent that may not have been applicable for the Roman army.

The status of *medici veterinarii* is uncertain, and there is no information as to how they came by their skills. They may have used whatever written information was available to them, combined with empirical knowledge acquired as they worked. It is possible that they trained as civilians and then entered the army, but this is simply once again to extend a modern parallel. Possibly some *veterinarii* were selected from within the army and trained by other army personnel. Inscriptions and other literature shed very little light on how and where *veterinarii* were educated. Knowledge passed down by means of handbooks is no substitute for practical training and carrying out treatments under the supervision of an experienced person who can correct mistakes as they occur.

By far the most frequent ailments affecting horses would probably be digestive problems and sore backs, and diseases of, and injuries to, the feet and legs. One of the most common causes of loss of condition in a horse is connected with diet. Insufficient feeding or bad quality food will be detrimental, but sometimes for various reasons horses do not digest their food properly even though there is enough of it and it is of good quality. The ancients did not fully understand the digestive process, and so any attempt to evaluate their veterinary remedies in the light of modern practice is of very limited use (Walker 1973, 334). Some symptoms are not always immediately obviously related to digestive problems, so without this understanding the symptoms are all that can be treated, rather than the root cause of the trouble. None the less, experience had taught, for example, that feeding of bad barley and hay, or overfeeding on barley resulted in laminitis, and the various types of colic were probably recognized (Vegetius *Ars Mulomedicinae* 1.49–51; Walker 1973, 332–4).

Sore backs were dealt with in Vegetius' second book, in which he first listed preventative measures such as ensuring that saddle-cloths were soft and washed to remove any abrasive material; above all, the saddle should fit properly. This should be well known to horsemen, but sometimes, due to loss of flesh, the best fitting saddle which was satisfactory to start with can cause sores and galls. Treatment according to Vegetius was by honey and linen cloths for sores, barley meal and colewort for callouses and hot onion poultices for swellings (*Ars Mulomedicinae* 2.60–3; Walker 1973, 332).

Regular care of the feet is essential, and farriers would be indispensible to any Roman unit. Some authorities would prefer to translate the term *veterinarius* as farrier. Farriery is a specialized task but not so wide-ranging as that of the *mulomedicus* proper. With suitable training it is possible that picked soldiers could be converted into farriers, which is how the British Army filled gaps in personnel during the First World War: over 400 men were trained between December 1915 and September 1918 (Blenkinsop and Rainey 1925, 33). In the US cavalry farriers ranked as corporals, paid at the relevant rate, and were responsible for about 70 horses (Rickey 1972, 110). As both Vigneron (1968, 43) and Walker (1973, 321) point out, the Roman instruments for paring and trimming hooves are remarkably consistent in design with those used up to the nineteenth century (Fig.80) except that the Roman versions are often elaborately decorated with statuettes of gods and goddesses and horses. Examples are known from Dorchester and Silchester in Britain, and Grenoble and Naples in Europe, all presumably of civilian origin (Walker 1973, 408 n.7).

Horseshoes

The question of horseshoes can be divided into two categories: firstly concerning the use of so-called hipposandals; and secondly whether Roman cavalry horses were shod in the modern sense.

Hipposandals are made of plaited straw or broom (*soleae sparteae*) or metal (*soleae ferreae*) (Fig.81). They were most likely used for keeping a dressing on a foot and protecting it from damage, like modern poultice boots. The *soleae sparteae* would presumably have been used only once and then discarded (Walker 1973, 322), whereas metal *soleae* would be both

80 Relief from Aix-en-Provence showing civilian veterinarians at work. The man on the left holds the reins of the horse in his left hand, together with an instrument that may be a pair of shears. On the right the vet is depicted possibly bleeding the horse (Espérandieu 1907 vol.1, no.104. Drawn by K.R. Dixon.)

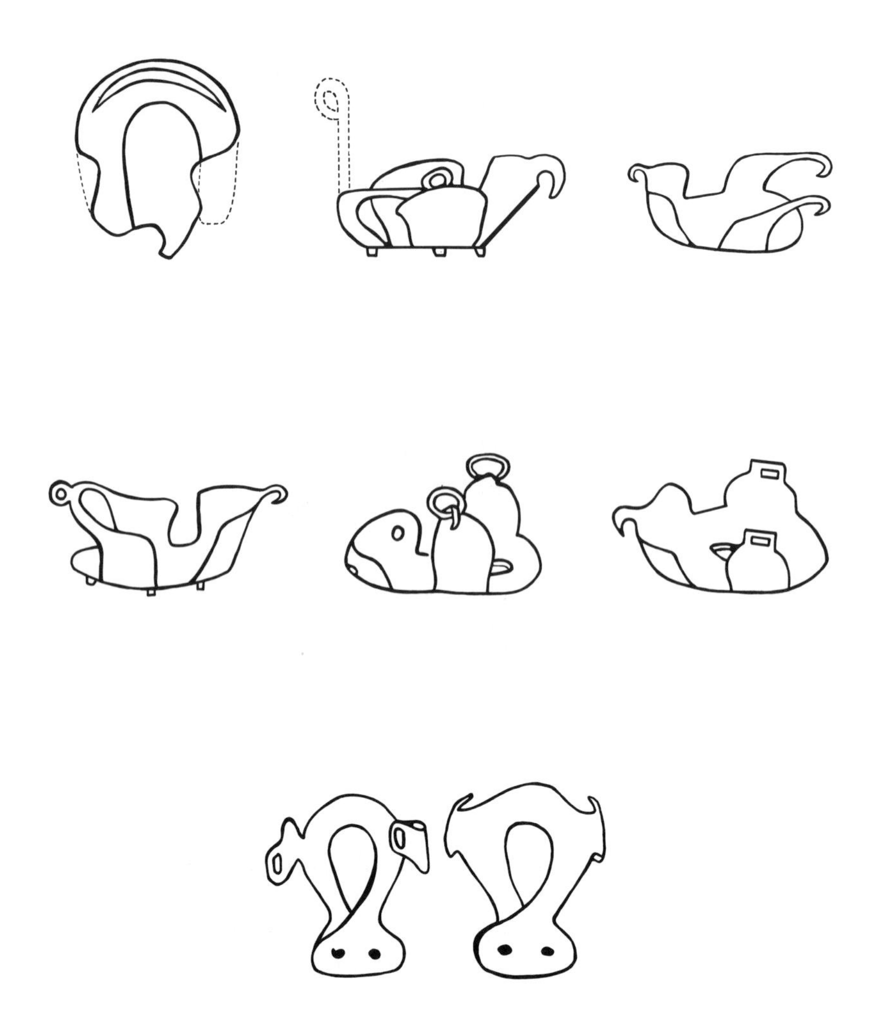

81 Various types of hipposandals or *soleae ferreae*. None of the examples so far discovered has nail holes. The metal tangs or rings may have been used to secure the shoe to the horse's hoof by means of cords (see Fig.82.) (Redrawn by G. Stobbs from Vigneron 1968.)

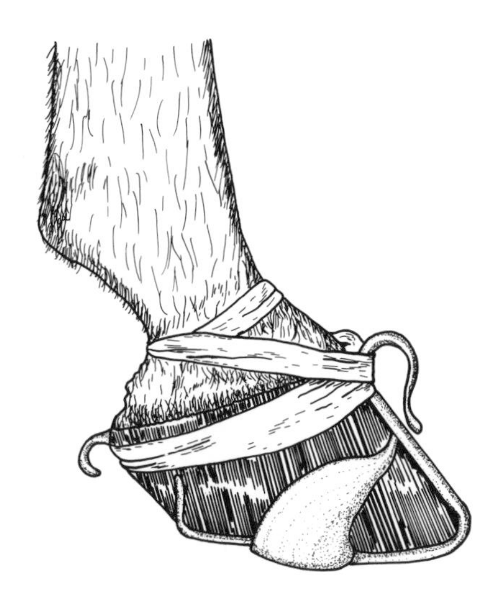

82 The open *so'leae ferreae* may have been attached to the horse's feet by cords. Experiments conducted by des Noëttes at St Germain-en-Laye in 1901 showed that the shoes would remain in place unless the horse was made to go at anything faster than a walking pace. It is possible that such shoes were employed to protect injured hooves and perhaps to keep medications in place. (Redrawn by G. Stobbs from Vigneron 1968.)

easier to put on and reusable. They were attached to the foot by means of cords or leather straps (Fig.82). Vigneron (1968, Pls.10–13) depicts several different types of *soleae*, but since they would be used for other animals and not exclusively for horses, it is to be expected that there should be variants in size and shape (Walker 1973, 322). Vigneron distinguished between two types of *soleae* on grounds of shape rather than material: one which left the sides of the hoof unprotected; and another which encircled the whole foot.

With regard to the first type, experiments carried out by des Noëttes in 1901, using modern copies of the open *soleae* from St Germain-en-Laye, showed that the hipposandal was well adapted to the horse's foot, and once tied on it stayed in place at a walk, but came off at a faster pace, because the metal tangs used to hold the cords got in the way of the other hooves. Thus it would seem that these *soleae* were used for convalescent animals which were not required for work (Vigneron 1968, 46).

The second type of *soleae*, which covered the hoof, would probably have been used temporarily to protect the feet of horses and mules in rough terrain. It is probable that they would remain attached to the foot rather better than the above type, which des Noëttes experimented with, and it is probably this kind of *soleae* to which Suetonius (*Nero* 30) referred when he described Nero's mules wearing silver shoes (Vigneron 1968, 46). Some of these shoes are provided with projections like outward facing nails, probably for use in icy conditions.

Some types of temporary shoes were probably made of leather, which would not survive as well as metal. Xenophon (*Anabasis* 4.5.36) refers to such shoes to give the horses extra grip in the snows of Armenia. Some North American Indian tribes protected their horses' feet by means of leather boots (Vigneron 1968, 45 n.8).

The subject of nailed horseshoes is one that is open to debate. Vigneron (1968, 48, Pl.13) discusses hipposandals that approach the shape of modern horseshoes but they do not have nail holes, so that they were most likely tied on like the other hipposandals. Arguments against the use of nailed shoes are firstly that the ancient authors do not mention them and secondly that there are few examples in art where horseshoes are depicted. Vegetius devotes several passages to the care of feet, but does not mention nailed shoes. It might be expected that since injuries can occur if nails are badly placed, a few authors would have discussed briefly how to treat such injuries.

It is possible that on Roman sculptures shoes would have been painted on later, much as the details of strap-work and reins may have been painted on the sculptures showing mules pulling carts and so on. But on medieval sculptures shoes are clearly depicted, complete with nails, so it is not impossible to show them in this fashion. On a sculpture from Vaison (Fig.83) one of the horses pulling a four-wheeled cart seems to be wearing a shoe on its left fore-foot, but this detail is lacking for its other hooves and also for those of its companion (Esperandieu 1907, no.293). The evidence is

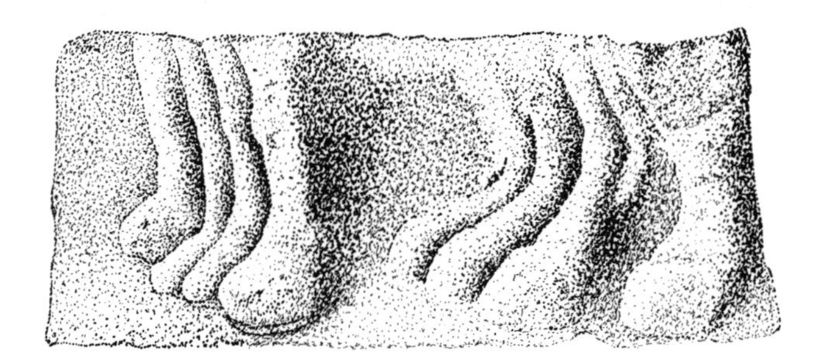

83 Detail from a sculptural relief from Vaison, France. The sculpture shows two horses pulling a four-wheeled cart. Close inspection shows that the left fore-foot of the nearest horse appears to be shod. This is a very rare example in Roman sculpture and it cannot be taken as conclusive proof that the Romans used nailed shoes (Espérandieu 1907 vol.1, no.293. Drawn by K.R. Dixon.)

thus inconclusive, but the possibility must not be discounted that this is an ordinary *soleae ferreae* tied on by cords which were painted on the monument, and no trace remains of the paint. Vigneron (1968, 49) allows that in certain areas of the Roman Empire some veterinary specialists may have experimented with a type of nailed shoe. If horses were regularly shod all over the Empire it is very surprising that shoes are not found in large numbers. In different parts of the Empire certain climatic conditions may have obviated the need for shoes. Horses which run on dry rocky ground can develop hard hooves, whereas softer, wetter ground can soften hooves so that they require some protection (Hyland 1990, 36).

Exact stratification and secure dating of the shoes that have been found in association with Roman material are very rare, and this fact was acknowledged by Ward in his article on Iron Age horseshoes: 'Very few of our museum specimens can stand the test of systematic enquiry' (Ward 1941, 9). A shoe from the Sheepen farm site at Colchester, and two shoes from Saffron Walden are the only examples that Ward accepted as Roman in date. A shoe from Gloucester, reputedly found *c.* 17.5–20cm (*c.* 7–8in) below the surface of the Roman road, was discounted because the circumstances of the find and its present whereabouts are not well documented. None the less Ward postulated that there was a traditional use of nailed shoes in Iron Age Britain and Gaul, but was forced to admit that no shoes have come to light from any undisturbed Iron Age site in Britain (Ward 1941, 15). The debate was continued by Green (1966), Dent (1967) and Littauer (1968) without definite conclusion.

Without further evidence it remains a possibility that even when found in association with finds of Roman date, horseshoes could have been lost at much later periods and worked their way deep into the ground, especially if a horse made vigorous efforts to extract its foot from a rut or fissure in the soil. At least some of the shoes found in supposedly Roman contexts may be medieval or later intrusions, a theory which is supported by the fact that some of them are in a very good state of preservation (Vigneron 1968, 50).

14 Baggage animals

Every unit of the Roman army, whether mounted or not, would depend in one way or another upon animals for its transport. Wagons and carts used to carry baggage would require animals to pull them. In some instances, oxen would pull wagons, as evidenced on Trajan's Column. The word *impedimenta* implies the baggage train as a whole, comprising oxen, horses, asses, mules, the wagons and carts and their drivers as well. *Iumenta* refers to the actual animals of all types.

Pack animals would be necessary in addition to wagons, and in certain terrain they would be the only form of transport which could be used. Both horses and mules were employed, but there is probably no need to identify automatically any small horse found on a military site as a baggage animal. The majority of pack animals would be mules. Although horses are more than adequate as beasts of burden, in general mules are hardier. They are less susceptible to disease than horses, their coats are finer and therefore more resistant to mange, and at the same time their skins are tougher so that although their pack-saddles can eventually cause sore backs this is less of a problem with mules than horses (Blenkinsop and Rainey 1925, 63). Furthermore they can survive on a smaller food ration than horses of comparable size and still keep fit and healthy. Their only disadvantage is that they cannot keep up with the fast pace of the cavalry, though if they are allowed to go at their own pace they can work incredibly long hours (Preston 1921, 326). But they cannot keep going indefinitely and are just as dependent on a water supply as horses are, as Afranius and Petreius found during the Civil War. Caesar cut them off from food and water, and eventually they had to kill all their baggage animals (*Civil War* 1.81).

Mules were highly valued in Roman times in civilian as well as military contexts. Columella divides horses into three classes (*De Re Rustica* 6.27.1). First he says there is the noble stock for the circus and the sacred games. Next there is the stock which is used for breeding mules, and then the ordinary riding horses. Since mules brought extremely high prices, the horses used to breed them could be rated almost as highly as the noble stock.

According to Varro (*De Re Rustica* 2.8.5) nearly all the road transport of the Roman world was pulled in carts or wagons by pairs of mules.

In military law the penalty for stealing a pack-animal was severe. If a man was caught stealing weapons he would be thrashed, but if he stole a pack-animal he would lose both hands by having them cut off, because weapons 'are useful only in battle, while pack animals are useful at all times' (Brand 1968, 163). The importance of pack animals had not changed in the nineteenth century, when a US army sergeant reported that his long trip through Indian territory had not been too bad: 'we lost a few recruits but none of the mules' (Elting 1988, 313).

The organization of a pack-train is not something which can be left to chance. Experienced staff who know how to load the pack-saddles are just as necessary as the mules or horses, and to achieve efficiency and speed at packing, the mule drivers have to practise frequently (Cabaniss 1890, 249). In the Roman army this task belonged to the *muliones*, or muleteers, which is their title both in literature and the official military papyri. Their status is unknown. They may have been ordinary soldiers seconded to this task, or they may have been civilians, or even slaves.

Numbers of baggage animals were possibly allotted to each cavalry *turma* or infantry century rather than to the auxiliary unit as a whole, but this is not definitely established, and on the march the baggage animals would presumably all march together. Troop B of the US Fourth Cavalry stationed in Arizona in the 1880s had ten mules for the troop baggage and two spare saddle mules in case of accidents. Seven men looked after the mule train on the march, the cook, the baker and one assistant at the head and four men bringing up the rear (Cabaniss 1890, 248). In the Roman army the ratio of animals and staff to each cavalry unit may have been lower, since it was considered that the Arizona troop was very well provided with baggage animals. Roman organization may also have differed and the number of pack animals may have varied according to the way in which the cavalry and infantry were employed in each province. In areas where more or less peaceful short-range patrolling was all that was necessary, pack-trains would probably not be necessary at all, or were quite small. For long-range patrols and in areas or circumstances where troops had to take the field at a moment's notice, baggage animals would probably feature largely in the military organization. For full-scale warfare such as Trajan's and Marcus Aurelius' Danubian campaigns, vast numbers of draught animals and pack-mules would be necessary. Probably extra animals would be needed, and circumstances would arise when there were insufficient numbers. When they requisitioned goods, the Romans did not use their own transport and everything had to be transported by the suppliers. For instance Caesar requisitioned corn from tribes in Spain to be brought to him on their own pack animals (*Civil War* 1.60).

Mules are shown on Trajan's Column pulling artillery in one scene, and a four-wheeled cart in another. Mules appear in seven scenes in all on Trajan's Column and in six scenes on the Marcus Column. One scene on Trajan's Column plainly shows a mule pack-saddle, and another shows panniers (Fig.84) (Toynbee 1973, 190–1; Vigneron 1968, Pl.56b; 56c). Mule trains could not operate without the proper saddles and harness, just as vital as mule-drivers. In preparation for war, Napoleon wrote to his chief of staff in April 1800, ordering him to have in readiness a thousand spare sets of draught and pack-harness 'which is always needed' (Howard 1961, 401 n.564). It is interesting to note that in Diocletian's *Edict* on prices (10.1–7) the mule harness is consistently more expensive than that for the horses. A military saddle should cost 500 *denarii*, whereas the mule saddle is listed at 800 *denarii*. A pack-saddle for an ass is listed at 250 *denarii* and that for a hinny at 350 *denarii*.

The amount of equipment and stores which the mules could carry can only be estimated. Each mule of a typical US cavalry troop carried about 66kg (145lbs), 2.25kg (5lbs) of which consisted of the protective covering for each load. These loads were considered light, because it was necessary to move at a fast pace to keep up with the cavalry, sometimes over very rough ground. The baggage carried was therefore reduced to a minimum. While the horses could be rested by the men dismounting and leading them or by stopping altogether and off-saddling for a while, the mules carried their dead weight all day long, often tightened up at each opportunity as the day wore on (Cabaniss 1890, 251).

Virtually nothing is known of how the Romans organized their baggage animals. Each fort would have accommodated some of them, but their numbers cannot be estimated and it is not known how they were housed, if at all. It has been suggested that the so-called stable at Gellygaer may have been for baggage animals but the function of the building is not definitely known and in general it is not understood how baggage animals were looked after. The annexes attached to forts on the Antonine Wall have also been proposed as shelters for baggage animals and wagons, at least in part. Some Roman forts, particularly in Dacia, had recesses in their encircling walls, which may have been used for storage or to provide shelter for animals, but this is only guesswork and would have been just as inconvenient as keeping the horses in the *intervallum* area. Mules may have been picketed outside forts, possibly with their respective troop horses so that they would become used to them. Papyrus records show that at least on campaigns some men were detailed to guard draught animals (Fink 1971,

84 A baggage mule with panniers from a scene on Trajan's Column. (Drawn by K.R. Dixon.)

n.63, 36). These were presumably outside the camp, in picket lines or in a corral. Walker (1973, 313) maintains that on the march the baggage animals would be herded together in the centre of the camp, in the area designated *veterinarium*, which is often translated as veterinary hospital. This is usually because the *valetudinarium*, *veterinarium* and *fabrica* and their staff are listed all together in the *De Metatione Castrorum* (4; 35), which leads to the assumption that sick men and animals were treated in the same area of the camp, but Walker disputes the identification of *veterinarium* as 'hospital'. The word *veterinarius* derives from *veho*, to pull, and was originally associated with draught animals, so that *veterinarium* might be better translated as transport park.

Mules and pack-horses were probably fed on barley like the horses of the cavalry. It is not known whether the hay and cereal ration of each *turma* included a portion for mules, or whether there was a separate organization for feeding baggage animals. In at least one case barley rations were drawn for both horses and mules together, when a detachment of cavalrymen and pack animals from *Cohors XX Palmyrenorum* were on detachment at Appadana (*P. Dur.* 64 A i). In an infantry unit barley and hay would be needed for pack animals but there is not enough information about ration scales, transport or storage.

On some occasions, mostly in emergencies, mules may have been used for riding. On Trajan's Column, a messenger seems to have just dismounted from a mule (Toynbee 1973, 192). At Gergovia Caesar mounted some of his *muliones* on their mules to make the enemy think he had more cavalry (*Gallic War* 7.45). On at least two occasions during the Republic, the Romans employed the same ruse, in 359 BC and 293 BC, when it was necessary to make the enemy think that cavalry was approaching (Livy 7.14.7; 10.40.8). On these occasions there was never any intention of using the mules and their riders as cavalry in battle, or indeed for any of the normal cavalry duties. Such a practice would probably not have been successful. In February 1877 it was decided to send 150 infantrymen from Fort Keogh in Montana on a five day patrol, mounted on mules. The officer in charge reported: 'with a good deal of fuss and worry, I got the men mounted on the mules at 1 pm . . . The sight was as good as a circus' (Rickey 1963, 225).

Glossary

Acetum sour wine.
Ad signa compulsory deduction made from a legionary's pay to the burial club.
Aerarium militare military treasury.
Ala milliaria cavalry regiment *c.*1000 strong.
Ala quingenaria cavalry regiment *c.*500 strong.
Annona militaris supply of provisions for the army.
Aquila eagle standard of a legion.
Aquilifer bearer of the eagle standard.
Artaba Egyptian corn measure equal to three-and-one-third *modii* (q.v.).
As basic unit of Roman coinage made of bronze. Four *asses* made one *sestertius* (q.v.).
Aureus gold coin, one of which was equivalent to 25 *denarii* (q.v.).
Auxilia cohorts and *alae* raised in the provinces from non-citizens; used later of infantry regiments raised in the fourth century to serve in the field army.
Barding armour covering body of a horse.
Basilica equestris exercitatoria colonnaded hall used for riding exercises.
Bucina horn used for ceremonies and regulating watch-guard changes.
Bucinatores men who blew the *bucina* (q.v.).
Campus level area suitable for cavalry exercises.
Campidoctor drill-instructor.
Capitum literally 'fodder'; in the later Empire, this was the term used for supplies of food for army horses, equivalent to *annona* (q.v.), or supplies for the men.
Capsa bandage box.
Capsarius wound-dresser.
Cataphractarii heavy-armoured cavalry. They may have differed from *clibanarii* (q.v.) by being equipped in a more western manner, carrying a lance and shield.
Centuria infantry unit nominally *c.*100 strong, but more usually *c.*80 strong.
Centurion commander of a *centuria* (q.v.).
Cervesa Celtic beer which was particularly popular in the north European provinces of the Empire.
Clibanarii heavy-armoured cavalry; the term derives from *clibanus* which means 'baking oven'. These troops may have been equipped in an eastern fashion, employing bow and lance.
Cohors equitata auxiliary unit of infantrymen with cavalry added to it, either *quingenaria* or *milliaria*.
Comitatus field army of the fourth century.
Constitutio Antoniniana legislative enactment of the Emperor Caracalla in AD 212, which admitted free-born inhabitants of the Empire to Roman citizenship.
Contarii cavalry units in the Roman army equipped with the *contus* (q.v.).

Contubernium tent party, or the number of soldiers sharing the same barrack room; usually eight men.
Contus heavy lance, approximately 3.6m (12 ft) long, which was held two-handed.
Cornicularius adjutant to a senior officer, often attached to headquarter's staff.
Cornu large curved horn.
Cuneus literally 'a wedge'; used of cavalry formations of the later Empire and of some units in Britain from the late third century.
Custos armorum literally 'keeper of the arms and armour'.
Decurio commanding officer of a *turma* (q.v.).
Denarius Roman silver coin worth four *sestertii* (q.v.).
Dilectus from the verb *diligere*, meaning to value or to favour, and used, not entirely accurately, of recruitment.
Diploma a Latin term, meaning a letter folded in two; used by modern scholars to describe the pair of small bronze tablets recording the privileges granted to a soldier on discharge from the *auxilia*.
Dona militaria military decorations.
Draco dragon standard believed to have been introduced into the Roman army by the Sarmatians.
Draconarius bearer of the *draco* (q.v.).
Dromedarius eastern troopers who were mounted on camels.
Duplicarius a soldier in receipt of double pay. The term is also used of the auxiliary cavalry officer second in command of a *turma* (q.v.).
Dux title given to a high-ranking officer in the third century, usually when he was performing duties normally above his rank.
Equites legionis cavalry attached to a legion.
Exploratores scouts.
Ex testamento phrase found on tombstones which denotes that it was erected by the heir/heirs of the deceased according to the terms of the will.
Fabrica workshop.
Frumentum grain; a term used of the corn supply in general.
Garum a good-quality fish sauce.
Gladius short stabbing sword of Spanish origin used by legionaries.
Gorytus Scythian-developed combined quiver and bow-case.
Gyrus circular course for training horses.
Hackamore a type of metal muzzle worn by horses to prevent them from 'getting away from the bit'.
Hasta spear.
Hiberna winter quarters.
Hippika gymnasia cavalry tournament of the Roman army in which both the men and horses were richly adorned.
Honesta missio honourable discharge from the army.
Hordeum barley.
Horrea granaries.
Imaginifer bearer of the *imago*, a standard which bore the image of the Emperor.
Immunes soldiers on special duties, excused ordinary fatigues; not a special rank.
Impedimenta the baggage train.
In numeros referre to enter names of recruits into the military records.
Intervallum the space between the back of the rampart and the internal buildings in a Roman fort.

Limitanei frontier troops of the later Roman Empire.
Lituus J-shaped horn believed to have been used specifically by the cavalry.
Lorica hamata mail armour constructed from interlinking rings of iron or, less frequently, copper alloy.
Lorica squamata armour constructed from scales of iron or copper alloy.
Medicus non-commissioned medical officer; sometimes used in conjunction with *veterinarius* (q.v.).
Medicus ordinarius commissioned medical officer.
Missio causaria soldiers who have been discharged before the end of their term of service through illness.
Missio ignominiosa dishonourable discharge.
Modius Roman corn measure; usually translated as a peck, or a quarter of a bushel.
Muria fish sauce of inferior quality to *garum* (q.v.).
Numerus literally 'unit'; used of troops raised from tribesmen, but can be applied to any military formation.
Optio second in command to a centurion (q.v.).
Origo place of origin.
Pecuarius soldier in charge of livestock.
Pedites infantrymen.
Phalerae military decorations.
Praefectus a title with several different meanings. Officer in command of an *ala* (q.v.) or cohort.
Praeiuratio first stage in the taking of the military oath (*sacramentum* q.v.), in which a chosen man recited the entire oath, followed by the others who each said *idem in me* ('the same in my case').
Praepositus an officer in temporary command of a unit, or of a vexillation (q.v.).
Praetentura area of a Roman fort in front of the *principia* (q.v.), as opposed to the *retentura* or rear half of the fort.
Praetorium commanding officer's house in a Roman fort.
Prata meadow land.
Pridianum military strength report.
Principia headquarters building in a Roman fort.
Probatio probationary examination to which all new recruits, and all remounts were subjected.
Pteruges leather straps used as fringing on armour.
Sacellum shrine for military standards.
Sacramentum military oath.
Sagittarius archer.
Scutum a shield. Modern scholars use this term to define the semi-cylindrical rectangular shield employed by legionaries.
Sesquiplicarius a soldier in receipt of pay-and-a-half; auxiliary cavalry officer, third in command of a *turma* (q.v.).
Sestertius Roman coin worth four *asses* (q.v.).
Signa a standard, one of which was carried by each century: it is not known if this also applied to each *turma* (q.v.).
Signifer bearer of the *signa*.
Singulares bodyguards. *Equites* and *pedites singulares consularis* were the guards of the governor of a province, while *singulares Augusti* were the bodyguard of the Emperor.
Stipendium pay, or a period of service.

Strator usually translated as 'groom', but this title could denote several different duties, some of them possibly connected with the remount service.
Strigil scraper used to remove oil and dirt from the body.
Tabula ansata name or unit identification tag.
Territorium land outside a fort on which the military or tenant farmers could graze livestock and grow crops.
Testudo literally tortoise; an infantry formation in which the men formed their shields into a shell.
Tirones recruits.
Torque a military decoration apparently awarded in pairs to individuals or a unit for valour. These rings, which were worn around the neck by the Celts amongst others, appear to have been worn by the Romans on either side of the cuirass below the collar bone.
Tuba long straight trumpet.
Tubicen man who blew the *tuba* (q.v.).
Turma cavalry unit, probably containing *c*.32 men, commanded by a *decurion* (q.v.).
Umbo shield boss.
Valetudinarium hospital.
Veterinarius a title used in both civilian and military contexts for a veterinarian or farrier; probably not a military rank.
Vexillarius bearer of the *vexillum* (q.v.).
Vexillatio detachment of troops drawn from an auxiliary unit or a legion.
Vexillum cavalry standard consisting of a square red or purple tasselled flag which was hung from a cross bar attached to a lance.
Via Sagularis the road which ran all round the inside of a Roman fort.
Viaticum literally means 'travelling-money', but it became associated with the payment which recruits received upon joining the army.

Bibliography

Abbreviations

AA	*Archaeologia Aeliana*
AE	*L'Année Epigraphique*
ANRW	*Aufstieg und Niedergang der Römischen Welt*. Berlin, de Gruyter.
Antiq. J.	*Antiquaries Journal*
Arch. J.	*Archaeological Journal*
BAR	*British Archaeological Reports*
BGU	*Berliner Griechische Urkunden*
Ch. LA	*Chartae Latinae Antiquiores*
CIL	*Corpus Inscriptionum Latinarum*
ETUD. PAP.	*Études de Papyrologie*
FIRA	*Fontes Iuris Romani Antejustiniani*
GAJ	*Glasgow Archaeological Journal*
IGR	*Inscriptiones Graecae Ad Res Romanas Pertinentes*
ILS	*Inscriptiones Latinae Selectae*. H. Dessau. Berlin. Three volumes.
JRS	*Journal of Roman Studies*
ORL	*Der Obergermanisch-raetische Limes der Römerreiches*
PBSR	*Papers of the British School at Rome*
P. Dur.	*The Excavations at Dura-Europos, Final Report V, Part I: The Parchments and Papyri*. C.B. Welles, R.O. Fink and J.F. Gilliam. New Haven (1959).
P. Mich.	*Papyri in the University of Michigan Collection*. C.C. Edgar, A.E.R. Boak and J.G. Winter *et al.* Ann Arbor (1931–).
P. Oxy.	*The Oxyrhynchus Papyri*. B.P. Grenfell, A.S. Hunt and H.I. Bell *et al.* London (1898–).
PSAS	*Proceedings of the Society of Antiquaries of Scotland*
PSI	*Papiri greci e latini*. G. Vitelli *et al.* Florence (1912–).
RIB	*The Roman Inscriptions of Britain* Volume I. R.G. Collingwood and R.P. Wright. Oxford (1965).
TDGNHAS	*Transactions of the Dumfriesshire and Galloway Natural History and Antiquarian Society*
ZPE	*Zeitschrift für Papyrologie und Epigrafik*

Ancient sources

AELIAN *De Animalia*
AMMIANUS MARCELLINUS
APPIAN *Civil War*
APPIAN *Roman History*
ARRIAN *Acies Contra Alanos*
ARRIAN *Ars Tactica*
CAESAR *The African War*
CAESAR *The Civil War*
CAESAR *The Gallic War*
CAESAR *The Spanish War*
CELSUS *De Medicini*
CODEX THEODOSIANUS
COLUMELLA *De Re Rustica*
DIGEST *Digest of Justinian* ed. T. Mommsen. Philadelphia: University of Pennsylvania. Four volumes. 1985.
DIO *Roman History*
FRONTINUS *Stratagems*
HELIODORUS *Aethiopica*
HERODIAN
HYGINUS *De Metatione Castrorum*
JOSEPHUS *Jewish War*
JUVENAL *Satires*
MAURICE *Strategikon*
LIVY
ONASANDER
PAUSANIAS *Description of Greece*
PLINY *Natural History*
PLINY THE YOUNGER *Letters*
PLUTARCH *Lives*
POLYBIUS *The Histories*
PROCOPIUS *History of the Wars*
SCRIPTORES HISTORIAE AUGUSTAE
SENECA *Moral Essays*
STRABO *Geography*
SUETONIUS
TACITUS *Agricola*
TACITUS *Annals*
TACITUS *Histories*
VARRO *De Re Rustica*
VEGETIUS *Ars Mulomedicinae*
VEGETIUS *Epitoma Rei Militaris*
VIRGIL *Georgics*
XENOPHON *Anabasis*
XENOPHON *The Art of Horsemanship*
XENOPHON *The Cavalry Commander*

Modern works

ANDERSON, A.S. 1984, *Roman Military Tombstones*. Buckinghamshire, Shire Archaeology.

ANGLESEY, Marquess of, 1973, *History of the British Cavalry Volume I. 1816–1819*. London, Leo Cooper.

APPLEBAUM, S. (ed.) 1971, *Roman Frontier Studies 1967: Proceedings of the 7th International Congress, Tel Aviv, 1967*. Tel Aviv, University of Tel Aviv.

APPLEBAUM, S. 1972, 'Roman Britain', in Finberg, H.P.R. (ed.) 1972, 3-277.

ATKINSON, D. and MORGAN, L. 1987, 'The Wellingborough and Nijmegen marches', in Dawson, M. (ed.) 1987, 99–108.

AZZAROLI, A. 1985, *An Early History of Horsemanship*. Leiden, Brill.

BARRETT, J.C. (*et al.*) (eds.) 1989, *Barbarians and Romans in North West Europe*. Oxford, BAR S471.

BÉDOYÈRE, G. de la 1989, *The Finds of Roman Britain*. London, Batsford.

BENNETT, P., FRERE, S.S. and STOW, S. 1982, *The Archaeology of Canterbury: Excavations at Canterbury Castle Volume 1*. Kent Archaeological Society, Maidstone.

BIRLEY, E. 1961, *Research on Hadrian's Wall*. Kendal, Titus Wilson.

BIRLEY, E. 1966, '*Alae* and *cohortes milliariae*', *Corolla Memoriae Erich Swoboda Dedicata* (*Römische Forschungen in Niederösterreich V*), 54–67.

BIRLEY, E. 1969, 'Septimius Severus and the Roman army', *Epigraphische Studien* 8, 63–79.

BIRLEY, E. 1976, 'An inscription from Cramond and the Matres Campestres', *GAJ* 4, 108–10.

BIRLEY, E. (*et al.*) (eds.) 1974 *Roman Frontier Studies 1969: 8th International Congress of Limesforschungen*. Cardiff, University of Wales Press.

BIRLEY, E. and RICHMOND, I.A. 1939, 'The Roman Fort at Carzield', *TDGNHAS* 22, 156–63.

BISHOP, M.C. (ed.) 1985, *The Production and Distribution of Roman Military Equipment: Proceedings of the Second Roman Military Equipment Seminar*. Oxford, BAR S275.

BISHOP, M.C. 1988, 'Cavalry equipment of the Roman army in the first century AD', in Coulston, J.C. (ed.) 1988, 67–196.

BISHOP, M.C. 1990, 'On parade: status, display, and morale in the Roman army', in Vetters H. and Kandler, M. (eds.) 1990, *Akten des 14. Internationalen Limeskongresses 1986 in Carnuntum*. Österreichische Akademie der Wissenschaften, vol.36, 21–30.

BISHOP, M.C. and DORE, J.N. 1989, *Corbridge Excavations of the Roman Fort and Town 1947–80*. London, HBMC.

BLENKINSOP, L.J. and RAINEY, J.W. 1925, *Veterinary Services (History of the Great War Based on Official Documents)*. London, HMSO.

BORGELIN, A.K. 1989, *Marine Molluscs as an Aspect of the Roman Seafood Industry*. Unpublished B.A. Dissertation. The University of Newcastle upon Tyne.

BOWMAN, A.K. 1974, 'Roman military records from Vindolanda', *Britannia* 5, 360–73,

BOWMAN, A.K. 1983, *The Roman Writing Tablets from Vindolanda*. London, British Museum.

BRAILSFORD, J.W. 1962, *Hod Hill Volume I: Antiquities from Hod Hill in the Durden Collection*. London, Trustees of the British Museum.

BRAND, C.E. 1968, *Roman Military Law*. Austin, University of Texas Press.

BRANDES, R. 1960, *Frontier Military Posts of Arizona*. Globe, Dale Stuart King.

BREEZE, D.J. 1969, 'The organization of the legion: the first cohort and the *equites legionis*', *JRS* 59, 50–5.

BREEZE, D.J. 1971, 'Pay grades and ranks below the centurionate'. *JRS* 61, 130–5.

BREEZE, D.J. 1976, 'Appendix: the ownership of arms in the Roman army', in Breeze, D.J., Close-Brooks, J. and Ritchie, J.N.G. 1976, 93–5.

BREEZE, D.J. 1979, 'The Roman fort on the Antonine Wall at Bearsden', in Breeze, D.J. (ed.) *Roman Scotland: some recent excavations*. Edinburgh, 1979, 21–5.

BREEZE, D.J. 1982a, 'Demand and supply on the northern frontier', in Clack, P. and Haselgrove, S. (eds.) 1982, 148–65.

BREEZE, D.J. 1982b, *Northern Frontiers of Roman Britain*. London, Batsford.

BREEZE, D.J., CLOSE-BROOKS, J. and RITCHIE, J.N.G. 1976, 'Soldiers' burials at Camelon, Stirlingshire, 1922 and 1975', *Britannia* 7, 73–95.

BREEZE, D.J. and DOBSON, B. 1969, 'Fort types on Hadrian's Wall', *AA*[4] 47, 15–32.

BREEZE, D.J. and DOBSON, B. 1974, 'Fort types as a guide to garrisons: a reconsideration', in Birley, E. (*et al.*) (eds.) 1974, 13–19.

BREEZE, D.J. and DOBSON, B. 1987, *Hadrian's Wall*. London, Penguin Books. 3rd Edition.

BRERETON, J.M. 1976, *The Horse in War*. Newton Abbot, David and Charles.

BRUCE, J.C. 1867, *The Roman Wall*. Newcastle upon Tyne, Andrew Reid. 3rd edition.

BRUCE, J.C. 1978, *Handbook to the Roman Wall with the Cumbrian Coast and the Outpost Forts*. Newcastle upon Tyne, Harold Hill & Son. 13th edition, edited and enlarged by C.M. Daniels.

BRUNT, P.A. 1950, 'Pay and superannuation in the Roman army', *PBSR* 18 n.s.5, 50–71.

BRUNT, P.A. 1974, 'Conscription and volunteering in the Roman Imperial army', *Scripta Classica Israelica* 1, 90–115.

BUCKLAND, P. 1978, 'A first-century shield from Doncaster, Yorkshire', *Britannia* 9, 247–69.

CABANISS, A.A. 1890, 'Troop and company pack trains', *Journal of the United States Cavalry Association* 3, 248–52.

CAMPBELL, B. 1978,'The marriage of soldiers under the Empire', *JRS* 68, 153–66.

CHANDLER, D.G. 1987, *The Military Maxims of Napoleon*. London, Greenhill Books.

CHARLESWORTH, D. 1976, 'The hospital, Housesteads', *AA*[5] 4, 17–30.

CHARLTON, B. and MITCHESON, M. 1984, 'The Roman cemetery at Petty Knowes, Rochester, Northumberland', *AA*[5] 12, 1–31.

CHEESMAN, G.L. 1914, *The Auxilia of the Roman Imperial Army*. Oxford, Clarendon Press.

CLACK, P. and HASELGROVE, S. (eds.) 1982, *Rural Settlement in the Roman North*. CBA Regional Group 3.

CONNOLLY, P. (ed.) 1981, *Greece and Rome at War*. London, Macdonald.

CONNOLLY, P. 1986, 'A reconstruction of a Roman saddle', *Britannia* 17, 353–5.

CONNOLLY, P. 1987, 'The Roman saddle', in Dawson, M. (ed.) 1987, 7–27.

CONNOLLY, P. 1988, 'Experiments with the Roman saddle', *Exercitus* 2:5, 71–6.

CONNOLLY, P. 1991, 'The saddle horns from Newstead', *Journal of Roman Military Equipment Studies* 1, 61–6.

COULSTON, J.C. 1985, 'Roman archery equipment', in Bishop M.C. (ed.) 1985, 220–366.

COULSTON, J.C. 1986, 'Roman, Parthian and Sassanid tactical developments', in Freeman, P. and Kennedy, D. (eds.) 1986, 59–75.

COULSTON, J.C. (ed.) 1988, *Military Equipment and the Identity of Roman Soldiers: Proceedings of the Fourth Roman Military Equipment Conference*. Oxford, BAR S394.

COUSSIN, P. 1926, *Les Armes Romaines*. Paris.

COWLES, V. 1983, *The Great Marlborough and his Duchess*. London, Weidenfeld and Nicolson.

CRUMMY, N. 1981, *Colchester Archaeological Report 2: The Roman Small Finds from Excavations in Colchester 1971–9*. Colchester Archaeological Trust Ltd.

CURLE, J. 1911, *A Roman Frontier Post and its People: the Fort of Newstead in the Parish of Melrose*. Glasgow, James Maclehose and Sons.

CURLE, J. 1913, 'Notes on some undescribed objects from the Roman fort at Newstead', *PSAS* 47, 384–405.

DANNELL, G.B. and WILD, J.P. 1987, *Longthorpe II*. London, Society for Promotion of Roman Studies. Britannia Monograph Series, no.8.

DAVIES, R.W. 1968a, 'The training grounds of the Roman cavalry', *Arch. J.* 125, 73–100.

DAVIES, R.W. 1968b, 'Fronto, Hadrian and the Roman army', *Latomus* 27, 75–95.

DAVIES, R.W. 1969a, 'The medici of the Roman armed forces', *Epigraphische Studien* 8, 83–99.

DAVIES, R.W. 1969b, 'The supply of animals to the Roman army and the remount system', *Latomus* 28, 429–59.

DAVIES, R.W. 1969c, 'Joining the Roman army', *Bonner Jahrbuch* 169, 208–32.

DAVIES, R.W. 1970, 'The Roman military medical service', *Saalburg Jahrbuch* 27, 84–104.

DAVIES, R.W. 1971a, 'Cohortes equitatae', *Historia* 20, 751–63.

DAVIES, R.W. 1971b, 'The Roman military diet', *Britannia* 2, 122–42.

DAVIES, R.W. 1974, 'Daily life of the Roman soldier under the Principate', *ANRW* II: 1, 299–338.

DAVIES, R.W. 1976, 'Singulares and Roman Britain', *Britannia* 7, 134–44.

DAVIS, R.H.C. 1983, 'The medieval warhorse', in Thompson, F.M.L. (ed.) 1983, 1–20.

DAVIS, R.H.C. 1989, *The Medieval Warhorse: Origin, Development and Redevelopment*. London, Thames and Hudson.

DAVISON, D.P. 1989, *The Barracks of the Roman Army from the First to Third Centuries AD*. Oxford, BAR S472. Three volumes.

DAWSON, M. (ed.) 1987, *The Accoutrements of War: Third Roman Military Equipment Seminar*. Oxford, BAR S336.

DENT, A. 1974, 'Arrian's array', *History Today* 24:8, 570–4.

DENT, A.A. 1967, 'The early horseshoe', *Antiquity* 41, 61–3.

DEWAR, M. (ed.) 1990, *An Anthology of Military Quotations*. London, Robert Hale.

DOBSON, B. 1981, 'Army organisation; Equipment; The army in the field', in Connolly, P. (ed.), 1981, 213–48.

DOBSON, B. and MANN, J.C. 1973, 'The Roman army in Britain and Britons in the Roman army', *Britannia* 4, 191–205.

DOMASZEWSKI, A. VON. 1900, 'Der Truppensold der Kaiserzeit', *Neue Heidelberger Jahrbücher* 10, 218–41.

DOMASZEWSKI, A. VON. 1967, *Die Rangordnung des römischen Heeres*, 2 durchgesehene Auflage. Einführung, Berichtigungen und Nachträge von B. Dobson. Cologne.

DRIEL-MURRAY, C. VAN. 1989, 'The Vindolanda chamfrons and miscellaneous items of leather horse gear', in Driel-Murray, C. van (ed.) 1989, 281–318.

DRIEL-MURRAY, C. VAN. (ed.) 1989, *Roman Military Equipment: the Sources of Evidence: Proceedings of the Fifth Roman Military Equipment Conference*. Oxford, BAR S476.

EDWARDS, E.H. and GEDDES, C. (eds.) 1973, *Complete Book of the Horse*. London, Ward Lock.

ELGOOD, R. (ed.) 1979, *Islamic Arms and Armour*. London.

ELTING, J.R. 1988, *Swords Around a Throne: Napoleon's Grande Armée*. London, Weidenfeld and Nicolson.

ESPERANDIEU, E. 1907, *Recuil General des Bas-Reliefs de la Gaule Romaine*. Paris. (Reprint 1965).

EWART, J.C. 1911, 'Animal remains' in Curle, J. 1911, 362–77.

EWER, T.K. 1982, *Practical Animal Husbandry*. Bristol, John Wright and Sons Ltd.

FABRICIUS, E. 1937, Das Kastell Niederbieber. *ORL* B1, 1a.

FARIS, N.A. and ELMER, R.P. 1945, *Arab Archery, an Arabic Manuscript of about AD 1500*. Princeton, Princeton University Press.

FINBERG, H.P.R. (ed.) 1972, *Agrarian*

History of England and Wales: Volume I: II AD *43–1042*. Cambridge, Cambridge University Press.

FINK, R.O. 1971, *Roman Military Records on Papyrus*. American Philological Association, Monograph 26.

FITZ, J. (ed.) 1977, *Limes: Akten des XI Internationalen Limeskongresses, Szekesfehervar, 1976*. Budapest Akademiai Kiado.

FORNI, G. 1953, *Il reclutamento delle legioni da Augusto a Diocleziano*.

FORSTER, H.H. and KNOWLES, W.H. 1911, 'Corstopitum: Report on the excavations in 1910', *AA*[3] 7, 143–267.

FOURNIER, A. 1914, *Napoleon I: A Biography*. London, Longman. Two volumes.

FREEMAN, P. and KENNEDY, D. (eds.) 1986, *The Defence of the Roman and Byzantine East*. Oxford, BAR S297. Two volumes.

FRERE, S.S. and ST JOSEPH, J.K. 1974, 'The Roman fortress at Longthorpe', *Britannia* 5, 1–129.

GARBSCH, J. 1978, *Römische Paraderüstungen*. Munich, C.H. Beck.

GARNSEY, P. 1970, 'Septimius Severus and the marriage of Roman soldiers', *California Studies in Classical Antiquity* 3, 45–53.

GENTRY, A.P. 1976, *Roman Military Stone-Built Granaries in Britain*. Oxford, BAR 32.

GICHON, M. 1971, 'The military significance of certain aspects of the Limes Palestinae', in Applebaum, S. (ed.) 1971, 191–200.

GILBEY, W. 1900, *Small Horses in Warfare*. London, Vinton and Co.

GILLIAM, J.F. 1950, 'Some Latin military papyri from Dura. I. Texts relating to cavalry horses', *Yale Classical Studies* 11, 169–209.

GILLIAM, J.F. 1965, 'Dura rosters and the Constitutio Antoniniana', *Historia* 14, 74–92.

GREEN, C. 1966, 'The purpose of the early horseshoe', *Antiquity* 40, 305–8.

GROENMAN-VAN WAATERINGE, W. 1967, *Romeins Lederwerk uit Valkenburg Z.H.* Groningen.

GROENMAN-VAN WAATERINGE, W. 1989, 'Food for soldiers, food for thought', in Barret, J.C. (*et al.*) (eds.) 1989, 96–107.

GSELL, S. 1901, *Les Monuments Antiques de l'Algérie*. Paris, Albert Fontemoing. Two volumes.

GUÉRAUD, O. 1942, 'Ostraca grecs et latins de l'Wâdi Fawâkhir', *Bulletin de l'Institut français d'archéologie orientale* 41, 141–96.

HARDMAN, A.C.L. 1976, *Young Horse Management*. London, Pelham.

HARTLEY, B.R. 1966, 'The Roman fort at Ilkley: excavations 1962', *Proceedings of the Leeds Philosophical and Literary Society* 12, 23–72.

HARTLEY, B.R. 1973, Discussion in *Roman Northern Frontier Seminar* 9, Nov. 1973, 6–7. Unpublished typescript.

HASELGROVE, C. 1982, 'Indigenous settlement patterns in the Tyne-Tees lowlands', in Clack, P. and Haselgrove, S. (eds.) 1982, 57–104.

HAYES, M.H. 1947, *Stable Management and Exercise*. London, Hurst and Blackett Ltd. 5th edition.

HIGHAM, N.J. 1989, 'Roman and native in England north of the Tees: acculturation and its limitations', in Barrett, J.C. (*et al.*) (eds.) 1989, 153–74.

HOBLEY, B. 1969, 'A Neronian-Vespasianic military site at 'The Lunt', Baginton, Warwickshire', *Transactions of the Birmingham Archaeological Society* 83, 65–129.

HOBLEY, B. 1974, 'The Lunt' Roman fort, England. Summary of excavations 1967–72', in Pippidi, D.M. (ed.) 1974, 361–79.

HOLDER, P.A. 1980, *The Auxilia from Augustus to Trajan*. Oxford, BAR, S70.

HOLDER, P.A. 1982, *The Roman Army in Britain*. London, Batsford.

HOLDER, P.A. 1987, 'Roman auxiliary cavalry in the second century A.D.', *Archaeology Today* 8: 5, June, 12–16.

HOWARD, J.E. 1961, *Letters and Documents*

of Napoleon. London, Cresset Press. Two volumes.

HYLAND, A. 1990, *Equus: the horse in the Roman world.* London, Batsford.

HYLAND, A. 1991, 'The action of the Newstead cavalry bit', *Journal of Roman Military Equipment Studies* 1, 67–72.

JACOBI, H. 1897, *Das Römerkastell Saalburg.* Germany.

JACOBI, H. 1934, 'Die Be-und Entwässerung unsere Limeskastelle', *Saalburg Jahrbuch* 8, 32–60.

JAHN, M. 1921, *Der Reitersporn.* Leipzig.

JAMES, S. 1986, 'Evidence from Dura-Europos for the origins of Late Roman helmets', *Syria* 63, 108–34.

JOHNSON, A. 1983, *Roman Forts.* London, A & C Black.

JOHNSON, D. 1978, *Napoleon's Cavalry and its Leaders.* London, Batsford.

JOHNSON, D. 1989, *The French Cavalry 1792–1815.* London, Belmont Publishing.

JONES, A.H.M. 1973, *The Later Roman Empire 284–602.* Oxford, Basil Blackwell. Two volumes.

JONES, F.P. 1987, '*Stigma*: tattooing and branding in Graeco-Roman antiquity, *JRS* 77, 139–55.

JONES, G.D.B. and WILD, J.P. 1968, 'Excavations at Brough-on-Noe (Navio) 1968', *Derbyshire Archaeological Journal* 88, 89–93.

KEIM, J. and KLUMBACH, H. 1951, *Der Römische Schatzfund von Straubing.* Munich, C.H. Beck.

KEPPIE, L. 1984, *The Making of the Roman Army from Republic to Empire.* London, Batsford.

KLINDT-JENSEN, O. 1961, *Gundestrup Kedelen.* Copenhagen, National Museum.

KLUMBACH, H. 1952, 'Pferde mit Brandmarken', *Festschrift des Römisch-Germanischen Zentralmuseums in Mainz zur Feier seiner hundertjährigen Bestehens* Band III, 1–12.

LATHAM, J.D. and PATERSON, W.F. 1979, 'Archery in the lands of Eastern Islam', in Elgood, R. (ed.) 1979, 78–88.

LEPPER, F. and FRERE, S.S. 1988, *Trajan's Column.* Gloucester, Alan Sutton.

LEWIS, N. and REINHOLD, M. 1955, *Roman Civilization. Sourcebook II: the Empire.* New York, Harper and Row.

LITTAUER, M.A. 1968, 'Early horseshoe problems again', *Antiquity* 42, 221–5.

LITTAUER, M.A. 1969, 'Bits and pieces', *Antiquity* 43, 289–300.

LIVERSIDGE, J. 1968, *Britain in the Roman Empire.* London, Routledge.

LUFF, R.M. 1982, *A Zooarchaeological Study of the Roman North-Western Provinces.* Oxford, BAR S137.

MACMULLEN, R. 1960, 'Inscriptions on armor', *American Journal of Archaeology* 64, 23–40.

MACMULLEN, R. 1963, *Soldier and Civilian in the Later Roman Empire.* Cambridge, Mass., Harvard University Press.

MANN, J.C. and ROXAN, M.M. 1988, 'Discharge certificates of the Roman army', *Britannia* 19, 341–7.

MANNING, W.H. 1975, 'Roman military timber granaries in Britain', *Saalburg Jahrbuch* 32, 105–29.

MANNING, W.H. 1985, *Catalogue of the Romano-British Iron Tools, Fittings and Weapons in the British Museum.* London, British Museum

MARSHMAN, J.C. 1876, *Memoirs of Major-General Sir Henry Havelock, K.C.B.* London.

MAXFIELD, V.A. 1981, *The Military Decorations of the Roman Army.* London, Batsford.

MEEK, A. and GRAY, R.A.H. 1911, 'Animal remains' in Forster, H.H. and Knowles, W.R. 1911, 78–125.

MITTEIS, L. and WILCKEN, U. 1912, *Grundzüge und Chrestomathie der Papyruskunde.* Leipzig and Berlin.

MOYSE-BARTLETT, H. 1971, *Louis Edward Nolan and his Influence on the British Cavalry.* London.

MÜLLER, G. 1979a, *Durnomagus: das Römische Dormagen.* Cologne, Rheinlandverlag GMBH.

MÜLLER, G. 1979b, *Ausgrabungen in Dor-*

magen 1963–1977. Cologne, Rheinisches Landesmuseums Bonn.

NIGHTINGALE, F. 1858, *Notes on Matters Affecting the Health, Efficiency, and Hospital Administration of the British Army*.

NOBIS, N. 1973, 'Zur Frage römerzeitlicher Hauspferde in Zentraleuropa', *Zeitschrift für Säugertierkunde* 38, 224–52.

NOLAN, Capt. L.E. 1853, *Cavalry: its History and Tactics*. London, Thomas Bosworth.

PAKENHAM, T. 1979, *The Boer War*. London, Weidenfeld and Nicolson.

PARKER, H.M.D. 1932, 'The antiqua legio of Vegetius', *Classical Quarterly* 26, 136–49.

PARKER, H.M.D. 1958, *The Roman Legions*. Cambridge, W. Heffer and Sons Ltd.

PARKER, S.T. (ed.) 1987, *The Roman Frontier in Central Jordan: Interim Report on the Limes Arabicus Project 1980–1985*. Oxford, BAR S340.

PETRIKOVITS, H. VON 1967, *Die Römischen Streitkrafte am Niederrhein*. Dusseldorf, Rheinland-Verlag GMBH.

PIGGOT, S. 1955, 'Three metal-work hoards of the Roman period from southern Scotland', *PSAS* 87, (1952–3), 1–50.

PIPPIDI, D.M. (ed.) 1974, *Actes du IXe Congrés international d'Etudes sur les Frontières Romaines*. Bucharest, Editura Academiei.

PIRLING, R. 1978, 'Die Ausgrabungen in Krefeld-Gellep 1977', *Ausgrabungen in Rheinland* '77, 136–40.

PIRLING, R. 1986, *Römer und Franken am Niederrhein*. Mainz, Phillip von Zabern.

PITTS, L.F. and ST JOSEPH, J.K. 1985, *Inchtuthill: the Roman Legionary Fortress 1952–65*. London, Society for the Promotion of Roman Studies, Britannia Monograph series no.6.

PLANCK, D. 1975, *Arae Flaviae I. Neue Untersuchungen zur Geschichte des römischen Rottweil*. Forschungen und Berichte zur Vor-und Frühgeschichte in Baden-Württemberg 6. Stuttgart.

PLANCK, D. and UNZ, C. (eds.) 1986, *Studien zu den Militärgrenzen Roms III: Vorträge des 13. Internationalen Limeskongresses, Aalen 1983*. Stuttgart, Konrad Theiss Verlag.

PRESTON, R.M.P. 1921, *The Desert Mounted Corps: an Account of the Cavalry Operations in Palestine and Syria 1917–18*. London, Constable.

RICHMOND, I.A. 1945, 'The Sarmatae, Bremetennacum veteranorum and the Regio Bremetennacensis', *JRS* 35, 15–29.

RICHMOND, I.A. 1968, *Hod Hill Volume II: Excavations Between 1951 and 1958*. London, British Museum.

RICKEY, D. 1972, *Forty Miles a Day on Beans and Hay*. Norman, University of Oklahoma Press. 4th Edition.

ROBINSON, H.R. 1975, *The Armour of Imperial Rome*. London, Arms and Armour Press.

ROBINSON, H.R. 1976, *What the Soldiers Wore on Hadrian's Wall*. Newcastle upon Tyne, Frank Graham.

ROGERS, H.C.B. 1959, *The Mounted Troops of the British Army 1066–1945*. London, Seeley Service and Co.

ROGERS, H.C.B. 1977, *The British Army of the Eighteenth Century*. London, George Allen and Unwin.

ROSTOVTZEFF, M.I., BELLINGER, A.R., HOPKINS, C. and WELLES, C.B. (eds.) 1936, *The Excavations at Dura-Europos: Preliminary Report of the 6th Season of Work, Oct. 1932–Mar. 1933*. New Haven, Yale University Press.

ROSTOVTZEFF, M.I., BROWN, F.E. and WELLES, C.B. (eds.) 1939, *The Excavations at Dura-Europos: Preliminary Report of the 7th and 8th Seasons of Work: 1933–34 and 1934–35*. New Haven, Yale University Press

ROSTOVTZEFF, M.I. 1942, 'Vexillum and Victory', *JRS* 32, 92–106.

ROSTOVTZEFF, M.I. 1957, *Social and Economic History of the Roman Empire*. Oxford, Clarendon Press. 2nd Edition.

RUGER, C.B. 1971, 'Kastell Gelduba', *Beiträge zur Archäologie des Römischen*

Rheinlands II. Düsseldorf.

SALWAY, P. 1965, *The Frontier People of Roman Britain*. Cambridge, Cambridge University Press.

SCHLEIERMACHER, M. 1984, *Römische Reitergrabsteine: Die kaiserzeitlichen Reliefs des triumphierenden Reiters*. Bonn, Bouvier Verlag Herbert Grundmann.

SCHÖNBERGER, H. 1975, *Kastell Künzing-Quintana: die Grabungen von 1958 bis 1966*. Limesforschungen 13. Berlin, Gebr. Mann Verlag.

SHORTT, H. de S. 1959, 'A provincial Roman spur from Langstock, Hants., and other spurs from Roman Britain', *Antiq. J.* 39, 61–76.

SIMPSON, F.G. (ed.) 1976, *Watermills and Military Works on Hadrian's Wall: Excavations in Northumberland 1907–1913*. Kendall, Titus Wilson.

SIMPSON, F.G. 1976, 'The latrine building in the south-eastern angle of Housesteads fort, 1922–12', in Simpson, F.G. (ed.) 1976, 133–43.

SIMPSON, F.G. and RICHMOND, I.A. 1937, 'The fort on Hadrian's Wall at Halton', *AA*[4] 14, 151–71.

SIMPSON, F.G. and RICHMOND, I.A. 1941, 'The Roman fort on Hadrian's Wall at Benwell', *AA*[4] 19, 1–43.

SMITH, D.J. 1976, 'A note on the water supply', in Simpson, F.G. (ed.) 1976, 143–6.

SMITH, G.H. 1978, 'Excavations near Hadrian's Wall at Tarraby Lane 1976', *Britannia* 9, 19–57.

SOMMER, C.S. 1984, *The Military Vici in Roman Britain*. Oxford, BAR 129.

SPEIDEL, M. 1970, 'The captor of Decebalus', *JRS* 60, 142–53.

SPEIDEL, M. 1973, 'The pay of the auxilia', *JRS* 63, 141–7.

SPEIDEL, M. 1974, 'Stablesiani: the raising of new cavalry units during the crisis of the Roman Empire', *Chiron* 4, 541–6.

SPEIDEL, M. 1976, 'The guards of the Roman provincial governors: an essay on their singulares', *American Studies in Papyrology*.

SPEIDEL, M. 1981, 'The prefect's horse-guards and the supply of weapons to the Roman army', *Proceedings of the XVI International Congress of Papyrology* 405–9.

SPEIDEL, M. 1984, 'Catafractarii clibanarii and the rise of the later Roman mailed cavalry: a gravestone from Claudiopolis in Bithynia', *Epigraphica Anatolica* 4, 151–6.

STEPHENS, G.R. 1985, 'Military aqueducts in Roman Britain', *Arch. J.* 142, 216–36.

STRACHAN, H. 1985, *From Waterloo to Balaclava: Tactics, Technology, and the British Army 1815–1854*. Cambridge, Cambridge University Press.

STRONG, D.E. 1961, *Roman Imperial Sculpture*. London.

SZILÁGYI, J. 1956, *Aquincum*. Budapest and Berlin.

TATTON-BROWN, T. 1979, 'Two Roman swords from a double inhumation burial. Canterbury', *Antiq. J.* 58, 361–4.

TAYLOR, A.K. 1975, 'Römische Hackamoren und Kappzäume aus metall', *Jahrbuch des Römisch-Germanischen Zentralmuseums Mainz* 22, 106–33.

THOMAS, J.D. and DAVIES, R.W. 1977, 'A new military strength report on papyrus', *JRS* 67, 50–61.

THOMPSON, F.M.L. (ed.) 1983, *Horses in European Economic History: a Preliminary Canter*. London, British Agricultural History Society.

TIMMIS, Maj. R.S. 1929, *Modern Horse Management*. London, Cassell and Co. Ltd.

TOMLIN, R. 1981, 'The Later Empire AD 200–450', in Connolly, P. (ed.) 1981, 249–61.

TOYNBEE, J.M.C. 1948, 'Beasts and their names in the Roman Empire', *PBSR* n.s.3, 24–37.

TOYNBEE, J.M.C. 1964, *Art in Britain Under the Romans*. Oxford, Clarendon Press.

TOYNBEE, J.M.C. 1973, *Animals in Roman*

Life and Art. London, Thames and Hudson.

TOYNBEE, J.M.C. and CLARKE, R.R. 1948, 'A Roman decorated helmet and other objects from Norfolk', *JRS* 38, 20–7.

TURNER, J.P. 1950, *The North West Mounted Police 1873–1893*. Ottawa, Edmond Cloutier.

TYLDEN, G. 1965, *Horses and Saddlery*. London, J.A. Allen and Co.

ULBERT, G. 1968, *Römische Waffen des 1. Jahrhunderts n.Chr.* Limesmuseum Aalen. Stuttgart, A.W. Gentner Verlag.

UNZ, C. 1971, 'Römische militärfunde aus Baden-Aquae Helveticae', *Jahresbericht Gesellschaft Pro Vindonissa*, 41–58.

UNZ, C. 1973, 'Römische funde aus Windisch im ehemaligen Kantonalen Antiquarium Aarau', *Jahresbericht Gesellschaft Pro Vindonissa*, 11–42.

UTLEY, R.M. 1973, *Frontier Regulars: the United States Army and the Indian 1866–1891*. New York, Macmullen.

VIGNERON, P. 1968, *Le Cheval dans l'Antiquité Gréco-Romaine*. Nancy, Faculté des Lettres et des Sciences Humaines de l'Universitaire de Nancy. Two volumes.

WALKER, R.E. 1973, 'Roman veterinary medicine' in Toynbee J.M.C. 1973, 303–43.

WAR OFFICE, 1899, *Regulations for Mounted Infantry*. London, HMSO.

WAR OFFICE, 1904, *Manual of Horse and Stable Management*. London, HMSO

WAR OFFICE, 1937a, *Remount Manual (war)*. London, HMSO.

WAR OFFICE, 1937b, *Manual of Horsemanship, Equitation and Animal Transport*. London, HMSO.

WARD, G. 1941, 'The Iron Age horseshoe and its derivatives', *Antiq. J.* 21, 9–27.

WARD, J. 1903, *The Roman Fort at Gellygaer in the County of Glamorgan*. London, Bernrose and Sons.

WARNER, P. (ed.) 1977, *The Fields of War: a Young Cavalryman's Crimea Campaign*. London, J. Murray.

WATERMAN, R. 1970, *Arztliche Instrumente aus Novaesium*.

WATSON, G.R. 1959, 'The pay of the Roman army: the auxiliary forces', *Historia* 8, 372–8.

WATSON, G.R. 1981, *The Roman Soldier*. London, Thames and Hudson. (Reprint of 1969 edition).

WEBSTER, G. 1985, *The Roman Imperial Army*. London, A. & C. Black. 3rd edition.

WELLES, C.B. (*et al.*) (eds.) 1959, *Excavations at Dura-Europos: Final Report V Part I: the Parchments and Papyri*. New Haven, Yale University Press.

WELLS, C.M. 1977, 'Where did they put the horses? Cavalry stables in the early Empire', in Fitz, J. (ed.) 1977, 659–65.

WHITE, K.D. 1970, *Roman Farming*. London, Thames and Hudson.

WILCKEN, U. 1899, *Griechische Ostraka aus Aegypten und Nubien*. Leipzig and Berlin.

WILD, J.P. 1981, 'A find of Roman scale armour from Carpow', *Britannia* 12, 305–6.

WYLLY, Col. H.C. 1908, *The Military Memoirs of Lieutenant General Sir Joseph Thackwell*. London.

YORCK VON WARTENBURG, Count 1902, *Napoleon as a General*. London, Kegan Paul. Two volumes.

Index

Index